Adventures Across Space and Time

Adventures Across Space and Time

A *Doctor Who* Reader

Edited by Paul Booth, Matt Hills, Joy Piedmont and Tansy Rayner Roberts

BLOOMSBURY ACADEMIC
LONDON • NEW YORK • OXFORD • NEW DELHI • SYDNEY

BLOOMSBURY ACADEMIC
Bloomsbury Publishing Plc
50 Bedford Square, London, WC1B 3DP, UK
1385 Broadway, New York, NY 10018, USA
29 Earlsfort Terrace, Dublin 2, Ireland

BLOOMSBURY, BLOOMSBURY ACADEMIC and the Diana logo are
trademarks of Bloomsbury Publishing Plc

First published in Great Britain 2024
Reprinted 2024

Copyright © Paul Booth, Matt Hills, Joy Piedmont and Tansy Rayner Roberts, 2024

Paul Booth, Matt Hills, Joy Piedmont and Tansy Rayner Roberts have asserted their right
under the Copyright, Designs and Patents Act, 1988, to be identified as Editor of this work.

For legal purposes the Acknowledgements on p. xvi constitute an extension
of this copyright page.

Cover design: Ben Anslow
Cover images: British police box similar to the one used as the Tardis in the TV series
Dr Who. (© Jeremy Pembrey / Alamy Stock Photo); Abstract trees blurred in circular motion
stock photo (© Kirill_Savenko / iStock)

All rights reserved. No part of this publication may be reproduced or transmitted in any form or
by any means, electronic or mechanical, including photocopying, recording, or any information storage
or retrieval system, without prior permission in writing from the publishers.

Bloomsbury Publishing Plc does not have any control over, or responsibility for, any third-party websites
referred to or in this book. All internet addresses given in this book were correct at the time of going to press.
The author and publisher regret any inconvenience caused if addresses have changed or sites have ceased to
exist, but can accept no responsibility for any such changes.

A catalogue record for this book is available from the British Library.

A catalog record for this book is available from the Library of Congress.

ISBN: HB: 978-1-3502-8838-6
PB: 978-1-3502-8837-9
ePDF: 978-1-3502-8840-9
eBook: 978-1-3502-8839-3

Typeset by Integra Software Services Pvt. Ltd.
Printed and bound in Great Britain

To find out more about our authors and books visit www.bloomsbury.com
and sign up for our newsletters.

Paul
To Katie, with love.

Matt
To the memory of Robin Hills (1942–2017), the original inspiration
for my lifelong *Doctor Who* passion. He lost interest towards the
end of the 'classic' series, and intermittently followed again post-2005, but
thanks to his immersion in the Pertwee and Baker years,
I was always destined for fandom.

Joy
To my fan family in NYC – thank you for always adding to
my pile of good things.

Tansy
For Caitlin, and her loving parents,
who found their family in fandom

Contents

List of figures xii
List of tables xiii
Foreword by Matthew Sweet xiv
Acknowledgements xvi
List of contributors xvii

Introduction 1

Section I Into the (Transmedia) vortex: From Dalekmania to *Time Lord Victorious* – Paul Booth 9

1 Transmedia *Doctor Who* I 11

From 'Canonicity in *Doctor Who*' by Paul Cornell 11
From '*Doctor Who* and the Convergence of Media: A Case Study in "Transmedia Storytelling"' by Neil Perryman 12

2 Early TV scholarship 17

From '*Dr Who*: Similarity and Difference' by John Tulloch 17
From '*Dr Who*: Ideology and the Reading of a Popular Narrative Text' by John Fiske 19

3 Production insights 23

From *The Making of Doctor Who* by Terrance Dicks and Malcolm Hulke 23
From *Triumph of a Time Lord: Regenerating Doctor Who in the Twenty-First Century* by Matt Hills 24

4 The (in)definite article 29

From *TARDISBound: Navigating the Universes of Doctor Who* by Piers Britton 29
From *Design for Doctor Who: Vision and Revision in Science Fiction Television* by Piers Britton 32

5 Bigger, louder and now in colour! 35

From 'Adapting Telefantasy: The *Doctor Who and the Daleks* Films' by John R. Cook 35

From 'Televisuality Without Television?: The Big Finish Audios and Discourses of "Tele-centric" *Doctor Who*' by Matt Hills 37

From *Love and Monsters: The Doctor Who Experience, 1979 to the Present* by Miles Booy 39

6 The legacy of *Doctor Who* literature by Stacey Smith? 41

7 The *Doctor Who* figurine collection by Ross Garner 47

8 *Doctor Who: Time Fracture* – Process, techniques and principles of an immersive experience production by Sarah Atkinson and Helen W. Kennedy 55

9 The costs of the Doctor: *Time Lord Victorious* and managing transmedia engagement by Elizabeth Evans 63

Section II Studying *Doctor Who's* audiences and fans – Matt Hills 71

10 The powerless elite 75

From *Science Fiction Audiences* by John Tulloch and Henry Jenkins 75

11 The powerless elite? 81

From 'Keeping the Elite Powerless: Fan-Producer Relations in the "Nu *Who*" (and New YOU) Era' by Leora Hadas and Limor Shifman 81

12 The eras of *Doctor Who* 87

From 'Periodising *Doctor Who*' by Paul Booth 87

13 Political *Doctor Who* 95

From 'Is *Doctor Who* Political?' by Alan McKee 95

14 Desiring *Doctor Who* 101

From 'Desiring the Doctor: Identity, Gender and Genre in Online Fandom' by Rebecca Williams 101

15 Feminist *Doctor Who* 109

From '"Finally, we get to play the Doctor": Feminist Female Fans' Reactions to the First Female Doctor Who' by Neta Yodovich 109

16 Fans as consumers: Psychographics and tribalism in *Doctor Who* fandom by Alison Lawson and David Lawson 117

17 The controversy of the Thirteenth Doctor announcement and *Doctor Who* fandom on Tumblr by Alice de Freitas Gomes and Polyana Inácio Rezende Silva 125

18 *Marginally Fannish*: Fan podcasts as alternative sites of intersectional education by Parinita Shetty 133

19 Casual fans and non-fans in *Flux*: The reception of 'Once, Upon Time' and *Doctor Who*'s return to serialization by Dominique Gagnon 141

Section III *Doctor Who* Fandom in the 21st Century – Joy Piedmont 147

20 Tumblr fandom is an unknowable anti-monolith cryptid by Lena Barkin 149

21 The police box 159

From 'Doctor Who's TARDIS Has a Different Meaning for Black Fans' by Constance Gibbs 159

22 Space isn't always for everyone: How unconscious racial bias in *Doctor Who* scripts affects fan perception of companions of colour by Amanda-Rae Prescott 163

23 'Martha Jones is a lesbian': Queer (re)interpretations of companions in *Doctor Who* by Océane I. Nyela and Anna Young 169

24 Fandom DIY: *Doctor Who* fans in Poland by Magdalena Stonawska 175

25 'The Day of the Doctor' and *Flux* in Latin America: The relationship between BBC's strategies and Brazilian Whovians by Eloy Vieira and Lilian França 181

26 Translating *Doctor Who* into Chinese: Fansubbing and *Doctor Who* fandom in China by Ting Guo 189

27 The girl who ~~waited~~ survived: Fan rewritings of Amy Pond by Bethan Jones 195

28 Forks in the fandom road: Divergent views on the social politics of *Doctor Who* by Talia Franks 201

29 Postcolonial *Doctor Who* 207

From 'Through Coloured Eyes: An Alternative Viewing of Postcolonial Transition' by Vanessa de Kauwe 207

Section IV *Doctor Who's* creative intersections – Tansy Rayner Roberts 213

30 Fans for hire 215

From 'Douglas Adams: The First Professional *Doctor Who* Fan' by Eddie Robson 215

31 The Doctor effect 217

From 'How Fanzines Helped Put *Doctor Who* Fans in Charge of *Doctor Who*' by Nolan Feeney 217

32 Fannish origin stories 223

From 'Dalek-Builders' by Peter Capaldi 223
From rec.arts.drwho Post by Steven Moffat 223

33 Poachers turned cartographers by Ian Potter 225

34 Within any fan's dream 233

From David J Richardson interviews Kate Orman 233
From 'Pop Between Realities, Home in Time for Tea 41 (rec.arts.drwho)' by Elizabeth Sandifer 235

35 Run fast, love hard, be kind: Twenty years in *Doctor Who* fandom by Lynne M. Thomas 239

36 Popping into fiction 245
From 'Where to Find the Doctor in All of My Historical Fantasy Novels' by Mary Robinette Kowal 245

37 Sexism in fandom 247
From 'The Uncomfortable Truth about Fandom Sexism' by Claudia Boleyn 247

38 When fans become showrunners by Julia Henken 253

39 Scripting fandom in twenty-first-century *Doctor Who* by Paul Driscoll 259

40 The legacy of the fanzine Renaissance by Leslie McMurtry 267

Index 273

List of Figures

7.1   Tessellated bases encouraging display (photo by author) 49
8.1   Liminauts in the second 'sandbox' phase of DWTF – include from left to right: the character of Robert Dudley, Leonardo Da Vinci and a Time Lord Guide. Photographs by Mark Senior 57
8.2   Examples of the different 'worlds' in DWTF. From left to right: UNIT Command, the Alien junkyard and market and Brolls' Salvage and Import Export Emporium. Photographs by Mark Senior 58
17.1 A diagram of the different topics and arguments brought up by users in the controversy surrounding the casting of Jodie Whittaker as the Thirteenth Doctor on Tumblr. Made by the authors, based on Gomes 129
20.1 Accessed from smooth-mccrimmonal, reblogged from untimelylord 151
20.2 Accessed from smooth-mccrimmonal, reblogged from reiqenarataka 153
20.3 Accessed from doctorwhorama 154
20.4 Accessed from doctorwhorama 155
23.1 Screen capture of a tweet by Ali Rae (@alistrair613) discussing the idea that Martha Jones' infatuation with the Doctor is the result of compulsory heterosexuality 171
23.2 Screen captures of a MARTHADONNA fan edit by Rory (@lesbiantardis) 172
25.1 Screenshot of tweets from account @DoctorWhoBrasil, indicating presence in Trending Topics list. Source: VIEIRA & FRANÇA (2018) 183
25.2 Screenshots of main results to the Boolean research combination on Stilingue: *Doctor Who* OR 'the flux' OR 'jodie whittaker' OR #doctorwhobr OR #doctorwho OR #DoctorWhoDay. Date: nov/dez/2021. Source: Stilingue (edited) 184
25.3 Screenshots of main results to the Boolean research combination on Stilingue: *Doctor Who* OR 'the flux' OR 'jodie whittaker' OR #doctorwhobr OR #doctorwho OR #DoctorWhoDay. Date: nov/dez/2021. Source: Stilingue (edited) 185
25.4 Screenshots of main results to the Boolean research combination on Stilingue: *Doctor Who* OR 'the flux' OR 'jodie whittaker' OR #doctorwhobr OR #doctorwho OR #DoctorWhoDay. Date: nov/dez/2021. Source: Stilingue (edited) 185
25.5 Akerman tweets. Source: Twitter 186
32.1 Reprint of letter from Peter Capaldi, *Radio Times* 224

List of Tables

9.1 List of *Time Lord Victorious* Elements. From www.doctorwho.tv-time-lord-victorious with some release dates updated from Hero Collector website 65
16.1 A Theoretical Typology of *Doctor Who* Fans 122
40.1 Gender Representation in Televised *Doctor Who* Creatives Between 1963 and 2021 270

Foreword

by Matthew Sweet

Matthew Sweet presents *Free Thinking and Sound of Cinema* on BBC Radio 3 and *The Philosopher's Arms* on BBC Radio 4. His most recent series was *1922: The Birth of Now*, a ten-part history of Modernism for Radio 4. He is the author of *Inventing the Victorians* (Faber, 2001), *Shepperton Babylon* (Faber, 2005), *The West End Front* (Faber, 2011) and *Operation Chaos: The Vietnam Deserters Who Fought the CIA, the Brainwashers and Themselves* (Henry Holt/Picador 2018). His film *Liberation Radio* screened in the 2021 London Film Festival and at the Manzi gallery in Hanoi. In 2017 he and the baker Frances Quinn achieved a Guinness World record that was, sadly, broken by Ant and Dec in 2022. He is currently writing a biography of Barbara Cartland.

In the last years of the twentieth century, when I was at university, new *Doctor Who* was *Dimensions in Time* and the internet was less than half its present size, my tutor sat me down for a talk about the Renaissance.

How, he asked me, did people know that it was happening? I didn't know. Fortunately, he did. People, he said, knew the Renaissance was happening because it was no longer possible for one person to have read every book in existence.

Two decades later, it is no longer possible for one person to have read every *Doctor Who* book in existence. If Light were attempting to catalogue the blooming, thriving transmedia enterprise begun by this modest BBC programme, the output of Big Finish audio plays alone would defeat him in a flash of lightning. Loss as well as plenitude makes completism impossible. As 1963 edges inexorably towards the Niagara of living memory, we will (barring a miracle in the basement of a Mormon church or a Nigerian film vault) soon arrive at a moment when there will be no one alive who has seen every TV episode of *Doctor Who*.

In 1981, when Barry Letts wrote a foreword for Jean-Marc Lofficier's two-volume *Doctor Who Programme Guide*, he did it with diffidence. The idea of such a work delighted him, but he also considered its existence slightly barmy. It was a 'work of eccentric but dedicated scholarship'. Today, I think, we can just call it scholarship. *A Doctor Who Reader* collects the fruits of all that labour – from John Tulloch's Cartesian analysis of the first Tom Baker title sequence to posts from the half-forgotten world of rec.arts.drwho to Constance Gibbs musing on the meaning of the TARDIS for Black fans.

The first scholars to turn their attention to *Doctor Who* were not film historians or media theorists. They were child psychologists. In 1967, John and Elizabeth Newson founded the Child Development Research Unit at the University of Nottingham, where they studied childhood and parenting, mainly through surveys and observational work in nearby communities. In their landmark book, *Four Years Old in an Urban Community* (1968), they noted the voices of Skaro in the playground. 'Don't push me', they heard one small nursery-age Dalek protest, 'Daleks don't push people'. 'Well', replied its friend, 'but they *exterminate* people'.

All forms of twentieth-century *Doctor Who* – the television episodes, the novelizations and short fiction, the movies and stage works, the comic strips and Chad Valley Give-a-Show projector slides – were opportunities for play. Perhaps the *TV Comic* strip registers it best. Clear characterization is not a high priority. Subsidiary characters are often nameless – unless they are Father Christmas, the Pied Piper or the Old Man of the Sea. Narrative logic is not prized. The protagonists ricochet from one life-or-death situation to the next – monsters loom, dinosaurs lunge, floors collapse, Trods do improbable things with conveyor belts and stories come to a halt as if someone had blown a whistle and told The Doctor, John and Gillian to come in for their tea. Twenty-first-century *Doctor Who* was made by people with experience of this play.

So too is the scholarship. The unfolding text of *Doctor Who* has now unfolded in ways that are too complex to fully capture. This book is a record of how it got too big to fully understand, and why that is no reason to stop trying, or stop playing.

Acknowledgements

This book would not have been possible without help from many, many people. First and foremost, the editors thank DePaul University's University Research Council and the College of Communication Summer Grant committees, both of which provided the funds to pay for the permissions for these reprints. We're also indebted to Brian DeHart at the DePaul University Library and Professor Michael Balfour at the University of New South Wales for help tracking down articles. We also thank all the authors of the original pieces in this volume. This book is definitely bigger on the inside.

Paul: I want to acknowledge with huge thanks Matt, Joy and Tansy, each of whom kept this project afloat (while also dealing with my periodic panicked emails!), as well as the regular ol' gang of *Doctor Who* Club students at DePaul, who continue to nurture the spark of love for this amazing show.

Joy: I am so fortunate to have made many friends through fandom who have become a professional and emotional support system: Graeme Burk, Kyle Anderson, Paul Booth, Stacey Smith?, everyone in the Black Nerds Create family, Nicole Hill and the WhoFUBU community, the Gallifrey Stands team and Deb Stanish, who first encouraged me to jump in.

Tansy: I appreciate the help and advice of my fellow Verities (and their fannish husbands/partners!), who cover the breadth of contemporary *Doctor Who* fandom between them, and are always there to help me check my privilege, my facts and whether or not I need a jelly baby. Shout-out to my son, my daughter and my three borrowed sons: Bailey, Jemima, Inigo, Oscar and Felix, whose clashing opinions about *Doctor Who, Torchwood* and/or *the Sarah Jane Adventures* (not to mention their games, cosplay, fan art, Lego, sonic screwdrivers, birthday cakes, etc.) have been the background noise (and sometimes foreground noise) of my life over the last few decades.

And thanks to my own fannish husband, who is always up for rewatching a Classic episode when important research needs to be done.

List of Contributors

Editor bios

Paul Booth is Professor of Communication at DePaul University. He is the author/editor of fifteen books, including *A Fan Studies Primer* (with Rebecca Williams, 2021), *Board Games as Media* (2021), *Watching Doctor Who* (with Craig Owen Jones, 2020), *Fan Phenomena: Doctor Who* (2013) and *Digital Fandom* (2010). He is currently enjoying a cup of coffee.

Matt Hills is Professor of Fandom Studies at the University of Huddersfield. He has published widely on *Doctor Who*, beginning with *Triumph of a Time Lord* (2010) about the BBC Wales' revival of the show. He has also edited/co-edited collections on *Doctor Who* including *New Dimensions of Doctor Who* (2013) and *Doctor Who – New Dawn* (2021) as well as publishing a monograph on the programme's fiftieth anniversary, *Doctor Who – The Unfolding Event* (2015). He has additionally contributed to ATB Publishing's *Outside In* book series and, most recently, to the Black Archive's set of essays on *Flux*.

Joy Piedmont is a librarian at a Manhattan independent school. As a freelance writer, she's covered pop culture for *Entertainment Weekly* and reviewed Young Adult literature for *School Library Journal*. She co-produces *Reality Bomb*, a *Doctor Who* podcast, and is the co-creator and co-chair of Gallifrey One's TARDIS Talks, a special track of programming giving space to big ideas and theories about *Doctor Who* and fandom. Follow her on Twitter @InquiringJoy.

Tansy Rayner Roberts is one of the co-hosts of the *Verity! Doctor Who* Podcast. She is an Australian writer and publisher of SFF and has won the Hugo Award twice, for Fancast and Fan Writer. Tansy's books include *Musketeer Space, Tea & Sympathetic Magic*, and the essay collection *Pratchett's Women*. She also has a (not so) secret life as Livia Day, author of cosy murder mysteries. She completed a PhD in Classics at the University of Tasmania.

Author bios

Sarah Atkinson is Professor of Screen Media at King's College London and co-editor of *Convergence: The International Journal of Research into New Media Technologies*. Sarah has published widely on the impacts of digital technologies on film, cinema and media audiences, and screen production practices and industries.

Lena Barkin completed her Master's in Film and Television Studies at Boston University. Her writing focuses on fan studies, cult television and media history. She is also a veteran of Xanga, Livejournal and Tumblr, and has published in *Polygon, Nerdist* and *SYFY Wire*. Nothing in ze world can stop her now.

Paul Driscoll is an Oxford University post-graduate, where he majored in theology. He currently lives in Leigh, Greater Manchester, in a crowded house of children, pets and *Doctor Who* memorabilia. He is on the editorial team of Obverse Books' acclaimed Black Archive range and has contributed his own volumes on 'The God Complex', the 1996 *TV Movie* and 'Vincent and the Doctor'. He is the co-owner of the Altrix Books imprint, which publishes a range of cult-related fiction and non-fiction works, including the *Doctor Who* essay collection *Army of Ghosts*. He is a regular contributor to the *Doctor Who* Appreciation Society fanzine *The Celestial Toyroom* and has penned various online *Doctor Who* articles for *What Culture* and *Doctor Who Worldwide*.

Elizabeth Evans is Professor of Screen Cultures at the University of Nottingham. Her research examines the intersection of screen audiences, screen industries and technology studies. She is the author of *Transmedia Television: Audiences, New Media and Daily Life* (2011) and *Understanding Engagement in Transmedia* Culture (2020) and co-editor of *Participations: The Online Journal of Audience Research*.

Lilian França earned a PhD in Communication and Semiotics and is Full Professor – Master in Cinema and Audiovisual – Federal University of Sergipe and Visiting Scholar at CUNY – New York; UMINHO and UBI – Portugal, UNICAMP and UFRGS – Brazil and author of *The Facebook Instant Articles Business Model*, among others.

Talia Franks is a writer, poet and podcaster from Massachusetts. They are the co-host and executive producer of *The Wibbly Wobbly Timey Wimey Podcast*, a retrospective deep-dive *Doctor Who* analysis podcast. Talia has contributed *Doctor Who* articles to *Nerdist* and has appeared on multiple *Doctor Who* podcasts including *Reality Bomb and Gallifrey Public Radio* to discuss diversity in fandom, prominent episodes and *Doctor Who* news.

Dominique Gagnon is a PhD student in Communication at the University of Quebec at Montreal (UQAM). She is interested in fan and anti-fan studies, videographic criticism and humour studies. Her PhD thesis will focus on anti-fans' discourses and practices in online fan spaces regarding gender-swapped franchises, such as *Doctor Who* and *Ghostbusters*. She is affiliated with the research group on international and intercultural communication (GERACII, UQAM) and the research laboratory on consumer and media culture in Quebec (LaboPop, UQAM).

Ross Garner is Lecturer in Media and Cultural Studies in the School of Journalism, Media and Culture at Cardiff University, UK. His research expertise concerns the spatial and material dimensions of media consumption. He has published many essays exploring these issues (and others) in relation to *Doctor Who* including articles in the journal *Popular Communication* and edited collections published by IB Tauris, SUNY Press and MacFarlane. He has been a *Doctor Who* fan since the final series of the 'classic' incarnation in 1989 and was an avid collector of the Eaglemoss Doctor Who range. He secretly believes he is Omega.

Alice de Freitas Gomes is a *Doctor Who* fan. She has a master's degree in social communication from the Federal University of Minas Gerais and a bachelor's degree in social communication, with a qualification in advertising, from the same institution. Her interests include participatory culture, fan studies, internet memes and transmedia dynamics. She is currently a collaborator researcher at the Research Group on Media, Semiotics, and Pragmatism – MediaAção.

Ting Guo is Senior Lecturer in Translation and Chinese Studies at the University of Liverpool. She has published widely in journals such as *Translation Studies*, *Translation and Interpreting Studies* and *Literature Compass*. Her research focuses on fan translation, translation of queer media texts and translation/interpreting history. She is particularly interested in the pivotal role of translator in the reproduction and dissemination of knowledge as well as in cultural and social change.

Julia Henken is a recent graduate of Boston University's Film and Television MFA programme. She has a background in education with a special interest in using media in the classroom.

Bethan Jones is Research Associate at the University of York. She has written extensively about anti-fandom, media tourism and participatory cultures, and is co-editor of *Crowdfunding the Future: Media Industries, Ethics, and Digital Society* (2015) and the forthcoming *Participatory Culture Wars: Controversy, Conflict, and Complicity in Fandom*. Bethan is also on the board of the Fan Studies Network and co-chair of the SCMS Fan and Audience Studies SIG.

Helen W. Kennedy is Professor of Creative and Cultural Industries at the University of Nottingham and co-editor of *Convergence: The International Journal of Research into New Media Technologies*. Helen has published widely on feminist interventions into digital games culture, live cinema and the broader immersive experience economy.

Alison Lawson is the Head of the Discipline of Marketing and Operations in Derby Business School at the University of Derby in the UK. She leads a team of academics and teaches marketing, specializing in social marketing, marketing communications and research methods. Her research focuses on social marketing for behaviour change and for social good. She is a lifelong *Doctor Who* fan and has had several short stories and an audio play published by Big Finish Productions. In the typology of fans proposed in her chapter, she is best described as an optimistic enthusiast.

David Lawson has over twenty years of marketing management experience and has worked for a range of organizations in the public, private, NGO and charity sectors in the UK and Ireland. As a chartered marketer, he was a director of a private marketing consultancy practice for many years and has also lectured on the MA Publishing degree at Anglia Ruskin University in the UK. He appears with his sister, Alison, in *Doctor Who Magazine* issue 558 and (at the time of writing) his favourite story is *The Keys of Marinus* or possibly *The Robots of Death*. He can't decide. He identifies most with the nostalgia buff in the typology proposed in his chapter.

Leslie McMurtry is Lecturer in Radio Studies at the University of Salford. She has edited the fanzine *The Terrible Zodin* since 2008. She has published on *Doctor Who* in *We the Neo-Victorians: Perspectives on Literature and Culture*, *Doctor Who: Fan Phenomena*, *Doctor Who and Race*, *The Unsilent Library: Essays on the Russell T Davies Era of the New Doctor Who* and in a forthcoming volume of *Outside In*. Her wedding ceremony included readings from *Survival* and 'Demons of the Punjab'.

Océane I. Nyela is a PhD student in the Joint Program in Communication & Culture at York and Toronto Metropolitan University. She graduated from the University of Ottawa with an Honours Bachelor of Social Sciences (BSocSc) in Criminology and Sociology. Her doctoral research investigates the proliferation of braided hairstyles in several West African countries and their diasporas. The practice is situated within a larger media ecology consisting of social, spiritual and communicative practices that act as embodied mathematical practices which mobilize the unconscious for moments of diasporic transindividuation. She is a recipient of the Joseph-Armand Bombardier Canada Graduate Scholarships (CGS-D) Doctoral Scholarship.

Ian Potter was a curator of Television at the National Museum of Photography, Film and Television for thirteen years. He has worked on a number of TV shows, and his book *The Rise and Rise of the Independents* charts the growth of UK TV's Indie sector from the 1950s into the early twenty-first century. He has written on *Doctor Who* for Manchester University Press and Obverse Books, and has scripted and sound designed a great deal of audio *Doctor Who* for Big Finish Productions. He is part of the problem.

Amanda-Rae Prescott is a Black and multiracial freelance journalist from Brooklyn, New York. She has contributed *Doctor Who* articles to *Den of Geek*, *Doctor Who Magazine* and *BlackTARDIS*. She has also appeared on several *Doctor Who* podcasts and convention panels to discuss diversity in fandom, cosplay and her favourite historical episodes. Alongside writing about *Doctor Who*, she has written extensively about racial representation on UK TV and period dramas. She can be found on Twitter @amandarprescott and on amandaraeprescott.com.

Parinita Shetty has worked with young people and children's books in India in various ways – as an author, a bookseller in a children's bookshop, a reading programme developer and a coordinator of a children's literature festival. She completed her MEd in Children's Literature and Literacies from the University of Glasgow in 2017. She launched a PhD podcast called Marginally Fannish to research intersectionality and public pedagogy in fan podcasts. In June 2022, she passed her PhD viva with no corrections from the School of Education at the University of Leeds. She is passionate about co-creating knowledge, including diverse voices in her research, and making academic research as accessible as possible to non-academic audiences in creative ways. She should currently be planning Season 2 of her fan podcast but is probably watching *Doctor Who*.

Polyana Inácio Rezende Silva has a doctoral degree in Social Communication from the Federal University of Minas Gerais and a master's degree in Communication from the Pontifical Catholic University of Minas Gerais, Brazil. She is a researcher, professor, Public Relations professional and photographer interested in the Internet and Social Networks, Activism, Technology and Digital Image. Her research relates to the Studies of Platforms and sociotechnical networks, open laboratories for prototyping with analogue supports, wearable technologies and Digital Media.

Stacey Smith? co-wrote *Bookwyrm*, a guide to the New Adventures, and is in the middle of writing *Bookwyrm II*, a guide to the Eighth Doctor Adventures. She also co-wrote the *Who Is the Doctor* Series of episode guides to the Modern Series and contributed a Black Archive on *Doctor Who and the Silurians* for Obverse Books. She's editor extraordinaire of the *Outside In* Series that examines pop culture with a twist. In her day job, she's a professor of disease modelling at the University of Ottawa. Even there, she sometimes links her work with pop culture, as she's an expert on zombies.

Magdalena Stonawska is book editor, translator and fan writer interested in SF&F literature and film, LGBTQ+ themes and everything human and alien. She became a *Doctor Who* fan in 2010, and since then, the show has taken her on numerous adventures, including research on Polish Whovians (leading to a master thesis in culture studies at Jagiellonian University), running several conventions and writing dozens of articles, essays and convention speeches. Currently, she can be found on Whosome.pl, a website about *Doctor Who* and other sources of joy. When not keeping busy with paid work or fan work, she enjoys coffee, baking, cosy video games and throwing a ball to her dog.

Lynne M. Thomas, ten-time Hugo Award winner, is the Head of the Rare Book & Manuscript Library and Juanita J. and Robert E. Simpson Rare Book and Manuscript Professor at the University of Illinois at Urbana-Champaign, one of the largest public university rare book collections in the country. She previously served as the Head of Distinctive Collections and Curator of Rare Books and Special Collections at Northern Illinois University. She co-authored *Special Collections 2.0* (2009) and co-edited *New Directions for Special Collections: An Anthology of Practice*, both with Beth Whittaker (2016), and is a founding member of the Digital POWRR project. An alumna of Smith College with a degree in French and Comparative Literature, she also holds an MS in Library and Information Science from the University of Illinois at Urbana-Champaign and an MA in English and American Literature from Northern Illinois University. https://orcid.org/0000-0002-3504-1836.

Eloy Vieira is Business Intelligence Supervisor at BETC-Havas and former guest professor at USP and Unisinos. He earned a PhD in Communication Sciences (Unisinos/2021) with CAPES-Print scholarship at Universitat Autònoma de Barcelona (UAB/Spain), and is a member of Pop Culture Research Group (Cultpop). He did MSc in Culture, Economy and Politics of Communication (UFS/2016) and a bachelor's degree in Social Communication/Journalism (UFS/2013).

Anna Young is a second-year PhD student on the York-TMU programme in Communication and Culture. Originally from the UK, she studied previously in London and is now based in Toronto. Her research straddles the related disciplines/approaches of material culture and body studies, with a focus on screens. She is broadly interested in spatiality, queer theory and the cultural aspect of technology.

Republished piece author bios

Claudia Boleyn is a singer/songwriter living in the UK. She is a former member of *Doctor Who Magazine*'s Time Team.

Miles Booy studied film, television and literature at the College of St. Mark and St. John in Plymouth, before doing post-graduate work in cinema at the University of East Anglia.

Piers Britton is Professor and Director of Visual & Media Studies at the University of Redlands, Southern California. He is the author of *Design for Doctor Who* (2021) and *TARDISbound* (2011).

Peter Capaldi is an actor and long-time *Doctor Who* fan. Among other roles, he has played the twelfth incarnation of the Doctor.

John R. Cook is an internationally known and respected academic expert in the study of the media, with particular research specialisms in aspects of television history, media institutions, screenwriting, television drama, documentary and film.

Paul Cornell is an award-winning writer of novels, comics, short fiction and non-fiction, as well as a TV screenwriter for *Doctor Who* and many other series.

Terrance Dicks was a long-time script editor on *Doctor Who* and wrote many of the novelizations. He was one of the most prolific *Doctor Who* authors and scriptwriters.

Nolan Feeney is a writer and editor based in Brooklyn. He was a senior editor at *Billboard* and staff editor at *Entertainment Weekly*.

John Fiske was a media scholar and cultural theorist whose work has influenced generations of scholars.

Leora Hadas is Assistant Professor in Culture, Film and Media at Nottingham University.

Malcolm Hulke was a screenwriter and author of many popular *Doctor Who* stories.

Henry Jenkins is Professor at the University of Southern California.

Vanessa De Kauwe has more than two decades' experience in the disability and education sectors and an honours degree in philosophy specializing in classical and postmodern philosophy. She has also completed studies in world theologies, pastoral care and ancient languages.

Mary Robinette Kowal is a Hugo-winning novelist and professional puppeteer.

Alan McKee is a Professor at the University of Sydney and is an expert on entertainment and healthy sexual development.

Steven Moffat is a writer and producer for many television programmes, most notably serving as showrunner for *Doctor Who* from 2010 to 2018.

Kate Orman is an Australian SF author who wrote several titles for the Virgin New Adventures and BBC Books range of *Doctor Who* novels.

Neil Perryman is an academic and fan of *Doctor Who*; he has written, with his wife, *Adventures with the Wife in Space*.

David J Richardson was editor of the *Doctor Who* fanzine *Sonic Screwdriver*.

Eddie Robson is a British writer and novelist and has written for Big Finish.

Elizabeth Sandifer is a media critic and writer, who wrote the blog *TARDIS Eruditorum*.

Limor Shifman is a professor at the Department of Communication and Journalism, The Hebrew University of Jerusalem, Israel.

John Tulloch is a British-Australian educator and university lecturer.

Rebecca Williams is Associate Professor in Media Audiences and Participatory Cultures at the University of South Wales.

Neta Yodovich is a fellow researcher and postdoctoral researcher at the University of Haifa, Department of Sociology.

Introduction

Paul Booth, Matt Hills, Joy Piedmont and Tansy Rayner Roberts

This collection brings together a wealth of academic articles and fan work published over the past half century about the television series *Doctor Who* and introduces newly commissioned chapters about the history, longevity and scope of the series. The perennially popular BBC series holds a unique place in the history of television: as the longest-running science-fiction series, academic research and fan discussion about the show track social and cultural changes over the past sixty years. A unique attribute of *Doctor Who* is its 'unfolding text',[1] its capacity to change over time. Some of the earliest writing about the show was journalistic in nature, with fans writing more sporadically until the start of the *Doctor Who* Appreciation Society in 1976. The earliest academic scholarship on *Doctor Who* was printed in the early 1980s, with the popularization of television studies in the academy. Each piece was written in a particular context, a certain time and place. As with any Reader, there will be disagreements among many about what to include – and what to exclude. Although we can never please everyone, we hope to have presented a wide array of academic and, especially, fan writing.[2] To date there have been no Readers or collections of previously published *Doctor Who* research, but as a field the study of *Doctor Who* has become a popular topic. Importantly, *The Doctor Who Reader* provides a useful guide for researchers and fans of *Doctor Who* about what has come before and what is yet to come.

The history of *Doctor Who* is almost as vast and complicated as the history of the Doctor themselves. Our focus in this book has been the way the text of *Doctor Who* (within its cultural context) has influenced and been influenced by the fandom. Like the character of the Doctor, the show and its many networked associations and intersections have 'regenerated' over and over again. While the average viewer of *Doctor Who* may not think of it as anything other than a television show, it might better be described as a wide network of texts, an intersection of viewpoints and a coming together of a variety of perspectives over the past sixty years. In this volume, we focus less on some abstract cohesiveness to *Doctor Who* and instead embrace the prismatic (and often contradictory) fan and audiences viewpoints that have shaped the social and cultural history of the show. We believe that the best way to describe *Doctor Who* is through an explication of the many perspectives it has generated over the past sixty years.

The importance of studying *Doctor Who* lies in the way it has changed and developed over time, for more than anything, *Doctor Who* represents longevity, devotion and transformation. As one of the editors of this volume, Matt Hills, has written, '*Doctor Who* is vital, multiple, and open to renewal and rejuvenation at every turn'.[3] Studying *Doctor Who* allows us to develop a keen awareness of what happens to a text as it changes, develops, renews and (yes) regenerates over sixty years of development. Key to the success of *Doctor Who*, as this volume illustrates, is the wide variety of intersections it represents: intersections between parts of the text through transmedia extensions, intersections between fans and industry professionals throughout the years as generative of creativity and intersections between fannish engagement and scholarly criticism.

Pat Harrigan and Noah Wardrip-Fruin have called *Doctor Who* a 'vast, fictional quilt'; a whole constructed of many different parts.[4] Like a fractal, we can see this quilting metaphor at many different levels. Purely at the level of the text itself, *Doctor Who* has had a continually changing set of producers, writers, directors and actors at the helm, meaning that a show that started in 1963 is now wholly different than the show at 1983 or at 2023.[5] But the quilt thickens with additional transmedia connections, as with the comics (which started in 1964), novels and novelizations, audio adventures and web content – all of which is equally (in)coherent within the skein of *Doctor Who*.[6]

Intersections between fan and creative personnel develop the show even further, as fans of the long-running programme eventually take over the production in the new series. But hints of this intersection come earlier in the programme's history as well, as the 1980s saw fan feedback as crucial for the show's development. Fans *are* the creative personnel, which both opens up and restricts the types of content that gets made.

And, as this volume demonstrates, the connections between academic and fan writing reflect (at least) two different but intersecting paths to understanding the role of *Doctor Who* in contemporary culture. The earliest fan writing of *Doctor Who* arguably can be traced back to the day after the airing of the first programme,[7] and fan clubs like 'William (Doctor Who) Hartnell Fan Club' (eventually 'The *Doctor Who* Fan Club') started as early as 1965. The official *Doctor Who* club, The *Doctor Who* Appreciation Society (DWAS), started in 1976.[8] Fan clubs encouraged critical engagement with the series – so much so that in the 1980s, fan writing could influence the series itself. But academic work on *Doctor Who*, first appearing in the early 1980s, also fed into the series, with nascent pop culture academics like John Tulloch and Manuel Alvarado words entering into the series itself (cf *Dragonfire*).

Importantly, as the editors of this volume – academics and fans all – will attest, the line between fan and academic can be thin (or even non-existent) at times. We believe one can be both a fan (re: emotionally engage with a text) and critical of that text (re: analyse it); and in fact, we hold that to truly understand *Doctor Who*, to truly get at what this show means both to millions of fans and to culture writ large, one has to do both.

A history of fan writing on *Doctor Who*

Doctor Who has a long history of fan writing. The longevity of the show, from 1963 through to today, has allowed not only for generational fandom (always changing, never staying still) but also for young fans of the show to grow up into creative professionals, many eventually contributing to licensed material or 'official' *Doctor Who* media.

The 1970s and 1980s saw a wave of fanzines from fan groups with access to staplers and mimeographs or photocopiers. Fanzines featured fanfic, fan art, reviews, critical writing, production notes and more. They allowed fans to write letters to each other. Fanzines were distributed by mail, as swaps, or sold cheaply at conventions and meet-ups.

Meanwhile, some of the show's followers expressed their thoughts in more mainstream publications, like young Peter Capaldi writing letters to that hallowed institution of British media journalism, the *Radio Times*.

Doctor Who Weekly, later *Doctor Who Magazine*, a professional magazine launched by Marvel Comics in 1979 (now published by Panini), provided a professional space for writing by fans, for fans – and many of its contributors crossed over from the fanzine world.

Then it came. The internet. Fans no longer needed letters columns to write to each other. All they needed was a dial-up connection.

And oh, how they typed.

One of the most famous (and infamous) *Doctor Who* forums of the 1980s/90s was rec.arts.drwho, which continued to be a centre for fannish writing and communications until the usenet format itself gave way to more popular developing online platforms in the twenty-first century.

In 2005, *Doctor Who* returned with a bang, becoming a mainstream TV hit beloved by millions, just as in the early 1960s. Fandom split and split again – not always into the more 'obvious' groupings of Classic versus New, or men versus women, or even Old Codger versus Newfangled Youngster. There were more women in fandom than ever before, and that shaped the conversation, as well as, rather disappointingly, the backlash.

There was more kissing in *Doctor Who*, in the fanfic as well as on screen. (Let's face it, mostly in the fanfic.)

Online resources developed, each with their own subset of fans. Did you make the leap from Livejournal to Dreamwidth? Have you ever got into an argument on Gallifrey Base? What even is a Tumblr?

Data was lost. So many stories, posts, conversations, simply disappeared as old servers went down, fan groups broke apart or new tech replaced older platforms. Not everything on the internet is forever.

Fic hubs like A Teaspoon and an Open Mind were created with the intent to be as permanent an archive as possible of fanfic on the internet.

Fan criticism sharpened. Flame wars burned. Everyone was blogging. Then no one was blogging. It was, as RTD himself said in his book *The Writer's Tale*, a decade where everyone typed furiously at each other.[9]

These days, *Doctor Who* criticism gets millions of eyeballs by happening lightning-fast across Twitter. Podcasts allow fans to chat to each other without anyone having to type at all. Zines made a comeback, because stapled paper is comforting and it's nice to have an outlet for fannish writing without being shouted at by strangers.

A new Doctor's coming, and a new Rose. We're likely to see a whole new wave of fanfic, written by children who weren't alive in 2005, featuring crossovers with *Heartstopper* and *Sex Education*. Fandom will never be the same again … again.

Who's writing about *Who*?

Doctor Who is one of the most documented TV series of all time, and it has likewise been capaciously discussed in academia. Its early mentions in nascent television studies were indebted to the 1970s/80s fashion for 'structuralist' analysis – this meant studying programmes for their narrative structures. John Fiske analysed *The Creature from the Pit* in this way in 1983,[10] and John Tulloch and Manuel Alvarado's book *The Unfolding Text* – also 1983 – cemented this 'structuralist' approach to *Doctor Who*; it was full of forbidding jargon intent on proving that popular television deserved to be on university reading lists (see Section I).[11]

However, in the wake of John Tulloch's co-authorship, with Henry Jenkins, of *Science Fiction Audiences: Watching Doctor Who and Star Trek* (1995),[12] *Doctor Who* began to be analysed in more 'poststructuralist' terms as a matter of different audience readings – fans' readings among them. Rather than arcane academic interpretations of *Who* being offered up, scholars instead began to show an interest in its 'reception', and viewers and fans with very different political views could find (or claim) 'their' version of *Doctor Who* by understanding the same stories in radically different ways – a situation that has only become more heightened in today's 'culture wars'.

Academic writing on the Doctor gradually found its way out of this structuralist-to-poststructuralist time tunnel, and with a generation of fans entering academia (as well as all sorts of other cultural production) the show began to be analysed in more diverse ways. It was studied as cultural history,[13] in relation to transmedial texts rather than purely as a TV show,[14] and importantly analysed via gender studies.[15] Academic publisher I.B. Tauris – now an imprint of Bloomsbury – set up a book series called 'Who Watching' to corral this variety of material. All arenas of *Doctor Who* were now fair game for scholarship, from Big Finish Audios[16] to *Doctor Who Monthly* and VHS releases.[17]

The variety of cross-disciplinary scholarly writing on *Doctor Who* means that there is no one 'master-narrative' of the programme's academic lives. Instead, *Doctor Who* has regenerated into countless academic forms/theories. A search might turn up *Who*'s analysis in religious studies[18] but also in linguistics,[19] in work on national identity[20] as much as philosophy.[21] Despite a recurring cast of academic-fan writers who have returned to *Who* on multiple occasions, there is arguably no absolute or strong sense of an 'academic canon' of work on the programme – what gets referenced depends to a large degree on what exactly a new author is looking at, what they're arguing and which discipline(s) they're calling home. Like *Doctor Who*'s own sense of canon, which tends to be overwritten by new creators as required, its academic canon is similarly subject to fluctuation.

That said, there have been reiterated concerns: *Doctor Who* has repeatedly been read critically as excluding and marginalizing forms of difference,[22] and as the programme itself opens up more and more to cultural identities that it has previously left out or downplayed, it could be suggested that critical strands of media scholarship have preceded, and gradually become aligned with, contemporary media production's own focus on greater diversity. The threads connecting TV scholarship and TV production may sometimes seem fragile, but both are shaped by the same cultures: *Doctor Who* in and out of the academy has benefited from the generational trajectories and careers of its fans; *Doctor Who* in and out of the academy has had to move with the times and respond to the powerful critique that it has, historically and recurrently, centred a white male narrative. Rather than viewing academic writing and *Doctor Who*'s cultural life as somehow disconnected, then, or as only tangentially related, we might very much view scholars and media creators as fellow (time and space) travellers. Both groups thrive on 'making it new' – just as Russell T Davies focuses on what new approaches, aspects and kinds of storytelling *Doctor Who* can incorporate, academic writers look for gaps in the literature. For instance, there is much less scholarship on *Who*'s casual audiences than its fans – hence Dominique Gagnon's contribution in this book – and there's not as much academic work as there should be on *Doctor Who*'s podcasters, YouTubers and contemporary content creators, something we have sought to address alongside reprinting influential book chapters and journal articles.

At the same time, it is vital to challenge the tribalism of some academic writing; much knowledge production occurs in *Who*'s 'para-academic' industry of reader-writers,[23] whether in Patreon and Kickstarter-funded spaces or through the catalogues of small presses like Obverse Books. Hybrid 'aca-fans' may have become the norm in academic work on popular/cult TV, but histories and theories of equally hybridized para-academic writing still remain to be fully explored for *Doctor Who*'s many worlds of fanzine, e-zine and fan press theorization.

Conclusion and summary of sections

Adventures Across Space and Time is organized into four sections, each of which focuses on a particular aspect of the *Doctor Who* writing and writers. Section I opens the book by discussing the transmedia connections that have emerged since the beginning of the series. Over the past sixty years, countless words from fans, scholars, journalists, creatives and many others have spilled across the pages of zines and papers, journals and books, sites and blogs. One could do worse in finding one text that effectively charts the development of fan writing and scholarship over half a century. But of course *Doctor Who* isn't just one text: it's a television series, but it's also book series, films, theatrical productions, merchandise, clothing, audio adventures, comics. It's a transmedia spectacular. In this section, we chart the growth of *Doctor Who* across media, from early work that focuses on *Doctor Who*'s televisual presence to work on *Doctor Who* across media, culminating in new work about live adventures (escape rooms, etc.) and the Time Lord Victorious transmedia experience.

In Section II, we focus on writing from and about fans. As *Doctor Who* has shifted and changed over time, so too have the fan audiences that have guided the multifaceted experiences of the show. This section ranges from early media studies' work on *Doctor Who*'s fans and followers through to new work on the contemporary fan 'blogosphere' represented by types of 'social media entertainment' such as podcasting and YouTubing. However, there has been far, far more work on fan activities and interpretations over the years than on what John Tulloch calls *Doctor Who*'s 'coalition' audience – that is, more casual and uncommitted, fleeting viewers alongside enduring fans. Therefore this section also includes groundbreaking work on this under-researched or even relatively 'invisible audience', present in BBC internal reports, perhaps, but rarely seriously studied in scholarship and fan writing alike. In terms of collecting together key readings, this section also explores how fans have read *Doctor Who* as representing all sorts of political ideologies, as well as critically assessing discourses of 'periodization', whereby various eras have been fannishly nominated as 'golden ages' (or nadirs for the series). It revisits John Tulloch's influential concept of fandom as a 'powerless elite' in the 'nu *Who*' era and considers the desires and cultural politics of both female and feminist fans, including recent work on reactions to Jodie Whittaker's casting as the Doctor.

In Section III, we focus on a new generation of fans discovering and exploring the programme. While *Doctor Who* is often conceptualized as a children's programme, the truth is more complicated: originally produced by the 'drama' department (rather than the 'children's' department), the show has always had a multi-generational audience. With the modern series' premiere in 2005, the fan generations split: many older fans returned to the show, joining children and young adults who were meeting the Doctor for the first time. Within this generation of fans there's a range of experiences that seem to fall along racial but also geographical lines, and as a whole, they're much more comfortable viewing the show through the lens of identity and politics. In this section, we explore the way that *Doctor Who* discussion has developed into silos for different generations and identities and highlight changing focuses of concern by the fan audience.

Finally, Section IV explores the intersections and crossovers between 'fandom' and 'professional'. In the history of *Doctor Who*, many fans went into writing, publishing and television production, even becoming part of the creative side of things. Even secondary texts like *Doctor Who Magazine* are spaces where fans are being paid professionally to cover their fannish love. There's a discomfort to those crossovers sometimes, with pros intruding on fannish spaces and vice versa. At what point does fan power get so large that it intrudes on the making of the show? How can fans salvage problems of the show's making? For example, fannish spaces helped to bring actors back to feeling positive about their role in *Doctor Who*, like Christopher Eccleston in 2019 and Caroline John in the 1990s, who thought everyone hated her until a convention convinced her otherwise. Professional production companies like Big Finish have taken fannish frustrations with some of the worst failings of the show and turned them around, but as fans become professionals, they stop being able to exist in those fannish spaces any more.

Ultimately, *Doctor Who* is not, and never can be, just one thing. We celebrate its complexity and contradictions, its vast and expansive history, and its many interpretations and meanings over time. It is what we set out to do in this volume: collect the voices of fans, scholars, creatives and professionals alike to offer the multifaceted and (yes) contradictory meanings that construct *Doctor Who* at its sixtieth anniversary and beyond. As we write this, we sit at the start of a new era of *Doctor Who*: Ncuti Gatwa is poised to take over the role, becoming the first Black male actor to portray the Doctor; Russell T Davies is back as showrunner, bringing a wealth of fan – and production-based knowledge back to the series. A new international partnership with Disney+ and the BBC heralds new opportunities (or new challenges) to the show in the years after its Sixtieth Anniversary.

Much is uncertain about what *Doctor Who* will become. But what is certain is that fans, academics and aca-fans will continue to write, to research and to develop new ideas about the show.

A note on reprints and new chapters

This volume collects classic writing about *Doctor Who* as well as newly commissioned pieces. In the interests of breadth, we have included shorter excerpts of many classic pieces. We have kept the citation styles authentic to the original piece, with the exception of adding full citations where needed. Newly commissioned work follows the same citation format, with all citations listed in the endnotes. We have opted to italicize the titles of *Doctor Who* stories from 1963–1996 and put in quotation marks titles of episodes for the 2005 series onwards.

Notes

1. John Tulloch and Manuel Alvarado, *Doctor Who: The Unfolding Text* (London: Macmillan, 1983).
2. We have included a few short primary sources, but in the main have opted for secondary sources. Interested readers of primary sources may want to explore Andrew Pixley's excellent work in the *Doctor Who: The Complete History* series, which was published by Panini UK, as well as a critical engagement with the BBC Written Archives in James Chapman's *Inside the TARDIS*.
3. Matt Hills, 'Foreword: The Eleven Fandoms?' in *Fan Phenomena: Doctor Who*, ed. Paul Booth (Bristol, UK: Intellect, 2013), 6.
4. Pat Harrigan and Noah Wardrip-Fruin, 'Introduction', in *Third Person: Authoring and Exploring Vast Narratives*, ed. Pat Harrigan and Noah Wardrip-Fruin (Cambridge: The MIT Press, 2009), 2.

5   As we write this, Russell T. Davies is coming back to showrun the programme a second time, although with a new Doctor (Ncuti Gatwa) in the role.
6   The BBC have never asserted a 'canon' of *Doctor Who*; our position is that all texts are valid, and we relish the contradictions!
7   See Paul Booth and Craig Owen Jones, *Watching Doctor Who* (London, UK: Bloomsbury, 2020).
8   Miles Booy, *Love and Monsters: The Doctor Who Experience, 1979 to the Present* (London: I.B. Tauris, 2012), 33.
9   Russell T. Davies, with Benjamin Cook, *The Writer's Tale* (London: BBC Books, 2013).
10 John Fiske, 'Dr. Who: Ideology and the Reading of a Popular Narrative Text', *Australian Journal of Screen Theory* 13, no. 14 (1983): 69–100.
11 Tulloch and Alvarado, *The Unfolding Text*.
12 John Tulloch and Henry Jenkins, *Science Fiction Audiences: Watching Doctor Who and Star Trek* (New York: Routledge, 1995).
13 James Chapman, *Inside the TARDIS: The Worlds of Doctor Who – A Cultural History* (London: I.B. Tauris, 2006).
14 Piers Britton, *TARDISbound: Navigating the Universes of Doctor Who* (London: I.B. Tauris, 2011).
15 Lorna Jowett, *Dancing with the Doctor: Dimensions of Gender in the Doctor Who Universe* (London: I.B. Tauris, 2017).
16 Discussed in *Time and Relative Dissertations in Space* (Manchester: Manchester University Press, 2007).
17 Thoughtfully analysed in Miles Booy's *Love and Monsters*.
18 See, for example, *Time and Relative Dimensions in Faith* (2013), edited by Andrew Crome and James McGrath.
19 Jason Barr and Camille D. G. Mustachio (eds), *The Language of Doctor Who* (Lanham, NC: Rowman and Littlefield, 2014).
20 Danny Nicol, *Doctor Who: A British Alien?* (London: Palgrave, 2018).
21 Kevin S. Decker, *Who is Who? The Philosophy of Doctor Who* (London: I.B. Tauris, 2014).
22 See, for instance, Lindy Orthia's edited collection *Doctor Who and Race* (Bristol: Intellect, 2013).
23 Ken Gelder, *Popular Fiction* (London: Routledge, 2004), 75.

SECTION ONE

Into the (Transmedia) vortex: From Dalekmania to *Time Lord Victorious*

Paul Booth

What is '*Doctor Who*'? Although obviously a television series that premiered in November 1963, the concept of '*Doctor Who*' as an entity has grown to encompass a grander, more multimedia existence that just the TV programme. Less than a year after the show premiered, the release of the first *Doctor Who* comic in *TV Comic* (Nov 1964), furthered the adventures of the Doctor (William Hartnell). But rather than include the Doctor's TV companions, Susan (Carole Ann Ford), Ian (William Russell) and Barbara (Jacqueline Hill), the comic featured two children, John and Gillian, with no mention of the traditional TARDIS crew. The lines of continuity had already grown murky, just one year into the series.

The continuity grows more complex as the series develops other spin-offs that both are and aren't connected to the television series. The novelizations of episodes proport to tell the same story, but often include additional information (or even complete alterations; e.g. *Doctor Who in an Exciting Adventure with the Daleks* by David Whitaker retells *and* changes the introduction of the first companions); the comics introduce new companions and stories, which may or may not come back in other media; Big Finish audio adventures; webcasts and later media including stage plays, original novels, video and board games, toys, websites and escape rooms each complicate (rather than re-mediate) the *original* of *Doctor Who*. Even additional television texts complicate the narrative exposition: simply mention *Dimensions in Time*'s complex continuity and a *Doctor Who* fan might become apoplectic!

Although the term 'transmedia storytelling' wouldn't appear until twenty-five years or so after this *TV Comic* appearance of John and Gillian, the seeds of it were already planted in *Doctor Who* fans' minds.[1] The term 'transmedia storytelling' refers to one story (or narrative) being told across multiple media. While many scholars have put their own stamp on the term, at its heart it explores the way that audiences piece together stories into a coherent whole.[2] Some transmedia texts (e.g. the Marvel Cinematic Universe) are heavily concerned with canon and coherence. There is top-down canonicity, where each part (film, television series, comic) builds on the others, and if one element contradicts some other element, it is often explained away in a later text. Other transmedia texts, like *Doctor Who*, are constructed in a more piecemeal, bottom-up manner. As Paul Cornell asserts, in a piece excerpted in this section, there is no authorized canon of *Doctor Who* – which means, of course, that both nothing and everything 'counts' as *Doctor Who*.

This section takes *Doctor Who* as a key exemplar of a transmedia text that emerges *before* these implications had become de facto. By examining the way *Doctor Who* blazes a trail in transmedia storytelling, we can see both antecedents for what transmedia storytelling has become today, and also some alternate histories of transmedia storytelling – deviations and diversions that tell a sideways story of 'could have been'. The chapters in this section explore this tension through their contrasts. Taken individually, each chapter in this section presents a slice of the *Doctor Who* universe; taken as a whole, they form their own transmediated understanding of the *wholeness* of *Doctor Who*.

Notes

1. See Henry Jenkins, *Convergence Culture: Where Old and New Media Collide* (New York: New York University Press, 2006) and Marsha Kinder, *Playing with Power in Movies, Television, and Video Games: From Muppet Babies to Teenage Mutant Ninja Turtles* (Berkeley, CA: University of California Press, 1991).
2. See Paul Booth, 'Transmedia Fandom and Participation: The Nuances and Contours of Fannish Participation', in *The Routledge Companion to Transmedia Studies*, ed. Matthew Freeman and Renira Rampazzo Gambarato (New York, NY: Routledge, 2019), 279–87.

Chapter 1
Transmedia *Doctor Who* I

From 'Canonicity in *Doctor Who*' by Paul Cornell[*]

First published 2007

Paul Cornell's discussion about the lack of canon in Doctor Who *is a persuasive look not just at the development of the series but at the way canon encumbers fandom. Canon is always about authority – going back to its biblical roots – and arguing for a canon is ultimately granting someone the authority to say* this counts *and* this doesn't. *But because* Doctor Who *has rarely had that authority figure saying so, and even when they do they dismiss canon concerns, Cornell argues that the show has only benefited from its absent canon.*

Not giving a toss about how it all fits together is one of *Doctor Who*'s oldest, proudest traditions, a strength of the series. [...] It's allowed infinite change, and never left the show crunched into a corner after all the dramatic options had already been done. [...] The fact that the BBC had never declared anything non-canonical is one of the reasons why canonicity is much fought over by *Who* fans. It's not just about presumed authority (I'll come to that), it's about worth.

The closest we ever got to a BBC pronouncement on canonicity was a couple of years after the end of the original series of *Doctor Who*. The show's last production team declared that Virgin's *Doctor Who* novels, the New Adventures, were an official continuation of the series, overseen by the last producer, John Nathan-Turner, with the last writing team onboard, heading towards the aims that that team had put in place.

Those who argue against the canonicity of the New Adventures miss having an authority to declare or reinforce canonicity. They wish, having once had such an authority declare against them, that such an authority was now on their side. In its absence, they feel they should and can do the job of that authority.

Russell Davies probably could utter a pronouncement about canonicity that would be accepted. If he wanted to. [...] He's come close, in that he's said that only what the general TV audience remembers is important in terms of what's referred to onscreen (I'm vastly paraphrasing here), and also that BBC

---

[*]Originally published online in 2007. https://www.paulcornell.com/2007/02/canonicity-in-doctor-who/.

television dramas must be whole unto themselves, and must not require extra purchases that 'complete the story', as per the BBC charter.

The first is a simple truth. You don't make stories about decades-old continuity points and expect to keep eight million tuning in. (I think fandom offhandedly understands that.) But the second is a more interesting bit of give and take. It says the show won't work out its continuity in other places, or finish off threads that were started in the old BBC *Doctor Who* novels or the Big Finish audio plays.

To deal with that […] Russell's quietly invented […] The Time War. Those who say that because the New Adventures are canonical, therefore the TV series shouldn't contradict them (and those people also are often inclined to abuse the opposition in search of false authority) are ignoring the fact that the TV series now has a licence to contradict *itself*, and has already used it, big time.

[W]hen you say 'the books just aren't "canon!"' or 'the books "happened" and the TV show can't ignore them!' you're not saying something like 'for every action there is an equal but opposite reaction', you're saying something like 'the South will never surrender'. You're yelling a battle cry, not stating the truth. Because there is no truth here to find. There was never and now cannot be any authority to rule on matters of canonicity in a tale that has allowed, or at the very least accepted, the rewriting of its own continuity. And you're using the fact that discussions of canonicity are all about authority to try to assume an authority that you do not have.

In the end, you're just bullying people.

Because in *Doctor Who* there is no such thing as 'canon'.

From '*Doctor Who* and the Convergence of Media: A Case Study in "Transmedia Storytelling"' by Neil Perryman[†]

First published 2008

Perryman focuses here on two competing threads: first, the BBC quite deliberately entered into an era of transmedia storytelling with the appearance of the new series of Doctor Who *in 2005 and, second,* Doctor Who *had always been using transmedia style in its storytelling. Of note, Perryman uses 'transmedia' in the sense of Henry Jenkins' concept of '"convergence culture", meaning "a new aesthetic that has emerged in response to media convergence", where audiences act as "hunters and gatherers, chasing down bits of the story across media channels" – a participatory process that can potentially result in a 'richer entertainment experience"'.[1] Transmedia is a corporate practice which, at least in terms of* Doctor Who, *is born from grass-roots, organic processes.*

[†]Originally published in *Convergence: The International Journal of Research into New Media Technologies* 14, no. 1 (2008): 21–39.

Doctor Who's first steps into convergence culture began, not during the transmission of the original series, but rather after its cancellation in 1989. [...] While grassroots amateur fan-fiction and semi-professional, low-budget video productions helped to plug the gap during the early years of Doctor Who's Interregnum,[2] the BBC also decided to take the unprecedented step of licensing professionally produced fan fiction for mainstream distribution. Virgin Publishing licensed the property of Doctor Who from the BBC in 1990, less than one year after its cancellation, and in 1991 they published their first original novel, Timewyrm: Genesis. However, unlike the Target novelizations, these novels were not aimed at children. Instead, these New Adventures (or NAs) were aimed squarely at a mature audience who had grown up with the show. In fact, early novels in the series controversially used the 'f-word' and depicted the Doctor's teenage companion engaging in sexual intercourse (ed.: see Smith?'s Chapter 6 in this volume).

Buoyed by the financial success of these original novels, and coupled with fans' thirst for new and officially sanctioned material, the BBC subsequently licensed the rights to produce original audio dramas for direct distribution on CD to the independent company Big Finish in 1999; a company once again staffed (administratively and creatively) by Doctor Who fans who already had established track records in grassroots fandom in general and the Virgin New Adventures in particular.

A good example of the levels of collaboration that existed between these fan-driven media platforms during the show's Interregnum period can be distilled via the multimedia project 'Shakedown' (1995). This story began life as a fan-produced video project which was then novelized and expanded upon in a Virgin New Adventure novel, while characters who featured in that novel (e.g. the archaeologist Bernice Summerfield) also featured in their own series of Big Finish plays and books. In short, this was a very early example of a transmedia collaboration between three different companies, which not only resulted in a coherent treat for the fans, it also displayed a level of complexity that almost certainly went unnoticed by the BBC itself.

When Doctor Who returned to British television in 2005 it was not as dormant as it may have first appeared. As Clayton Hickman, editor of Doctor Who Magazine, explains: 'for any one month between Doctor Who ending and the new series coming on you could get up to five or six separate Doctor Who stories a month, which is a lot more than you ever got when it was on the telly'.[3] This could explain why Doctor Who was chosen by the BBC to be its flagship for transmedia storytelling. The franchise had been successful in a variety of different media platforms (books, CD, radio, comics and the web), while the writers and producers of the new series had written for all of them.

One of the most complex forms of transmedia storytelling occurred via a series of meta-textual websites and blogs that were produced by the BBC to accompany the return of Doctor Who.

When season two was transmitted in 2006 the games between producer and fan became even more complex. James Goss, content producer for the official Doctor Who website, boasted, 'this year we're producing the most ambitious online fictional world ever' (Goss, 2006: 66), and an example of this intertextual complexity can be traced via the 'Leamington Spa Lifeboat Museum Website' (Leamington Spa is 60 miles away from the nearest coast, which immediately raised alarm bells). The site told the story of a family killed by a 'mad wolf' (harking back to the 2005 'Bad Wolf' meme), and it included a hidden interactive game where the player could hunt for alien artefacts that had appeared in the show (BBC, n.d.a). Furthermore, the Museum was opened by Queen Victoria, and buried deep within the site was a seemingly innocuous link to the 'Millingdale Organic Ice Cream' website (BBC, n.d.b), which offered some rare flavours such as 'Silver Giant' (a reference to the Cybermen), 'Henriks' Surprise' (Henriks was the shop where Rose originally worked) and 'Madame Du Pompadom' (a reference to

Madame De Pompadour who would appear in the 2006 episode 'The Girl in the Fireplace'). More links were revealed as the series continued, inviting viewers to return and search for more clues and content. For example, after the episode 'Army of Ghosts' had aired, the link to the flavour 'Ghost Glace' suddenly revealed a restricted area that contained hidden video clips for that episode.

Fans have also questioned the validity of these websites in terms of canonicity. Is the information provided by these metasites really a genuine and legitimate part of the fictional fabric of the programme? While James Goss suggests that the production team vets every decision suggested by the BBC's new media division, continuity errors do complicate the relationship between the television text and the sanctioned metatext. The most infamous example of this occurred on Mickey's blog after the episode 'Father's Day' was transmitted. This story took place in an alternative timeline where Rose's father survived what should have been a fatal hit-and-run car accident. However, by the end of the episode her father bravely surrenders to his preordained fate and the timelines re-establish themselves until none of the events actually happened. However, Mickey's website contradicts this fact by showing photographic evidence of events that should have been erased from both Earth's timeline *and* Mickey's memories.

However, these metasites have also been used to correct continuity errors that have appeared within the television show. For example, following the broadcast of the *Torchwood* episode 'Cyberwoman' (13 November 2006), the official *Torchwood* website provided information about 'The Fall of Torchwood One' that attempted to correct – via 'additive comprehension'[4] – what some fans had regarded as a glaring error in the plot. Fans had asked how the eponymous Cyberwoman was not sucked into the void along with the rest of her kin during the climax to the *Doctor Who* episode 'Doomsday' (8 July 2006) and the site retroactively explained away the problem: 'The only exceptions were those being converted with material entirely derived from this side of the void', which allowed the events of 'Cyberwoman' to take place without contradicting what viewers originally saw in the episode.

There are limitations to how far the BBC, as a public service broadcaster, can take the concept of transmedia storytelling. For example, in the months leading up to the programme's return in 2005, the Eighth incarnation of the Doctor was embroiled in a series of multimedia adventures, both in print (the BBC books and the official comic) and on audio (the Big Finish CD releases). When news of the series' return to television was announced in September 2003 each range of adventures carefully placed its particular version of the Eighth Doctor into a position where he could seamlessly regenerate into his successor. For example, the Big Finish audio plays had exiled the Eighth Doctor to an alternative universe but as soon as the new series was announced the company swiftly brought him back again. The final Eighth Doctor novel, *The Gallifrey Chronicles*, was originally scheduled for release in February 2005, one month before the show returned to BBC1 with the episode 'Rose': however, two weeks prior to its publication the novel was mysteriously delayed until June. The show's producer, Russell T. Davies, explained the reason for this unexpected delay in the May 2005 issue of *Doctor Who Magazine* (Davies, 2005: 67):

> The BBC's Editorial Policy – a mighty and powerful department – realized that, with its title alone, *The Gallifrey Chronicles* would imply that the book was a necessary purchase in order to understand the narrative of 'Rose'. *Doctor Who* is produced by a Public Service Broadcaster and it is paid for by you, the licence payer. As a consequence of this status, the BBC has to be very careful with its merchandising. We are happy for you to enjoy the Doctor off-screen and read the novels but we must never make that purchase necessary. If you had to buy a BBC novel in order to understand the plot as transmitted on BBC1, then we would be breaking the BBC's guidelines.

In other words, while these satellite formats can complement the parent programme they can never be integrated into the over-arching narrative to such an extent that it impacts directly upon it. In short, these platforms must stand alone.

While the intuitional limitations laid down by the BBC certainly apply to merchandise that must be purchased (books, comics, CDs and so on), do the same rules apply to transmedia programming that is free to access? According to Jenkins (2006), part of what makes for good transmedia storytelling experience is when the producers successfully build an entire world that can be experienced across many different platforms and media channels. Jenkins (2003) says, 'A good character can sustain multiple narratives and thus lead to a successful movie franchise. A good "world" can sustain multiple characters (and their stories) and thus successfully launch a transmedia franchise'.

The result is that the BBC has successfully created a transmedia world that supports demographic-spanning spin-offs that straddle media platforms and storytelling techniques. It allows passive audiences to simply sit back and enjoy the parent show in blissful isolation, while at the same time it gives active, migratory and participatory audiences opportunities to engage in a rich and extended multimedia experience unparalleled in British broadcasting at the time of writing. It has also illustrated to the BBC how transmedia storytelling makes sound economic sense, not only in terms of ancillary merchandising and branding but in production costs as well.

Notes

1. Henry Jenkins, *Convergence Culture* (New York: New York University Press, 2006), 20–1.
2. The term 'Interregnum' was used by the scriptwriter (and fan) Mark Gatiss, and then adopted by fandom, to describe the programme's sixteen-year gap from active television production.
3. *Doctor Who Confidential: Bringing Back the Doctor* (broadcast BBC3, Saturday 26 March 2005).
4. Ed.: a key component of transmedia storytelling, where different media components add up to a cohesive understanding of a single narrative.

References

From '*Doctor Who* and the Convergence of Media'

BBC. 'Leamington Spa Lifeboat Museum' (n.d.a): http://www.leamingtonspalifeboatmuseum.co.uk/ (accessed 9 January 2007).
BBC. 'Millingdale Ice Cream' (n.d.b.): http://www.millingdaleice.cream.co.uk/ (accessed 9 January 2007).
Davies, Russell T. 'Production Notes'. *Doctor Who Magazine* 356 (May 2005): 67.
Goss, James. 'Face Forward'. *Doctor Who Magazine* 367 (2006): 66.
Jenkins, Henry. 'Transmedia Storytelling'. *Technology Review* (January 2003): http://www.technologyreview.com/Biotech/13052/ (accessed 9 January 2007).
Jenkins, Henry. *Convergence Culture*. New York: New York University Press, 2006.

Chapter 2
Early TV scholarship

From '*Dr Who*: Similarity and Difference' by John Tulloch*

First published 1982

> *Tulloch's 'Dr Who: Similarity and Difference' might just be the very first published academic writing on* Doctor Who. *While more common today (if still not completely accepted), academic studies of popular culture were considered avant-garde at the time. It is perhaps for this reason that the academic language and 'jargon' of the piece heighten its academic credentials. Tulloch's argument is an ultimate one that* Doctor Who *has always wrestled with: how to balance* change *in the series with connection to and reliance on* continuity. *The Doctor will change faces and personalities, the stories will change, so how do we know the programme we see in 2023 is the same one that was seen in 1983 or 1963? For Tulloch, the power of* Doctor Who *lies precisely in this balance of novelty and uniformity.*

The success of the programme (its audience size, its longevity) must depend on this other 'success' (its tension between novelty and sameness) – the latter's terms defined according to the discourse of television professionals.

These professional assumptions of 'something similar but different' relate casually to what Heath and Skirrow have called 'the central fact of television experience', which is 'much less flow than flow and regularity', a succession which is also 'repetition' generating 'terms of movement and status' which are to be found' within the single programme as within the evening's viewing'.[1]

Against the dissolution the text must work especially hard. To tie together its discourses *Dr Who* draws heavily on its noted articulacy ('probably the most articulate science fiction drama on television', 'the plot operates very much on what he says'; 'it becomes much more intellectual ... in most other programmes it's just kill the aliens').[2] Even in the case of the judo-Who, events are ultimately decided by intellectual rather than naked action, and this in turn draws on generic and narrative themes and

---

*Originally published in *Australian Journal of Screen Theory* 11/12 (1982): 8–24.

conventions of science fiction. But as well as this dependence, *Dr Who* has recently increasingly striven for its continuity and coherence via a particular mode of address, incorporating a consciously allegorical dimension. In the Graham Williams era as producer, for instance, its stress on inter-textuality became a sign of its style, and via this unity-as-style the programme masked other inter-textual references which could have been more divisive.

Theoretically, the simplifying quest for a single, homogeneous meaning in the text is disturbed in two ways. (1) By the fact that, as Ellis says, to determine the possibilities of any text – the possibilities which construct its 'preferred' reading – it is necessary to consider it as crossed by a variety of material, technological, aesthetic and ideological codes which (each with their own history and narrative presence) are by no means inevitably harmonious.[3] (2) Because these potentially contradictory codes may then be de-coded differently by different class, sub-cultural and institutional groups.

Textual meaning occurs as an interaction of discursive processes, since both text and reader are only a matter of relative coherence. As the point of intersection of potentially antagonistic discourses, each is a site of struggle and negotiation. Neither in the text nor in the reading of the text, and thus certainly not in the space between them, can one every assume a simple, uncontradictory meaning.

The opening titles of *Dr Who* foreground its generic context: 'This is science fiction'. But in doing so they reproduce visually the centripetal/centrifugal opposition fundamental to S.F'.s play of meaning. Each changing shot of the title sequence – of the Doctor, of the Tardis and of the hole in time, in turn at the centre of centrifugal lines of force – is structured visually on S.F'.s principle of centring and diffusion. The Doctor is both human centre and, through the hole in time represented by the vortex, a ceaseless explorer and peace-keeper of the universe. In Descartes the vortex, the rotary movement of atoms of matter around an axis, accounts for the formation of the universe; and the opening image of *Dr Who* with lines of force spreading outwards from his forehead potentially recalls the idealist principle that the universe exists because man thinks it exists. 'I think therefore I am'.

One of the successes of the programme has been its ability to replace *Dr Who*'s lead actor several times, each of the first four Doctors emphasizing contrast. There has been a regular alteration of Doctors – straight/comic straight/comic. This acting against institutionalized type threatens the coherence of the programme with the effect of actor-as-text – what Dyer refers to as the 'structured polysemy' of the star images which is generated by the prior construction of the star via other (promotional, filmic and critical) texts.[4] This partially countered where, as is generally the case in *Dr Who*, lead actors are encouraged to present 'themselves' or act against type. Jon Pertwee's liking for action, stunts and 'fine living', for instance, were incorporated characteristics of the Third Doctor. This unusual degree of personalization in *Dr Who* also works to protect the text-as-institution from the 'anything goes in S.F. syndrome'.

There are two recurring themes in *Dr Who*: (i) the threat of human defilement; (ii) the liberation of the oppressed … Both themes have the same project: the nomination of what it means to be human. And they draw on what I have called the master images of science fiction over the last thirty years: the fragile human organism, and the potent human lawgiver.

However, whether or not intertextuality operates semantically for some audience groups is, I would suggest, irrelevant to the mode of address of *Dr Who*. Even at the most simplistic level – of simple recognition of references to Greek myth, Shakespeare, the Bible, 'history', Lang's *Metropolis*, 'science', etc. – *Dr Who* establishes a 'complicit' relationship with its audience, which is much closer to the conventions of theatrical vaudeville (or, more recently, of the northern English working men's club) than to those of 'realism'. In the case of the tertiary educated audience – an important target group for *Dr Who* – these 'double meanings' (where the 'allegorical' reference is in fact to another 'high art' text) may have as much to do with the pleasure derived from the text as its 'scary' quality has for younger children.

However, this is not a case of a text meaning 'all things to all people'. *Dr Who*'s emphasis on its own textuality is re-tied to the fictional world insofar as most of the foregrounding devices have ... a direct relevance to the dominant generic and narrative values of the program. The syntagmatic and paradigmatic play between similarity and difference, purity and defilement, quest and hubris, thought and will, science and power is formed present is formally presented as a play between a 'realistic' and an allegorical form.

From '*Dr Who:* Ideology and the Reading of a Popular Narrative Text' by John Fiske[†]

First published 1983

Building on Tulloch's argument about novelty and uniformity, which he quotes in this piece, John Fiske's 'Dr Who: Ideology and the Reading of a Popular Narrative Text' explores the relationship between storytelling in Doctor Who *and the experience of watching/enjoying it as an audience member.* Doctor Who, *as all television does, creates ideological meanings (cultural values) for its audience through stories; but in order to appreciate those meanings (Fiske calls them 'discourses'), the audience has to accept them. Fiske argues, the irony is that the audience is so vast and diffuse that any meanings must themselves be vague enough to be acceptable! Fiske's piece here, like Tulloch's before him, uses academic language to analyse popular culture like* Doctor Who (*specifically* The Creature from the Pit) *in order to explore the connection between production and consumption of cultural texts.*

In this paper I intend to explore two closely related concerns – (i) the relationship between the syntagmatic, onward thrust of the story through time and the paradigmatic, a-temporal discourses through which it is realized, and (ii) the notion of popularity, which I define as 'an easy fit between the discourses of the text and the discourses through which its model readers articulate and understand their social experience'.

Popular texts are constructed from those areas of a discourse where consensus is high enough to be taken for granted – thus we have *Dr Who* defined partly through democracy in the political discourse and his adversaries through totalitarianism, because these signs can be taken for granted.

Our social experience is, therefore, harder to read than a text, because it is fraught with the internal contradictions and sites of ideological struggle that are excluded from a popular text by its conditions of production and reception. Reading social experience is a struggle, and because of its open nature we find it difficult to be finally sure that our reading is adequate: reading a text, however, is easier by far, and the greater closure within it is constantly working to reassure and convince us that this easy reading is adequate – totally adequate. Such an easily read text, then, becomes, I submit, popular when its readings, which are confidently believed to be adequate, fit neatly and naturally with readings of social experience that we use the same discourses to understand, but which are by definition, more complex contradictory and thus harder to read. Popular narratives prove in their own closed world the

---

[†]Originally published in *Australian Journal of Screen Theory* 14 (1983): 69–100.

adequacy of discourses as explanatory mechanisms: this adequacy is then transferred to the use of those discourses in the social world to the ultimate relief and reassurance of the reader.

Of the discourses of knowledge in this narrative, the first, and most obvious, is that of science: but science is not the value-free objective discourse it claims to be in society. As John Tulloch (1982) has pointed out, pure science is finally totalitarian – it allows no alternative, no oppositional view. In story after a story in *Dr Who*, 'pure', or 'cold', science is used to maintain or establish a totalitarian political order. Science is a means of power in an intergalactic version of feudal society. The Doctor typically defeats a totalitarian, scientific antagonist and replaces him or her with a liberal democratic humane scientist to take over and bring justice and freedom to the oppressed serf class.

The text then faces the inherent ideological problem of its genre – science fiction. It needs to reconcile the objective, inhuman values of science with the individualistic and moral values of popular fiction. It does this by a careful structuring of heroes, villains and discourses.

The TARDIS exemplifies this meeting perfectly: on the inside it is pure science, on the outside idiosyncratically individualistic (see Tulloch, 1982); it is the mechanical equivalent of the Doctor, who also clothes his science in the garb of eccentric individualism. It is also a metaphor for control – spatial physics expands its interior presumably ad infinitum, whereas externally it is not only compact, but a police box – a metonym of social law and order.

The use of these value-laden objectives brings us on to [another] crucial discourse, that of morality. The BBC is specific and precise about the morality of the show – the Doctor must be clearly good, and his adversaries clearly bad. The story admits of no blurred value judgements in the main characters, though minor ones may undergo a transformation through their meeting with the Doctor from apparently bad to really good (e.g. the Huntsman and Irato).

In the narrative, however, the constant killing and capturing by the villains takes a variety of exciting forms that disguises the fundamental monotony or at least homogeneity. But this is typical of television where an attractive variety of signifiers commonly overlays a restricted range of signifieds and a simple repetitive self-reinforcing structure. Indeed, the attractiveness of the signifier is essential for the ideological effect because without it, the internal repetition of the structure would become manifest with the result that it would cease to be the hidden organizing device, and would then become apparent and therefore propaganda.

Here, the onward syntagmatic flow of the narrative serves to restrict the potential range of the discourses, and thus the range of positions from which the reading subject can make sense of the text. I do not wish to take up the over-determined position of some of the early screen theorists, which over-emphasized the power of the text to construct the subject, but I agree with them in their identification of the hegemony of the text in the enterprise of making sense. This text, in common with other popular narratives, constructs a restricted space within which the reading subject must be positioned if she/he is to make the preferred sense, which is the easy natural sense of the text.

This text may be closed in its sense of delimiting the space within which a preferred reading can be arrived at. But within this space the reader has a certain amount of freedom. Schoolboys can use the discourses of science and morality to validate their school experience, and may subordinate those of politics and economics to the suspense of the plot. More sceptical adults can read the science discourse as a parody, but use the text's conflation of morality with capitalist democracy to validate their social experience. Different readers can place the discourses in a different hierarchical order, foregrounding them and relating them differently within the limits proposed by the text. But these limits are crucial: the text does not encourage us to correlate despotism with free market economics via the concept of the slavery of the one who may be exploited in the trading deal: neither does it allow us to perceive that the Doctor's liberal democracy requires dominant and subordinate classes just as clearly as does Adrastra's totalitarianism. These readings are radically opposed, ones that would be produced by readers who dislike the text, that is who put themselves outside the realm of its popularity.

My point is that the popularity of a text is directly attributable to the collapse of the difference between author and reader: the appropriate discourses by which the text is constructed and read are part of the commonsense experience of both. Popularity then is not just the willing consent of the model reader to the hegemony of the text, it involves a more active assessment of the effectiveness of the discourses in making sense of both the text and the world.

The classic realist text of which this *Dr Who* story is an example is by definition a closed text, and it therefore becomes politically necessary to prise it open by this sort of semiotic or structuralist analysis. [...] The author in the realist text may be invisible, but he is not absent. Discourses are visual as well as verbal, and ideology is the framework of meaning that holds the discourses together. [...] The events of the story demonstrate that the Doctor and his helpers are successful because they are better scientists, but the structure of the discourses proposes that their success derives from their morality, politics, economics and individualism.

The popularity of the text derives from the reader's ability to transfer this uncontradictory reconciliation easily between text and society, a transference that becomes conventional, because it is generic to the series of Dr Who and even to the genre of science fiction. [...] The aesthetic structure of the text is satisfying only to the extent that it performs an ideological function in society. [...] This theory implies that popular art is not escapist, but mythic: it does not merely provide an imaginative refreshing alternative to the hard grind of an industrial existence; rather it enables and encourages the reader to make a particular kind of sense of that existence.

These relationships between discourse, text and world constitute a system, for each element affects and is affected by the others. Texts and social experience enter a mutually supportive relationship, and each, and both, affect the discourses by which they are structured and understood.

Popular artworks generally, but not, I believe, necessarily, in favour of the status quo. What we now need is an understanding of popularity, of the intertext between work of art and social experience and that is what I have attempted to move toward in this paper. The next enterprise is, for my money, the crucial one: it is to discover and analyse just how a work of popular art can be other than reactionary.

Notes

1 Stephen Heath and Gillian Skirrow, 'Television – a World in Action', *Screen*, Summer 1977, p. 16.
2 *Dr Who* audience research project: 'Nucon' (Science Fiction organization) group; responses recorded at the New Crest Hotel, Sydney, 11 May 1981.
3 Ed.: See John Ellis, 'Made in Ealing', *Screen*, Spring 1975.
4 Richard Dyer, *Stars* (London: British Film Institute, 1979), 72.

References

From '*Dr Who*: Similarity and Difference' by John Tulloch

Dyer, Richard. *Stars*. London: British Film Institute, 1979.
Dr Who audience research project: 'Nucon' (Science Fiction organization) group; responses recorded at the New Crest Hotel, Sydney, 11 May 1981.
Ellis, John. 'Made in Ealing'. *Screen* (Spring 1975): 78–127.
Heath, Stephen, and Gillian Skirrow. 'Television – a World in Action'. *Screen* (Summer 1977): 7–60.

From '*Dr Who*: Ideology and the Reading of a Popular Narrative Text' by John Fiske

Tulloch, John. '*Dr. Who*: Similarity and Difference'. *Australian Journal of Screen Theory* 11, no. 12 (1982): 8–27.

Chapter 3
Production insights

From *The Making of Doctor Who* by Terrance Dicks and Malcolm Hulke*

First published 1976 (original publication 1972)

The first edition of The Making of Doctor Who, *mainly written by script-writer Malcolm Hulke, was almost entirely a diegetic (internal) history, told through fictional documents from the Time Lords and UNIT about The Doctor as a fictional character. When Terrance Dicks developed the second edition, he decided to include much more information about the actual making of a television series, turning this into the first professionally published non-fiction book about* Doctor Who. *As such, it was hugely influential on fans in the 1970s, for many of whom this may have been the first exposure to a 'behind-the-scenes' account of television production. We can see this in the repetition of the quote 'never cruel or cowardly', used to describe the Doctor in this non-fiction work and applied by Steven Moffat in the fiction.*

Is it any wonder that so many Doctor Who *fans have become media professionals today?*

Television is something of an 'instant' medium. Yesterday is already history; last year is lost in the mists of time. So it is no easy matter to reconstruct something that happened over twelve years ago. But here, as accurate as painstaking research can make it, is an account of the origins of *Doctor Who*.

In television, the Producer has complete and overall charge of his own particular show. Each individual episode, or group of episodes, will have its own Director, responsible for 'getting the show in the can', i.e. for carrying out a successful studio recording. Individual Directors come and go with each serial. The Producer remains with his own show, working with each Director in turn.

This is a very demanding and time-consuming job, and in one very important area the Producer gets a full-time assistant. Everything starts with a script. No show can be a real success unless the script is sound. But numbers of freelance writers work on each show, each one writing a different serial. Someone is needed to find the best writers for the show, co-ordinate their efforts, evaluate different story ideas,

---

*Originally published in *The Making of Doctor Who* (London: Target Books, 1976), 2nd edition.

help writers to develop their ideas and cope with various script crises. Scripts prove to be too long or too short at the last moment, actors have difficulty with a scene or a line, writers fall ill and can't complete their assignments ... All this is another full-time job. Although the final decisions are his, the Producer will delegate most of the work directly concerned with the writing of the show to his Script Editor.

Although we've been referring above to the Producer as 'he', in fact the very first Producer of *Doctor Who* was a young woman called Verity Lambert. The first script editor was David Whitaker, himself a very experienced television writer.

... The Doctor believes in good and fights evil. Though often caught up in violent situations, he is a man of peace. He is never cruel or cowardly. In fact, to put it simply, the Doctor is a hero ...

In appearance, a television studio is like a very big room (some are as big as a football pitch). In this huge empty space the sets are built, mainly all round the walls so as to leave a big space in the middle for the cameras to move about. A set might be a bedroom, or an office, or the inside of the TARDIS. Sets usually have only three walls. The cameras 'look' into the set through where the fourth wall should have been.

At the end of the studio day, the Director has hundreds of feet of video tape (this is like tape-recorder tape only wider; it carries both sound and vision in electrical impulses). The Director can play this back to himself and select the shots he wants to keep. This is called editing. Music and sound effects, such as explosions, can be added afterwards to the edited tape.

In nearly every *Doctor Who* adventure there is one moment everyone is waiting for. Up till then, you have only seen hints of the monster, a scaly foot or a mechanical hand. But now the moment has arrived! The monster is revealed. Here it comes, lurching from the shadows, eyes flashing, ray-gun blazing, advancing on to the brave Doctor and his terrified companions! However, what you don't see is the man from the BBC's Visual Effects department who is trailing behind the monster, turning off and on those flashing eyes. Nor do you see the perspiring actor who is staggering along inside the heavy costume of this terrifying alien invader from Space.

Next time you see a *Doctor Who* monster, give a thought to the actor inside, and a special thought to all the hardworking people who turned the writer's idea into what you actually see on screen.

From *Triumph of a Time Lord: Regenerating Doctor Who in the Twenty-First Century* by Matt Hills[†]

First published 2010

But if Dicks and Hulke helped inspire those fans from the 1970s to enter the media industries, what did they do when they got there? Hills' influential 2010 Triumph of a Time Lord *explores the way that fandom helped bring the series back to the screen in 2005, through Russell T Davies' production, David Tennant's influential Tenth Doctor and the many screenwriters that helped develop the very show that influenced them. Hills also explores a shift in fan studies from seeing the fans as powerless entities, at the mercy of large media corporations, to when fans actually have power in the industry.*

[†]Originally published in *Triumph of a Time Lord* (London, UK: IB Tauris, 2010).

And, in using that power, they have turned the Doctor Who *brand into a multimedia franchise. The 'Doctor Who* mafia' *that brought the show back continues to dominate its text even fifteen years later.*

Doctor Who's fan culture has undoubtedly been instrumental in its return to TV screens. As Clayton Hickman, then editor of Doctor Who Magazine [DWM], told Guardian journalist Andy Bodle in 2004, 'The Doctor Who mafia ... That's why the show's coming back. If it wasn't for all the fans in high places, it would have just faded away'.[1]

Davies ... posits that fans' love of the show has inspired their desire to go into the media industry. In contributions to special editions of DWM, Davies developed his thesis that Doctor Who was always structured through absences and gaps, both textually and extra-textually (many early episodes having been junked by the BBC). As a result, he depicts Who fans as being forced to use their imaginations. [...] Doctor Who fandom has seemingly had a closer link to professional media production, writing or performance, rather than inspiring careers in science.

Now, 'official' producers are fans who combine communal knowledge with professional industry-insider status, making the programme for BBC Wales – and as a flagship BBC show, no less. Poachers have turned gamekeeper at the highest levels of official TV production aimed squarely at the mass market.

Prior to the show's triumphant return, fans sought to distance themselves symbolically from pathologizations of fandom as 'sad', infantile and living in the past. After all, in the wilderness years, Doctor Who was definitively an 'old', 'dead' show, popular in the 1970s. At that time, admitting to Who fandom seemed to imply that devotees had failed to grow up and move on, instead becoming trapped in regressive, infantile tastes.

'Fanwank' has a specific meaning within Doctor Who fandom, being 'a continuity reference thrown into a story and having little relevance to the plot, but there purely as a device to please fans'.[2] [...] BBC Wales' Doctor Who effectively deconstructs the concept of 'fanwank'. It does so by critiquing the binary logic that sustained it – that of 'fans' versus the 'general audience', and 'continuity' versus 'new stories'.

New Who has embraced continuity as a multi-layered and polysemic tool that can be equally meaningful for old fans, new fans and more casual 'followers' of the series.[3] [...] Fan 'gamekeepers' have, however, extended specific fan-cultural discourses (e.g. the notion of multiple authorship considered previously). And Russell T Davies has elaborated on his thesis that Doctor Who uses textual gaps to incite fans' imaginative play, arguing that he has no final authority over the programme.

However, Davies' disavowal of textual authority, and his fannish romanticization of absence and imagination as Doctor Who's key values, appears somewhat disingenuous. [...] The information that Davies chooses to provide and endorse does carry symbolic authority, however much he may resist this discursively in order to align himself as a 'collaborationist' with fandom.[4] Indeed, his relationship with socially organized and online fandom has not always been harmonious.

One of the major industrial shifts accompanying Doctor Who's return has been its repositioning as a modern TV franchise. Although the classic series was merchandised heavily across its existence – and continues to function as a largely separate brand – Doctor Who has now been firmly re-conceptualized within the contemporary TV industry's 'will-to-brand'.[5] [...] The BBC terminology for this brand immersion is '360-degree commissioning', which aims to integrate a single commission's multi-platformed presence.[6] Indeed, Doctor Who has been applauded as a key success story within the BBC's pursuit of this multi-platforming ambition.

Brand management follows a different set of corporate discourses from those of *Doctor Who*'s 'creatives', implying, as Henry Jenkins has argued, that corporations can oscillate between contradictory approaches to fan collaboration and prohibition.[7]

The classic series is marked frequently by startling variations in textual consistency and tone. New *Who*, run by fans, sets out to avoid this fate. The BBC Wales production team may have left diegetic continuity wrangles alone, but they were evidently keen to evade problems of episodic consistency. Russell T Davies, as a fan, would have been keenly aware of the problems created by, say, just one risky visual effects decision in an otherwise startling story (as with, for example, the Skarasen in *Terror of the Zygons*, 1975).

In an implicit critique of the classic series – particularly its unevenness across and within stories – Davies thus instigated a production practice of 'tone meetings', bringing all key production staff together for a discussion of every story's intended identity. Seeking to even out tonal variation within stories, tone meetings ensured that all the different production departments were tasked with achieving similar meanings and textual effects. Asked to focus on a single, guiding word, the intent was that distinct areas of design and direction would then cohere stylistically, avoiding conflicts of interpretation between members of the production team.[8]

Such inconsistencies were captured by what became the most infamous theoretical statement in *Doctor Who*'s history, cited in the 1987 story *Dragonfire*: 'Tell me ... what do you think about the assertion that the semiotic thickness of a performed text varies according to the redundancy of auxiliary performance codes?'[9] This was paraphrased from Tulloch and Alvarado's *Doctor Who: The Unfolding Text*,[10] when *Who*'s then script editor Andrew Cartmel was asked for some 'technical-sounding gibberish'.[11] By virtue of its textual inclusion, the quote has become emblematic of *Doctor Who* scholarship.[12]

Drawing on the work of drama and theatre theorist Keir Elam,[13] Tulloch and Alvarado argued that:

> What Elam calls the semiotic 'thickness' (multiple codes) of a performed text varies according to the 'redundancy' (high predictability) of 'auxiliary' performance codes. Thus, for instance, if the sets, music and so on were simply to reinforce the actors' performance without adding to it or inflecting it in the direction of new associations, but simply overlaid the acted 'pace' and 'drama' with their own, they would be relatively redundant.[14]

Tulloch and Alvarado are tackling the subject of how *Doctor Who*'s multiple codes (set design, costume design, music) work together, or against each other, to create meaning. Redundant codes don't add new meanings to the text, but simply underscore meanings communicated elsewhere, and hence don't add to the semiotic thickness of the programme. By contrast, where 'auxiliary' codes add new meanings to major codes – such as acting styles and performances – then the text is said to have been 'thickened': 'in the Williams/Adams story, *The City of Death* [1979], the use of music and sets ... was more entropic, drawing on motifs which some audience members recognised as "very forties" ... therefore potentially relocating the "stolen art" theme in terms of, say, *The Maltese Falcon*'.[15] As Lance Parkin has noted of the 'semiotic thickness of the text':

> [H]ow do you measure it? There's no SI unit of semiotic thickness ... After all, roughly the same number of people worked on all the *Doctor Who* stories of a given era – they all had a writer, actors, directors, costume people and so on ... So you'd think there would have to be a roughly consistent 'thickness'.[16]

Though fully quantified scores for semiotic thickness may indeed be impossible, the term still has some comparative merit, because it indicates that new *Who*, with its tone words and meetings, aims to reduce semiotic thickness. Rather than 'entropic' production decisions leading to clashes between different sign systems (or varied production choices leading to wild fluctuations in the tonal impact of special effects, practical design and acting styles), new *Who* aims to coordinate its multiple codes. Increased textual consistency means avoiding the embarrassments and disappointments familiar to *Doctor Who*'s established fan culture, though it also militates against the 'amateur aesthetic' and unruliness of stories such as *City of Death* so loved by fans.

The 'fanbrand' of BBC Wales' *Who* is thus not just a matter of fan culture's collaborative emphasis on a 'cohesive fictional world' being brought into the multi-platformed sphere of official production. More than this, *Doctor Who*'s 'fanbrand' is also a fannish critique of classic *Who*'s unevenness, leading to the 'semiotic slimness' of newer texts. Characteristically it aims to iron out the old series' production inconsistencies rather than correct its diegetic continuity errors.

Notes

1. Clayton Hickman in Andy Bodle, 'Who Dares, Wins', *Guardian*: G2 (23 March 2004), 4.
2. Craig Hinton cited in Keith Topping, 'Craig Hinton' (6 December 2006): http://keithtopping.blogspot.com/2006/12/craig-hinton.html (accessed 3 September 2008).
3. John Tulloch and Henry Jenkins, *Science Fiction Audiences* (New York: Routledge, 1995), 23.
4. Henry Jenkins, *Convergence Culture: Where New and Old Media Collide* (New York: New York University Press, 2006), 169.
5. Paul Grainge, *Brand Hollywood: Selling Entertainment in a Global Media Age* (London: Routledge, 2008), 43.
6. BBC, 'BBC Reorganises for an On-demand Creative Future', press release (19 July 2006), available online at http://www.bbc.co.uk/pressoffice/pressre-leases/stories/2006/07_july/19/future.shtml (accessed 3 September 2008).
7. Jenkins, *Convergence Culture*, 170.
8. See, for example, Benjamin Cook, 'Favourite Worst Nightmares!', *Doctor Who Magazine* 384, 45.
9. In Tat Wood, *About Time 6* (Des Moines, IA: Mad Norwegian Press, 2007), 217.
10. John Tulloch and Manuel Alvarado, *Doctor Who: The Unfolding Text* (London: Macmillan, 1983).
11. Andrew Cartmel, *Script Doctor: The Inside Story of Doctor Who 1986–89* (London: Reynolds and Hearn, 2005), 78.
12. See Wood, *About Time 6*, 209.
13. See Keir Elam, *The Semiotics of Theatre and Drama* (London: Methuen, 1980), 45.
14. Tulloch and Alvarado, *The Unfolding Text*, 249.
15. Ibid.
16. Lance Parkin, 'Re: Time and Relative Dissertations in Space' (18 December 2007), 7:29pm: http://www.doctorwhoforum.com.

Chapter 4
The (in)definite article

From *TARDISBound: Navigating the Universes of Doctor Who* by Piers Britton[*]

First published 2011

Britton's focus in his 2011 TARDISBound *is to explore the 'multifarious' narrative(s) of* Doctor Who *not as a cohesive whole but rather as a diverse and divisive palimpsest – a piece of art that is continually re-written, and written over. For Britton, then, the success and power of* Doctor Who *lie precisely within its contradictions, illogic and inconsistencies. In this short excerpt, he uses productive terminology from Matt Hills' work on cult narratives, including 'endlessly deferred narrative' (defined as a narrative that embraces a central mystery that will never have closure) and 'hyperdiegesis' (meaning a self-contained narrative world that is vaster than we'll ever see on screen). Britton's work ties together much narrative, fan and media studies work to examine the fractured wholeness of* Doctor Who.

The purpose of this short chapter is to outline some of *Doctor Who*'s primary characteristics as a narrative and more particularly as a 'vast narrative'.[1] It introduces structuring motifs and patterns, cumulative thematic concerns and also internal breaches or shifts in the texts. I shall argue here and in later chapters that ongoing elements in *Doctor Who* have been significantly recoded in texts produced since the demise of the classic series in 1989. This is true especially of the various series of novels produced between 1991 and the television revival in 2005. I do not mean to suggest that there is an absolute fissure between the classic series and later texts, or that *Doctor Who* cannot be theorized as a narrative whole. Yet it seems to me that what makes the different textual universes of *Doctor Who* interesting to study in tandem is the fact that the narrative has accommodated so many alterations in ideology and taste without recourse to such devices as *Star Trek*'s introduction of 'next generation' and 'prequel' series, and without any absolute rupture in consistency at a motivic level.

---

[*]Originally published in *TARDISBound* (London, UK: IB Tauris, 2011).

Doctor Who is an unwieldy skein of texts, partly by virtue of the fact that it has endured in one form or another almost continuously for forty years, but more particularly because there's no clear hierarchy within its various media manifestations.

The lack of any such ruling means that both the novels and the audios have at various stages been *understood* as the official continuation of the classic series of *Doctor Who*, even if they are now all supposedly trumped by the new series. This has fundamentally defined what is at stake in *Doctor Who*'s storytelling in these licensed media and constrained the types of stories told.

Chronological analysis of the *Doctor Who* narrative is not particularly useful unless conditions of production and reception are the main focus ... It is inherently problematic to imply that the *Doctor Who* narrative is defined by the imprints of its various transient stars or producers. Moreover, any analysis based around a 'line-of-succession model' clearly cannot accommodate the current multiplicity of textual universes, with six actors simultaneously playing the Doctor in licensed productions and original tie-in novels regularly being published. For present purposes, it is more useful to theorize *Doctor Who*'s narrative organization in terms of the recently developed critical model of the 'vast narrative', articulated in Pat Harrigan and Noah Wardrip-Fruin's *Third Person: Authoring and Exploring Vast Narratives*.[2] This can be usefully supplemented with aspects of Matt Hills's model of the 'cult text' from his *Fan Cultures*.[3] As I argued below, both approaches accommodate the essential multi-vocality of *Doctor Who* texts (which obtains even in the early 2010s, at a moment of massively focused branding), and both provide a context for understanding the transformations of narrative trajectory and ethos which *Doctor Who* has undergone in the last twenty years.

Unsurprisingly, given its endurance and the enormous complexity of its diegetic universe, *Doctor Who* is one of the textual sets most prominently discussed in Harrigan and Wardrip-Fruin's collection of essays on the 'vast narrative'. As a 'multi-authored cross-media phenomenon' *Doctor Who* falls squarely within their (deliberately loose-knit) conceptual framework, which is designed to incorporate a range of recent fictions, textual forms and media interactions.[4]

In another way, *Doctor Who* also thrives more than many series on the studied tension between change and continuity, and true to a now-venerable cliché it has shown a prodigious capacity for repeated self-transformation. Attempts to refresh the narrative have been regular and sometimes radical, from the time of the Doctor's first on-screen physical 'regeneration' onwards. Hills has therefore suggested in his analysis of cult texts that *Doctor Who* represents a prime example of the *endlessly deferred narrative*. As the term implies, this storytelling form, proper to many television series, is as potentially limitless as soap opera. But Hills argues that unlike soap opera, with its diffuse serial structure, the endlessly deferred narrative is focused on a central theme or character which is inherently mysterious.[5]

Another key characteristic of the cult text, according to Hills, is the *hyperdiegesis*. This is the intricate universe of the text, a self-contained world with its own laws and history, whose scale and complexity is hinted at but never fully explored. This hyperdiegesis serves as a conceptual anchor, a consistently implied, coherent framework for events, inspiring the audience's or readers trust and ongoing interest in the narrative.[6] *Doctor Who* certainly developed its own hyperdiegesis, but (as noted by Harrigan and Wardrip-Fruin) this has proven to be increasingly unstable. In spite of going through periods of obsessive reference to its own past, *Doctor Who* has much more often breached its own internal continuity. This is partly due to its sheer length of duration and proliferation, partly due to the fact that its narrative has always been open and haphazard in nature. Yet, as I shall argue, the failure of its hyperdiegesis also points to one of *Doctor Who*'s idiosyncratic strengths: its capacity for the rich and complex accretion of ideas in what amounts to a narrative palimpsest.

Endlessly deferred narrative, though peculiarly accommodating to the enthusiasm of fans, is a property of many series or serials, whether or not they become cult texts. The device of endless deferral is calculated to secure audience loyalty without necessarily requiring intense engagement. In other words, it is quite possible to be actively curious about the way the Doctor's relationship with companions such as Rose Tyler or Sam Jones may turn out, or eagerly anticipate his next rematch with the Daleks, without sharing in the kind of affective play which characterizes fan interaction with a cult text.

In *Doctor Who*'s case, at least, the same cannot be said of hyperdiegesis: the complex self-suspending universe of a cult text, of which we only ever see portions in the narrative. The maintenance, ordering and enhancement of the *Doctor Who* hyperdiegesis have almost entirely been the work of fans. Nearly all sustained fictional exploration of the Whoniverse belongs to the phase of the texts' history in which audience and authors were arguably the most homogenous, which is to say, the lifespan of the NAs [New Adventure novels] and MAs [Missing Adventure novels]. The NAs became increasingly interdependent as the series progressed, but they also alluded to an array of details from the established history of the worlds of *Doctor Who* on television, sometimes picking up on the most fleeting of references or obscure of characters. The MAs by definition filled in some of the blanks and could even be designed specifically to paper over cracks in the classic series narrative.[7]

The principle of retroactively shaping continuity around newly stated 'facts' is by no means peculiar to *Doctor Who*; in fact, one might argue that it is another common (if not quite leading) characteristic of cult texts. What is striking about *Doctor Who* is the extent to which the process of defining the texts' internal universe is *palimpsestic.* In other words, key elements have not always simply been brought into alignment with existing 'truths', or vice versa; some of them have effectively overwritten earlier histories, albeit leaving the original elements partially visible. The most notable example of this is provided by 'facts' concerning the Doctor's people, the Time Lords of Gallifrey. In *The Three Doctors* (1973), a quasi-mythic figure called Omega was introduced as the originator of Time Lord technology. A few years later, in *The Deadly Assassin* (1976), the previously unmentioned engineer and architect Rassilon was credited as the author of Gallifrey's time-travel capability, and Omega apparently forgotten. Rassilon immediately and definitively eclipsed Omega, emerging as *the* linchpin figure of Gallifreyan history. In nearly every subsequent script or novel referring to Time Lord culture and lore, Rassilon is designated with tedious predictability as the proprietor of anything powerful, mysterious, venerable or merely first rate in Gallifreyan culture, from the Black Scrolls of Rassilon to 'Rassilon's Red', apparently a favourite wine in taverns beneath the Time Lord citadel. Although Omega is not only mentioned but also returns and later *Doctor Who* texts, he always stands in the shadow of Rassilon.

Harrigan and Wardrip-Fruin's metaphor of the vast narrative as 'fictional quilt' stresses non-linear and thus non-hierarchical relationships within sprawling media-crossing texts such as *Doctor Who*. This model encourages us to understand seemingly ill-assorted or contradictory elements in the *Who* narrative as parts of a multifarious whole rather than problems requiring unification. In short, the quilt metaphor can serve to highlight not merely *Doctor Who*'s famous flexibility of narrative premise but rather its inherent and often productive lack of narrative constraint and coherence.

From *Design for Doctor Who: Vision and Revision in Science Fiction Television* by Piers Britton[†]

First published 2021

In this second of Piers Britton's excerpts, he explores how traditional art and aesthetic design considerations cannot always be effectively employed to discuss a shifting and changing narrative like Doctor Who's*. He argues the best way to examine design in* Doctor Who *is through genre, mode and atmosphere. In the rest of the book, he offers an historical view of* Doctor Who's *iconic designs, and chooses thirteen of them as key to understanding the series.*

Scholars of design for film have tended to regard anything which smacks of spectacle with a measure of suspicion, at worst condemning it for its shallowness and escapism, at best chiding it for failing in its supportive function. Thus, the most developed taxonomy of design for the screen produced to date, Charles and Mirella Jona Affron's *Sets in Motion: Art Direction and Film Narrative*, identifies 'set as artifice' as the second-to-highest level of 'design intensity' – and this ranking is not an accolade.[8] The 'artificial set', in the Affrons' critical framework, is design which consistently 'calls attention to itself', most often evident in screen fiction with a high fantasy quotient, such as the musical, the fairy-tale, the horror movie, the superhero film and science fiction.[9] Such design, according to the Affrons, is apt to be *too* intense, 'challenging the force of plot and character'. For them – and, they claim, most practising designers – the 'good set' is one which is 'modestly denotative' of time, place, mood and culture.[10]

According to this view, which is broadly endorsed by most other scholars writing about production or costume design, nearly all the *Doctor Who* episodes discussed in this chapter are tainted one way or another. 'Rosa' would probably pass muster, as just possibly might 'The Zygon Invasion' and 'The Zygon Inversion', by virtue of their emphatic mundanity and very limited, low-key use of the titular aliens. Yet the Affron model simply can't accommodate the kind of bifurcated design idiom of a serial like *The Masque of Mandragora*, where the overall realism of the palace sets and period costumes is offset, courtesy of Hieronymus's purple cult robes and gold mask, with something closer to the brightly coloured, simplified costume imagery in Roger Corman's film adaptation of *The Masque of the Red Death* (1964).

There have been several episodes in revived *Doctor Who* which are in design terms much more internally inconsistent than *The Masque of Mandragora*. For example, 'Twice Upon a Time', Peter Capaldi's Christmas 2017 swansong, runs the gamut from unabashed artifice to finely tuned historical realism. The episode culminates with a respectful recreation of the Ypres trenches and no-man's-land during the 1914 Christmas Truce. Yet the action starts amidst improbably sculptural snowdrifts in an Antarctic landscape, and then veers further into the irreal. Of the other two main environments, one is the set for the interior of an unusual spaceship, which appears to be a vast, circular stone tower of superimposed arcades with a grand staircase running up steeply to a control chamber in the midst. The whole thing is dizzying and operatic enough to grace one of Peter Jackson's *Hobbit* films. More daringly,

---

[†]Originally published in *Design for Doctor Who* (London, UK: Bloomsbury, 2021).

'Twice' juxtaposes the realism of the Second World War [sic] scenes directly with highly stylized sets for the ruined world of Villengard, which depend for their impact primarily on suffusing fanciful, theatrical structures with intense, primary-coloured light.

On inspection, the Affrons' notion of the 'modestly denotative' proves less neutral and reasonable than it claims to be: as already implied in the foregoing, it speaks to an entrenched bias in favour of realism and understatement. So if the Affrons' taxonomic model is built on unacknowledged prejudice and implied hierarchy, then how might it be possible to establish a less tendentious framework for evaluating the work of design in *Doctor Who*? Rather than use absolute benchmarks or supposedly universal taxonomies, it seems to me best to think about the morphology of design imagery in *Doctor Who* texts in terms of genre, mood and atmosphere. These are all imprecise and to an extent fungible categories, but they accommodate the variety – not to say the sometimes wild inconsistency and internal contradictoriness – of design for *Doctor Who*.

While genres are certainly not immune to hierarchization, implicit in the very idea of genre is *multiplicity*. As a basis for inquiry, genre theory allows for the idea that verisimilitude and appropriateness are relative terms.[11] [...] If the benchmark is *generic* verisimilitude (as opposed to socio-cultural verisimilitude),[12] it is logically meaningless to condemn science fiction for showing alternative or projected worlds which draw the eye because they are unlike our world.

Yet even a genre-based approach is problematic in the case of *Doctor Who*, since the series is not a homogeneous phenomenon.[13] Quite apart from adjustments in tone which have occurred with successive authorial regimes, *Doctor Who*'s shifts across genre were effectively built into its storytelling foundations, allowing it from the very outset to undergo regular and radical idiomatic change.[14] As we have seen, even episodes which belong broadly to the same genre may vary wildly at the level of mood and atmosphere, as in the cases of 'Rosa' and 'Robot of Sherwood'. With this in mind, it is useful to reach beyond genre-based analysis to narrative theory, for this can help specify design's role not within clusters of texts, but within given, individual texts.

[A]ssessing a single episode as an isolated narrative ignores the fact that *Doctor Who* is open-ended, long-form television fiction. The narrative against which design imagery's indicial effectiveness is judged may in the first instance be the episode in question, but the claims of the ongoing series-narrative cannot be denied. This is especially true in the age of story arcs, where we are invited to connect episodes in a variety of ways which might arguably require some level of visual consistency to uphold them. Key images which recur or are updated, such as the Doctor's costumes, the TARDIS and the various iterations of the Cybermen, also inevitably invite comparison with precedents within the larger narrative. Such comparison arguably trumps questions of how effective such a design is within any given scenario.

All this seems to suggest that we are at an impasse. Design in the macro-narrative context might reasonably be expected to index what can only be called '*Doctor-Who*-ness' – a mood or atmosphere which makes the series in toto distinctive and always recognizably itself, in spite of changing imperatives in its production or larger cultural context. Yet *Doctor Who* seemingly resists the application of any unitary standard for assessing the effectiveness of design, beyond what visual imagery indexes within a given micro-narrative.

Responses to *Doctor Who*, such as fan criticism of camp design elements and journalistic persiflage about the original series' rubber monsters and wobbly walls, matter not in terms of how 'right' they are but in terms of how they may have come to define expectations of the show. In short, such clichés may have influenced how *Doctor Who* has adapted and changed, especially since the revival. After all, the new series has been consistently shaped by professionalized fans, and it is hard to believe that Russell

T Davies, Steven Moffat and Chris Chibnall, or any of the other long-standing *Who* devotees working on the programme with them, were wholly immune to the existing tenets of fan criticism.

Notes

TARDISBound

1. See Pat Harrigan and Noah Wardrip-Fruin, 'Introduction', in *Third Person* (Cambridge, MA: MIT Press, 2009), 2.
2. See Harrigan and Wardrip-Fruin, 'Introduction', 2.
3. Matt Hills, *Fan Cultures* (London: Routledge, 2002), 131–8.
4. Harrigan and Wardrip-Fruin, *Third Person*, 2, 5.
5. Hills, *Fan Cultures*, 134.
6. Ibid., 138.
7. For example, David Banks's 'Iceberg' (London, 1993) represents an attempt to consolidate the history of the Cybermen.

Design for Doctor Who

8. Charles Affron and Mirella Jona Affron, *Sets in Motion: Art Direction and Film Narrative* (Englewood Cliffs, NJ: Rutgers Univeristy Press, 1995), 35–40.
9. Ibid., 39.
10. Ibid., 44.
11. On generic verisimilitude, see Steve Neale, *Genre and Hollywood* (London & New York: Routledge, 2000), 27–35, esp. 28.
12. Ibid.; Catherine Johnson, 'Telefantasy', in *The Television Genre Book*, ed. Glen Creeber, 3rd edition (London & New York: BFI/Bloomsbury Publishing, 2015), 57–8.
13. Matt Hills, 'Doctor Who', in, *The Television Genre Book*, 67.
14. Cf. Kim Newman, *Doctor Who* (London: BFI, 2006), 21.

Chapter 5
Bigger, louder and now in colour!

From 'Adapting Telefantasy: The *Doctor Who and the Daleks* Films' by John R. Cook[*]

First published 1999

The three pieces in this chapter each tackle different media forms of Doctor Who *as they relate to the television text and to each other. In Cook's piece from 1999 about the Doctor Who and the Daleks films, the cinematic representation of* Doctor Who *is deliberately set in contrast with the television series. The movies from 1964 and 1965 retell two television stories, but introduce new companions, new narrative adventures and a new actor playing the Doctor (Peter Cushing). Yet there are similar themes in both representations of what* 'Doctor Who' *might be.*

[The] first appearance of the Daleks became a phenomenon, changing the whole course of *Doctor Who*. Something about these metal monsters clicked with the general public at the time. […] Despite being precisely the 'bug-eyed monsters' he had wished to avoid, the Daleks ensured the success of [Sydney] Newman's original commissioning goal for *Doctor Who*: … attracting eight- to fourteen-year-olds to BBC-1 but at the same time, by not 'talking down' to its audience, it did not alienate elder siblings and parents while they waited for the later programmes.

While the … *Doctor Who and the Daleks* film is essentially a remake of Nation's 'The Mutants', some of the key revisions and abridgements which [Milton] Subotsky made to the original provide crucial clues as to his intentions for the film, as well as his perceptions of where its audience might lie. Together these offer a telling illustration of some of the widespread assumptions about what was deemed commercially possible for British science fiction in the cinema during this period as opposed to on television. If the

---

[*]Originally published in *British Science Fiction Cinema*, edited by IQ Hunter (London: Routledge, 1999), 113–27.

BBC and Sydney Newman saw the *Doctor Who* concept as a means of fulfilling a public service remit by 'reaching across' to as wide a cross-section of the audience as possible, in the cinema, Subotsky perceived his best hopes lay in refashioning it into a vehicle specially 'niche-marketed' for children.

In this way, *Doctor Who and the Daleks* irons out much of the adult content that might be thought 'troublesome' for children.

Right from the start, Subotsky's version of *Doctor Who* makes a direct equation between science fiction and the 'magical' world of the child's imagination.[1] [...] When [the Doctor] pits himself against the machine-like Daleks, his is the old romantic image of the 'good scientist': the quirky, enquiring, free spirit committed to science as a means of individual emancipation and progress versus the more modernist image of science gone wrong in the form of the coldly rational, dehumanizing Daleks. In short: 'good' science as old-fashioned magic versus 'bad' science as new-fangled terror.

Compared to the dream of science as the progress of humanity embodied by the Doctor, [the Daleks] represent the corresponding nightmare vision of science as the road to utter dehumanization. In *Doctor Who and the Daleks*, these two competing visions are well illustrated by the difference between the Daleks and their enemies, the Thals. Borrowing heavily from images of the gentle, surface-dwelling Eloi versus the hideous subterranean Morlocks in *The Time Machine*, the Thals are represented as essentially peace-loving and agrarian. [...] Everyone is accorded the status of an individual and all are in complete harmony with nature. By contrast, in the Daleks, we find creatures that have utterly estranged themselves from the natural world to such an extent that they can no longer survive anywhere other than in special cities constructed entirely of metal. Moreover, they progress through collective, ant-like colonies, in which there are clear lines of structure and hierarchy – a wholly 'rational' order – but where any sense of individuality or emotion has been completely expunged. Theirs is the nightmare of urban dehumanization in a mass society.

If this may be one reason why the Daleks achieved such iconic status in the decade of the 'white heat' of technology, at the same time, it does not explain why thousands of fans actually loved them [...] The Daleks were so successful not so much because they could be frightening but because they were so easily imitable to an extent that children came to identify with them. [...] Just like children in the exuberance of play, the Daleks really could not 'help it' if they did things of which 'responsible' human adults often did not approve.

All of this was quite a long way from Terry Nation's conception in the original TV version of the machine-like Daleks as 'the ultimate Nazis' (Howe et al., 1992: 31). Interestingly, however, both films retain the sense, tangible in Nation's TV plots, of offering a partisan perspective on Britain's experience in the Second World War. Thus in *Doctor Who and the Daleks*, the inhumane collectivity of the Dalek 'reich' is pitted against the brave, plucky Thals who may not have the cold efficiency nor military might of their ruthless opponents but who more than make up for it in their willingness to stand up against all odds in defence of their freedom. There are also echoes of the Holocaust. The Daleks' war cry is 'exterminate, exterminate', while the Thals, at first, resemble the Jews: an innocent 'wandering tribe' who are tricked into entering the metal city on the pretext of receiving food, only to be slaughtered en masse by the Daleks.

From 'Televisuality Without Television?: The Big Finish Audios and Discourses of "Tele-centric" *Doctor Who*' by Matt Hills[†]

First published 2007

Hills' discussion of the Big Finish audios focuses on the tension between what he calls the 'tele-centric' attributes of the stories with the unique audio attributes they provide. On the one hand, the early Big Finish audios attempted to replicate some traditional aspects of Doctor Who *on television, including providing original actors and faux* Radio Times *listings. But on the other hand, the audios continued to evolve their own unique language for* Doctor Who *on audio, providing content that replicated the spirit of* 'Doctor Who' *in a new medium. Hills ultimately argues that the televisual elements of the audios reveal more about* Doctor Who *than the audio-centric ones, although Big Finish now recording new series episodes (post Hills' publication) might complicate these notions.*

Doctor Who's continued and still unfolding existence as a series of audio stories raises intriguing questions about the text's 'televisual' identity. ... I will suggest that *discourses of televisuality* are more important than essentialist notions of media-specificity when analysing the Big Finish *Doctor Who* audios. That is, I am arguing that how these sonic adventures imitate structures and formats of televised *Who*, as well as how they utilize fan experiences and memories of *Who* on TV, are all more important to understanding and analysing these adventures than an essentialist notion of what audio 'has' to be or do, where it is assumed that it *has* to work essentially in certain ways. What is significant about these adventures, as an act of fan-producer 'textual conservationism' (Hills, 2002: 37–8), is the way that 'authentic', 'traditional' and 'televisual' (i.e. tele-centric) *Doctor Who* is realized entirely without the technology of television. In other words, one thing Big Finish are (re)creating for their target market of fan-consumers is a specific *experience of Doctor Who:* the phenomenology ... of consuming an episodic format, complete with cliffhangers and opening and closing theme music, as well as including faux *Radio Times* entries, up to and including release number 33 'Neverland', for each 'week's' episode.

Although efforts may be made to capture the spirit of certain seasons or Doctor-companion partnerships, the ageing of actors' voices partly works against this; rather than seeking to perfectly recreate certain periods of the show (as do many of the BBC's Missing Adventures novels), the audios seem instead to focus on recreating an *archetypal fan experience* ... of the TV programme.

There is certainly a type of 'textual conservationism' on show here, but it is not that of obsessive continuity, nor does it indicate an eternal sameness of characterization. Quite to the contrary, Big Finish audios have developed new companions for various Doctors, such as Evelyn Smythe (Maggie Stables), who appears with Colin Baker's Sixth Doctor in a range of stories, and Charlotte Pollard (India Fisher), who accompanies Paul McGann's Eighth Doctor.

[†]Originally published in *Time and Relative Dissertations in Space: Critical Perspectives on Doctor Who*, edited by David Butler (Manchester University Press, 2007), 280–95.

But these variations on a theme have, nevertheless, sought to create moments that many fans wish could have happened on TV, such as the Sixth Doctor encountering the Brigadier, thereby restoring a pattern that had held true since the era of Patrick Troughton's Second Doctor (and which Big Finish further continue by having the Brig appear in a 2001 Eighth Doctor story, 'Minuet in Hell').

If these adventures can be described as tele-centric, then this is seemingly a matter of fan nostalgia, being a textualized marker of the desire to re-experience 'classic' *Doctor Who* as it was as an ongoing TV programme. The ironic 'as-if' televisuality of these audio stories suggests that where fan sub-cultural memories and narratives of consuming *Doctor Who* are concerned, television culture (Fiske, 1987) can be faked, if you like, or commemorated/memorialized without the presence of TV itself.

Perhaps a certain section of fandom is never going to get past the '*Doctor Who* only exists on TV' perspective. For media-essentialist fans, televisuality and being-on-telly are condensed into one seamless experience; the supposed 'essence' of *Who* is carried in its *tele*snaps, or perhaps in its non-VIDfired video and non-CGled DVD releases. Thus, while fan debate may still rage over the relative merits of specific stories or eras, for many fans the 'telly' question tends to play like a trump card, defining *Who*ness beyond all other murky areas of dispute.

If the Big Finish audios variously work to recreate fan memories of experiencing TV *Who*, drawing on discourses of televisuality and at the very least becoming tele-centric, then this still does not exhaust how they play with different media. A number of audio adventures strongly emphasize their lack of visuals by carrying out narrative conceits that would be difficult to sustain in filmed or televised versions. For example, shock twists at the end of 'Omega' (2003) episode three, or at the conclusion to 'Natural History of Fear', hinge on audience making certain assumptions on the basis of what (or who) they are hearing. Nev Fountain has said of his script for 'Omega' that 'I realized I could do an "audio *Fight Club*"! As someone who writes a lot of radio, writing a story that could only work in the audio medium greatly appealed to me' (in Cook, 2003: 215).

Other Big Finish stories have made exaggerated use of sound design to construct meaning: 'Deadline' (2003) is particularly notable in this respect, where incidental music is repeated so that it becomes uncanny, stilted and mechanical-seeming, adding greatly to the surrealism of Rob Shearman's script, and capturing the story's blurring of fantasy and reality. Much earlier in the Big Finish range, in the third release, 'Whispers of Terror' (1998), the audio in 'audio adventures' was also being stressed. The writer of this story, Justin Richards, has suggested that '[i]f there's a single *Doctor Who* audio adventure that simply couldn't be done in another medium […] no question, *Whispers of Terror* it is' (in Cook, 2003: 23). This tale features a sound creature and the Museum of Aural Antiquities, and makes repeated use of recorded, replayed and distorted sound in line with Richard's original notion to 'fully use (exploit?) the medium' (in Cook, 2003: 21).

Such a story may seem to radically contradict the notion that these audios are tele-centric in terms of seeking to recreate televisual and TV-industrial forms of the original series, but it is worth considering that even this story repeats the episodic form of the original TV series.

Perhaps unsurprisingly, the Big Finish range has most consistently moved away from 'traditional' tele-centric *Doctor Who* in its Eighth Doctor adventures starring Paul McGann, beginning with 2001's 'Storm Warning'. After all, in a sense, these BF audios do not possess a sustained and televised 'era' to recapture, beyond relating to the one-off 1996 *TV Movie*. Unusually, they create new *Who* without referring back to a nostalgia-laden template, and without consistently citing an archetypal fan experience of watching *Doctor Who*.

From *Love and Monsters: The Doctor Who Experience, 1979 to the Present* by Miles Booy[‡]

First published 2012

Booy's discussion of the fan experience from the 1970s onwards helps establish the narrative connections between media forms. In this small excerpt from his book, he discusses the way narrative information in the home releases, like the novelizations from the 1980s and the DVDs from the mid-2000s, helps complete some story moments. At the same time, much Doctor Who *media takes fan theories (like Season 6B) and actualizes them, turning them into so-called canonical moments.*

[The Classic series later seasons' complexity] necessarily changed the relationship between the programme and its major merchandising. The McCoy stories were all novelized by their own authors (save *Battlefield*, which was done by *Ghost Light* author Marc Platt), with many of the excised scenes reinstated and the themes expanded. Moreover, since the show's writers had been encouraged to share ideas at large meetings, the themes of the individualized stories started to bleed into each other in their novelized form. Ace's Asian friend Manisha, mentioned only in *Ghost Light* on screen, gets several references in the novelization of *Remembrance of the Daleks*. That same book's immersion in memories of World War Two (though it is set in 1963) means that it often covers the same thematic ground as *The Curse of Fenric*; Alan Turing is mentioned; one character's father was 'lost at sea', as is the husband of a young woman in '*Fenric*'.

The search was on for a less compromised version of what became known by fans – but not the production office – as 'The Cartmel Masterplan'. When novelizations didn't quite reveal it, there were videos, and later DVDs, with excised footage returned to the proper positions, or included as extras. The DVD of *Battlefield*, released in 2008, re-edits the story, replaces some cut material and adds a small amount of new CGI shots, becoming in the process a substantial improvement upon the transmitted version. DVDs like this, or *Ghost Light* and *The Curse of Fenric*, came loaded with authorial interviews and interpretive extras, revealing the obscured intentions more than a decade after their original transmissions. 'Millington and Judson are gay. Well, if I ever thought that then I've long since forgotten it', declared *DWM*'s reviewer, Vanessa Bishop, upon watching the extras on *Fenric*.[2] When original novels were produced from 1991 onwards, they provided more clues, and Cartmel wrote several comic strips for DWM. All took their readers closer to the mythic master plan, but none ever quite delivered.

As the example of Judson's sexuality suggests, fans were searching not only for a narrative meaning but also a political one, in Cartmel's *Who*. That was something which could be rendered more completely in niche-marketed novelizations than in prime-time television where the BBC would face accusations of ideological bias. Most producers and script editors had been content to keep the programme's liberal/soft-left biases as vague as possible, often blurring political edges.

So many stories, so many Doctors: canonicity was the debate which consumed fandom in the 1990s. 'Canonicity' in these debates doesn't refer to a canon of worthy texts acclaimed for their quality (though *DW* fandom has those as well, of course), but to the assertion about which stories 'actually happened'

[‡]Originally published in *Love and Monsters* (London, UK: IB Tauris, 2012).

in the *Doctor Who* universe. Whilst the TV series had been in production, these debates, insofar as there were any, had mostly concerned the status of the uncomplete story *Shada* and whether the extra material added to books like *Doctor Who and the Doomsday Weapon* 'counted' or not. The novelizations of the McCoy era, which seemed to offer much more substantial account of the era than the televised versions, stretched the question further. As niche-marketed *Who* proliferated, strict canonicity (already under strain in the most playful of fanzines and fictions) collapsed completely in professional products. The BBC were less concerned than Virgin with using the books to create a coherent *Who* universe which would cross reference between volumes and dropped whatever barriers between continuities remained. Frobisher the Penguin, a companion of the Sixth Doctor in mid-80s *DWM*, appeared in BBC books and Big Finish audios. Novels were set during series 6B, the fan-contrived extra season to explain why Patrick Troughton looked so old in *The Five Doctors*; Gary Russell's *Placebo Effect* incorporated the short-lived *Radio Times* strip into novel continuity … Kim Newman's novella *Time and Relative* extended the story backwards, being set several months before the events of the programme's first episode … Jim Mortimore's *Campaign* … was set in the programme's earliest years and found the TARDIS inhabited by all versions of the earliest crew including those drawn from the Dalek films, the comic strip, the earliest novelizations and some abandoned ideas from early production documents.

Notes

1. Ed.: something that Steven Moffat's *Doctor Who* does in 2011 as well.
2. Vanessa Bishop, 'Review: The Curse of Fenric' DVD, *Doctor Who Magazine* 336 (12 November 2003).

References

From 'Adapting Telefantasy: *The Doctor Who and the Daleks* Films' by John R. Cook

Howe, David J., Mark Stammers, and Stephen James Walker. *Doctor Who: The Sixties*. London: Virgin, 1992.

From 'Televisuality Without Television?: The Big Finish Audios and Discourses of "Tele-centric" *Doctor Who*' by Matt Hills

Cook, Benjamin. *The New Audio Adventures: The Inside Story*. Maidenhead: Big Finish, 2003.
Fiske, John. *Television Culture*. London: Methuen, 1987.
Hills, Matt. *Fan Cultures*. London and New York: Routledge, 2002.

Chapter 6
The legacy of *Doctor Who* literature by Stacey Smith?

Original to this volume

The corpus of Doctor Who *texts is vast and broad – not just the episodes we've seen on television but also comics, films and audios mentioned in the previous chapters. Smith? unpacks the history of the Target, Virgin and BBC Book* Doctor Who *novels and literature, focusing here on the way they impact the larger* Doctor Who *framework.*

It's all Paul Cornell's fault.

Long before the advent of media recording, novelizations were one of the few permanent records of an insubstantial medium like television that most people had access to. Television was something you watched, usually once; books were something you could re-read. It was a perfect vehicle for fans who revisited material. At the same time, interest in the show could be kept alive through further adventures, such as those published in comic-strip form or in the form of short stories in Annuals and the like.

Doctor Who's relationship with its print media grew from a few hardback novelizations published in the 1960s, along with an ongoing comic strip, to regular novels churned out, mostly by Terrance Dicks, both a master of efficiency and willing to do the job when few of the original scriptwriters were interested in writing novels for children.

At the same time, fan fiction was alive and well, being published in obscure fanzines across the world, with tiny readerships. With limited episodes per year (shrinking as the show moved into its final phase) and relatively few avenues to consume print adventures, fans did what they always do: they created their own. This would turn out to have a very happy outcome not only for the hard-core fans but for everyone else.

The novelizations had been hugely successful worldwide, selling 50,000–100,000 copies per book, but they had a very obvious limitation: they were entirely dependent on televised episodes. As the show moved into the 1980s, original scriptwriters were lured to the novelization side, producing works that were deeper than the Terrance Dicks throwaways. The final run of books saw original writers adding greater depth than ever before, laying the seeds for original books in novelizations such as *Remembrance of the Daleks*, *Battlefield* and *The Curse of Fenric* (ed.: see Booy in Chapter 5).

In 1991, *Doctor Who* was at a crisis point. Viewership had fallen, but fan interest was still alive and well – only the fans had run out of episodes to watch. Target Books had been experimenting with other options – original adventures featuring companions, novelizations of scrapped stories – but the loss of the TV show put more weight on the print output than it had ever borne. It was time for books that were, as the advertising suggested, too broad and deep for the small screen.

In retrospect, it's a wonder they didn't just stick to 140-page output books. That model had worked well, but the switch to the New Adventures was accompanied by a change of production company (Target Books were renamed Virgin Publishing) and an increase in length (books were now regularly 250 pages). Target Books' final editor was Peter Darvill-Evans, who negotiated the switch to original novels. Darvill-Evans imposed a vision of a novel line with its own continuity, something that could appeal to the discerning science fiction reader, beyond the *Doctor Who* fan base, and with moral complexity in abundance. The plan was longer, deeper – broader, one might say – stories featuring the current TARDIS crew that could move forward.

That last one was crucial, because this wasn't just nostalgia for its own sake. Without a TV show, these books could have forward momentum and character development. They could have cliffhangers and recurring characters. In short, they were new; they were original – and they were *dangerous*.

Well, not at first, of course. At first, the New Adventures were full of soft continuity and told children's adventures with added nudity (*Timewyrm: Genesys*) or grown-up adventures with the Doctor battling alternate-universe Nazis (*Timewyrm: Exodus*) or plain-old children's schlock sci-fi (*Timewyrm: Apocalypse*). These were written by established authors and were essentially bigger versions of the novelizations – that is, until the avalanche occurred.

One person was in the right place at the right time. *Doctor Who* fan Paul Cornell pitched one of the early novels and had it accepted. John Nathan-Turner, the final producer of *Doctor Who*, was briefly consulting for the range and recommended against published Cornell's first book, thinking it wasn't at all what the New Adventures should be about. Luckily for all of us, nobody listened.

The reason that *Timewyrm: Revelation* was the pebble that started the avalanche was largely because it was fanfic, and few people had realized just how powerful that could be. Whereas the preceding three books had continuity in them, *Revelation* actually did something with that continuity. The TARDIS, for instance, materializes in the single most inventive place it has ever landed, before or since: the Doctor's mind.

The power of fan writing is that fans have thought long and hard about the show they love, deconstructing it and determining just what makes it tick. That kind of familiarity means that risks can be taken and changes made, safe in the knowledge that they aren't destroying the series we all love. *Revelation* was the ideal vehicle for that, as it showed us a version of *Doctor Who* that had never existed in professional output before.

This massively changed the direction of not only the New Adventures, not only *Doctor Who* literature as a whole, but of how we understand and consume *Doctor Who* today.

Once they'd figured out how to forge ahead, the New Adventures picked up that ball and ran with it. At the time, they were one of only two ongoing *Doctor Who* outputs (the other being the comic strip that was published in *Doctor Who Magazine* every month; the two even synched up for a while). They took risks, they developed both character and continuity, they grew, and they changed. Authors worked with each other to create ongoing storylines and inter-book continuity, while the editorial hand was firmly on the rudder: Darvill-Evans left, and Rebecca Levene took over, with an even stronger vision of the line as a coherent series, with its own story arcs, new companions and character development for the Doctor.

Thanks to the success of Paul Cornell's avalanche, they encouraged new writers to submit proposals, finding multiple gems in the slushpile. Writers such as Mark Gatiss and Gareth Roberts, who went on to write for TV (and eventually *Doctor Who* when it came back), found their start here. Others became well-respected novelists.

The New Adventures wrote out TV companions (Ace leaves twice) and introduced their own, including archaeologist Bernice Summerfield, who became beloved, eventually starring in her own spin-off series for decades (and inspiring the character River Song). They gave the Doctor an actual arc, complete with resolution: the master manipulator from the TV series was developed even further, finding himself on a treadmill of intervention and doing questionable things in the name of the greater good that led to a lot of angst … and a lot of excellent stories.

One of the key parts of the backstory was the so-called Cartmel Masterplan, which had been developed for TV but barely used. With writers such as Andrew Cartmel, Ben Aaronovitch and Marc Platt being part of the writing stable, the New Adventures were able to delve into the Doctor's past deeper than had ever been developed before, drawing on a comic-strip sensibility for hidden backstory that suggested there was far more to the Doctor than we'd ever known.

Sales were excellent (they boomed in a recession, regularly selling 20,000–30,000 copies per book) and readership loyal. A sister line, The Missing Adventures, was launched, featuring more traditional tales set within the earlier eras, while the New Adventures continued to experiment. They were beautiful and powerful and were – for many people, myself included – *Doctor Who*'s ultimate golden age.

They ended in a blaze of glory, with a single novel featuring the new Eighth Doctor … and a desperate last-minute publication of the climactic book to a huge story arc from five months earlier, which had been lost in Ben Aaronovitch's hard disc crash and hurriedly rewritten by Kate Orman, despite the consequences of the storyline having already been published. The last few books were only on sale for a few weeks but later ended up selling for hundreds of pounds on eBay, because of their rarity.

In the end, the New Adventures were a victim of their own success. By the late nineties, the *TV Movie* had failed to launch an ongoing TV series, but multiple forces were circling, hoping to monetize fan enthusiasm. The BBC took the book licence back, producing their own line of Past Doctor Adventures (which were essentially the Missing Adventures with the serial numbers filed off) and an ongoing line, the Eighth Doctor Adventures.

Sadly, the new lines never quite took off in the same way. Part of the problem was editorial: there was noticeably less care put into the books due to overburdened and limited editorial staff. Nuala Buffini helmed the line initially, but there was no particular vision from the outset. Steve Cole took over shortly afterwards, but there was never the editorial cohesiveness that the New Adventures had enjoyed, not least of which was because he was also responsible for overseeing all *Doctor Who*–related merchandise as well as the books. Distribution to North America was bungled, meaning many fans were unable to buy them. And the central companion was an entirely generic one, Sam, whose likeness never even appeared on a cover. It got even worse for the next guy, Fitz, who was introduced without a description and didn't receive one for over a year!

The Eighth Doctor was very much defined by the *TV Movie*, in the sense that the major beats established there were entirely verboten in the novels: on no account could the Doctor be half human or kiss anyone. Oh, and he had to be the opposite of the master manipulator from the New Adventures, which was fair enough, except that no one appeared to have decided what character traits he should actually have, so the end result was what was often termed the congenital idiot, as he floundered around, babbling at people in a way that's only Doctorish when the Doctor actually has some kind of plan underneath it all.

Where the New Adventures had looked to the Doctor's past, the Eighth Doctor Adventures looked to his future, as led by Lawrence Miles (who wasn't a TV writer or anything, but he was well known among the dwindling readership). Unfortunately, Miles didn't play well with others, so this story arc tended to be convoluted and contradictory, as authors fought to undo each other's developments, retconning things left, right and centre. The arc was finally junked once and for all when they blew Gallifrey up and stranded the Doctor on Earth for six books.

What followed at this point was a renaissance for the BBC Books, helped by a switch in editorial teams behind the scenes, as Justin Richards took over from Steve Cole and had a story arc planned out: the Eighth Doctor had his memory wiped and lived out more than a century trapped on Earth, with no companions. Eventually, he rejoins Fitz and takes off... with no memories and with Fitz's memories on the blink as well. Further adventures continued, although many of them took place in parallel universes, which became a bit of a trope after a while. It was better than the congenital idiot, but the two lead characters with no memories exploring universes that weren't ours wasn't a whole lot of fun either.

Meanwhile, the Past Doctor Adventures were more of a steady hand, as the traditional fare was at least competent. And such stories weren't just limited to the BBC. The *Doctor Who* print world split again when Telos Publishing decided to release a set of hardback novellas, some of which were written by published science fiction writers who weren't solely drawn from the *Doctor Who* literati crowd. They didn't last long, but they span off into their own series (*Timehunter*). Meanwhile, the fan dollar was strained yet again, as Big Finish turned up with actual TV actors and stories you could experience in ninety minutes, which sorely bit into the diminishing returns of the BBC Books.

Virgin had published a couple of short-story collections called *Decalog*s, with the BBC producing a few more (called *Short Trips*). These featured past Doctors or some tales beyond (such as chronicling the family of one of the New Adventures companions). Big Finish, as was their wont, saturated the market with a massive output of short-story collections.

By the time the New Series was announced, *Doctor Who*'s print output had massively balkanized, with multiple competing past-Doctor stories (the Past Doctor Adventures, the comic strip, the majority of Big Finish, the Telos novellas, short stories) and only a poorly executed Eighth Doctor Adventures line still pushing forward... only now they couldn't push any more, because there was a Ninth Doctor on the horizon.

The Eighth Doctor Adventures wrapped up their arcs and finished with a final run of six books ... that are lovely and beautiful, but nobody was still reading by that point. Indeed, the very final book, *The Gallifrey Chronicles*, had to be delayed because the BBC charter forbade tie-in material that was required for viewing of a TV show. It wasn't, but the back cover blurb led everyone to believe that it was (ed.: see Perryman in Chapter 1).

With the New Series came new books, but these were quite different from the full-length novels of the earlier eras. They were written with one eye for children and had very little that tied into the ongoing show. Occasionally, they pushed the envelope, such as *The Story of Martha* featuring tales set during her year walking the Earth during *Last of the Time Lords*, but most had no connection to the ongoing TV series aside from the regulars and almost no inter-novel continuity. As the revival spawned spin-offs, so too did novelizations (in the case of the *Sarah Jane Adventures*) and original books for those spin-offs appear. *Class* might have been a massive failure as a TV production, but its three original novels make the premise work on its own terms, integrating modern-day school drama with science fiction thrills in much more thoughtful ways than seen on TV.

Occasional other novels were published here and there, sometimes with big names recruited. Science-fiction celebrities such as Michael Moorcock or Stephen Baxter contributed some, while *Doctor Who* celebrities like Tom Baker or Sophie Aldred contributed others. Short-story collections continued to appear sporadically.

Eventually, the Classic Series novelizations were completed and select ones written for New Series episodes. One avenue that opened up was the works of Douglas Adams, with hardcover, long-form editions of novelizations of his TV stories, as well as the unmade story *Doctor Who and the Krikkitmen*. These had a much broader appeal, as they could trade on the Adams name to a wider audience than just the *Doctor Who* fan base.

What's interesting is that the relationship with the TV adventures wasn't just one way. Several TV stories built off various New Adventures. 'Human Nature/The Family of Blood' is a direct retelling of Paul Cornell's novel *Human Nature* (considered one of the highlights of the New Adventure range). The Chelonians, recurring tortoise-like monsters from the New Adventures, rate a mention in 'The Pandorica Opens'. Professor Arthur Candy, created by Steven Moffat for a short story in *Decalog 3*, became the only character from *Doctor Who*'s print adventures to find his way onscreen (he interviews River Song [Alex Kingston] for graduate admissions in 'Let's Kill Hitler').

However, it's more than just a few cameos and the one rewritten script. The ethos of the New Adventures massively informed what *Doctor Who* could be, which is very much what the New Series became as well. Stories that were broader and deeper, which were about character as well as plot and written by fans like Russell T Davies and Steven Moffat, who had thought long and hard about what *Doctor Who* was and could be, and who knew how to change it in ways that would work, while still being true to the show we all loved.

Like I said, it's all Paul Cornell's fault.

Chapter 7
The *Doctor Who* figurine collection by Ross Garner

Original to this volume

For many fans of Doctor Who *(see Section II), the main way of interacting with the series is through action figures and collectibles. In this chapter, Garner explores the legacy of the* Doctor Who Figurine Collection *from Eaglemoss, Ltd., a series of more than 200 scale model figures, and their intersection with the main television text.*

Eaglemoss, Ltd'.s *Doctor Who* Figurine Collection (*DW*FC) launched in 2013 and ran until mid-2022, when the company entered financial administration. The *DW*FC consisted of a fortnightly release of a die-cast, hand-painted figurine depicting a character from the show's history in a 1:21 scale. Most retailed at UK£13 (approx. USD$15) and were accompanied by a short magazine exploring the character depicted and the story where they featured from a production and design perspective. Echoing Tim Holmes and Liz Nice's comments on partwork magazines, the *DW*FC represented 'a vehicle for delivering sets of collectibles' to a small niche of dedicated fan-collectors.[1]

The range began with a strong emphasis on contemporary *Doctor Who* characters: Matt Smith's Eleventh Doctor launched the range, and early inclusions were the Weeping Angels, the revised Silurians from 'The Hungry Earth/Cold Blood' (2010) and Davros from 2008's 'Journey's End'. However, Issue 15 expanded the range by depicting Omega from 1973's *The Three Doctors*, acknowledging characters from the 'classic' series. Reflective of how commercial pressures guided the range's development, the contemporary series – and newly released episodes especially – took precedent. Nevertheless, 'new' characters linked to the recently broadcast series were supplemented by alien creatures like the Voord (1964) and the Borad (1985). Over 200 issues were released in the core range, as well as additional supporting lines focused on aspects like TARDIS consoles and a continuing series of Special Editions, which continued the dual focus on contemporary and classic series but offered larger figures at a higher price point (retailing at between £25–40, approx.$30–50).

This chapter examines the *DW*FC primarily in relation to its handling of the 'classic' series. First, the discussion explores the collection's difference to other forms of *Doctor Who* collectibles and intersections with discourses of transmedia remembering. I argue that the *DW*FC offered a democratization of the programme's remembrance that challenges how fan canons and tastes have been co-opted and commodified by concurrent licensees. The analysis then reads the *DWFC* through transmedia historiography.[2] This perspective allows for the *DWFC* to be interrogated for its areas of absence and how these omissions further demonstrate the relationship between canonicity, fan remembrance and commercial concerns.

Commerce, canonicity and transmedia historiography

Doctor Who fandom has a long-standing alignment with material cultures of collecting, indicative of an enduring desire on behalf of certain subsections of fans to accumulate and own elements related to the show's history. In terms of commercial merchandise, collector cultures date back to the mid-1960s wave of 'Dalekmania'[3] and indicate how fans have sought out replicas of characters such as the titular Time Lord, their companions and adversaries.[4] The character-centric focus of these lines points to an enduring relationship between *Doctor Who* and commercial ideologies operating at the level of the show's merchandising. John Fiske noted that television drama 'is typically presented in terms of its leading characters' as this aids in promoting individual shows through appeals to discourses of consumer individualism and agency.[5] *Doctor Who*'s focus on iconic and distinct characters such as the Doctor's multiple regenerations and the Daleks, both 'then' and 'now', enables this form of engagement and so its alignment with commercial ideologies in terms of marketing and promotion.

The *DWFC* partly differed from other lines of collectibles, especially Character Options' action figures, because of the material affordances that the figurines offered. That is, *DWFC* figurines were *not* action figures: they offered neither points of articulation nor opportunities for (fan-)posing.[6] Instead, the figurines demonstrated *immobility* through being attached to a hexagonal base which encouraged display by tessellating the bases of individual figures together (Figure 7.1).

DWFC figurines, however, still demonstrated the potential for expanding *Doctor Who*'s narrative worlds through imaginative forms of transmedia play. As Jonathan Rey Lee argues, 'story toys are constituted by a tension between *play* – the activation of the toy in dynamic, playful performance – and *dis-play* – the pacification of the toy into a static representational commodity'.[7] *DWFC* figurines embody this tension by simultaneously providing material connections to specific moments in the *Doctor Who* storyworld through the character (and story) depicted, whilst also supporting the possibility for generating new, owner-created narratives that either complement or extend the storyworld's parameters.

A further point of differentiation, and therefore significance, between the *DWFC* and other contemporary figure lines concerns the former's attitude towards *Doctor Who*'s history. Memory is essential to any processes of transmedia expansion as audiences are directed towards remembering previous encounters with the intellectual property through the characters and locations selected for inclusion.[8] At the same time, these processes of cross-media remembering are structured by commercial processes such as how licensing – the commercial use of intellectual property – grants access to specific aspects of the property.[9] Licensing deals thus set parameters concerning what established elements of an intellectual property can be used by the licensee.

This point can be demonstrated by comparing the *DWFC* with Character Options' engagement with the show's history. Character Options has been attempting to maximize financial returns on its license through foregrounding the period of *Doctor Who*'s history with the highest levels of audience recognition

Figure 7.1 Tessellated bases encouraging display (photo by author).

and therefore commercial saliency. For example, to date there have been nine different figures of the Third Doctor (Jon Pertwee, reflecting the character's flamboyant wardrobe) and fifteen of the Fourth Doctor (Tom Baker). In comparison, there have been four different figures of both the First (William Hartnell) and Second (Patrick Troughton) Doctors, six of the Sixth (Colin Baker) and five of the Seventh (Sylvestor McCoy).[10] From a commercial standpoint, this selectivity makes sense as the 1970s saw *Doctor Who* achieve widespread popularity within the UK, cementing *Doctor Who*'s 'narrative image' by establishing the images and characters through which 'classic' *Who* endures.[11] Prioritizing the decade when the 'classic' series achieved its highest levels of popularity is indicative of how commercial ideologies engage with and appropriate cultural memory.[12]

More than this, and highly appropriate given the small-but-valuable market that fan-targeting collectibles represents, Character Options' selective reading of 'classic' *Who* constitutes the appropriation and commodification of fan perceptions of aesthetic 'value'. The 1970s is regularly celebrated among 'classic' *Who* fans by constructing author functions around executive producers Barry Letts and Philip Hinchcliffe and script editors Terrance Dicks and Robert Holmes. As James Chapman observes, Holmes' period as script editor, working alongside executive producer Philip Hinchcliffe, 'represents the "golden age" of *Doctor Who*', and this point has been restated in numerous publications,[13] both academic and scholar-fan facing.[14] Similarly, the 'Barry Letts-Terrance Dicks' era (1970–4) is often celebrated for developing 'a particular type of story … [and] tone' alongside the contributions that both made to the show's wider history.[15] Cumulatively, these statements indicate fans '*power to gloss* and write the aesthetic history of the show' through hierarchizing particular decades, production teams, actors and/ or writers.[16] By demonstrating a similar attitude towards 'classic' *Who*'s history, Character Options' strategies for selecting and releasing action figures indicate the co-opting of fan canons for the purposes of commodification and reflecting fan tastes back to their target market.

In contrast, Eaglemoss' approach to character inclusion within the *DWFC* can be read as a democratization of the 'classic' show's history. Since achieving a foothold, the core line had recognized more niche-appeal and ephemeral elements from the show's history such as the Monoids, the widely disparaged Nimon, and the Navarino. Although a few non-returning monsters (the Fendahleen from *Image of the Fendahl* and Scaroth from *City of Death*, both Fourth Doctor monsters) have featured in Character's range, most figures have been incarnations of the Doctor, companions, Daleks, Cybermen and Sontarans. Certainly, when it comes to the 'classic' series' progression into the 1980s, Character has shown no willingness to recognize stories such as *Arc of Infinity* or *Dragonfire*. The *DWFC* therefore represented a challenge to, and expansion of, dominant fan canons and taste formations by acknowledging and accepting both the successes and perceived failures from the show's history. By doing this, a more inclusive attitude towards the show's history was adopted, both motivated by commercial concerns (such as sustaining Eaglemoss' market share) and recognizing a wider range of fan taste formations such as camp and kitsch.

In addition, analysing *DWFC*'s magazine supplements invites debates concerning transmediality. *DWFC*'s magazine content exemplified what Phillip Dominik Keidl names 'transmedia historiography', or 'a subset of transmedia storytelling ... [that] describes the making of a storyworld's production and cultural history across multiple platforms, with each medium making distinctive contributions to the audience's understanding of the franchise's past'.[17] Demonstrating a different 'logic' to Henry Jenkins' concept of transmedia storytelling,[18] transmedia historiography 'is less concerned with contributing new meaning to a fictional story than with guiding engagement with the franchise's history'.[19] Relevant material for examining transmedia historiography constitutes 'behind-the-scenes features, making-ofs, and other paraproduction materials'.[20] The *DWFC* contributed to *Doctor Who*'s transmedia historiography by introducing or reaffirming established narratives of the show's production, whilst also taking individual costume or creature designs on their own terms and confronting dominant fan critiques by contextualizing the design, materiality and performance style enabled by the costumes within the context of that story's production.

The 'Your Figurine' article accompanying Mestor from *The Twin Dilemma* (1984) demonstrated this point. Readers were informed that 'BBC costume designer Pat Godfrey had never worked on any sci-fi series, let alone *Doctor Who* ... Godfrey revealed that the budget for Mestor had been a mere £200 to £300'.[21] Elsewhere in the article, Godfrey was also quoted concerning the materials used for creating the costume and the constraints these produced during recording:

> It consisted of three layers of material mounted on calico, the top layer being organza to give it a shiny look. The back was covered in a textured latex, with a fibreglass carapace which was also covered in textured latex on them ... Edwin Richfield, who played Mestor, wore the costume only for short periods at a time, but whenever we removed it he and the costume would be soaked in perspiration.[22]

The article thus encouraged readers to re-evaluate aspects of this frequently panned story by inviting reconsideration of the story's production circumstances and conditions. Moreover, detailing the costume's materiality and construction encouraged fans to reconsider how these aspects inhibited and encouraged performance styles. However, these historical narrative constructions represent 'cultural memory management' in that they are 'top-down' impositions by licensees that regulate what aspects of a franchise are deemed worthy of remembering alongside how the tone of those remembrances should be conducted.[23] As the case of Mestor demonstrates, the suggested tone is one of appreciation and reconsideration which works in service of BBC brand management by silencing 'bottom up' fan critiques.

Another way that the *DWFC*'s performed 'cultural memory management' concerns its contributions to reinforcing what constitutes the show's 'proper' history. For example, the *DWFC* positioned the broadcast *Doctor Who* television series as the primary site of storyworld canonicity. In fact, only one release in the core range acknowledged *Doctor Who*'s other transmedia iterations. This was Issue 167, which featured a figurine of the Sixth Doctor in a light-blue version of the character's outfit from the 2002 BBC animated webcast 'Real Time'. Alternatively, Big Finish's audio dramas were only included in a satellite manner, appearing infrequently and outside of the main fortnightly range. There were two separate three-figure sets, each including a variant of both the Eighth Doctor (Paul McGann) and a Dalek alongside a figurine of companion that is solely tethered to the audio dramas (Lucie Miller [Sheridan Smith] and Liv Chenka [Nicola Walker], respectively).

The absence of Lucie or Liv from the core range, alongside the omission of other popular Big Finish-originating characters like Dr Evelyn Smythe (Maggie Smith) or Charley (India Fisher), speaks to another inflection of how licensing exerted power over how the *DWFC* constructed and commodified the show's history. The *DWFC* was produced under licence from BBC Studios, as are Big Finish's audio dramas. To what extent, then, did the terms of Eaglemoss' licence cover access to characters created by Big Finish? Answering such a question requires access to confidential documents like licensing contracts that are frequently not made accessible to either cultural studies researchers or the public. However, the infrequency with which Big Finish-derived characters were released, as well as their status as stand-alone sets outside of the core range, suggests how commercial-industrial practices like inter-corporate licensing agreements installed boundaries concerning how the *DWFC* could construct the show's history. Although Big Finish audio dramas were acknowledged in some magazine articles alongside other non-televised transmedia expansions like comics and official novels (e.g. the New Adventures), these mentions were only ever brief and so demonstrated the primacy of televised *Doctor Who* over its extension in other media.

Conclusion

In summary, the *DWFC* was a significant addition to *Doctor Who*'s cultures of collecting and processes of transmedia expansion as its longevity allowed fans to collect figurines of characters that were hitherto viewed as commercially unviable due to concurrent licensees prioritizing the commodification of dominant fan canons. The range has therefore destabilized established fan hierarchies and tastes by granting visibility and materiality to the entire span of the show's history, recognizing both the beloved and the disparaged, the fan-friendly and the often overlooked. However, the transmedia historiography constructed by the range remained subject to commercial pressures including the re-evaluative attitude that magazine articles encouraged towards fan appraisals of the show's aesthetic history and the primacy afforded to televised *Who* over other transmedia iterations. The myriad relationships between merchandising, memory and commercial interests are therefore elements that analyses of any forms of merchandising – *Doctor Who* or otherwise – should address.

Notes

1. Tim Holmes and Liz Nice, *Magazine Journalism* (Los Angeles: SAGE Publications, 2012), 27.
2. Philipp Dominik Keidl, 'Between Textuality and Materiality: Fandom and the Mediation of Action Figures', *Film and Merchandise* 42, no. 2 (November 2018): https://doi.org/10.3998/fc.13761232.0042.207; and Philipp Dominik Keidl, 'Franchising the Past: Transmedia Historiography, Cultural Memory Management, and the Fanboy Historian', *Journal of Cinema and Media Studies* 61, no. 5 (2021–22): 159–82.
3. For an academic commentary on 'Dalekmania', see Jonathan Bignell, 'Space for Quality: Negotiating with the Daleks', in *Popular Television Drama: Critical Perspectives*, ed. Jonathan Bignell and Stephen Lacey (Manchester: Manchester University Press, 2005), 76–92. For a fan commentary on this phenomenon, see Christopher Hill, 'Toy Stories', *Doctor Who: Chronicles 1965*, February 2021, 44–51.
4. See Victoria L. Godwin, 'By Any Other Name: Gender and Doctor Who Barbie Dolls, Adventure Dolls, and 1:6 Scale Figures', in *Doctor Who – New Dawn: Essays on the Jodie Whittaker Era*, ed. Brigid Cherry, Matt Hills and Andrew O'Day (Manchester: Manchester University Press, 2021), 189–205. See also Panini Comics, *Doctor Who Magazine – Special Edition #60: Action Figures – The Essential Guide 1963–1996*, April 2022.
5. John Fiske, *Television Culture,* 2nd Edition (London: Routledge, 2011 [1987]), 150.
6. Jason Bainbridge, 'Fully Articulated: The Rise of the Action Figure and the Changing Face of "Children's" Entertainment', *Continuum* 24, no. 6 (2010): 829–42.
7. Jonathan Rey Lee, *Deconstructing LEGO: The Medium and Messages of LEGO Play* (Basingstoke: Palgrave MacMillan, 2020), 159.
8. Colin B. Harvey, *Fantastic Transmedia: Narrative, Play and Memory across Science Fiction and Fantasy Storyworlds* (Basingstoke: Palgrave Macmillan, 2015).
9. Avi Santo, *Selling the Silver Bullet: The Lone Ranger & Transmedia Brand Licensing* (Austin: University of Texas Press, 2015), 7.
10. The figure of four Second Doctor action figures excludes the 'Androgum' variant from a box set themed on *The Two Doctors* story. It is difficult to pin down the exact number of Fifth Doctor action figures as variants have pivoted around whether the character's hat and stick of celery are included, as well as the stripe design employed on both the jumper and trousers.
11. See, for example, Matt Hills, *Triumph of a Time Lord: Regenerating Doctor Who in the Twenty-First Century* (London: I.B. Tauris, 2010), 204.
12. John Ellis, *Visible Fictions: Cinema, Television, Video* (London: Routledge, 1982), 145–60.
13. James Chapman, *Inside the TARDIS: The Worlds of Doctor Who* (London: I.B. Tauris, 2006), 98.
14. See Alan McKee, 'Which Is the Best Doctor Who Story? A Case Study in Value Judgements Outside the Academy', *Intensities: The Journal of Cult Media* 1 (December 2001): http://intensities.org/Essays/McKee.pdf and Kim Newman, *BFI TV Classics: Doctor Who* (London: BFI, 2006), 62, 78 and 80 for evidence of this discourse in academic publications. See Laurence Miles and Tat Wood, *About Time 4: The Unauthorized Guide to Doctor Who, 1975–1979 Seasons 12 to 17* (Illinois: Mad Norwegian Press, 2004) for evidence in fan-facing material.
15. Chapman, *Inside the TARDIS*, 83.
16. John Tulloch and Henry Jenkins, *Science Fiction Audiences: Watching Doctor Who and Star Trek* (London: Routledge, 1995), 145.
17. Keidl, 'Franchising the Past', 160.
18. Henry Jenkins, 'Transmedia 202: Further Reflections – Henry Jenkins', Confessions of an Aca-Fan, last modified 31 July 2011: http://henryjenkins.org/blog/2011/08/defining_transmedia_further_re.html.
19. Keidl, 'Franchising the Past', 162.

20　Ibid., 164.
21　Simon Guerrier, Eddie Robson, Jim Smith and Tom Spilsbury, 'Your Figurine: Mestor', *Doctor Who Figurine Collection – Part 196: Mestor, Leader of the Gastropods* (2021): 4.
22　Ibid., 6.
23　Keidl, 'Franchising the Past', 162.

Chapter 8

Doctor Who: Time Fracture – Process, techniques and principles of an immersive experience production by Sarah Atkinson and Helen W. Kennedy

Original to this volume

The history of Doctor Who *in the theatre is vast; from early examples (*Curse of the Daleks *[1965] and* Seven Keys to Doomsday *[1974]) to much more recent productions like* Time Fracture *(2021). Atkinson and Kennedy discuss* Time Fracture *specifically in their chapter, exploring the limits of* Doctor Who *on stage and the immersive experience.*

Doctor Who: Time Fracture (DWTF) is an immersive theatre experience which opened in London, UK, in May 2021. With a cast of forty-three and a crew of thirty-seven, DWTF brought together the internationally recognized creative expertise of professionals from UK-based Secret Cinema. As well as drawing on this sector-leading talent pool, DWTF was underpinned by collaborations with the original BBC creative team. This chapter draws from exclusive interviews with those who have written, designed, created and delivered DWTF. We illuminate the ways in which these sector leaders have evolved the latest techniques, processes and principles which are shaping the wider immersive experience industry by adapting *Doctor Who* into a transmedia experience that is faithful to the original IP, celebrates and honours the artistry of its original creators, and is mindful of the desires and needs of its dedicated and diverse fan base.

DWTF can be considered a pandemic success story, developed during a national lockdown in 2020 in the peak of the first wave of Covid-19 infections and launched at the tail end of the second wave in 2021 under strict social distancing measures. This extraordinary context enabled access to world-class creative talent, as Brian Hook, chief creative officer of Immersive Everywhere/Hartshorn-Hook, explains:

> There really isn't a person on that team who isn't an A grade, world class theatre maker. I think we ended up with a cast that you otherwise couldn't get. It's an amalgamation of Punchdrunk, Les Enfants, Secret Cinema. They're absolutely incredible and they've done it all. They've seen it all. There's nothing you can't throw at them.

The key creative team had the benefit of considerable extra development time, as Luke Swaffield, the Secret Cinema/DWTF sound designer, explained:

> We have a very strong working relationship and a very tight workflow that we have developed over the years of doing these shows [...] we had both the horrible experience and the advantage of COVID, in that we had three months of exclusive availability for all of us to do nothing more than sit on zoom.

This time frame also supported an intensive period of textual research, as Daniel Dingsdale, the DWTF writer and Secret Cinema alumnus, explained:

> I undertook six months of research which included two watches of the complete thing from the (19)60s to present day, which was about 400 hours of TV and then going back to other stuff – some of the novels, some of the audio plays, so it was a real immersion in the world [...] I mean when you're going for an intellectual property, normally [...] it doesn't cover 60 years!

The production drew from this rich history, using transmedia worldbuilding techniques to weave together a multi-layered tapestry of references into the experience including a homage to every single Doctor.

DWTF both consolidated and advanced immersive experience production techniques, process and principles, making notable contributions to the form in three significant ways: through performance and character design; through the automation and synthesis of stage management, lighting and sound; and through embedding principles of inclusion within the entire production.

Transmedia techniques

Through the development of new storylines and characters, DWTF involved the creation of what we have elsewhere described as 'interstitial IP': the elaboration of key characters and situations that are true to the 'lore' of the world of the originary Intellectual Property (IP) but are distinct in their own right.[1] This interstitial IP has the potential to form part of a new 'canon' related to the IP, particularly if it is well-received by pre-existing fans. This is already in evidence with the DWTF.[2] The close relationship between the new DWTF creative team and those responsible for the original IP and the lore of the world[3] is an essential element to the success, believability and durability of the new experience. Dingsdale explains the complex back and forth that was required between himself and the BBC during the writing phase, which occurred

> ... every time I had a question such as – 'I want to resurrect someone in Gallifrey, I want to bring back a Time Lord – is there a ritual that does that?' [...] 'what do all of the items in Rassilon actually do? 'is there equivalent of lightspeed in the *Doctor Who* universe ... ?'

In addition, for all characters that were used from the TV show in DWTF, the BBC signed off on both the casting decisions and the proposed dialogue – a major challenge for an experience that was also building in space for improvisation and audience participation.

In the case of DWTF, the interstitial IP is based on the premise that a time fracture – a rift in space and time – has been created by a bomb explosion during the 1940 blitz of London. The fracture has become increasingly unstable over the past eighty years. This information is conveyed to the audience through news reports playing on multiple screens in the secret 'UNIT' Command. UNIT are the organization which have sought to conceal the time fracture's existence and the danger it poses to the universe. Audience members are addressed in a dual register as both a ticket holder and as a civilian volunteer selected by the Doctor to attend UNIT Command. On arrival, audience members are addressed in-character and welcomed into UNIT by a number of assistants in white lab coats. The importance of the fidelity and familiarity of the interstitial IP is underscored by Dingsdale:

> The audience coming in need to know at least something to be able to hang their hat on. You're asking a lot of an audience that comes to immersive theatre, not to the same degree as your performers, but you're asking them to play another part, so if they can come in with some kind of knowledge, it helps them meet you halfway.

Due to the complex narrative spatialization that is central to this 'freeform' immersive experience, this interstitial IP also builds in characters who play the role of a 'liminaut'[4] who support audience access to the new world. There are two types of liminaut present within DWTF. The first populate the entry stage of the experience, assisting the audience in 'traversing the limen' from the 'real world' (i.e. accessing the venue, locating the cloakroom, etc.) to the created world of DWTF, the 'cross-fade' moment in Punchdrunk's immersive theatre productions.[5] In DWTF, the liminauts are the UNIT assistants, and their communication includes a briefing video from Chief Scientific Office Kate Lethbridge-Stewart (Jemma Redgrave), a character already featured in the wider *Doctor Who* universe.

Once the time fracture has been opened, audience members are led down two flights of stairs into the second segment of the experience which plays out in an area of multiple rooms and spaces described as

> Sandbox play. [...] you can do whatever you want in the area. You can go and talk to people. You can get a drink. You can spend all your time with one character, or you could run about exploring the set. It's up to you.
>
> (Sophie Cairns, Assistant Stage Manager)

The second liminaut character is fully embedded in the world and acts to support participants in moving between the narrative vignettes that exist within the navigable spaces of the experience. These liminauts are distinct from the other performers in their freedom to move across and throughout the experience drawing participants with them and stimulating further engagement and activation of the missions embedded within the designed experience (see Figure 8.1). To manage the complexity of the multiple

Figure 8.1 Liminauts in the second 'sandbox' phase of DWTF – include from left to right: the character of Robert Dudley, Leonardo Da Vinci and a Time Lord Guide. Photographs by Mark Senior.

character arcs, all actors follow a detailed beat-sheet of their own narrative pathway of the key points that they are required to hit throughout the experience.

Process

The designers of DWTF explained the scale and complexity of the experience. It was conceived as if a feature-length television episode, structured in three sections of forty-five minutes, with the audience entering in three 'waves' of ninety people. There are seventeen 'worlds' within the venue, comprising of differently-sized spaces, rooms, corridors and walkways (see Figure 8.2). These include UNIT Command, Torchwood's hub, Queen Elizabeth I's Court, Leonardo da Vinci's studio, Shakespeare's office, a basement of Weeping Angels and a luxury spaceship liner 'ZZ1', which serves as the interval bar.

Dingsdale explained that it is unlikely that a single audience member would be able to experience every space in one 135-minute performance. DWTF involves up to fourteen different narrative tracks, thus rendering the experience highly repeatable for fans, since each visit would entail a different set of exchanges. The team were aware of the new ground they were breaking: '… it just makes it this beast of a show. I've never worked on anything so complicated in my life, because we fit three types of shows together' (Sophie Cairns, assistant stage manager). These three shows are an interactive promenade performance, an exploratory sandbox and a traditional theatrical experience. Lorna Adamson, deputy stage manager, explains the logistical complexity of managing the three separate waves of audience members:

> I'm cueing three shows on top of each other. In the first section I've got five cues and then the audience move into the next section and I've got 10 cues in there, but obviously I've still got to do those five cues on top of those ten cues, and then when the third ones come in, I've [now also] got those next five cues on top, because everything needs to be to time. But if the third audience are delayed coming in, I've got to shift those cues into different times while also cueing these ones and those ones! I must admit that I think they underestimated how complicated it was going to be.

This complexity is intensified when sound and lighting are introduced. As Swaffield explains:

> We had to automate a lot of it because the capacity for the venues was quite small […] we have to keep each section to 40 minutes or they're going to crash into each other.

Figure 8.2 Examples of the different 'worlds' in DWTF. From left to right: UNIT Command, the Alien junkyard and market and Brolls' Salvage and Import Export Emporium. Photographs by Mark Senior.

This requires complex management when the audience are divided across multiple performance spaces and engage with numerous performers. Terry Cook, lighting designer, describes:

> … of course the cast get distracted. It's an immersive show, they might be in deep conversation with a customer who's really enjoying it. But then forget that at 16.41 they have to walk everyone over here – they tend to be what we call signifiers in lighting and audio terms – where we might change the colour of the room or flash some lights to tell the cast – 'you're two minutes away from the next big sequence – wrap up your conversations!'

Cook went on to explain the new way of working that he developed for DWTF:

> [We have] 17 different shows all running simultaneously, and it's repeated three times in a night so I have 4291 lighting cues across a night. That is a ridiculous amount and it's too many to operate […] so using MIDI – a sound effect will have various elements attached to it, so the sound operator triggers multiple sound and lighting cues at once.

Cook goes on to reveal the tricks and tools that have been brought in to manage these triggers:

- We have hidden buttons, pressure plates, sensors, there's a door sensor when you open a particular door, it triggers a two-minute sequence, we know that the audience have opened that door, so we can build that sequence at that time.

In addition to streamlining the technical parameters of the show control software, DWTF evolved documentation to support the flow and clarity of information between the different members of the department:

> We developed a very user-friendly document so that the operators can very quickly see what's happening because there's so many different things happening at once – all buried!
>
> (Swaffield)

The move towards automation and synthesizing performance, lighting and sound cues together into one show system signals a key advance in the techniques of immersive theatre production, as Cook affirms: 'The technical has taken a real step forward in immersive – it's become a character of the show, much like your principal artist or cast member'.

Principles

Inclusion is a core principle underpinning the DWTF production, not least, because of the fans:

> the fan base is so lovely, it's unique. I think *Doctor Who* is a very inclusive place and it's for all the family. It's where a lot of people who sometimes feel unwelcome in different places always feel welcome.
>
> (Dingsdale)

The creative team developing DWTF were determined to build on some of the challenges they had encountered with earlier immersive experiences (notably *The Wolf of Wall Street* and *The Great Gatsby*) particularly in relation to safeguarding their performers and their audiences. Dan Gammon, company manager, outlined a specific set of contextual factors that impact upon performers within immersive productions:

> You're often in basements that have been converted that aren't necessarily built for this kind of thing […] sometimes it's quite difficult when everything is very loud and especially with *Doctor Who*, you've got people that are in masks and costumes that are very restrictive. It can be quite an intense experience and you have to make sure that you're checking up on people and making sure that they're OK.

Furthermore, immersive performance demands two contrasting approaches – improvisation and repetition. When multiple audience groups are brought through the experience, performers are required to repeat the same small narrative vignettes for batch after batch of audience members *whilst also* responding to a range of unpredictable audience interactions. DWTF rotates their cast through these 'vignettes' to counter the negative impacts of this repetition.

In terms of audience inclusion, Hook explains:

> we've really tried to make the show as accessible as possible. There's a huge neurodiversity in our audience and people with all sorts of different physical abilities. […] But it's been an absolutely incredible privilege to put a show together with that in mind …

DWTF included the engagement of an accessibility and inclusion consultant who outlined the very specific needs of the *Doctor Who* audience, explaining that there was

> … a consciousness that this is a show about inclusion. This is a show that orbits itself around being about all different types of people, about aliens and cosmic entities, where everyone should feel welcome and positive and loved. Inclusion was such a big part of its philosophy as a show. We knew that was going to be a real focus area, but I don't think any of us were prepared for just how many people from the very first opportunity would dive in.
>
> (Bayley Turner)

The DWTF team were trained in consent protocols and to recognize neurodiverse responses to the complexity of the environment and the sensory demands of the experience. The team can direct audience members to quieter spaces should they become overwhelmed. DWTF also includes the design and development of a wheelchair-accessible narrative track. Dingsdale explains his motives:

> I wanted it to be something special that only those audience members get […] it's completely unique. We put love into that, because the show is just as much for you as it is for everybody else. Not only that, when you share the anecdotes afterwards, nobody else is going to have done that experience.

Gammon explained how the creation of this narrative track responded to the logistical necessity for the access patron to be taken back through the experience along a wheelchair accessible route. This was narrativized as travelling back through time accompanied by a Time Lord Guide to undertake a mission for Davros:

> They had to go back the way they'd come to access the final area – they would have to go back through the waves of audience behind them – they come back to Elizabeth's court and the market and the same thing is happening to wave two that they've seen already, but it's like they're going back in time and then they have to go through wave three in the first area, and then they get recognized by a scientist. And that's like they're going back in time again to what has already happened to them, which was brilliant, it's bespoke and it made a really tricky situation very special for those patrons.

Conclusion

By adapting the *Doctor Who* IP to create an immersive experience that pitches *accessibility* as a core design principle, DWTF has set a high bar for future productions to ensure they are attentive to the accessibility requirements and neurodiversity of their audiences. In the evolution of the process, techniques and principles of immersive experience design, DWTF is a landmark production, an exemplar to build upon which has advanced the potential for scalability, replicability and repeatability of immersive experiences. The affordances of the immersive experience format for the *Doctor Who* fan base are clear. As Hook explains:

> The BBC are absolutely head over heels with the work. The beautiful thing *about Doctor Who* is that every fan wants to be a part of their own *Doctor Who* story. That's all fans ever wanted to do with the brand. And that is 100% what we offer them.

Acknowledgements

Kind thanks to our generous interviewees from the DWTF team: Lorna Adamson, Sophie Cairns, Terry Cook, Daniel Dingsdale, Daniel Gammon, Brian Hook, Danny Nolan, Luke Swaffield and Bayley Turner, and also to Frankie Bunce and Iain Fraser-Barker at Hartshorn-Hook Enterprises.

Notes

1. Sarah Atkinson and Helen W. Kennedy, *Secret Cinema and the Immersive Experience Industry* (Manchester: Manchester University Press, 2022).
2. A detailed breakdown of DWTF has been compiled on 'Tardis Date Core: The *Doctor Who* Wiki': https://tardis.fandom.com/wiki/Time_Fracture_(stage_play).
3. Including James Goss – Executive Producer of 'Time Lord Victorious', writer of both *Doctor Who* and *Torchwood*, and 'Lore Consultant' and Script Editor on DWTF (see Evans' chapter 9).

4   The term Liminaut has previously been used to refer to the ideal player subjectivity required within Live Action Role Playing (LARPing) as 'a free explorer of the threshold realm' (See Martin Ericsson, 'Play to Love', in *The Foundation Stone of Nordic Larp*, ed. Eleanor Saitta, Marie Holm-Andersen and Jon Back (Stockholm: Knutpunkt, 2014), 54). Here we adapt this original conception to capture the expert role played by these characters in immersive experiences, drawing participants across the threshold into the fictional world and supporting their navigation of these spaces as guides and activators.

5   Josephine Machon, ed., *The Punchdrunk Encyclopaedia* (London: Routledge, 2018), 69–70.

Chapter 9

The costs of the Doctor: *Time Lord Victorious* and managing transmedia engagement by Elizabeth Evans

Original to this volume

Wrapping up this section, Elizabeth Evans discusses Doctor Who's *sprawling 2020–21 transmedia epic,* Time Lord Victorious (TLV). *The first deliberately transmedia campaign for Doctor Who, TLV, utilized television, DVD, audio, comics, literature, figurines and even T-shirts to tell a story about the Doctor and the Kotturuh, an alien race that introduced the concept of death to the universe. Evans explores the success and failures of transmedia* Doctor Who.

In April 2020, BBC Studios announced the launch of a massive transmedia *Doctor Who* narrative, *Time Lord Victorious* (*TLV*), involving over thirty pieces of content and building up to the opening of immersive theatre experience *Time Fracture* in May 2021. Despite *Doctor Who*'s long history of transmedia storytelling,[1] *TLV* was the corporation's most ambitious attempt to expand the Doctor's adventures beyond television and constructed a story that was deliberately and inherently told across platforms rather than expanding from a core pillar of television episodes. Narratively, it built on a moment from the 2009 episode 'The Waters of Mars' when the Tenth Doctor (David Tennant) proclaimed himself the 'Time Lord Victorious', able and willing to change time despite a Time Lord edict not to. *TLV* sees him subsequently travel back to the early years of existence to change time and stop the Kotturuh, the race who impose life spans across the universe. The consequences of the Kotturuh's defeat were explored across numerous transmedia components featuring several versions of the Doctor. Stories were told across novels, audio dramas, web videos, short stories, comics, videogames, action figures, an escape room and *Time Fracture*. The vast majority of *TLV* content was new, but it also included retrofitting existing television episodes into the overarching story via a Blu-Ray special box set. From a licensing perspective, *TLV* was a feat of industrial cooperation and organization, bringing together BBC Studios, existing licensees including audio drama producers Big Finish, publishers Penguin Random House, games company Maze Theory and Titan Comics and new partners working in immersive experiences (Escape Hunt and Immersive Everywhere).

The narrative and logistical ambition of *TLV* raises a number of issues relating to transmedia storytelling experiences, most notably the 'costs' that are demanded of audiences when content is expanded from a core narrative pillar. This chapter will map the cognitive and contextual costs that emerge in various forms when experiencing the entirety of *TLV* and the various strategies employed to mitigate them. In doing so, it will establish the challenges that emerge from balancing transmedia storytelling ambition with the demands such ambition places on audiences.

Mapping the costs of *TLV*

No media experience is 'free', and 'in return for each engaging experience, audiences make a sacrifice'.[2] This sacrifice comes in the form of costs. Whilst the most obvious engagement currency is money, non-monetary currencies such as time and attention are also 'paid' by audiences in return for an engaging experience.[3] These currencies coalesce around 'cognitive costs', which relate to how easy or difficult it is to follow and comprehend media experiences, and the 'contextual costs' created through the effort of accessing them. Audiences complete a mental cost to engagement 'equation' in which 'the perceived time and attention that content requires is balanced against the expected value and enjoyment of the experience it offers'.[4] Is the potential enjoyment that a piece of content offers an audience member worth the various costs associated with accessing and understanding it?

These costs increase with transmedia experiences that are spread across different media formats and platforms. Steve Benford and Gabriella Giannachi's model of 'transitions' in what they label 'mixed reality' is useful here. They identify 'critical moments … at which users must cross between spaces … take on new roles, or engage with interfaces, which need to be carefully designed if continuity and therefore coherence is to the maintained'.[5] This idea of transitions aligns with moments where the costs of transmedia engagement increase. Moving from an audio drama to a novel, then a game and then to an immersive experience involves shifts in space, behaviour, perception and mode of interpretation that require increased effort from the audience. It is easier to keep watching television than to turn it off, turn on another device and play a game. If an experience asks audiences to turn off the television, go to a completely different building and participate in an immersive experience, then the effort and costs become even higher. If the promised engagement is worth it, then that effort becomes no problem for the audience. If that promised engagement is vague or unfulfilled, then these moments become high risk for audience *dis*engagement.

Engaging with *TLV* generated a range of costs from both the contextual effort of finding and successfully experiencing each component and the cognitive effort of following the narrative. Table 9.1 maps out each component of *TLV* to demonstrate its scale and to support the following discussion of where and how costs were attached to engaging with it. For ordering purposes, it follows the 'Release Timeline' made available via the *Doctor Who* website (doctorwho.tv/time-lord-victorious), though we will return to how the correct content 'order' was presented later.

The most immediate costs that become apparent when looking at the scale of *TLV* were financial. To purchase access to every piece of *TLV* content, including merchandise which contained small snippets of narrative information, costs just over £300. There were also further financial costs that need to be acknowledged. Whilst the *TLV*-specific download for *Edge of Time* was free, it required access to a

Table 9.1 List of Time Lord Victorious Elements. From www.doctorwho.tv-time-lord-victorious with some release dates updated from Hero Collector website

Title	Story Order No.	Media	Price	Other information
The Hollow Planet	20	At home escape room	£14.99	Not listed in 'Release Timeline'; 60 minutes
'UNIT Field logs'	N/A	Web video	Free	Not listed in 'Release Timeline' or 'Story Order'; 11 minutes
A Dalek Awakens	22	Escape Room	£28	Only available in certain UK cities; 60 minutes
Defender of the Daleks #1	3	Comic		Later released as graphic novel
Doctor Who Annual 2021		Book		'Release Timeline' lists Annual, not story; 'Story order' lists story, not Annual
→ 'River Song's Guide to the Dark Times'	10	Short story		
Brian the Ood		T-shirt	£10	
Monstrous Beauty #1	11	Comic	£7	Part of *Doctor Who* magazine
Comic Creator – Tales of the Dark Times	15	Comic + game	£2.49	
The Knight, The Fool and the Dead	12	Book	£10	
Master Thief	4	Audio	£5	Released together; 82 minutes
Lesser Evils	4	Audio		
Defender of the Daleks #2	3	Comic		Later released as graphic novel
He Kills Me, He Kills Me Not	6	Audio	£9	75 minutes
Monstrous Beauty #2	11	Comic	£7	Part of *Doctor Who* magazine
Dalek Emperor and Dalek Drone	1	Action figure	£20	Includes 'The Last Message' short story
Edge of Time TLV update	23	Game	£15	Free update; requires *Edge of Time* game
Dalek Commander and Dalek Scientist		Action figure	£20	Short story included in packaging
→ 'Mission to the Known'	16	Short story		
Road to the Dark Times:	N/A	Blu-Ray	£16	Re-release of older episodes; 11 hours 29 minutes
→ *Planet of the Daleks*				
→ *Genesis of the Daleks*				
→ *The Deadly Assassin*				
→ *State of Decay*				
→ *The Curse of Fenric*				
→ 'The Runaway Bride'				
→ 'Waters of Mars'	8			
The Enemy of My Enemy	7	Audio	£9	78 minutes

'Daleks!'	2	Web video	68 minutes
Monstrous Beauty #3	11		*Doctor Who Magazine*
Defender of the Daleks collection	3	Graphic novel	£15
Dalek Executioner & Dalek Strategist		Action figure	£20
→ 'Exit Strategy'	19	Short Story	£20	Not included in Release Timeline
The Minds of Magnox	14	Audio	£21	73 minutes
Mutually Assured Destruction	18	Audio	£9	77 minutes
All Flesh Is Grass Part 1	13	Novel	£10	
All Flesh Is Grass Part 2	17			
Genetics of the Daleks	21	Audio	£9	80 minutes
The Time Lord Victorious & Brian the Ood		Action Figure	£20	
Echoes of Extinction A	5	Audio	£9	Dual release told from two perspectives; 78 minutes
Echoes of Extinction B	26			
Time Fracture	24	Immersive Theatre	£45	Only available in London; 2 hours 15 minutes
'Dawn of Kotturuh'	9	Short story	Free	Short story made available to DW newsletter subscribers
'Canaries'	25	Short story	Free	Published on website and with (non *TLV*) *The Winter Paradox* book

VR headset and the original game, which involved significant financial investment. *A Dalek Awakens* was only available in certain UK cities and *Time Fracture* was only available in London, meaning they also involved transport and accommodation costs for those not living nearby or were simply not available to fans outside the UK.[6] *TLV* required an expensive monetary commitment.

Further logistical and temporal contextual costs emerged in accessing much of the content. Content was released over ten months from August 2020 to May 2021, requiring audiences to keep paying attention to when and how new components were appearing. Global release dates varied, adding further confusion for non-UK-based fans. Experiencing those elements of *TLV* with fixed durations took at least twenty-six hours plus however long it took to read or play novels, comics and games. Attending *A Dalek Awakens* and *Time Fracture* involved the additional effort of booking tickets, determining how to get there and liaising with friends to go with, ultimately requiring significantly more time than each experience's duration. Cognitive costs emerged in relation to following and understanding the story across different narrative forms, using different types of engagement behaviour (watching, listening, reading, playing) and tracking how the story fits with the non-*TLV* storylines of the Fourth (Tom Baker), Eighth (Paul McGann), Ninth (Christopher Eccelston), Tenth and Thirteenth (Jodie Whittaker) Doctors. Some components, such as novel *All Flesh Is Grass* and audio drama *Echoes of Extinction*, featured events from multiple points in both the *TLV* narrative and the overall narrative of *Doctor Who*, requiring audiences to keep several narrative moments and strands in their head at once. To return to Benford and Giannachi's model of 'transitions', each time *TLV* required audiences to shift from watching a web video, to reading a short story, to playing a game, to participating in an immersive experience, it asked audiences to take a shift in the kind of narrative mode they were experiencing, where that narrative fitted into their wider knowledge of *Doctor Who* and what they were required to do as an audience member. Although these shifts may seem minor, they required an increase in effort on the part of the audience member and so brought with them additional cognitive costs.

Managing the costs of *TLV*

BBC Studios and *TLV* creative lead James Goss employed several strategies to mitigate and manage the above costs. The most straightforward was the use of branding to give a linguistic and visual connection point between different parts of the *TLV* narrative, allowing easier identification of items that belonged to the transmedia experience. Branding maintains coherence within transmedia storytelling,[7] and appeared in *TLV* in two main ways. Each component was labelled as part of a connected narrative called *Time Lord Victorious*, following the series' long tradition of telling multi-part stories under a single title and giving *TLV* a specific name to create a sense of a coherent *single* narrative. This was taken further through a second strategy of visual branding. Each component featured not only the *Doctor Who* logo but also an additional *Time Lord Victorious* logo. Recurring images further set *TLV* content apart from wider *Doctor Who* storylines. Most prominent was an image of David Tennant's Tenth Doctor wearing a set of Time Lord robes and large gold collar rather than his usual suit and converses. This was not only a costume that his version of the Doctor had never been seen in before but also reminiscent of those worn by senior Time Lords that the Doctor regularly comes into conflict with, thereby distinguishing the *TLV* version of the Tenth Doctor from his appearances elsewhere. The repetition of these *TLV*-specific visual cues worked to position each piece of content as a part of a single *TLV* narrative.

If branding was used to provide a sense of coherence and connection across different components of *TLV*, the production team took the opposite approach in promotional discourses in order to reassure audiences about the costs involved. When asked about criticisms of how expensive *TLV* would be, Goss described it was 'like a patchwork quilt – the idea is that you can explore any chunk of the quilt and go "this is really cool!"'[8] Goss' comments specifically respond to the considerable economic costs of experiencing every piece of *TLV* content by claiming that audiences do not have to access, and therefore pay for, everything. At the same time, his comments manage expectations of how much audiences were *required* to engage with the storyline, reassuring them that if they only want to devote their time and attention to *part* of *TLV*, they will still have a fulfilling and engaging experience. This seeks to balance the 'cost-engagement equation' discussed above in favour of engagement rather than disengagement. However, while the aim was to be reassuring, in doing so Goss acknowledges that *TLV* is actually expensive in terms of money and time and even undermines its coherence by saying that any component could be easily missed. The metaphor also, more problematically, implies that anyone who does not experience all of it will have a lesser experience. After all, a few squares of a quilt will not do the job as well as a full one.

The final strategy used to manage the high costs of engaging with *TLV* was also ultimately problematic. A website hub offered two guides to its constituent components: 'Release Timeline' and 'Story Order'. The latter divided the narrative into three parts: 'The Fractured Universe', 'The Dark Times' and 'The Victorious Days'. A database then allowed audiences to search for specific pieces of content, with links to where they could be purchased. The website seemed, on the surface, to act as a vital tool for reducing the effort that would be involved in piecing together and then accessing the full *TLV* narrative. However, a number of issues with the website impacted on its ability to function in this way. The database of purchase options required the user to search or browse for individual pieces of content, rather than linking from the two guides, resulting in extra effort to jump between the two in order to find and purchase content. The database equally did not contain entries for every item listed in the guides, and some links became broken, potentially causing further confusion and frustration.

The two guides only added to this confusion and frustration. Several pieces of content listed in one guide were missing from the other. The previously existing episodes were included in the 'Release Timeline' guide but not (apart from 'The Waters of Mars') in the 'Story Order' guide, leaving audiences to figure out what their relationship to the *TLV* narrative is. Other pieces of content, especially short stories, were listed but without any indication of where they could be found. 'River Song's Guide to the Dark Times' is listed in the 'Story Order' guide but with no indication that it could only be found in the *Doctor Who Annual 2020* listed in the 'Release Timeline'. Other entries were only available in the *Doctor Who* magazine. 'Dawn of Kotturuh', which shows the first planet the Kotturuh visit, is missing from the 'Release Timeline' and has no source listed the 'Story Order' guide. It was in fact only available to subscribers of the *Doctor Who* newsletter, making it difficult for nonsubscribers to track down. These hints at story components but with no indicator of where to find them required audiences to make further effort to try and find out more about them. Further, while the 'Story Order' guide offered a seemingly coherent order for content based on narrative progression, as Table 9.1 indicates, content was not released in that order, with some stories being sequels, others prequels and some featuring events from two different points in the 'Story Order'. Audiences must then figure out how different components fit together themselves. Whilst this kind of narrative complexity is not uncommon, it must be recognized that it involves a significant amount of work in looking between and making sense of the two guides to really understand how the different story pieces fit together. Rather than easing the time and attention costs that audiences must pay in order to experience *TLV*, the official guides actually increased them.[9]

Each of the above strategies were attempts to minimize or ease the high financial, cognitive and contextual costs of engaging with *TLV*. However, through the rhetorical tool of a 'patchwork', the production team undermined their own coherence and ambition. Equally, attempts to guide audiences through the full range of content were incomplete and difficult to follow, ultimately increasing the costs being asked of the *Doctor Who* audience. As a case study of complex, large-scale transmedia storytelling, *TLV* highlights the importance of careful strategies for managing the work that goes into transmedia engagement.

Notes

1. See Chapter 1 in this volume; Elizabeth Evans, *Transmedia Television: Audiences, New Media and Daily Life* (London: Routledge, 2011); Elizabeth Evans, 'Learning with the Doctor', in *New Dimensions of Doctor Who: Adventures in Time, Space and Television*, ed. Matt Hills (London: I.B. Tauris, 2015).
2. Elizabeth Evans, *Understanding Engagement in Transmedia Culture* (London: Routledge, 2020), 36.
3. Ibid., 105–9.
4. Ibid., 107–8.

5   Steve Benford and Gabriella Giannachi, *Performing Mixed Reality* (Cambridge, MA: MIT Press, 2011), 231.
6   This situation was exacerbated by *TLV*'s release during Covid-related travel restrictions. See Chapter 8 in this volume for a further discussion of *Time Fracture*.
7   Carlos Scolari, 'Transmedia Storytelling: Implicit Consumers, Narrative Worlds, and Branding in Contemporary Media Production', *International Journal of Communication* 3 (2009): 586–606; Evans, *Transmedia Television,* 33.
8   Hugh Fullerton, 'How Doctor Who Fans Created Time Lord Victorious – Without Even Realising It', *Radio Times* (13 August 2020): https://www.radiotimes.com/tv/sci-fi/doctor-who-time-lord-victorious-fans/ (accessed 15 February 2022).
9   An unofficial guide to *TLV* was produced by fans on tardis.fandom.com, which provides more detail than the official guides.

SECTION TWO

Studying *Doctor Who's* audiences and fans

Matt Hills

This section begins with the first academic study of *Who*'s audiences, *Science Fiction Audiences* (1995). Its chapters on *Doctor Who* were written by John Tulloch, who studied *Who* audiences including young mothers reflecting on the programme's suitability for children; university students watching via an interest in literary SF and international fan club members. Our extract focuses on Tulloch's analysis of fans as a 'powerless elite'. Fans make up a small percentage of the audience, yet possess detailed knowledge of the programme; this combination makes them both 'elite' readers and ones who seemingly have little power to influence 'their' show.

The next chapter revisits Tulloch's 'powerless elite'; where Tulloch was looking at 'classic' *Who*, Leora Hadas and Limor Shifman (2013) consider fans on LiveJournal responding to the first few seasons of 'Nu *Who*' under showrunner Russell T Davies. It may be assumed – with a fan in charge of the programme and with fans having a visible presence online – that fandom would be notably empowered. But Hadas and Shifman demonstrate that the LiveJournal fans maintained distinctions from the 'mainstream' audience, arguing that Davies should *not* cater to fandom. The 'powerless elite' was alive in a new way.

Though Tulloch considered audiences beyond fandom, *Doctor Who* scholarship has focused more on fan interpretations and the next two extracts exemplify this. Both are 'poststructuralist' (focused on multiple readings). Paul Booth (2014) draws on the archive-oriented theories of Jacques Derrida, whereas Alan McKee (2004) is in dialogue with John Fiske's (1983) 'structuralist' understanding of *Doctor Who*, which identified it as supposedly carrying a specific 'ideology' (structuralists believed that fixed textual structures could be identified by analysis). Where Booth questions how *Who* has been divided up into 'eras' by fans, McKee questions whether fans read the show as meaningfully 'political'. These extracts argue for the diversity of fan interpretations; periodization might split *Doctor Who* up into preferred/ devalued phases, but doing so limits its readings. And positing any fixed political meaning to *Who* makes it impossible to understand how fans can read the show as leftwing, rightwing or not as political at all.

Despite his data challenging any singular idea of '*Doctor Who*'s politics', McKee suggests that the programme's genderings may be interpretable with greater uniformity. This question of *Doctor Who* and gender is taken up via fan studies in the next extracts. Rebecca Williams (2011) examines fan reactions to David Tennant's Doctor, showing that female fans identified, on the *Doctor Who* Forum, as the 'squee squad' were subjected to critique from established male fans. However, fans who discussed their desire for Tennant fought back against depictions of them as 'not real fans'.

Neta Yodovich (2020) brings us into the current (and just ending) 'era' of *Who*. Yodovich's (2022) book *Women Negotiating Feminism and Science Fiction Fandom* shows how fandom can be about 'conditional belonging' (2022: 108); female feminist fans encounter gatekeeping which questions their fan authenticity and challenges expressions of feminism. The last of this section's six reprints demonstrates that a kind of conditional belonging was evident in how female feminist fans defended Jodie Whittaker's casting, using points from *Doctor Who* canon to perform 'true' fandom. Yodovich argues that her respondents were simultaneously keen on the first female Doctor not being 'girly', implying that the Doctor's characteristics should be continuous with earlier incarnations. She cites Tulloch's foundational (1995) work, demonstrating that her interviewees used some of the same reading strategies as Tulloch's, arguing that the Doctor was a Time Lord and should be understood through this.

Four newly commissioned pieces begin with Alison Lawson and David Lawson's 'Fans as Consumers: Psychographics and Tribalism in *Doctor Who* Fandom'. This illustrates how studies of *Who*'s audiences have become multi-disciplinary rather than just the preserve of media studies, using marketing theory to identify fan 'tribes'. Such tribalism may be particularly evident through social media, and many of Lawson and Lawson's proposed categories might strike the reader as immediately recognizable. Rather than leaving such typologies to those selling *Who* as a commodity, however, they could be useful within debates surrounding fans' self-understandings.

Although traditional fan practices (fanfiction; cosplay; fanzines) have been well analysed by fan studies, there is a need for more work on how fandom plays out across social media and across new types of textual productivity. The following chapters tackle these topics. In 'The controversy of the Thirteenth Doctor announcement and *Doctor Who* fandom on Tumblr', Alice de Freitas Gomes and Polyana Inácio Rezende Silva revisit the same event analysed by Neta Yodovich, but from the perspective of Tumblr fandom. Given Tumblr's reputation for being a pro-social-justice space, Gomes and Silva find, perhaps unsurprisingly, a lack of negative responses to Whittaker's casting in terms of gender. At the same time, the 'controversy' of Whittaker's casting contained – again – multiple, diverse interpretations, displaying the heterogeneity of fandom in one social media context.

As Gomes and Silva note, Tumblr has been studied for its 'pedagogies' and Parinita Shetty extends this into podcasting in '*Marginally Fannish*: Fan Podcasts as Alternative Sites of Intersectional Education'. Showing how fandom and academia themselves can intersect, Shetty created a fan podcast, *Marginally Fannish*, in her PhD. The podcast hosted discussions where fans were able to 'restory' *Doctor Who*'s canon via their own experience, showing the importance of how fandom, and *Who*'s readings, are situated. Shetty's work enacts how politicized criticisms of *Doctor Who* can become a form of public pedagogy, extending fans' experiences so that these can be empathetically understood by others.

The section closes with Dominique Gagnon's chapter on 'casual' audiences for the serialized series 13, *Flux*. Gagnon addresses another gap in studies of *Doctor Who* audiences – that we know relatively little about how less committed viewers interpret the show. Fans, as a 'powerless elite', have worried about how popular *Who* is with the mass audience. And while fans were concerned about how the seriality and complexity of *Flux* would impact on its success, Gagnon shows – via an analysis of Twitter responses to the episode 'Once, Upon Time' – that more casual audiences were willing to go along for the ride, trusting that serial developments would bring clarity.

Overall, this section emphasizes key strands in previous work on *Doctor Who*'s audiences and fans ('the powerless elite;' poststructuralist or multi-interpretive approaches to *Who*'s periodization and politics; analyses of gendered conflicts within post-2005 fandom). And it illuminates the potential for new cross-disciplinary work exploring scholarly gaps and audience developments (fan tribalism; platform-based community and podcasting pedagogy; casual/non-fan readings). Perhaps of all *Who*'s audiences and fans, though, it is the child audience which remains least studied. It can only be hoped that future doctorates on *Doctor Who* will generate expertise in this 'dark dimension' of academia.

Chapter 10
The powerless elite

From *Science Fiction Audiences* by John Tulloch and Henry Jenkins*

First published 1995

Foundational work by John Tulloch (1995) analysed a wide range of Doctor Who *audiences. This extract focuses on fans' interpretive power – for example, the power to define 'golden ages' of the show – and how this is aligned with a lack of influence over whether or not* Who *proves successful with the mass TV audience.*

Golden ages and the 'unforgivable'

What, then, constitutes a 'good' episode that would keep the 'floating voter' (and the fan) switched on? This question plays a central role in the fans' reading of individual texts.

Doctor Who fans' sense of a good episode is constructed in terms of quite a precise aesthetic: it should not 'leave things unexplained' (in order not to lose the wider audience); and it should adhere to the history and continuity of the series (in order not to lose the fans). [*Doctor Who* Appreciation] 'Society' fans are, in effect, situated as a privileged group with few powers – a powerless elite with little control over the floating voter on one side, the producers of the show on the other. Consequently their explanation and evaluation of any one episode is strongly determined by this positioning as experts who have little control over either the conditions of production or reception of 'their' show.

In the absence of this, their power is the power to gloss, and to write the aesthetic history of the show – dividing its twenty-five years into a series of 'golden ages' and 'all-time lows'. They, thus, establish an officially constituted reading formation, which supervises reading of the show. Ian Levine, for many years a very senior British fan (and at one time unofficial continuity historian to the producers), had this to say[:]

---

*Originally published by Routledge (London and New York), 1995.

Levine: 'The series had a mood, and a charisma and atmosphere and a sort of gripping drama to it during Philip Hinchcliffe's era. The stories were meticulously made. A TV play or TV series like *Doctor Who* can turn out to be a work of art if everything comes together in the end which a lot of Hinchcliffe's were and a lot of John Nathan-Turner's are. Hardly any of Graham Williams's were, and if they were it was by accident'[...]

'Unforgivable' was a word that sprang easily to the lips of fans when they were being critical, and it is a word used especially often by *Doctor Who* fans about 'the Graham Williams era' (1977–80). For instance, Ian Levine noted that

> facts they have given in one story clash grossly in the next .... We are told in one story that only the Doctor can fly the Tardis and in the next story he has got the savage Leela, who has no grasp of electronics at all, asking the Doctor what the co-ordinates are and flying the Tardis herself. That was unforgivable, that really was unforgivable.

Similarly another senior English fan Jeremy Bentham (author of *Doctor Who: The Early Years*) observed, 'I can't forgive Williams for the line he gave to the Sontarans in *Invasion of Time* [1978], "primitive rubbish"';[...] Levine adding, 'We know the Sontarans aren't as advanced as the Time Lords, so how could a Sontaran walk into the Tardis and say, "This machine is a load of obsolete rubbish"? – that is the exact line'. The producer behind both of these 'unforgivable' examples was Graham Williams.

'Errors in continuity' (which Levine spotted throughout the series) entered, in his view, a qualitatively new stage as they became systematic under producer Graham Williams (1977–80). Under Williams, 'errors in continuity' combined with a 'send-up' style which most fans disliked intensely[:]

> [Levine again:] Under Graham Williams the decline set in as a rot .... The three stories in a row, *The Creature from the Pit* [1979], *The Nightmare of Eden* [1979] and *The Horns of Nimon* [1979–80], *Doctor Who* reached an all-time low then and the ratings plummeted.

Despite Levine's error of fact here (current fans note that the ratings were very high for these stories, *Horns of Nimon* rating 11 million), we should nevertheless recognize the integral link in fan consciousness between programme aesthetics and ratings 'outside the Society'. Fans quite generally agree with Levine that Williams's 'seventeenth season' was the worst in the show's history.

Australian fan Pat Fenech writes in the fanzine *Zerinza* about their 'worst stories' survey results[:]

> The most notable feature here is the placing of 4 out of the 5 stories broadcast in the 17th season as amongst the worst stories ever. This season is reputed to be the worst in *Doctor Who* history. These results certainly suggest ADWFC [Australasian *Doctor Who* Fan Club] members consider it so [...]

Of those four stories, Australian fans rated *The Horns of Nimon* the worst story ever, *Destiny of the Daleks* (1979) second worst, *Nightmare of Eden* (1979) fifteenth and *Creature From the Pit* (1979) sixteenth worst.

Fans are thus far from being uncritical or sycophantic about their show. Rather, they establish an aesthetic history of 'classics' and 'worst ever' episodes which they circulate through the fanzines. This aesthetic is articulated quite self-consciously in their discourse about 'continuity'[...].

Continuity: Textual exegesis and the fans' power to gloss

The fans' particular competence is their intimate and detailed knowledge of the show; consequently, any producer or script editor who needlessly breaches the continuity and coherence of that knowledge is 'insulting their intelligence'. Many fans particularly enjoy episodes which call up that knowledge and so address them directly as fans. Levine, for instance, 'loved *Logopolis*' (produced by Nathan-Turner) because

> events in *Logopolis* revolved around the myth itself of *Doctor Who*. In other words, the whole story started because the Doctor wanted to change his broken chameleon circuit which has been broken since the very first story – and even the reference back to Totters Yard which was in the first story, to explain it.... Bring in anything from the series' past and you get my vote anyway.

The 1981 DWAS [*Doctor Who* Appreciation Society] president, David Saunders, and secretary, Gary Russell, described *Logopolis* as 'a nice fannish story' and 'all fandom and padding'[:]

> Saunders: 'It started off with a policeman looking around which is supposed to be reminiscent of the very first episode'.
> Russell: 'The reintroduction of the Master and the fight at the end on top of a radio telescope which was completely taken from the original Master's very first story where there was a fight on top of a telescope ... '.
> Saunders: 'The Tardis, within a Tardis, within a Tardis is straight out of *Time Monster* [1972]'.
> Russell: 'It's a fan story'.
> Saunders: 'We love it. But it's made for our thousand [DWAS members] instead of made for the BBC's millions'.[...]

As Levine put it, *Logopolis* was especially enjoyed by fans because 'the entire plot of *Logopolis* arose inside the myth of *Doctor Who* rather than taking the myth of *Doctor Who* to an outside planet'.

Fans on the other hand do not usually enjoy episodes which overtly undercut that myth. One of the 'most hated' *Doctor Who* stories in the ADWFC poll was Douglas Adams's first as script editor under Graham Williams, *Destiny of the Daleks*. Mary Tamm, who played the companion Romana, had unexpectedly quit the show, leaving the producer with a number of scripts featuring her. As Romana was, fortuitously, the first companion who was also a Time Lord, the decision was taken to make Romana 1 regenerate as Romana 2, and thus plausibly explain a new actress playing the part. The way in which this was done infuriated many fans.

> Levine: 'I could never forgive Graham Williams for the regeneration scene.... It has been clearly established that a Time Lord can only have twelve regenerations, clearly established. In many stories that fact has been stated. So how can they have some supposedly responsible female Time Lord in the Tardis trying on about six different faces before she decides which one she wants? – which is obviously wasting [...] regenerations. It is just ludicrous. It is that sort of non-attention to the detail of the series that gives me no regard for Graham Williams at all'.

Jeremy Bentham agreed:

> It was something that was done purely for a laugh – there is no other justification for it. If he knew that Mary Tamm wanted to leave, well at least you could have written something a bit more doom-laden – there is an outlet for it in *The Armageddon Factor* [1979] where the Shadow is torturing her very severely. The idea of that could have triggered off an involuntary regeneration.

And in Australia, fan Stephen Collins wrote:

> There is no good reason for this regeneration. The body of Romana I is functioning perfectly at the end of *Armageddon Factor*, there is no hint of a decay in the bodily functions. Neither is Romana I very old – *City of Death* (1979) establishes her as only 120. This is not a natural regeneration, Romana has forced it upon herself in a display of extravagance (considering she only has twelve to fool around with) […]

Rather desperately, Collins looks for reasonable explanations within the history and myth of *Doctor Who* to explain this 'extravagance'[:]

> There appear to be three valid approaches to the question. One stems from Baker's comment in *Robot* about the stability of his regeneration. If you assume from that there is a period of instability around every Time Lord regeneration, during which the new physical appearance may change, and clearly that is what Baker is suggesting in *Robot*, then the changes Romana makes as she searches for the correct body can be construed as occurring during that period.
>
> The second theory … concerns 'The Key to Time' (1978–79). The White Guardian, having utilised the power of the key whilst it was assembled in the Tardis, decided to relocate the Sixth segment. He decided to rest the segment in Romana, triggering her regeneration cycle. Romana then utilises the ability of the segment to 'try on' the other bodies – *Stones of Blood* (1978) established the ability of individual segments to allow transmutation of the possessor of the segment.
>
> Finally, it is possible that the ability displayed by K'anpo Rinpoche in *Planet of the Spiders* (1974) provides the solution. After regenerating into her new form, Romana shows the Doctor the finished result. He is not pleased, but she has no intention of changing her appearance to make him happy. So she retires from the control room and summons up possible future projections of herself, sending them to the Doctor to receive his appraisal. After she thinks the Doctor has had enough, Romana returns to the control room in her Princess Astra form – the only one she regenerated into […]

Whichever the right answer might be, Collins insists that

> Romana was not utilising normal powers of regeneration when she 'tried on' the three bodies to please the Doctor. Romana is far too intelligent to waste valuable regenerations on such a frivolous enterprise […]

This degree of exegesis of the 'holy writ' of *Doctor Who* may seem humourless to some, positively medieval to others. However, Collins is reading the episode in the same way as the university students discussed [… elsewhere in *Science Fiction Audiences*] – inter-textually, the only difference being the degree to which fans call up series history in their quest for meaning. What Collins's analysis indicates is that the power of *Doctor Who*'s executive fans (i.e. fans who are executives of the fan club and its magazines) is discursive rather than institutional. In this aspect of series continuity, the fans are clearly in the hands of the producers, who responded to the situation differently. John Nathan-Turner, according to Levine, was 'careful to consult the facts to make sure that he is not clashing with anything' […] – and during this period Levine 'helped out the *Doctor Who* office with continuity errors and continuity problems' (which is one reason for Levine's initial view that Nathan-Turner had 'restored *Doctor Who* to a golden age again'). Other producers, like Graham Williams, kept the 'Society' fans (who, numbering not more than 1,000 in the UK, constituted a tiny part of his audience) in their place. Williams told us that, as regards influence on the programme, fans had 'none whatsoever' even though 'they would rather like to think they have' […] We also asked DWAS executives David Saunders and Gary Russell whether they had an influence on the production of the show:

> Russell: 'I think there is a straight answer – one has to take in the BBC's approach which … is "fob them off with a few stories". No, they don't take a great deal of notice…. The fans don't make up the complete viewing public of *Doctor Who*'.
> Saunders: 'When all is said and done we hop around the thousand mark, and *Doctor Who*'s audience is millions. We are in some respects only a speck in the ocean'.

But in the absence of power over either production of the series or over the wider viewing public, these senior fans do have discursive power in establishing the 'informed' exegesis for their subculture of fans. Thus they establish and control an important reading formation. Stephen Collins, for instance, as letters editor of the Australian fanzine *Zerinza*, specialized for a while in 'regeneration theory'. In this way, editors of fanzines can have an important agenda-setting function. Thus *Zerinza* editor, Tony Howe, noted after the latest skirmish between a correspondent and Stephen Collins: 'as *Zerinza* editor I think it is time that more attention be given to discussing other topics such as the new stories soon to be seen, the Survey results, the Season Reviews; Regeneration has been well covered for the present' […]

So executive fans' opinions matter within the subculture – on, for instance, which issues are controversial at any one time as well as the way in which these issues are interpreted and closed off. It is in the pages of the fanzines that the unfolding myth of *Doctor Who* is articulated, positioned and circulated – the view, for instance, that Tom Baker polarized the fans between, as Collins put it, 'the ones who are fans of *Doctor Who*' (who hated Baker for 'sending up' the show) and 'the ones who are fans of Tom Baker'; or the view that Sarah-Jane Smith [Elisabeth Sladen] and Tegan Jovanka [Janet Fielding] were the 'all-time favourite companions' because of their 'strong, well-defined characters' (whereas, in Australia, Tegan was much less popular because of her 'pseudo-Australian character'); or the view (especially strong in Australia) that *Doctor Who* – far from being in a new 'golden age' under producer John Nathan-Turner – was 'going down the drain' […]

Chapter 11
The powerless elite?

From 'Keeping the Elite Powerless: Fan-Producer Relations in the "Nu *Who*" (and New YOU) Era' by Leora Hadas and Limor Shifman*

First published 2013

> Later work in fan studies would revisit Tulloch's work on fans as a 'powerless elite'. This example from Leora Hadas and Limor Shifman (2013) analyses how sections of online fandom responded to the first few Russell T Davies' series in the noughties, stressing fans' continued difference from the mass audience, and therefore arguing that to be successful, Doctor Who should not be targeted at fandom.

What fans want, what fans demand: The community's perception of its power

Much of the [doctorwho LiveJournal] community's discussion about Russell T Davies revolves around the posting of relevant news items, mainly interviews with Davies or the production team. [...] Davies can be highly aggressive in his condemnation of online fandom, and so these interviews have a great potential for creating uproar. Two elements of Davies's attitude generate great volumes of fan reaction: derogatory remarks about fans, and his assertion that fan views must never be taken into account when making production decisions. These vitriolic comments pose a challenge to the fans of [LiveJournal or LJ] doctorwho, since they bring up the trauma of a show brought down by fan involvement, and force them to cope both with fandom's dark past and the potential dangers of its changing status.

We identified three main strategies employed by [LJ] community members to deal with Davies's assaults [studying 17 relevant posts generating 1564 comments between 26 March 2005, and 25 December 2008]: counter-attacks, concession and critical self-inquiry. The first coping strategy is the simplest and most immediately visible: Initial responses to articles and interviews are usually made by angry fans out to dismiss or disprove Davies's derogatory statement of the day, often by claiming that

---

*Originally published in *Critical Studies in Media Communication* 30, no. 4 (2013): 275–91.

he cannot cope with honest criticism. Since this response is not as complex and multi-faceted as the others, we won't elaborate on it here.

The second coping strategy, tagged by us as concession, was formed mainly in response to Davies's comments about ignoring fans' opinions and desires for the series. From the first discussions, posters raised the argument that writing the series to please fandom is inherently a hopeless endeavour:

> Fandom is a strange creature, with many many heads, none of which can agree. It also has many many hands with which it pokes itself repeatedly in the eye and therefore gets nothing done. It's not *possible* to listen to fandom and give it what it wants, because it doesn't KNOW what it wants. Even if it did know, it would change its mind ten minutes later.
>
> (LiveJournal, 2006b)

Another idea that gradually becomes more salient in these discussions is that fans are innately impossible to please. This does not refer to differing tastes between fan groups, but to an imagined common mentality of fans that can never be satisfied. This idea is succinctly summarized in a not entirely humorous definition of a *Doctor Who* fan as 'someone who hates *Doctor Who*', to quote one particularly cynical community member (LiveJournal, 2006c). Criticizing the show they love is what fans do, part of their raison d'etre. To be a fan is to be chronically dissatisfied with production decisions, rather than celebrate them (as Davies would prefer). This, according to some fans, is more relevant to *Doctor Who* than to other shows. *Doctor Who*, as a series, invites thought and scrutiny, and, as such, criticism; the competent and knowledgeable audience is expected to be able to analyse the show and point out flaws as well as merits. 'Gushers' who welcome every episode with nothing but praise are thus no more fully functional fans than the ever-critical 'haters', and the [LJ] community clearly lets them know as much.

The third responsive strategy we identified, tagged here as 'critical self-inquiry', goes beyond this acknowledgement. It involves a more serious discussion of fans, their self-perception and their ideas about power. Specifically, it highlights the gap between fans' taste and what they perceive as legitimate demands from the producer of a mainstreamed, rating-dependent show.

The self-disempowered elite

> Fan opinion these days is that you should never listen to fan opinion.
>
> (LiveJournal, 2006d)

The third strategy espoused by doctorwho members in response to Davies's assertions is somewhat surprising. It posits that there is a fundamental difference between fans and non-fans, but, surprisingly, it's the taste of non-fans that fans defend. In other words: writing to please fans would be detrimental to the success of the show among a wider audience, and hence to its ability to stay on air. Ironically, doctorwho members echo the fanwank argument that troubled the BBC and the Nu *Who* creative team: the assumption that should they write the show to appeal to *Doctor Who* fans, it would be filled with continuity references, obscure characters and places from the classic series that no one but the fan community would be equipped or inclined to appreciate. Repeatedly, Davies's supporters point out his great success in making *Doctor Who* a massively popular show, at absolutely no risk of cancellation. Rather than calling attention to fan references in the text where these do exist, they seem to [...] remind their fellows that this success was achieved with complete disregard for the online fan community. They encourage Davies to continue on that same track – even to carry on with what they view as deliberate goading of the haters[:]

> The creators of any fantasy show would be stupid to take what the message board massive might want into account because they're a tiny, completely unrepresentative fraction of the viewership it takes to keep a primetime programme from cancellation. […] If the direction of the new *Who* had been left to fandom it would have been an imdb nightmare with special guest stars like Davros and Romana in every episode and it would have been cancelled already.
> (LiveJournal, 2006c)

While his condemnation of online fandom seems to be all-inclusive and absolute, Davies is not, as has been mentioned, entirely against fandom; in saying that fandom is 'larger than' the problematic element, and furthermore that the complaining online fans are not 'real fans', he cues listeners in to the idea that they are not, in fact, the 'bad fans', or at least they can choose not to be. Gradually, doctorwho members come to adopt this practice, using it as an effective strategy for reflecting and redirecting the most problematic comments. In a growing number of threads, they accuse the vocal complainers of wishing to see the show dragged back to the problematic cult status of the 1980s. While directly accusing another poster of not being a true fan remains taboo – an act met with outrage not just from the accused party but from other participants in the discussion – the idea that Davies's Others are also the community's Others does take root[:]

> I don't think he's referring to people with legitimate criticism, obviously no one's going to think that the show is fantastic for them every single week. But he's talking about the 'fans' that do nothing but complain about how all of new *Who* is terrible, yet keep on watching and complaining to the rest of us.
> (LiveJournal, 2008)

The 'moaning minnies' are not 'us', but fans of a different sort who truly are as unpleasant and destructive to the show as Davies paints them. These other fans supposedly populate other sites, most often the forums at http://gallifreybase.com/forum/ (formerly The *Doctor Who* Forum and […] Outpost Gallifrey). The pinning of the moaning minny image on this forum is not coincidental: to doctorwho, the DWF is the home of the 'anoraks', the old-school fanboys – again distinctly male – who, according to fan folk wisdom, really do resent any and all changes to their show and prefer it in its cult form. These fans were Othered by doctorwho members long before Davies gave them additional reason; making them his legitimate targets is not only easy and convenient, but also lends the viewpoint of doctorwho members a certain prestige – a seal of approval for their fandom authenticity from the powers that be.

This form of division, contention even within fan communities, has been repeatedly observed and identified as counter to what later scholars saw as an idealization of fandom in early fan studies. Both Jancovich and Hunt (2004) and Hills (2002) have described how cult audiences are engaged in an ongoing bid to define themselves through Othering both the mundane audience and the pathological fan. Jancovich further notes that fans' most radical Othering is of rival fan groups imagined as less than 'true' fans. Discussing community construction through Othering specifically among *Doctor Who* fans, both Williams (2011) [see the later extract from Rebecca Williams' work in this section] and Hadas (2009) find the fandom to be rife with disputes along these same lines described by Jancovich. It is interesting to note that while the different targets of this Othering – Williams's fangirls, Hadas' anti-moderation campaigners and the members of the Outpost Gallifrey forums as portrayed by doctorwho posters – are wildly divergent crowds, they seem to have in common an unruliness, a refusal to be contained. The women who loudly express their attraction to actor David Tennant, the writers who deny the need for moderation in fan fiction archives and the fans who demand to be catered to are all seen by their rival communities as 'fandom out of place' and out of bounds, and as such deeply problematic.

Hills' (2010) conceptualization of powerless duality [where showrunners such as Davies are fans themselves, yet although fandom takes on a new dual role across audience and producer, types of fandom and fan pleasure are still disempowered as irrelevant to 'mainstream' TV success] assumes a new meaning when applied to fan discourse. From the fans' perspective, the gap is [...] between what they as fans want and what they feel themselves entitled to demand, between the sense of shared ownership [of *Doctor Who*] and the need to let go of the desire for involvement for the show's own good. There is no outright rejection of fan pleasures, but an insistent rejection of the power to realize them: a conscious return to powerlessness. As we shall now see, the same logic of fandom out of bounds is at work in the cases in which [LJ] community members do feel comfortable calling out production decisions, informing not just relations between fans but also the stance toward the blurring of borders between producers and fans.

Fanwank re-invented

Users of doctorwho acknowledge that fans, themselves included, want continuity nods and references to the classic series. Yet when it comes to the question of what they feel comfortable demanding of the production – the changes they believe must be implemented to improve the show – we find that their main concern relates to something else entirely. They believe that Davies is himself practising fandom out of bounds in the form of problematic, potentially destructive fanwank, as in writing for fannish pleasure; however, his alleged 'Nu' fanwank is not manifest through continuity or nods to the fans – which, as mentioned, pass without incident – but through issues related to genre.

A major source of fannish conflict and criticism in regard to Davies's writing is his leaning towards the dramatic and soap operatic at the expense of plot and science fiction elements – a style that he credits with the success of the series outside its traditionally male fan base. Early writings about fandom established that fans tend to see a strict contrast between character drama and science fiction plots. Scholars from Jenkins (1992) onwards have described the former as brought into the realm of the latter by female fandom reappropriating a male genre, and the resulting clashes between male and female modes of fannish reading. This plot/drama duality is intensely problematic to fans, and the decision to include explicit romantic situations and relationships appears to be the most controversial of the changes made to the series upon its relaunch [...]. In the present context, it is associated by fans with the duality of canon/fanon, and in a broader sense with the roles and interests of producers versus those of fans.

Interestingly, the inclusion of continuity references and nods to fandom in Nu *Who*, which Hills [2010 ...] notes as deconstructing the binary between fan interests and the tastes of the mainstream audience, go uncommented on by doctorwho members. In contrast, the focus on romance and relationships, associated with female fan fiction writers, is pegged by doctorwho members as Davies's own special brand of fanwank. He may not write as the continuity-obsessed male fan that makes fandom dread a return to cult days, but he writes as a fan nonetheless – a feminized unruly fan who refused containment, to the disapproval and distress of doctorwho posters[:]

> Usually in fandom the show is plot-heavy, and then you have to leave it to spin off media and fanfic to flesh out all the touchy feeling relationship stuff. Then Rusty [the fans' nickname for Russell T Davies] comes along and glosses over the plotty bits about the aliens and stuff so he can tell stories about how much Rose loves and depends on the Doctor and the Doctor's loneliness issues and all that crap. He's got it backwards!
>
> (LiveJournal, 2006e)

The inclusion of romantic storylines in Nu *Who* – at the expense, as fans see it, of plot and science fiction and adventure content – sees fans commenting that for this sort of content, they could read fan fiction, rather than watch the show. Particularly aggressive responses on this issue were generated by the fourth season finale, in which a human clone of the Doctor remains in an alternative universe along with companion and love interest Rose Tyler [Billie Piper], a twist that posters blatantly complained seemed to be taken from a 'bad fanfic'[:] 'For me, I enjoyed a lot of the finale, but found the whole clone/Rose thing quite unbearable and, to be honest, quite rubbish. It was a fanfic ending for a mary sue' (LiveJournal, 2008).

One poster asked outright if Davies 'just fanwank[ed] the finale' – fanwank in the sense of writing a resolution that would only appeal to fans, in this case, to one in particular: Davies himself. That members use […] the specific term fanwank is telling. Davies's fannish writing is a source of deep concern to doctorwho posters, who are troubled by their perception of the show being dominated by the sort of self-indulgent stories that are better suited to the realm of fan writing, where the writer needn't appeal to a mass audience. Ironically, it is Davies's unwillingness, or inability, to write a science fiction plot, the staple of this genre long associated with having only cult appeal, which is feared to be driving away the general audience. In one particularly contested interview comment, Davies explained his reluctance to set stories on alien planets by claiming that the viewing public doesn't care about 'Planet Zog' and the 'Zog people' […]. In response, posters accused Davies of having no personal interest in such stories and of using – in fact abusing – supposed public opinion as an excuse to write the series according to his own tastes, instead of what the viewing public would actually like to see. In trying to distance himself from the stereotype of the fan who supposedly desires an emotionless series of pure convoluted plot, Davies, according to his critics, ends up valorizing fanwank of a different but equally dangerous sort. Williams's (2011) discussion of the infantilization of the female 'fangirl' fills in here for Hills's […2010] description of fanwank as associated with regression […], yet the principle remains the same, […] one of fandom out of bounds.

[…] *Who* fandom as reflected in our study is constantly wary of the dangers of a creator who is also a fan. The principle of fanwank as signifying a clear break between fan and mainstream taste still rings true to the fans on doctorwho, despite the apparently proven ability of cult features to appeal to a wider audience. The prevalent view among them is thus that Davies is not supposed to write as a fan, neither as a continuity detailed anorak nor as a romance-oriented fan fiction writer. He is also, as we have seen, not supposed to write for the fans, whether they are viewed as conflicting communities or as a single community with contrary tastes. Both views lead us towards a single conclusion: In an era of seemingly blurring borders between fans and producers, intensive boundary work is carried out by fans to make sure they remain apart.

References

Hadas, Leora. 'The Web Planet: How the Changing Internet Divided Doctor Who Fan Fiction Writers'. *Transformative Works and Cultures* 3 (2009): http://journal.transformative-works.org/index.php/twc/article/view/129.

Hills, Matt. *Fan Cultures*. London: Routledge, 2002.

Hills, Matt. *Triumph of a Time Lord: Regenerating Doctor Who in the Twenty-first Century*. London: I.B. Tauris, 2010.

Jancovich, Mark, and Nathan Hunt. 'The Mainstream, Distinction and Cult TV'. In *Cult Television*, ed. Sara Gwenllian-Jones and Roberta Pearson. Minneapolis: University of Minnesota Press, 2004, 27–43.

Jenkins, Henry. *Textual Poachers*. New York, NY: Routledge, 1992.

LiveJournal. 'Can't Get Away to Marry You Today, My Wife Won't Let Me!' (2006c): http://community.livejournal.com/doctorwho/1542252.html?thread=25140076#t25140076 (accessed 2013).

LiveJournal. 'Doctor Who and Newbies' (2006d): http://community.livejournal.com/doctorwho/1312183.html?thread=20588727#t20588727 (accessed 2013).

LiveJournal. 'Dr Who and Russell T. Davies and L.A. Times' (2006b): http://community.livejournal.com/doctorwho/691450.html?thread=8354042#t8354042 (accessed 2013).

LiveJournal. 'No Alien Planets?' (2006e): http://community.livejournal.com/doctor-who/1192271.html?thread=17944911#t17944911 (accessed 2013).

LiveJournal. 'RTD Interview' (2008): http://community.livejournal.com/doctorwho/3494960.html?thread=56376112#t56376112 (accessed 2013).

Williams, Rebecca. 'Desiring the Doctor: Identity, Gender and Genre in Online Science Fiction Fandom'. In *British Science Fiction in Film And Television*, ed. James Leggott and Tobias Hochscherf. Jefferson, NC: McFarland, 2011, 167–77.

Chapter 12
The eras of *Doctor Who*

From 'Periodising *Doctor Who*' by Paul Booth[*]

First published 2013

Where the earliest scholarship on Doctor Who *was structuralist textual analysis – expert readings of the program – after Tulloch and Jenkins'* Science Fiction Audiences *(1995), a poststructuralist turn gathered pace, focused on multiple audience readings. This extract, from Paul Booth's 'Periodising* Doctor Who'*, uses Jacques Derrida's theory of the 'archontic' (archival textuality) to stress how splitting the show into 'eras' can problematically fix fans' and critics' interpretations.*

The *Doctor Who* corpus

Periodization highlights the changing evaluative and contextual understandings of *Doctor Who* across multiple cultural/historical moments. […] There are more than just production personalities at the heart of the periodization, as 'stark contrasts … need to be explained in terms of the forces much more powerful than individual whim or intention' (Tulloch and Alvarado 4). *Doctor Who*'s eras help to determine the audiences they engender; as Sandifer describes: 'all attempts to cobble together pet theories out of existing evidence are as much a product of their own eras as the "errors" that they attempt to correct' (*Volume 3* 172). Although a useful heuristic in *deepening* segmented forms of knowledge, periodization also acts reductively, *disciplining* various contextual meanings into particular articulations of significance.

Multiple discourses are necessary for a more coherent picture of *Doctor Who* (see Hills *Triumph* 14–15). This multi-discursive approach was also illustrated in the first major academic analysis of the series, John Tulloch and Manuel Alvarado's *Doctor Who*: *The Unfolding Text,* where they investigate the program through a 'wide range of institutional, professional, public, cultural and ideological forces' (2). Such discursive categorization is also a classic precedent in Foucauldian theories, in which [Michel Foucault …] argues that the *way we articulate determines what we know.* We understand knowledge through different discursive lenses. Each colours what we see and how the various discourses inform us, eliding 'an origin or transcendental subject that would confer any special meaning on existence' (White 105). Hills looks

---

[*]Originally published in *Science Fiction Film and Television* 7, no. 2 (2013): 195–215.

at *Doctor Who* via Foucault to establish that 'the text of *Who* is inevitably "caught up in a system of references to other ... texts ... it is a node within a network ... It indicates itself, constructs itself, only on the basis of a complex field of discourse"' (*Triumph* 15, citing Foucault *Archaeology* 23). To examine *Doctor Who*'s eras is to prescribe meaning to each era; to examine the *Doctor Who* corpus through one particular lens is to delimit the terms of analysis. Periodizing underscores – but does not create – the mechanisms by which categories are established.

Expanding on this point in his analysis of the new series of *Doctor Who*, Hills describes the difference between traditional fan analysis of the show (which he terms 'intratextual') and scholarly analysis (which tends to be 'intertextual') (*Triumph* 4 ...). Fannish intratextual analysis tends to look inwards, examining what makes the show 'unique' – it is an ontological assessment of *Doctor Who*. In contrast, a scholarly, intertextual approach looks at the relationship between *Doctor Who* and other texts, often reading the show through specific theoretical frameworks. Hills's attempt to combine intra- with inter- approaches

> can allow *Doctor Who* fandom to sidestep one of its bugbears: the issue of what counts as 'authentic' *Who* ... Fan criticisms involve shaping an image of 'ideal' *Who*, a kind of Platonic essence of the series (which may never have been realized fully in any one story).
>
> (*Triumph* 5)

This 'unattainable' goal is the approximation of the quintessence of *Doctor Who*, something that one could point to and say, 'this is what *Doctor Who* is'. Different fans may be able to articulate particular eras as the most ideal (e.g. the Hinchcliffe–Holmes 'gothic horror' era: Chapman 98 ...), but no value judgement can be said to be authoritative. If one particular era of *Doctor Who* may or may not be described by a particular fan as the essence of *Doctor Who*, then *any* era could be said to be ideal *Who* – and therefore none actually is [...].

Periodizing as discourse

Periodization emphasizes division rather than continuity, encouraging the development of criteria of differentiation rather than unity. Any type of categorization brings with it assumptions that discipline and determine our understanding of the whole. If *Doctor Who* is a 'vast fictional quilt' (Britton 5 ...), then, stretching the metaphor a bit, the more we categorize the quilt via its individual blocks, the less we know about the blanket. The more attached one gets to a particular type of block, the more fractured the view of the entire quilt one gets. In other words, a non-generic, anti-hierarchical view of *Who* elides the Platonic ideal of periodization to focus on the show's ability (like its protagonist) to shape-shift as a key factor in its longevity. As David Butler suggests:

> it is this openness to diversity and change that is one of the great strengths of the programme ... What makes *Doctor Who* particularly notable, and has perhaps enabled it to last so long, is its blurring of boundaries. *Doctor Who* has defied easy classification.
>
> ('Introduction' 8)

Hills takes this to its logical conclusion, that fans and academics alike could explore 'new *Who* without getting hung up on its "essence" and on whether a given episode is "really" *Doctor Who*' (*Triumph* 8). [...]

Doctor Who is, and always has been, about change, renewal and development (see Butler 'Introduction' 7; Sandifer *Volume 1*). *Doctor Who* is never standard, which makes it always in-process.

But if periodization becomes the lens through which all *Doctor Who* is interpreted, then that too reductively facilitates a specific reading of the corpus – a reading itself based on periodization as the totalizing principle. Focusing on periodization in *Doctor Who* makes periodization a central, connective tissue across the text, eliding periodization *within* the corpus as well. Thus, periodization brings with it a disciplining procedure; periodizing *as* that procedure reinforces what fans may think of a particularly favoured era, and what judgements to bring to any intra- fandom or inter- scholarly debates. Although previous academic research into fandom has described the homogenous groups of fans that provide useful models of community […], especially online […], other studies have shown a more fractious relationship between groups of fans and audience members […]. As Lindlof, Coyle and Grodin illustrate, 'a typical media audience is not a cohesive membership that behave according to a shared code'; instead, they 'use and interpret the "same" text in divergent ways and decide when, where, and how they will engage a medium, subject to the demands and constraints of their social order' (219–20). Audience engagement with *Doctor Who* is based not just on 'social order' but also on the key paradigms exposed and accentuated by periodization. Making periodization itself the key characteristic reifies and accentuates these paradigms.

The periodizing consistency of *Doctor Who* fans emerges through the ascription of value to particular eras, stars, producers or functions of the text. Any assertion of value is thus 'specific to the particular regime that organizes it' (Frow 145), the text shaping the 'social hierarchy' of the fan community that follows (Hills *Fan* 46). To emphasize one particular moment or series of moments fragments meaning within a text. Following a text with a fifty-year history, the 'community' of *Doctor Who* fans must create strata in order to self-actualize. The positioning of individual membership in any fandom depends on the relationship with others' organizational principles, highlighting the impact of periodization on viewers as well. However, by examining alternative conceptions of meaning-making of *Doctor Who*, a more polyvocal understanding of the text can be revealed.

Archives, palimpsests and periodization

Thus, reconciling periodization within and about *Doctor Who* means seeing ruptures as both meaningful and unimportant to the larger serial frame of the text. […] Thinking around this paradox as a totalizing force for categorization, however, Abigail Derecho's 'archontic literature' defines an alternate system. Archontic *Who* – looking at the archive-like qualities of *Doctor Who* – provides a mechanism for integrating periodizing tendencies within a continually expanding corpus. Archontic literature provides a post-structuralist methodology for conceptualizing *Doctor Who*'s 'unfolding' text. […]

The term 'archontic' comes from Jacques Derrida, who describes the properties of an archive that allow it to continually open up to allow new and varied inclusions. An archive can never be completely closed, for it must always allow the continual renewal of new information. As Derecho describes in her analysis of the archontic properties of cult texts, 'any and every archive remains forever open to new entries, new artefacts, new contents' (64). She uses the term to connect fan fiction to a larger corpus, as 'the archontic principle never allows the archive to remain stable or still, but wills it to add to its own stores' (64). In other words, the existence of an archive *encourages* contributions to enlarge and develop that archive […]. I would make a correlated argument: that the archontic properties of *Doctor Who* allow it to be continually added to as an archive, not (just) through ancillary texts but also through canonized and retconned information [...].

For Derrida, the primary 'archontic principle ... is also a principle of consignation' (3). Thus, the first archontic principle is the 'breakdown' of memory into *inscription* (11). For *Doctor Who*, inscription is key to the way periodization functions: individuals and communities group the 'endless transformations and complex weavings' (Tulloch and Alvarado 5–6) together, inscribing meaning into each 'entry' as a unique unit of data within a *Doctor Who* 'database'. The archive is not just a thing but a process; it is not just a device for reproduced information but for production itself (Booth *Digital* 108) [...].

The second property of the archive in its relation to *Doctor Who* is its ability to be *rewritten as it goes*. Archives record but they also work to construct the nature of the content. 'Archive' is both a noun and a verb, and to archive something means to write its place within an already-extant structure (Derrida 17). This inherent rewritability applies as *Doctor Who* continually reinvents itself: the notion of particular eras thus flourishes under archontic principles. As Britton notes about *Doctor Who*'s continuity:

> What is striking about *Doctor Who* is the extent to which the process of defining the texts' internal universe is palimpsestic. In other words, key elements have not always simply been brought into alignment with existing 'truths', or vice versa; some of them have effectively overwritten earlier histories, albeit leaving the original elements partially visible.
>
> (23)

The notion of the palimpsest highlights not just the archive's inscriptive properties but also its *re-inscriptive* ones as well as well. Changing the categorization does not alter the text; it alters the category into which the text has been placed. Thus, re-categorization invites, rather than elides, re-evaluative discourses. *Doctor Who* thrives on this re-evaluative situation. Each era of the show – however it is defined – undergoes a 'cycle of evaluation', in which its value is 'continually reworked' (McKee 12–4) [...]. *Doctor Who* never had a 'production bible' with the history of the Doctor, Gallifrey and the Universe neatly laid out. Rather, such diegetic canonization has usually occurred after the fact [...].

This cycle of evaluation leads naturally to a third archontic principle of *Doctor Who*: namely, that archives *are paradoxically expansive and limited in scope*. As Derrida describes, archives always 'open out to the future' (68). The inclusion of new material naturally engenders the desire to include more material. But an archive must necessarily exclude some material in order to be separate from the culture that created it. We know *Doctor Who* because there are things that are *not Doctor Who*, and they firmly remain outside the scope of the show.

Lance Parkin describes the desire of *Doctor Who* fans to continually add to or adjust what counts as 'canon' within *Doctor Who*. Although he talks about the books and comics predominantly, his argument can extend to the nominally canonized material of the show itself ('Truths'). With periodization, problems over quality 'always exclude parts of the whole': some eras of *Doctor Who* are 'less "proper" than other examples' (Hills *Triumph* 6–7). One relevant example is the 1996 *Doctor Who* television movie (TVM). As a singular text situated within the heart of the largest rupture in the series' history, it is an exemplar of a Derridean *différance*, situated between and betwixt eras, marking a point of estrangement that reveals the artificiality of periodization. Any information within it might fall prey to the categorical tendencies that elide information within a non-canonized text. For example, it reveals that the Eighth Doctor is half-human. Within a periodization of *Doctor Who*, such information would taint the entire Eighth Doctor period, underscoring our reading of the era as a whole. Even showrunner Russell T Davies reveals this discourse. In his *The*

Writer's Tale, a book chronicling his writing of the series, he describes an original draft of 'The End of Time' (25 December 2009–1 January 2010), [...] which [...] included a line that jokingly referred to this half-human assertion. However, Davies says the line was cut as a 'silly reference – and kind of confusing, since most of the audience will remember the Doctor being human in "Human Nature" rather than the 1996 *TV Movie*' (627). Even in its erasure, the Eighth Doctor's half-human nature affects the corpus. Such a reductive move illustrates the way individual elements within a period can overshadow larger concerns.

Through an archontic lens, however, the expansive archive 'always produces more archive, and that is why the archive is never closed' (Derrida 68). There is no finality to the archive, which means an individual element can and will 'always work, and *a priori*, against itself' (12). The half-human nature of the Eighth Doctor can thus *exist within the same system as the information that he is fully Gallifreyan*. Davies could or could not include it equally, as it is always-already inscribed within the archive. The units of information that are prescribed and described within an archive thus *individually* reflect the category but do not *transfer* that meaning to other entries. Both elements become part of the archive as equally concomitant but contradictory facts. Through a dialetheistic methodology, in which 'both the thesis and the antithesis ... must be true', paradoxes are maintained within both the *Doctor Who* narrative (Booth *Time* 112) and its context.

The paradox of expansion/exclusion arrives with *Doctor Who*'s placement in a particular contextual time and space. Although it is constantly expanding, the *Doctor Who* canon must be limited within its archive to be recognized. We recognize *Doctor Who* not only for what it is but for what it is not, and make arguments about canonicity to determine this placement in the archive. There can be no canon without a sense of inside and outside the archive. For example, what do we make of a single 25-minute episode that features no regular cast, introduces new main characters and is situated chronologically between two unrelated serials? Such an episode exists in *Doctor Who*: 'Mission to the Unknown' (9 October 1965) is the 'prequel' episode to the mammoth *The Daleks' Master Plan* (13 November 1965–29 January 1966). As such, it becomes 'part' of the archive because it is both 'inside' *Doctor Who* and because it reveals an 'outside' to *Doctor Who* as a text – it is bounded by interstitial titles, promos and other extra-diegetic material. Another example of a similarly liminal *Doctor Who* text is the thirtieth anniversary special, 'Dimensions in Time' (26–7 November 1993) – a one-off charity special that, while featuring all the surviving Doctors, many of the most popular companions, and even some returning enemies, is [sometimes and contestably] considered less canonized than 'Mission to the Unknown' (Jones). Yet it is still part of the archive. Further, *The Scream of the Shalka* (13 November–18 December 2003), the animated fortieth-anniversary episode, features a Ninth Doctor played not by canonized Christopher Eccleston but rather by Richard E. Grant (Jones). Known as the 'Shalka Doctor', Grant's portrayal is non-canon, but has received its own DVD release in the official BBC *Doctor Who* line, archiving it within a non-canonized but recognized liminal space.

For Derrida, '*There is no archive ... without a technique of repetition, and without a certain exteriority*' (11). Alec Charles argues that *Doctor Who* is inherently defined by 'relativity and relativism ... not continuity but discontinuity' ('Ideology' 111). There must be elements that are outside the canon that provide a lens to examine within. 'Mission to the Unknown', 'Dimensions in Time' and *Scream of the Shalka* are all liminal texts, whose positioning either inside or outside the canon allows a lens through which the archive can be perceived. Drawing from what it is *not*, the television programme tells us more about our contemporary archival construction of it than it does about the show itself. This 'inherent paradox at the heart of the archive' engenders the periodizing problem: 'by archiving, one must necessarily leave something out'; an archive can only record within a culture, within a particular context (Booth *Digital* 109).

Thus, an archontic examination of *Doctor Who* offers a way of envisioning the television series' ruptures between eras not as periodizing, nor as categorizing, but as part of a continuous archival *process* by which individual discourses and frameworks of meaning become *part of* rather than *constituent to* the development of *Doctor Who*. Ruptures take no more precedence than any other form of archived material. This also avoids the common articulation of *Doctor Who*'s discontinuity as its *most* relevant factor, a feature exemplified in Britton: the 'metaphor of the vast narrative as a "fictional quilt" … can serve to highlight not merely *Doctor Who*'s famous flexibility of narrative premise but rather its inherent and often productive lack of narrative constraint and coherence' (26). Discontinuity and continuity work together to cohere the *Doctor Who* archive. Ultimately, the archontic methodology allows us a way to see around textual incoherence, a way to see discourse about the ruptures between eras as *equally* productive as that between continuities and a way to see divisive discourse about different eras as *cohering* an archontic fandom rather than dividing a periodized hierarchy. […]

An archontic principle does not differentiate between professional and amateur – everything becomes added to the ongoing enlargement of an archive. […] We make artificial separations with any scholarly or fan analyses, and thus help to create the very meaning that we are attempting to elucidate. Instead of viewing *Doctor Who* as a 'vast, fictional quilt' where the very bricolage nature of the programme becomes its greatest asset, we can instead assert that however we view, analyse or discuss, *Doctor Who* becomes the argument by which we know the show. The discursive lens delimits the view, but using the infinite lenses available via archontic principles develops multiple discourses simultaneously. Periodization creates meaning; we need to think around this meaning in order to construct an ontology of television.

References

Booth, Paul. *Digital Fandom: New Media Studies*. New York: Peter Lang, 2010.
Booth, Paul. *Time on TV: Temporal Displacement and Mashup Television*. New York: Peter Lang, 2012.
Britton, Piers. *TARDISBound: Navigating the Universes of Doctor Who*. London: I.B. Tauris, 2011.
Butler, David. 'How to Pilot a TARDIS: Audiences, Science Fiction and the Fantastic in Doctor Who'. In *Time and Relative Dissertations in Space: Critical Perspectives on Doctor Who*, ed. David Butler. Manchester: Manchester University Press, 2007, 19–42.
Chapman, James. *Inside the TARDIS: The Worlds of Doctor Who*. London: I.B. Tauris, 2006.
Charles, Alec. 'The Ideology of Anachronism: Television, History and the Nature of Time'. In *Time and Relative Dissertations in Space: Critical Perspectives on Doctor Who*. ed. David Butler. Manchester: Manchester University Press, 2007, 108–22.
Davies, Russell T., with Benjamin Cook. *The Writer's Tale: The Final Chapter*. London: BBC, 2010.
Derecho, Abigail. 'Archontic Literature: A Definition, a History, and Several Theories of Fan Fiction'. In *Fan Fiction and Fan Communities in the Age of the Internet*, ed. Karen Hellekson and Kristina Busse. Jefferson: McFarland, 2006, 61–78.
Derrida, Jacques. *Archive Fever*, trans. Eric Prenowitz. Chicago: University of Chicago Press, 1996.
Foucault, Michel. *The Archaeology of Knowledge*, trans. A.M. Sheridan Smith. New York: Pantheon, 1972.
Frow, John. *Cultural Studies and Cultural Value*. Oxford: Clarendon, 1995.
Hills, Matt. *Fan Cultures*. New York: Routledge, 2002.
Hills, Matt. *Triumph of a Time Lord: Regenerating Doctor Who in the Twenty-First Century*. London: I.B. Tauris, 2010.
Jones, Craig Owen. 'Life in the Hiatus: New Doctor Who Fans, 1989–2005'. In *Fan Phenomena: Doctor Who*, ed. Paul Booth. Bristol: Intellect, 2013, 38–49.

Lindlof, Thomas R., Kelly Coyle, and Debra Grodin. 'Is There a Text in This Audience? Science Fiction and Interpretive Schism'. In *Theorizing Fandom: Fans, Subculture and Identity*, ed. Cheryl Harris and Alison Alexander. Cresskill: Hampton, 1998, 219–47.

McKee, Alan. '"Which Is the Best Doctor Who Story?" A Case Study in Value Judgments Outside the Academy'. *Intensities: The Journal of Cult Media* 1 (2001): http://intensitiescultmedia.files.wordpress.com/2012/12/mckee.pdf.

Parkin, Lance. 'Truths Universally Acknowledge: How the "Rules" of Doctor Who Affect the Writing'. In *Third Person: Authoring and Exploring Vast Narratives*, ed. Pat Harrigan and Noah Wardrip-Fruin. Cambridge: MIT Press, 2009, 13–24.

Sandifer, Elizabeth. *TARDIS Eruditorum – An Unauthorized Critical History of Doctor Who Volume 1: William Hartnell*. CreateSpace, 2011.

Sandifer, Elizabeth. *TARDIS Eruditorum – An Unofficial Critical History of Doctor Who Volume 3: Jon Pertwee*. Smashwords, 2013.

Tulloch, John, and Manuel Alvarado. *Doctor Who: The Unfolding Text*. New York: St Martin's, 1984.

White, Hayden. *The Content of the Form: Narrative Discourse and Historical Representation*. Baltimore: Johns Hopkins University Press, 1987.

Chapter 13
Political *Doctor Who*

From 'Is *Doctor Who* Political?' by Alan McKee*

First published 2004

Another key example of the turn to 'poststructuralist' study of Who *fans is Alan McKee's (2004) 'Is* Doctor Who *Political?' (a question which has become more pressing in the era of fandom-focused 'culture wars'). This excerpt shows convincingly that fans have variously read the classic series as leftwing, rightwing and not as political at all, issuing a curse of fatal death to earlier approaches that were based on expert academic textual readings (e.g. Fiske, 1983).*

I [...] conducted interviews with members of the *Doctor Who* audience who have studied the programme in detail and spent time considering its interpretation in order to gather information on the political position that the programme takes. I interviewed thirty-nine *Doctor Who* fans about their own political thinking, their thinking about the politics of *Doctor Who* and the relationship between these aspects of their lives. Of these interviews, nineteen were conducted at the 'Resurrection' *Doctor Who* convention in Stoke-on-Trent, UK, in September 2001. Seven were conducted with *Doctor Who* fans who are also fan producers of *Doctor Who* stories and novels, accessed through acquaintances involved in this fan production. Twelve were conducted electronically with *Doctor Who* fans sourced through the online notice board www.rec.arts.drwho. Of the sample, thirty subjects were male and nine were female. A number were queer (although a specific question in relation to this fact was not asked in the data gathering). Thirty-four lived in the UK, four in the United States and one in Finland. This sample is neither generalizable to all *Doctor Who* fans; nor to all *Doctor Who* viewers; nor to all TV viewers; nor to all consumers of culture. This is not the purpose of this study. It is neither sociology nor ethnography (Moores, 1993: 4); rather, it is an attempt to discover some 'available discourses' about the politics of *Doctor Who* for engaged viewers (Muecke, 1982); whether, for them, it is reasonable to talk about the programme's political thinking.

In the interviews, I used an approach that might be called 'interview textual analysis'. I did not take a naïve realist approach to this data: I did not attempt to measure the 'authenticity' or 'truth' of the

---

*Originally published in *European Journal of Cultural Studies* 7, no. 2 (2004): 201–17.

speaking positions. On the other hand, I did not want to look for hidden deep meanings of which the interviewees themselves would be unaware (Probyn, 1996: 145). Rather, I treated the interview data as a text to be subjected to poststructural textual analysis, making 'an educated guess at some of the most likely interpretations that might be made of that text' (McKee, 2003: 1). I asked these fans a variety of questions designed to illuminate their responses to, and uses of, the stories of revolutions and uprisings presented in *Doctor Who*. In designing these questions, I wanted to find ways to articulate my (academic) mode of thinking about cultural politics with that of a (largely) non-academic audience sample. The question 'Does *Doctor Who* function as vernacular state political philosophy?' would likely have been meaningless to a group unfamiliar with academic vocabulary. However, I suspected that the concept involved – that *Doctor Who* might have something to say about the way that a state should be run – would be meaningful to these fans if I could find a way to articulate it in language that did not require academic training to be understood. As well as data about their own political thinking, I asked interviewees 'Is the Doctor political?'; and, in case that was not meaningful, other questions that would make sense within the diegesis of the programme: 'What does the Doctor fight for?'; 'If the Doctor had landed outside a polling booth just before the last British election, who would he have voted for?'; and 'Do you ever think the Doctor is wrong to interfere in other societies?' [...]

A good range of state political positions were articulated with clarity and intelligence by these fans. When asked how they voted in the last general election in their country, seventeen of them voted for the major leftwing party in their country (Labour in the UK, Democrat in the United States); three voted for the Liberal Democrats, the 'third', 'middle' party in the UK. Five voted for the major rightwing party in their country (Conservative in the UK, Republican in the United States) and two for an unspecified rightwing party. Eight didn't bother voting in the last election. One voted for an Independent Party candidate, one for a Green Party candidate, while two did not supply an answer to this question.

There was no simple correlation between people's voting practices and their politics. One Conservative voter insisted that, although he voted for the party, he disagreed strongly with what he saw as its racist policies (10), while another insisted that he was a 'leftwing Conservative' (3). A Labour voter explained that they only voted for the party because 'I didn't trust any of them ... but I did vote because I thought it would be silly just to waste a vote' (16). Others felt that the Labour Party was too right wing, but voted for them strategically (27), naming themselves as Marxist in the process (26). The politics of those who chose not to vote could not simply be read as despair or disengagement. One interviewee, whose first response to the question about his politics was 'God. Ehm. I'm quite lazy, in the sense of watching things and being cross' (a wonderful definition of 'traditional' state politics), went on to explain that he didn't vote because 'I just morally found that I couldn't. I am much more Neil Kinnock than I am Tony Blair' (21).

These *Doctor Who* fans represent a selection of political positions, extending from Marxist to the so-called 'extreme right' (in the case of one fan who was strongly anti-immigration and pro-death penalty). The most popular voting option was for the mainstream leftwing party in their country, although seven voted for rightwing parties. A good number did not vote, while a small number went for Independent or Green candidates. Even accepting that this sample is statistically insignificant, it does allow us to state with some certainty that the fact that these people all love the same texts and consume them repeatedly does not seem to be linked to their political thinking and practice. [...]

[I]nterested in accessing their interpretations of the programme's politics, I pushed the interviewees towards discussing stories that have (or seem to me to have) explicit allegorical state political elements. These include *The Curse of Peladon*, a story that was written at the time of, and (perhaps) comments on, Britain's entry to the Common Market; and *The Sun Makers*, in which the villains are an evil, unscrupulous and exploitative capitalist multiplanetary corporation. [... A] number of interviewees explained that these stories are not state political, that they do not relate to that part of culture:

> Actually, I don't think *Peladon*'s a political story at all ... it can only be seen as a political story ... if Britain had tried to join the Common Market and found that Belgium was trying to drop statues on the head of the Prime Minister. No. What a load of old nonsense.
>
> (23)

> *The Sunmakers* [sic] is not all about the fucking tax system. What Robert Holmes [the writer] did is he went ... 'I'll make puns of the Inland Revenue stuff' ... the story has got nothing about an attack on the tax system.
>
> (27)

Throughout these interviews, the *Doctor Who* fans returned to the difficulty of trying to discuss the programme's relationship to 'politics' because its generic status, as an adventure serial, meant that it was not supposed to be read in that way [...].

A large number of the interviewees were quite open to thinking through politics with *Doctor Who*; it is, after all, another way to continue talking about their favourite texts. This openness to the idea, combined with their surprise at the questions, suggest that these interviewees have never thought about the programme in this way before. In some of the conversations that we had, once they had taken to this idea, the interviewees enjoyed thinking through their political interpretations of the programme. For one interviewee, the series was based on the politics of Amnesty International (12); for another, its politics most strongly represented various Thatcherite ideas in the 1980s (21); for another, its political position was strongly analogous to Conservative foreign policy (22). For many fans, it is possible, when the unusual idea is introduced to them, to make political interpretations of the programme. It is also important to note that there was no consistency in the political interpretations of the programme that emerged in these conversations. Interviewees reached the conclusion that the vernacular state political thinking of this text, in which they all had great expertise, was anything from extremely leftwing through to quite radical rightwing. [...]

It is possible for the fans of *Doctor Who* to have a wide range of attitudes towards state politics and still attend to the same text because:

> It's kept incredibly vague. I find that in most stories, the Doctor's politics are written in such a way that almost anyone would agree with them and see them as being compatible with his or her own. A Conservative will see the Doctor as conservative. A Liberal will the Doctor as liberal. A socialist will see the Doctor as socialist. An anarchist will see the Doctor as an anarchist.
>
> (32)

> The interesting thing about *The Sunmakers* [sic] is that although it purports to be a political satire, it doesn't actually take a political stance at all. Leftwing viewers watch it as a parody of capitalism gone mad; rightwing viewers watch it as a parody of bureaucracy gone mad. It's neither and both at the same time.
>
> (29)

I raised this point with some fans, asking them whether there were any moments in the programme wherein they disagreed with the Doctor's actions or stances. The majority of the interviewees said that there were not: whether leftwing, rightwing, centrist, apolitical or one of the other messy political affiliations sketched out above, most were able to find ways to interpret this text that did not conflict with their own political beliefs – partly by generic interpretations that insisted that this programme had nothing to do with any aspect of culture outside of itself. […]

Discussion

The results of this research disprove my hypothesis that *Doctor Who* engages in vernacular state political philosophy. It seems that, in fact, it does not. The findings also have some implications for thinking about cultural politics more widely that I didn't expect when I began the research.

> Any attempt to transpose the concept [of ideology] to the fictional realm, via the concept of 'preferred reading' … always runs the risk of reducing the fictional text to the mere vehicle of a banal substantive proposition which can then be labelled as 'ideological' … [we must] recognise … the question of … the relevance/irrelevance … dimension of decoding rather than being directly concerned with the acceptance or rejection of substantive ideological propositions.
>
> (Morley, cited in Tulloch, 2000: 189)

John Fiske argues that the 'hidden … ideological effect' (2004: 86) of *Doctor Who* promotes 'the values … of … capitalist democracy' (2004: 99). But its political thinking (its work as vernacular state political philosophy), as understood by viewers, is not so simple. For the audience members interviewed, it is not really political at all. When pressed to use their expert knowledge of the programme to produce a political reading, some fans believe it is arguing for anarchist politics, while, for others, it is a communitarian leftwing political tract and, for others still, it is a right-wing Thatcherite piece of thinking. What is the relationship between these interpretations of the text – Fiske's 'structuralist' attempt to read its deep meanings and my own 'poststructuralist' examination of its apparent function? What status does the interpretation of the text as a promoter of capitalist values have if that interpretation is not made by viewers and does not lead them to think about either the programme or their own value systems in such a way?

One answer to this question would be to say that it depends on whether you accept a structuralist or a poststructuralist model of culture. This is true, of course. My own personal axioms about cultural politics are indeed poststructuralist rather than structuralist. From that perspective, structuralist interpretations such as Fiske's do not reveal a hidden truth about texts; rather, they take on the status of one of a range of possible interpretations. Fiske's reading of the programme's capitalist ideology, from that perspective, is no more the 'truth' of the text than is a fan's interpretation of its anarchist or Marxist credentials.

But such an answer seems too glib. There is, I feel, a certain responsibility to explain why I prefer such a poststructuralist response. Partly this is to do with my own personal history and experiences (McKee, 2003: 10–11). But I also feel that if we take a structuralist approach and accept the hidden capitalist ideology that Fiske uncovers as something more than just another interpretation – as, in fact, some kind of truth about the political work of the text – then we reach an impasse. How do we explain the relationship between the deep interpretation made by Fiske and the everyday interpretations made by viewers?

In claiming that the programme carries a hidden capitalist ideology, we are not, of course, suggesting that viewers will consciously recognize this. We are not suggesting that it will automatically make them pro-capitalist. We are not suggesting that it will unconsciously push them towards being capitalists. We are not suggesting that it will become an element in their thinking about state politics. We are not suggesting that they will use material from the programme in their own formation of political views. We are not suggesting that it will affect their party affiliation. And we are not suggesting that it will change the way they vote. So, what exactly *are* we suggesting is the articulation between this interpretation of the text and everyday conscious political thinking?

The advantage of a poststructuralist perspective is that it allows us to make sense of both sets of interpretations (Fiske's and the fans') as possible interpretations made within different discourses associated with different institutions. We can explain Fiske's interpretation here as being made within the (peculiarly limited) institution of academic cultural theory (whose Marxist prehistory leads us still to interpret the politics of popular texts by looking for the ways in which they are not Marxist), while the interpretations made by fans are informed by the discourses of *Doctor Who* fandom, generic rules for interpreting popular culture and their own range of political thinking (wider than is generally the case for cultural studies academics). From this perspective, Fiske's interpretation of *Doctor Who*'s 'capitalist' nature is perfectly reasonable. But he is wrong to call it 'ideology' and thus imply that this interpretation of the show's politics has a truth status beyond that of viewers' interpretations of *Doctor Who* as a Marxist or a Thatcherite text – or, most importantly, as a text that has nothing to say about state-level politics.

By contrast, if we take the structuralist approach of privileging one political interpretation as being 'deeper' and more true (ideology, hegemony, dominant discourse), then I am not sure what we can do with the fans' responses. We can call them 'false consciousness', but that seems too dismissive of the often intelligent, informed and articulate explanations of politics that the viewers presented. Or we could appeal to the notion of the 'ideology' working at some unconscious level, but this simply avoids the question by pushing it into the unknowable.

This is not to say that *Doctor Who* is not political. I suspect that there are other kinds of political work in the programme that are much more readily articulated to everyday political thinking. To return to the consideration of different kinds of politics that opened this article, I suspect that many fans of *Doctor Who* would be able to articulate the programme's gender politics quite explicitly. We could interview them and ask, for example, 'Which of the following actors would make a good Doctor?', including some women on the list, and examine responses to this. These would, I suspect, tell us that the programme relies on a hierarchy of genders and that feminist fans would be aware of the need to rework the programme to some degree in order to overcome this. That is to say, it would make sense, I think, to talk about the programme's gender ideology (although the research might also disprove that hypothesis). But it seems that it simply does not make sense to talk about the programme's ideology in relation to the traditional politics of 'the form, organisation and administration of a state'. John Fiske, from this perspective, is wrong to find a capitalist ideology at work in the programme because even to look for such a thing is a category error.

To reiterate, this is not to argue that popular culture is mere entertainment or that it is apolitical. *Doctor Who* sustains examination for some forms of politics. And, importantly, other parts of popular culture may well bear examination for their state political ideologies (and their vernacular state political philosophies). One interviewee made this point:

There is something about *Doctor Who* which doesn't have connections with particular political persuasions – of the underdog, of cleverness and inventiveness winning out over brute force. And you can just as much be pro-death penalty and believe in that as you can be a Buddhist. And that's why [other fans] can watch the same programme as I do and not agree with me. It's so woolly, the programme. And it's a BBC show that was half made for kids, and they pulled back from politics, they shy away from 'should you sacrifice one for the many?' ... whereas *Star Trek* absolutely knows what it is [politically], they're crossing the Midwest and the Indians are going to die because they are bad people. And it's really clear.

(20)

Kate Mulgrew (who played Captain Kathryn Janeway in *Star Trek: Voyager*) states that *Star Trek* fans must have a certain politics to enjoy that show: '"If you consider yourself a [*Star Trek*] fan you will vote Democrat", she says. And *Trek* is perceived as a liberal-leaning show. Does she find the fans more left wing? "Oh yes", she asserts' (Golder, 2001: 79).

By contrast, when an attempt was made to produce an American version of *Doctor Who*, one reader on the pilot script commented that it 'never find[s] the political or philosophical resonance that has brought the *Star Trek* series such successes' (Segal and Russell, 2000: 69). An encyclopaedia of TV comments that *Doctor Who*'s 'aliens ... were less ... political than their *Star Trek* counterparts' (Hockley, 2001: 30). It is not surprising that a number of *Star Trek* fans have written books in which they explicitly explore the political philosophical issues raised by that programme (see, for example, Hanley, 1997; Hassler and Wilcox, 1997; Marinaccio, 1994: 16–17; McCrone, 1993), while nobody has written on *Doctor Who* in the same way. It makes sense to do this for *Star Trek*; it is part of the programme's meaning.

In the end, it may be that in the move from a structuralist search for ideology to a poststructuralist examination of vernacular political philosophy, we find that not all texts are political in the same way. When we are talking about state politics, as I did in this research, we may find that some texts simply do not have an ideological position at all.

References

Fiske, John. 'Popularity and Ideology: A Structuralist Reading of *Doctor Who*'. In *Critical Approaches to Television* (2nd ed), ed. Leah R. Vande Berg, Lawrence A. Wenner and Bruce E. Gronbeck. Boston, MA: Houghton Mifflin, 2004 [1983], 86–109.
Golder, D. 'The Female Frontier'. *SFX* 84 (November 2001): 78–9.
Hanley, Richard. *The Metaphysics of* Star Trek. New York: Basic Books, 1997.
Hassler, Donald M., and Clyde Wilcox, eds. *Political Science Fiction*. Columbia: University of South Carolina Press, 1997.
Hockley, Luke. 'Science Fiction'. In *The Television Genre Book*, ed. Glen Creeber. London: BFI, 2001, 26–31.
Marinaccio, Dave. *All I Really Need to Know I Learned from Watching* Star Trek. London: Titan Books, 1994.
McCrone, John. *The Myth of Irrationality: Science of the Mind from Plato to* Star Trek. London: Macmillan, 1993.
McKee, Alan. *Textual Analysis: A Beginner's Guide*. London: Sage, 2003.
Moores, Shaun. *Interpreting Audiences: The Ethnography of Media Consumption*. London: Sage, 1993.
Muecke, Stephen. 'Available Discourses on Aborigines'. In *Theoretical Strategies*, ed. P. Botswan. Sydney: Local Consumption, 1982, 98–111.
Probyn, Elspeth. *Outside Belongings*. New York: Routledge, 1996.
Segal, Philip, and Gary Russell. *Doctor Who: Regeneration*. London: Virgin, 2000.
Tulloch, John. *Watching Television Audiences: Cultural Theories and Methods*. London: Arnold, 2000.

Chapter 14
Desiring *Doctor Who*

From 'Desiring the Doctor: Identity, Gender and Genre in Online Fandom' by Rebecca Williams[*]

First published 2011

One area where there has been greater consensus surrounding the cultural meanings of Who *concerns its gender representations. This extract, by Rebecca Williams (2011), examines the gendering of fan audiences, analysing how post-2005 online fandom was policed in order to position younger female fans 'squeeing' about David Tennant as 'not proper' fans, whilst the 'squee squad' resisted such gatekeeping moves and asserted its fan-cultural presence.*

David Tennant, Geek Chic and masculinity

Although [some] male fans [...] appear to dismiss female viewers who support on-screen relationships or display unacceptable excitement towards the show, the fact remains that David Tennant has attracted a significant female fan base. Given the hostility of many male fans, why do fangirls continue to overtly display their attraction to him and to perform this identity so consciously on the *Doctor Who Forum*? One answer might be to view their fan practices as overt performances of femaleness, as exaggerated displays of appropriate hegemonic femininity. There have been clear links made between the figure of the fan and the 'nerd' or the 'geek', which suggests that fangirls may also be aligned with these archetypes. Furthermore, nerd identity (and, we can also argue, fan identity) is closely linked to issues of gender and sexuality as: 'nerdism in both men and women is held to decrease sexual attractiveness. [...] In women, lack of sexual attractiveness is a far greater sin'.[1] Indeed, 'nerds are presumed male [...] This connection between nerdism and masculinity may be what makes a nerd identity so damaging to women's potential and perceived sexual desirability'.[2] Fanboys similarly need to negotiate threats to their gender identity as 'the fan-boy clearly shares some of the (albeit stereotypical) characteristics of the [...] failed masculinity of

---

[*]Originally published in *British Science Fiction Film and Television*, ed. Tobias Hochscherf and James Leggott (Jefferson, NC: McFarland, 2011), 167–77.

the nerd'.³ Given the close links between fans and the figures of the nerd and the geek might we not be able to view the performance of a fangirl identity as a way to counter both this apparent desexualization but also to ward off any defeminization which occurs via the correlation of the geek/fan/nerd figure with masculinity? If [...] fan identity is performative and not natural, then assuming the mantle of the fangirl might actually offer a space for enactment of culturally feminized and devalued traits such as displaying attraction to desirable male figures.

In addition to the common focus on David Tennant as a figure of desire is a tendency towards discussion of the type of masculinity which he and his Doctor embody. There is a sense that his portrayal of The Doctor through costuming and styling, which connotes a 'geek chic', contributes to his appeal for many female fans. The masculinity and desirability of Tennant's Doctor appears to resonate with cultural constructions and stereotypes of the nerd or the geek but also relates to *Doctor Who's* status as a specifically British science fiction programme.

To deal with the first of these issues we need to consider popular cultural constructions of 'the fan', a figure who, despite the alleged mainstreaming of fandom, is still often prone to negative stereotyping, stigma, and ridicule. [... F]ans who express libidinal attraction for celebrities/characters often form one of these groups, but the wider stereotype of the fan as 'sad and pathetic, lacking a grasp of reality and obsessed with the unimportant' also endures.⁴ Indeed, 'Fans, geeks and nerds – overlapping but not identical social and cultural categories – have long been vilified in the mass media with "get-a-life" stereotypes and marginalized by images of social, sexual and economic incompetence'.⁵ Given this ongoing cultural denigration it is perhaps unsurprising that fans often gravitate towards fan objects which seem to reflect traits associated with fandom or which appear sympathetic to them. For example, in discussion of *Buffy the Vampire Slayer* actor James Marsters, Hills and Williams note that the actor often situates himself as an outsider or a 'freak', positioning himself as similar to fans in order to engender their support.⁶ Whilst it can surely be argued, given Tennant's self-identification as a long-time fan of *Doctor Who*,⁷ that he is positioned as 'close to' fans of the show, I am more interested here in how his characterization of the Tenth Doctor as 'geeky' and intelligent might work to encourage fan identification and, in the case of female fans, attraction and desire.

Despite cultural stereotyping, representations of the geek or nerd are not always associated with technology and computing, nor are they always linked to notions of failed masculinity.⁸ For example, within the rock and indie music scenes there has been a reappropriation of 'geek cool' which displays and valorizes being 'introspective, insecure and self-deprecating'.⁹ Thus, indie and geek chic can offer 'an alternative articulation of masculinity' which opposes the more aggressive males of rock and punk music.¹⁰ Here, the label of the geek is actively claimed and performed and used to construct a softer and more welcoming masculinity. Similarly, one way in which geeks and nerds can address potential stigma surrounding their identities is to 'embrace their outsider status and assert "geek pride" as an exercise of power and resistance',¹¹ and this is often achieved by wearing clothing which emphasizes one's geek status, by dressing stylistically in 'geek chic'. Thus, the notion that the geek chic which Tennant's Doctor embodies might actually engender attraction and desire from certain female viewers no longer seems so implausible. In fact, given the strong cultural linkage between the figures of the fan, the geek and the nerd, the fact that female fans might be attracted to male characters or actors who appear to embody similarities with them makes sense. If fangirls are positioned as largely devalued and as 'sad', much like the discursively constructed geek, then their reading of *Doctor Who* via Tennant's portrayal of The Doctor suggests a level of identification, as well as emotional investment and libidinal attraction. In 'The Record Long David Tennant Appreciation Thread', for example, fans debate their attraction to the actor.

One states, 'I dont think DT has conventional Good Looks either. I like that [actor John] Barrowman said DT is not what you would call Classically Good Looking, but that he is a sexy Guy. That's soooo true',[12] whilst another attests 'SEXY is definitely the right adjective for DT'.[13] Such comments suggest that part of Tennant's appeal is that he is not typically good-looking or unattainably handsome. His lack of stereotypical 'good looks' are valued by these fans who remain attracted to him even though he does not typify cultural norms of attractiveness and is not, as these fans note, 'classically good looking'. However, Tennant's own star persona may play a further part here, given his high cultural links to the Royal Shakespeare Company and his playing of Hamlet in 2008–2009[14] which might further feed into his construction as an intelligent, non-traditional figure of masculinity that female fans could identify with. Finally, given that 'the character [of The Doctor] has become wedded to imagined notions of British cultural identity',[15] it may be that part of Tennant's appeal for some female fans is his embodiment of a very British masculinity which is softer, more feminized and more accessible. Furthermore, fan attraction to the actor can also be linked to current trends in contemporary science fiction television more broadly as, whilst early science fiction depicted 'handsome American heroes [fighting] against evil, the genre's current representations of masculinity are rather less stable'.[16]

Policing the genre: British science fiction and 'appropriate' readings

Having outlined some of the ways in which female fans of 'new *Who*' read the show through David Tennant, I now consider the distinctions which operate within this online fan space, paying particular attention to how debates over appropriate readings of the show are gendered. Drawing on the case study of *Doctor Who* as a British science fiction show, this section considers how the issues examined in this chapter might relate more broadly to fan debates about science fiction as a genre and to wider discussions over *what* can be discussed and *who* can be permitted to speak.

[…M]ale and female fans often diverge in their discussions of fan objects since online male fans tend to dislike 'frivolous' chat[17] and, in MacDonald's study of *Quantum Leap* fans, objected to 'long discussions of the characters' relationships' and off-topic chat about posters' real lives.[18] However, such attempts to restrict 'female' conversations or to drive women to their own separate message boards clearly demonstrate fans' attempts to police the boundaries of acceptable conversation. Indeed, one of the most common ways in which fandom has been theorized is through analysis of how subcultures form their own distinctions, appropriate behaviour and discourses which tend to replicate the cultural hierarchies of mainstream culture.[19] This is often achieved by determining who is part of a fan culture, and fans make 'constant attempt[s] to project internal purity by identifying inauthentic outsiders who must be rejected and shunned'.[20] [… A] common way in which some fans of *Doctor Who* attempt to police the boundaries of the fandom is through devaluing those who display attraction to David Tennant, dismissing them as not being 'true' lovers of *Doctor Who* and being unfamiliar with the show's prior history. It is here that the label of the fangirl is often deployed as a derogatory term which aims to discursively feminize and infantilize those who perform their fandom in this way. Indeed, whilst the gendered element of the term is clear, invoking the notion of the 'girl' suggests childishness and immaturity; traits which are often disavowed within other fan cultures.[21]

For example, in a thread entitled 'New school fans – too much self-loving?', one poster suggests that many of these fans 'just say "ugh classic is boring, new is best, David Tennant OMGLOLBESTDRSEXGODLOL,"'[22] whilst another comments, 'I agree that there's a hugely irritating trend amongst some New fans to equate "talented actor playing a compelling character" and "omg so haaaawt!!!!11one" [...]. There's a certain giggling schoolgirl mindset to a particular kind of New Who fan'.[23] Comments such as these demonstrate fans' irritation with female fans' attraction to David Tennant which is here stereotyped as [resembling] 'giggling schoolgirls' [... with] a tendency to substitute coherent language for text-speak and enthusiastic declarations of attraction. This indicates the infantilization of such fans and their responses, characterizing them as childish and somewhat ridiculous. By rendering those who deviate from apparently masculinized 'proper' readings of *Doctor Who* (i.e. respecting the history of the programme, offering rational argument, suppressing emotional responses) as both feminized and immature, certain groups of fans work to enforce 'an officially constituted reading formation which supervises reading of the show'.[24] This dismissal of Tennant fans continues in a debate over whether certain fans would keep watching after the actor departed the show. Notions of fangirls as obsessive and concerned with the attractiveness of the lead character are clearly displayed in the following posts:

I don't think he was referring to actual fans more the kinda people that're like: 'David Tennant is the best Doctor ever ^_^! Matt Smith will be rubbish because he isn't sexy! He's so damn ugly, am I right Middle Aged Housewife Number 7?' They'll all be gone come next year, those people aren't fans. I can't understand the mentality of somebody who watches a show just 'cus the main character is hot.[25]

I'd be surprised if the fangirls creeping him out and his reputation as a pin-up didn't factor into his leaving. Wasn't there one report of them having to stop filming cus the squeers took their obsession with him too far? I find people discussing the paint on the TARDIS more endearing than people slagging off his girlfriends and digging and obsessing over his life to feel closer to him.[26]

Clearly here certain readings and behaviours are deemed appropriate within the science fiction genre whilst others are not. However, many female fans of David Tennant do not retreat from the battlefield over meaning and interpretation. One female poster angrily responds by devaluing the discussions of older fans and those who watched pre-2005 *Doctor Who*:

im sorry you dont get to choose who are fans of this show and personaly its a good thing you dont, the so called squee squad bring a different aspect to fandom that i for one love hearing about the reading about and its good for fandom to not just be 40 year olds talking about tardis paint and how its different now than it was in the key to time![27]

For this fan, and others like her, it is the reading of *Doctor Who* through the figure of Tennant that is 'appropriate', and it is the more masculinized responses of discussing minutiae such as the colour of the TARDIS which are deemed to be deviating from the norm. Furthermore, instead of treating the term fangirl as an insult or an attempt to belittle them, many seek to reclaim the identity and use it as a badge of defiance against those fans whose readings differ from their own. One female fan responds with 'There is nothing wrong with being a "middle-aged squeeing fangirl", it's not a "men only" fanclub after all. Mind you, some men do seem to be a bit intimidated and fed up with all the squeeing (which will only make us SQUEEE even louder!)'.[28] Another replies to the suggestion that fangirls and 'squee squads' occupy a 'dank corner of fandom'[29] by rejecting the male poster's attempt to belittle and devalue female fan practices through sidelining them. She posts, 'The Squee section of fandom is not dank, neither is it in a **corner.** It's here, full bloodied and to stay. Welcome to your worst nightmare!'[30]

However, practices such as squeeing and lusting over David Tennant are not always unproblematically embraced by female fans. Indeed, the term fangirl has always been open to contestation and ambiguity with many fans operating a dual usage of the label as a fan might 'post a diatribe about a "stupid fangirl" on her/his Livejournal one day, but may write a very excited and only semi-coherent entry another day and clearly label it as being "fangirl-mode".'[31] For example, some fans worked on a project to present to David Tennant, with one commenting 'perhaps I should put something about how I objected because he is so much more handsome with all his face showing, and his hair too. I don't want to get too "obsessed stalker fangirl" ish though!'[32] Even though this fan is posting in the 'David Tennant appreciation thread' and is obviously enough of a fan of the actor to contribute a lengthy letter to the project, she still works to maintain a line between herself and the constructed 'Other' of the fangirl. Here, fangirls are characterized as obsessive and as potential stalkers and the threat of association with this clearly comes from the fan's discussion of how handsome Tennant is. Here the link is clear – too much attention paid to the attractiveness of a celebrity is characteristic of the fangirl, a figure which this fan still seeks to maintain a distance from. Another thread, which although titled 'Could *Torchwood* survive without Jack?' discusses *Doctor Who*, debates the definition of the term fangirl and the assumptions associated with it. One male fan states,

> In general terms I don't like people equating being a 'fangirl', 'fanboy', 'fanperson', whatever, with having a crush on the actor/actress/being. Certainly not the case with myself considering I'm readily identified as a 'Freema fanboy' and can assure myself that I don't have anything in the realm of a crush on her.[33]

For this poster, it is not the label itself which is problematic (he quite happily identifies as a Freema Agyeman fanboy) but, rather, the implication that such an identity is based solely on attraction and desire. What this poster imagines other aspects of fanboy identity to be remains unclear but this comment clearly illustrates that fans themselves negotiate the terms of 'fangirl' and 'fanboy'. Furthermore, other (female) fans comment:

> Another reason I took exception to [the] generalization about fangirls is the immediate, negative connotation of 'fangirl' […] I've liked John Barrowman since I saw 'The Empty Child'. I've enjoyed sci-fi and fantasy for decades. So saying only 'JB fangirls' think [*Torchwood*] wouldn't work without him? No.[34]

> Well DT is my first Doctor so speaking as a 'middle-aged squeeing fangirl' I have to say that while I think he's fabulous (and fanciable) and I am sorry he's leaving, what I'm most appreciative of is the fact that he led me to this wonderful show. […] I'm most definitely going to stick with DW no matter what. I enjoyed Eccleston too and I look forward to Matt Smith.[35]

For these female posters being a 'fangirl' and being attracted to certain celebrity figures stands in clear opposition to their longer standing fandom of the science fiction genre more generally. For the first fan, her opinion that *Torchwood* would not work without the presence of actor John Barrowman is apparently based on her knowledge of the genre, rather than on any personal interest in the star. Of course, we cannot take this declaration at face value and it must be viewed, as with all online postings, as a performative display of fan identity. In this case, then, it might be that, well aware of the negative connotations of 'fangirl', these fans seek to remove their interest in *Torchwood* and *Doctor Who* from the devalued realm of female fandom by aligning themselves with the more culturally masculinized genres of science fiction and fantasy, or by describing how initial interest in the figure of David Tennant has led to a wider appreciation of the 'wonderful show' of *Doctor Who* more generally.

Notes

1. Lori Kendall, '"OH NO! I'M A NERD!" Hegemonic Masculinity on an Online Forum', *Gender & Society* 14 (2000): 265.
2. Ibid., 266.
3. Jacinda Read, 'The Cult of Masculinity: From Fan-boys to Academic Bad-boys', in *Defining Cult Movies: The Cultural Politics of Oppositional Taste*, ed. Mark Jancovich, Antonio Lazaro Reboll, Julian Stringer and Andrew Willis (Manchester: Manchester University Press, 2003), 64.
4. Nathan Hunt, 'The Importance of Trivia: Ownership, Exclusion and Authority in Science Fiction Fandom', in *Defining Cult Movies: The Cultural Politics of Oppositional Taste*, ed. Mark Jancovich, Antonio Lazaro Reboll, Julian Stringer and Andrew Willis (Manchester: Manchester University Press, 2003), 185.
5. Ed Wiltse, 'Fans, Geeks and Nerds, and the Politics of Online Communities', *Proceedings of the Media Ecology Association* 5 (2004): 1. http://www.mediaecology.org/publications/MEA_proceedings/v5/Wiltse05.pdf (accessed 20 March 2009).
6. Matt Hills and Rebecca Williams, 'It's All My Interpretation: Reading Spike through the "Subcultural Celebrity" of James Marsters', *European Journal of Cultural Studies* 8 (2005): 350.
7. BBC, 'Tennant to Take Over the Tardis', *BBC News UK* (2005): http://news.bbc.co.uk/2/hi/entertainment/4450285.stm (accessed 13 April 2009).
8. Lori Kendall, 'Nerd Nation: Images of Nerds in US Popular Culture', *International Journal of Cultural Studies* 2 (1999): 262.
9. Marion Leonard, *Gender in the Music Industry* (Hampshire: Ashgate Publishing, 2007), 48.
10. Ibid.
11. Jason Tocci, 'The Well-dressed Geek', *Media in Transition* 5 (2007): 6. http://web.mit.edu/comm-forum/mit5/papers/Tocci.pdf (accessed 14 February 2009).
12. 'The Record Long David Tennant Appreciation Thread [part 132]', Post #221: http://www.doctorwhoforum.com/showthread.php?t=217628&highlight=Record+David+Tennant+Appreciation+Thread+%5BPart&page=6 (accessed 5 March 2009).
13. Ibid., Post #174.
14. Matt Hills, *Triumph of a Time Lord* (London: I.B. Tauris, 2010), 159.
15. Matt Hills, 'Doctor Who', in *Fifty Key Television Programmes*, ed. Glen Creeber (London: Arnold, 2004), 76.
16. Rebecca Feasey, *Masculinity and Popular Television* (Edinburgh: Edinburgh University Press, 2008), 56.
17. Susan Clerc, 'DDEB, GATB and Ratboy: The X-Files Media Fandom, Online and Off', in *Deny All Knowledge: Reading the X-Files*, ed. David Lavery, Angela Hague and Marla Cartwright (London: Faber and Faber, 1996), 41.
18. Andrea Macdonald, 'Uncertain Utopia: Science Fiction Media Fandom and Computer Mediated Communication', in *Theorising Fandom: Fans, Subculture and Identity*, ed. Cheryl Harris and Alison Alexander (New Jersey: Hampton Press Inc., 1998), 148.
19. Cornel Sandvoss, *Fans: The Mirror of Consumption* (London: Polity, 2005), 32–42.
20. Mark Jancovich and Nathan Hunt, 'The Mainstream, Distinction and Cult TV', in *Cult Television*, ed. Sara Gwenllian-Jones and Roberta E. Pearson (Minneapolis & London: University of Minnesota Press, 2004), 28.

21 See, for example, Will Brooker, *Using the Force: Creativity, Community and Star Wars Fans* (New York & London: Continuum, 2002); Matt Hills, 'Putting Away Childish Things: Jar Jar Binks as an Object of Fan Loathing', in *Contemporary Hollywood Stardom*, ed. Thomas Austin and Martin Barker (London: Arnold, 2003), 74–89.
22 'New School Fans – Too Much Self-loving?', Post #21: http://www.doctorwhoforum.com/showthread.php?t=157933&highlight=giggling+schoolgirl (accessed 6 March 2009).
23 Ibid., Post #34.
24 John Tulloch and Henry Jenkins, *Science-Fiction Audiences: Watching 'Doctor Who' and 'Star Trek'* (London: Routledge, 1995), 145.
25 'Anyone Looking Forward to a Future of Doctor Who NOT Involving David Tennant?', Post #17: http://www.doctorwhoforum.com/showthread.php?t=221598&highlight=school (accessed 5 March 2009).
26 Ibid., Post #80.
27 Ibid., Post #76.
28 Ibid., Post #99.
29 Ibid., Post #88.
30 Ibid., Post #99.
31 Sandra Youssef, *Girls Who Like Boys Who Like Boys: Ethnography of Online Slash/Yaoi Fans*, Dissertation, Department of Anthropology, Mount Holyoke College (2003): http://yuuyami.com/luce/thesis.pdf (accessed 8 March 2009), 51.
32 'The Record Long David Tennant Appreciation Thread [Part 130]', Post #510.
33 'Could Torchwood Survive without Jack?', Post #36: http://www.doctorwhoforum.com/showthread.php?t=218265&highlight=fangirl (accessed 5 March 2009).
34 Ibid., Post # 37.
35 'Anyone Looking Forward to a Future of *Doctor Who* NOT Involving David Tennant?', Post #62.

Chapter 15
Feminist *Doctor Who*

From '"Finally, we get to play the Doctor": Feminist Female Fans' Reactions to the First Female Doctor Who' by Neta Yodovich[*]

Originally published 2020

> *The casting of Jodie Whittaker underpins two pieces in this section – here, Neta Yodovich (2020) draws on interviews with feminist female fans. She argues that these fans defended Whittaker's casting by emphasizing their fan credentials and downplaying their feminist identities (avoiding online conflict with male interlocutors). Such fans also wanted the female Doctor not to be 'girly', desiring an incarnation that fitted with earlier portrayals and so devalued types of femininity.*

This study is based on twenty-two semi-structured in-depth interviews with self-identified feminist female fans of *Doctor Who* between the ages of nineteen and fifty-five. Interviews were combined with a brief follow-up email correspondence with participants a year after the original fieldwork. […]

Fieldwork took place between September and December 2017, shortly after the Thirteenth Doctor announcement in July 2017. This time was pivotal since interviewees were in the midst of heated online and offline debates. The regeneration into the 13th Doctor occurred in the 2017 Christmas special after fieldwork concluded. Conducting interviews after the casting, but prior to the airing of the new season, provided a fascinating opportunity to explore feminist fans' expectations of the first female Doctor. It offered them an invitation to project their values and interpretations of gender and feminism onto her. In December 2018, a year after the original fieldwork and towards the end of the first season with the female Doctor, I contacted interviewees again via email to learn if their expectations were met. Eleven participants replied. These emails are also used as data in the analysis, alongside the original interviews.

Interviews were transcribed, coded and thematically analysed by myself. Thematic analysis assisted in finding patterns and recurring trends in the collected data […].

---

[*]Originally published in *Feminist Media Studies* 20, no. 8 (2020): 1243–58.

Findings: 'She's a Time Lord, not a Time Lady'

In the following sections, I reveal interviewees' conflicted engagement with the first female Doctor. On the one hand, they eagerly supported the casting shift in heated discussions with their opponents, who were usually male fans. On the other, they expressed their hopes that the female Doctor would not possess feminine characteristics. I will later argue that despite their feminist identities, interviewees valued masculine attributes over feminine ones, associating femininity with weakness and a lack of agency.

'PC gone mad': Fighting against the backlash

When casting was first announced, interviewees expressed joy and excitement. The primary cause for respondents' happiness was that a woman would now play one of the most prominent role models in popular culture. Interviewees were excited about the new generation of feminist fans that the new female Doctor can potentially raise:

> I talked to one of my cosplay friends […] she said, 'finally, we get to play the Doctor' […] I'm thinking about 6, 8-year-olds who will say 'that's the Doctor, I can relate to that'.
>
> (Stephanie, 29, UK)

However, interviewees' celebrations of the announcement were swiftly cut short by a backlash. The casting controversy was heated and signified much more than a simple dispute over a television series. According to participants, it had broader implications for society's approach to gender representations, gender roles and openness towards female leaders in the 'real' world. This was feminist female fans' Battle of the Sexes.

The primary objection against the female Doctor, raised by fans and media, centred on the potential damage of political correctness. Opponents opined that producers were forcing diversity on franchises as a marketing move to demonstrate their 'progressiveness'. Such a drastic change might cost the franchise its quality and commercial success (BBC, 2017; Duff, 2017). Interviewees strongly contested this claim and argued that women are merely starting to get their fair share in an arena which traditionally discriminates in favour of white men:

> When Jodie got the part, I said, 'you know what, there are an awful lot of people in this world who get film roles solely on the basis of their gender and their race, but guess what? They're white dudes!' Those are the ones that get jobs based solely on their ethnicity and their sex.
>
> (Donna, 46, UK)

To fight against PC claims, interviewees provided carefully worked through justifications that substantiated their arguments in favour of the new female Doctor. These included proof-based examples from *Doctor Who*'s canon:

> In 'The Night of The Doctor', the Doctor is given a choice who he wants to regenerate as, and one of the choices was a woman. In 'The Doctor's Wife', the Doctor talks about other friends of his whom regenerated as a woman. It's not a brand new idea.
>
> (Samantha, 46, UK)

Interviewees also addressed […] the Master's (one of *Doctor Who*'s nemeses) gender-swap, which […] proves that regenerating from male to female is possible in the series […]. According to participants, if the canon justifies the existence of a gender alteration through regeneration, it is reasonable to have a female Doctor.

I suggest that interviewees' heavy reliance on the canon was a strategy to avoid criticism that they support the female Doctor because of their feminist identities, as Ramona (31, UK) explains:

> Putting feminism aside, there had to be a female Doctor eventually […] the fact that you can talk about it without feminism coming up and just say 'this needed to happen' is something I kind of stress because, you know, people are saying, 'oh, it's just PC, blah, blah' and I like to use my knowledge to say 'no, this needed to happen'.

Establishing their arguments on the canon, instead of their feminist agenda, allowed feminist fans to provide intellectual justifications for the existence of a female Doctor and avoid being stereotyped as hysterical, irrational feminists.

Canon-related justifications are common in fandom backlashes against casting (Proctor and Kies, 2018). When reviewing the controversy regarding casting Michael B. Jordan (an African-American actor) as Johnny Storm (a white superhero) in the reboot of *Fantastic Four*, Jenkins explained that fans sometimes take advantage of their connoisseurship of the canon to reinforce 'white male entitlement' (2018: 17). Following this line, feminist female fans felt that their reading of the text was dismissed. Despite providing examples where characters changed genders in *Doctor Who*, interviewees experienced incidents in which male fans took ownership of the canon in order to dictate how it should be read while invalidating their interpretations. The shutting down of feminist reading of *Doctor Who* by emphasizing particular elements of the canon was also found by Tulloch (Tulloch and Jenkins, 1995: 131). In his study, male fans stressed that the Doctor is an alien Time Lord to block feminist readings that criticized the Doctor's role in perpetuating patriarchal conceptions, especially by treating female companions as his inferior.

A further example of male fans' domination of the *Doctor Who* franchise is found in another claim against casting a female Doctor: the loss of a role model for boys. Interviewees shared that male fans lamented the loss of a positive male role model for young boys during arguments and discussions. Participants challenged these claims by asserting that a female heroine could be inspiring for both girls and boys:

> What I didn't get is the 'we're losing a male role model'. You have so many to choose from, all these seasons of men playing this role. Why do you need one in this role? Get a female role model. Why not?
>
> (Anaya, 19, UK)

According to interviewees, women are more accustomed to relating to male characters, in comparison to men with female characters. Participants discussed a plethora of male characters and actors they looked up to over the years, from Han Solo (*Star Wars*) to Bruce Lee, but asserted that men seldom appreciate or identify with female characters. Zoe (32, UK) thought the regeneration of the Doctor into a woman was an opportunity for men to learn how to relate to female characters and women in general, claiming: 'women had to mentally gender-swap themselves into lead roles forever. If there are really good female characters, why wouldn't you want to be them?' This is a further example of feminist female fans' struggle to find their place in fandoms of franchises that are traditionally associated with and created for men. After quietly embracing and looking up to male protagonists for years, interviewees wanted protagonists that looked like them.

In light of the massive backlash after the announcement, some feminist fans expressed apprehension about a woman leading *Doctor Who*:

> I think that because we have a new scriptwriter if it doesn't work and the fans stop watching the show, it won't be because the scriptwriter changed, it would be because they cast […] a woman and that will put into a halt any chances that any woman will be involved in a lead role ever.
>
> (Stephanie, 29, UK)

Wendy (50, UK) also shared this worry, explaining that since *Doctor Who*'s ratings have been decreasing for years, 'to put a woman in at this point […], she'll get the blame for taking the show down'. Participants dreaded that if ratings dropped, it would deter other franchises from featuring women in leading roles, leading to repercussions beyond the *Doctor Who* franchise.

When the new series finally aired, worries dissolved; ratings were solid, and the new female Doctor was approved by most critics and fans (Hooton, 2018; Mangan, 2018) […]. Subsequent correspondences with participants revealed they were content and relieved by the generally positive reception of the 13th Doctor:

> She seems to have become in a very short time a beloved Doctor, and it's such a huge relief to not have to battle the 'I don't hate women, but …'crowd anymore. She's won the battle for us.
>
> (Samantha, 46, UK)

Samantha's vicarious victory over antagonistic male fans through the popularity of the 13th Doctor demonstrates the symbiosis between female fans and the characters they love. Having a female Doctor meant that women were acknowledged as part of the fandom community and that *Doctor Who* was not just a show for men, created by men, led by men.

In his study about football fans, Sandvoss (2004) differentiates between sports and popular culture fans by asserting that football fans express identification with their beloved team by addressing them as 'we', whereas popular culture fans use third-person pronouns. While Samantha referred to the 13th Doctor as 'she', she also used 'us', which I argue demonstrates the deep identification interviewees shared with the female Doctor, similar to the one experienced by football fans. Parallel to winning a football tournament, interviewees felt they had 'won' the fandom war because fans and media embraced the 13th Doctor. If the 13th Doctor had not become well-liked, as many feminist fans initially feared, it would have been their defeat too.

[T]he initial adverse reactions to the female Doctor demonstrated the challenges feminist female fans face when trying to claim their stakes in their fandoms and push for equal representation. To them, a female Doctor signified more than a character on television, [… and represented] a step towards the inclusion of women in positions of power and influence in popular culture and beyond. After standing united in their support of the female Doctor, the following subsection reveals interviewees' surprising expectations of her characterization.

'Please Not Girly': Expectations of the 13th Doctor

[… My] fieldwork commenced after the first female Doctor was announced and before the new series aired. During the time interviews were conducted, the first promotional shot of the female Doctor was released, uncovering her costume, which included high-waist trousers attached with suspenders and rainbow-colored stripes printed on a dark t-shirt, hinting to gay pride. The team of new companions, now called 'friends', was also announced: a young Asian woman, an older white man and a young Black man. The lack of details regarding the new Doctor allowed fans to project their hopes and expectations onto her character. Examining interviewees' expectations of the 13th Doctor also provided the opportunity to scrutinize their feminist stances and attitudes on femininity and masculinity.

Paradoxically, after fighting against the backlash and justifying the necessity of casting a woman as the Doctor, interviewees' primary demand was that she retained the masculine qualities associated with her previous male incarnations. Participants did not want the Doctor to be written differently as a woman or [to] be too 'feminine':

> Please, not girly! At her heart, she is a Time Lord […] I mean she has to be an assertive kick-a** Time Lord because that's how they survive […] please don't have her falling in love.
>
> (Angela, 55, UK)

> She's a Time Lord, not a Time Lady.
>
> (Bernie, 50, UK)

> She's the Doctor. I don't want her to be a female Doctor. I don't want her to be a lady Doctor.
>
> (Ruby, 38, UK)

Participants rejected the prospect of having a Doctor with stereotypical, traditional female characteristics. They stressed that she is a Time Lord ('not Time Lady') and were happy she would be wearing 'almost an androgynous dress […] not wearing *a* dress' (Emily, 34, UK). Participants also wished that the regeneration into a woman would not be explicitly addressed or written as an extraordinary event, despite stressing the significance of having a female lead:

> It shouldn't be treated as a big deal. They should just say 'this is the Doctor, this is the companion, this is everything you need to know'.
>
> (Stephanie, 29 UK)

Similar to Tulloch's (1995) findings reviewed earlier, interviewees turned to the canon and emphasized the fact the Doctor is a Time Lord and, therefore, should not be too feminine. Here, feminist female fans embraced an argument that was once used by veteran fans to shut them down. Furthermore, it is possible that interviewees rejected the potential stereotypical characterization of the female Doctor because this will erase queer representations of the male Doctor that were featured before. Throughout the years, different incarnations of the Doctor challenged conservative masculinity through representations of asexuality, geekiness or peaceful approaches to conflict (Britton, 2011). Perhaps, since the Doctor was not a conventional male character to begin with, participants were reluctant to embrace a traditionally feminine Doctor.

Another reason that goes beyond representations of female characters in popular culture relates to an inherent devaluation of femininity in society, even among some feminist women. According to gender and feminism scholars, femininity, or what is traditionally understood as such, does not encapsulate a desired set of values and practices. In her seminal work, Simone De Beauvoir [1949] 2011 asserts that 'woman' is conceptualized as man's other; her existence and definition are relational and dependent on that of the man's, while he exists as an independent social agent. While masculinity offers varied forms of expression and practice, femininity appears limited and restricting (Connell, [1987] 2003; Holland, 2004; Nicholls, 2018; Schippers, 2007). Femininity, especially the 'girly' kind, is perceived as 'try-hard' and inauthentic (Holland, 2004; Nicholls, 2018), whereas masculinity is automatically associated with effortless authenticity (Thornton, 1995).

Feminism has also demonstrated ambivalence towards traditional femininity. 'For many feminists', Joanne Hollows explains, 'in becoming feminine, women are "colonized" by patriarchy and become implicated in their own oppression' (Hollows, 2000: 10). Despite current branding of feminine practices as 'fun' and 'attractive', postfeminism also encouraged women to take part in activities that would make them seem 'cooler'. These usually include traditionally masculine practices such as drinking or frequenting strip clubs (Levy, 2005; McRobbie, 2009). Thus, despite promoting women's rights, certain feminist strands [of thought] encourage masculine attitudes, values and practices and prioritize them over the feminine. 'I don't want to be a girl', confesses feminist writer Laurie Penny, 'being a girl is understood to be somewhat less than being a person' (2013: 5).

These [... arguments] crystallize feminist fans' hesitant reactions towards a feminine Doctor. Traditional femininity, even through certain feminist eyes, is a stigmatized identity, associated with weakness, dependency and passivity (Budgeon, 2011; Nielsen, 2004; Rich, 2005). Interviewees longed for an inspirational female Doctor that would be embraced by women and men alike. Therefore, she could not be feminine, and her becoming a woman should not be explicitly celebrated in the series. Feminine qualities [...] are not influential and impressive according to many participants, but attract critique or antipathy.

Interviewees' expectations were met when the series featuring the 13th Doctor aired from October 2018 to January 2019. During follow-up correspondence, participants applauded Jodie Whittaker's portrayal of the Doctor. They praised her readiness to be 'a bit goofy and graceless' (Jane, 46, UK) and the ability to create her own sonic screwdriver (a technological device used by the Doctor). Interviewees were pleased with the nonchalant writing of the female Doctor's regeneration, emphasizing that the Doctor's gender does not matter:

> It makes no difference to me to see a woman. It could have been a man as well [...], and her character is not making a big deal about the fact that she's been a man for centuries [...] it seems that it wasn't important to the Doctor, and it wasn't important to me.
>
> (Anna, 27, France)

While participants were pleased with the female Doctor's masculine characteristics and behaviours, such as her knowledge in STEM and blasé approach to her looks, they were also supportive of the Doctor's new compassionate side. Nina (25, UK) detailed how she gradually warmed [...] to the Doctor's new feminine qualities:

My initial approach towards the new Doctor included a concern that her character would be overly sexualized or feminized. However, after seeing how the feminine themes of humanity, compassion, and peaceful negotiation have been entwined throughout the season, I've realized the importance of showing strong, feminine traits in popular culture, rather than expecting women to 'integrate' into the brooding, angry stereotype of the masculine hero.

Like Nina, other interviewees repented their hesitance from feminine qualities and saluted the 13th Doctor's fresh take on leadership.

The 13th Doctor was also received with scepticism by some participants. While many were pleased with the Doctor's new set of friends, others questioned why the female Doctor needed so many to accompany her. These interviewees argued that the ensemble of friends implicitly suggests that the female Doctor is unable to save the day on her own. Respondents also questioned why the female Doctor had to be the 'nice' one out of the entire cadre of Doctors:

I'm very interested by the very overt characterization of Jodie's Doctor as 'nice'. The way this has been stressed by the show makes it look to me like it is driven primarily by a dislike of the way previous Doctors have been characterized as, well, a bit of a d***. It looks like Chibnall [Chris Chibnall, the then-current showrunner] very explicitly wants to say you can be a hero without riding roughshod over those around you. It's a little unfortunate this coincides with the introduction of a female Doctor since it plays into stereotypes of women being more caring and doing more emotional labor.

(Jane, 46, UK)

Interviewees were in awe of the 13th Doctor's new style of leadership and heroism, which combined both masculine and feminine qualities while underscoring the importance of compassion and warmth. However, some worried that the 13th Doctor's feminine qualities perpetuated stereotypes about women and femininity, which they were eager to eradicate.

References

BBC. 'Doctor Who: Fans React to Jodie Whittaker Casting'. *BBC News* (17 July 2017): https://www.bbc.co.uk/news/entertainment-arts-40626224 (accessed 7 August 2019).

Britton, Piers. *TARDISbound: Navigating the Universes of Doctor Who*. London: I.B. Tauris, 2011.

Budgeon, Shelly. *Third-Wave Feminism and the Politics of Gender in Late Modernity*. New York: Springer, 2011.

Connell, Raewyn W. *Gender and Power*. Cambridge: Polity, [1987] 2003.

De Beauvoir, Simone. *The Second Sex*. New York: Vintage, [1949] 2011.

Duff, Seamus. 'BBC Face Furious Sexist Backlash after Announcing Jodie Whittaker as First Female Doctor Who', *Mirror* (16 July 2017): https://www.mirror.co.uk/tv/tv-news-doctor-who-jodie-whittaker-reaction-10811248 (accessed 7 August 2019).

Holland, Samantha. *Alternative Femininities: Body, Age and Identity*. Oxford: Berg, 2004.

Hollows, Joanne. *Feminism, Femininity and Popular Culture*. Manchester: Manchester University Press, 2000.

Hooton, Christopher. 'Jodie Whittaker's First Full Doctor Who Episode: What the Critics Are Saying', *Independent* (8 October 2018): https://www.independent.co.uk/arts-entertainment/tv/news/doctor-who-jodie-whittaker-series-11-episode-1-review-reaction-critics-a8573696.html (accessed 7 August 2019).

Jenkins, Henry. 'Fandom, Negotiation, and Participatory Culture'. In *A Companion to Media Fandom and Fan Studies*, ed. Paul Booth. Oxford: Wiley, 2018, 13–26.

Levy, Ariel. *Female Chauvinist Pigs: Women and the Rise of Raunch Culture*. UK: Pocket, 2005.
Mangan, Lucy. '*Doctor Who* Review: Great Jodie Whittaker Debuts in New Series with Heart(s) and Soul', *The Guardian* (7 October 2018): https://www.theguardian.com/tv-and-radio/2018/oct/07/doctor-who-review-great-jodie-whittaker-debuts-in-new-series-with-hearts-and-soul (accessed 7 August 2019).
McRobbie, Angela. *The Aftermath of Feminism: Gender, Culture and Social Change*. London: Sage, 2009.
Nicholls, Emily. *Negotiating Femininities in the Neoliberal Night-Time Economy*. London: Springer, 2018.
Nielsen, Harriet Bjerrun. 'Noisy Girls: New Subjectivities and Old Gender Discourses'. *Young* 12, no. 9 (2004): 9–30.
Penny, Laurie. *Cybersexism: Sex, Gender and Power on the Internet*. London: A&C Black, 2013.
Proctor, William, and Bridget Kies. 'On Toxic Fan Practices and the New Culture Wars'. *Participations* 15, no. 1 (2018): 127–42.
Rich, Emma. 'Young Women, Feminist Identities and Neoliberalism'. *Women's Studies International Forum* 28, no. 6 (2005): 495–508.
Sandvoss, Cornel. *A Game of Two Halves: Football Fandom, Television and Globalisation*. London: Routledge, 2004.
Schippers, Mimi. 'Recovering the Feminine Other: Masculinity, Femininity, and Gender Hegemony'. *Theory and Society* 36, no. 1 (2007): 85–102.
Thornton, Sarah. *Club Cultures: Music, Media and Subcultural Capital*. Middleton: Wesleyan University Press, 1995.
Tulloch, John, and Henry Jenkins. *Science Fiction Audiences: Watching Doctor Who and Star Trek*. London: Routledge, 1995.

Chapter 16
Fans as consumers: Psychographics and tribalism in *Doctor Who* fandom by Alison Lawson and David Lawson

Original to this volume

The first newly commissioned piece in this section, Alison Lawson and David Lawson use marketing theory on 'consumer tribes' to propose an initial, speculative typology of Doctor Who *fan tribes. This illustrates both how studies of Who fandom have moved beyond media/audience studies and how fandom cannot be understood monolithically, but must be analysed via its full heterogeneity.*

Traditional marketing uses the theory of segmentation to divide markets into target groups with similar characteristics so that marketing communications can be tailored to those being targeted. Segmentation may use a number of bases, such as demographics, socio-economics or geographic considerations. However, fandom is not tied by these considerations and is more appropriately described by psychographics, which describe consumers in terms of their values, opinions, beliefs, motivations and attitudes, and behavioural segmentation, which describes the way consumers behave in purchasing situations. This chapter uses the concepts of psychographic and behavioural segmentation and consumer tribes to develop a theoretical typology of *Doctor Who* fans as consumers.

Doctor Who fans as consumers

Doctor Who fans, in common with other fan groups, are often referred to in ordinary language as if they were one homogeneous mass (and for more discussion on this, see Chapter 17). This is, of course, not the case. Fans may be any age, from any country, of any socio-demographic, of any gender, any religion, any political persuasion, any race and so on. Indeed, fan studies has sought to analyse fandoms as multiple, diverse communities, but has still often downplayed the consumer status of fandom.[1]

Conversely, marketing theory has considered fandoms as 'subcultures of consumption',[2] making fans part of an ethnography of brands' 'interpretive communities'.[3] 'Brand fans' or even 'brandoms' have been analysed for the ways in which marketing can target and seek to channel their activities.[4] Increasingly, 'fan identity has been [...] analyzed, synthesized, and regenerated as a strategic objective of contemporary marketing managers'.[5] But how might those working in marketing describe and classify the varied types of fans within a TV programme's fandom? One of the first principles of marketing is to understand the consumer: what makes them behave the way they do, what informs their decisions, what are their preferences – essentially, who exactly are they?

Describing and categorizing consumers

Segmentation is one of the basic principles used in marketing, as part of a marketing strategy that starts with analysis and segmentation then moves on to targeting and positioning. The idea is that the total market for a product or service is not homogeneous and may be divided into different segments.[6] Each segment describes consumers with similar characteristics. The marketer then considers these segments and selects one or more as the target market. Last, the product or service is positioned in the market to meet the needs and wants of the target market, thereby encouraging them to buy the product or use the service.

Segmentation can be achieved in various ways, using different bases:

- Demographics – using age, gender and stage of life, physical characteristics and attributes
- Socio-economics – income, social class and levels of education
- Geographic – where people live
- Behaviour – what people buy, how often they buy, how they use products/services, what features or benefits they look for and whether they are loyal to brands, keen to try new things or prefer to stick to what they know
- Psychographics – personality traits, values, perceptions, attitudes and beliefs and the kind of lifestyle they have.

Demographics and socio-economic bases are clearly useful when marketing a product or service that is designed specifically for a particular age group or those earning a salary high enough to afford the product or service in question; examples might be investment products for those with enough money to invest or holidays for families with young children. Geographic segmentation is useful for products and services tied to a specific location, such as a window cleaning company that works within a radius of ten miles to recruit clients. But *Doctor Who* fans can be any age, of any social class, any income level, any level of education and literally anywhere in the world, so this kind of segmentation will not work to describe and classify such fans. Behavioural and psychographic bases are much more useful in this case. These methods of segmentation recognize that consumers are individuals with their own decision-making power, but may be grouped using similar psychological or behavioural characteristics. Although segmentation may be argued to be overly individualizing – after all, fandom is often about being part of a social group – as we'll show, it can incorporate communal or factional dimensions into individual fan psychographics.

Fan behaviour

To consider fans as consumers involves understanding what it is that they consume. First there is the television programme itself (and recordings of the programme), second there is the plethora of official and unofficial merchandise and third there is the fan community whether in person or online.

It may be assumed that all *Who* fans are consumers of the television programme, even if there are perhaps a very few highly unusual 'non-consuming fan[s]'[7] who take part in the fan community but no longer watch new episodes. But setting aside this rare, limited case, even among fan consumers of TV *Doctor Who* there are bound to be differences. There are those who prefer the original series (1963–89) to the new series (2005–present), or vice versa, those who like both and those who may like a particular era of one or both series. Some may watch the programmes repeatedly, either in transmission order or at random, choosing favourites. Many fans enjoy discussing the programme, teasing out plot details, critiquing the direction, special effects, costumes, music and so on, theorizing, examining minutiae, writing or reading about it in blogs, making or enjoying podcasts or videos on social media, writing for or reading fan websites and official publications. This takes the simple watching and enjoying of a television programme to the fan level – it is not enough simply to watch.

Being active consumers of the merchandise can become an expensive habit for the fan as there is a lot to choose from, covering a range of media (books, magazines, CDs/downloads, DVDs/BluRays), board games, computer and online games, jigsaws, records, action figures, cosplay outfits, wallets, cups, teapots, watches … There is too much to list here. Suffice to say that a fan who wished to buy all available merchandise would need a huge budget and an aircraft hangar in which to store it all. In this area, then, almost all fans must make discriminating purchasing decisions.[8] Some may buy only licensed merchandise, some will enjoy the unlicensed products, some will buy all the books but may not collect the action figures and some may prefer the free podcasts to the DVDs with their documentaries and other extras. The decision-making in this area is complex and will be an individual matter, depending on the need or want that the fan seeks to meet.

Being part of the fan community involves activities that may be free and those that attract a cost. Friendship groups on social media, engaging with Twitter or Instagram and meeting fans in your local group, may all satisfy the need for community at no extra cost. Attending conventions and visiting attractions such as the *Doctor Who Experience*, *Doctor Who at the Proms*, *Doctor Who Escape Rooms* or the immersive *Time Fracture* (see Chapter 8) attract a cost but promise an exciting and memorable experience to be shared with fellow fans. Decision-making here will mean consideration of several factors (such as price, availability, timing, distance, even accommodation) and, again, will be an individual matter for each fan. It is also perhaps worth noting under 'behaviour' that while some fans are quite open about their love of the program, others may not be, and may choose instead only to allow their inner fan to show when they are with other fans. The very strong feelings held by some fans can cause discord in communities although there is also understanding that this mix of likes and dislikes is all part of fandom's rich tapestry.[9]

Fan psychographics

The lifestyle we live allows us to express our personality, our values, beliefs, attitudes and opinions. This includes decisions we make about what we buy or use, actions we take around issues such as sustainability and the environment, how we present ourselves to others, how we respond to situations and so on. Fans cannot hope to emulate the Doctor's lifestyle but they can lead their lives in ways that reflect similar attitudes and values, or even interpret the Doctor as reflecting their own pre-existent value systems (see the Alan McKee extract included earlier in this section).

Of course, it is impossible to describe the values, beliefs, attitudes, opinions and perceptions of fans accurately without undertaking a full research study on the matter, but it is possible to make some assumptions based on the values and attitudes exemplified in the programme itself, and this is partly how marketing scholar Robert Kozinets has previously analysed the 'utopian enterprise' of *Star Trek* fans, for instance.[10] The character of the Doctor demonstrates that they are driven by a need to do what is right and to be kind. The Doctor accepts and celebrates difference, takes joy in all kinds of life and is curious to learn more about everything. They have a strong sense of justice, abhor violence and prejudice and are willing to fight against these to protect others, whether an individual or the whole universe, even if it means making sacrifices. The Doctor is outgoing and selfless, putting others first when difficult decisions are to be made. The Doctor is not completely virtuous, however, and can also be tactless, emotionally unaware, reckless, arrogant and childish. On balance, the Doctor is a positive character who is admired, respected and liked by others, so it tends to be the more positive character traits that are mentioned when they are described. These character traits are often displayed in the programme, and it may be possible that those who are loyal to it are likely to have sympathy for these traits at the very least, or aspire to them, even if not actually/always displaying them. The stories told within the programme also sit within a set of values that similarly celebrate difference, abhor prejudice and violence, promote sustainability and equality, and encourage kindness.

Perhaps, then, we may describe fans as potentially sharing the Doctor's own values of having a strong sense of justice, being good-natured, unprejudiced, helpful and kind. As Paul Booth and Craig Owen Jones have demonstrated in their study of *Doctor Who* fandom, there has been an established norm of 'convivial evaluation', whereby fans ordinarily defuse conflict by recognizing different individual viewpoints.[11] This may be easier to achieve in-person at conventions, however, and fan personalities, values and attitudes may be rather more tribally discerned on social media platforms.

Impact of social media and the formation of consumer tribes

Back in the days before social media, fans would gather at each other's houses, in schools, at pubs, universities and other places to share their love for the programme. As fandom became more organized, the *Doctor Who Appreciation Society* (DWAS) offered a 'home' for fans, particularly through its local groups and its conventions. Conventions grew in number, popularity and size and became a great place for fans to mix not only with stars and members of the production team from the programme but also with each other. These gatherings provided a place to feel safe, relaxed, known and accepted. They provided a space for people to share ideas and opinions, to discuss, debate, laugh and enjoy each other's company. The advent of the internet and then social media allowed fans to do this virtually as well as in person, but it also enabled something else – one voice on social media could be heard by thousands of people, rather than the handful of friends at the DWAS local group or the larger group at a convention. Suddenly, fans had access to hundreds of thousands of other fans and, of course, they didn't all agree with each other about everything.

Since 2005, many fans have been delighted at the way the show has progressively embraced LGBTQ+ characters has covered societal issues such as racism, sustainability and mental illness and, perhaps most significantly, has cast a woman in the lead role. However, other fans have not been so happy, finding the tone overbearing and preachy and not taking to a female Doctor. The #NotMyDoctor hashtag on Twitter emerged as some long-standing fans declared they would no longer watch, presumably placing them in the 'non-consuming fan' category highlighted by Sarah Kate Merry.[12]

Social media has enabled fans to communicate their likes and dislikes with total strangers, emboldening them with anonymity, freedom and the ability to reach a huge number of people, and allowing them to feel that their opinions are justified because they are shared. Social media works through algorithms detecting what individuals say, like and share, using keywords and other indicators to increase more of the same in the individual's feed. It is possible, arguably, to live in a kind of fandom echo chamber in which one rarely hears a dissenting voice. When and if a dissenting voice is heard, the backlash can be fierce, as users are anonymous and will never meet in real life. Some of the attacks on strangers that are seen on social media would never have happened at the DWAS local group at the pub. What we have seen develop on social media is well described by the ideas of tribal marketing.

The theory of consumer tribes holds that we may be individuals, but we are also social beings and that purchasing of products does not define us but instead allows us to have meaningful social relationships with others. These relationships – the belonging to tribal communities – are more important than the commodities purchased. Consumer tribes share a passion for a particular brand, product or service and/ or consumption behaviour. The tribe itself becomes an important part of the consumer's life.[13] There is a clear link here with fan behaviour.

Towards an initial typology of *Doctor Who* fans

There is a well-known typology of consumers based on their values and lifestyles known as VALS[14] that segments people into groups with similar characteristics based on whether they have high or low resources and their primary motivations. VALS uses a survey to categorize people as innovators, achievers, strivers, thinkers, experiencers, believers, makers or survivors. Each category is described in detail and may be used to describe and predict the behaviour of that group. Might it be possible to develop something similar to describe fans? Although we cannot yet draw on VALS-esque survey data for *Doctor Who* fans, an initially speculative and theoretical typology of fans might look something like Table 16.1.

For now, this is purely hypothetical, of course, and deliberately sets to one side the issue of the self-declared or genuinely 'non-consuming fan' (though the pessimist, as a category of still-consuming fan, is moving in this direction). Knowing that fans may be reading this proposed typology, it is sure to generate discussion and debate. The reality is probably even more complicated, with fans identifying with parts of several of the types suggested (or even none of them!). A major research project remains much needed in order to make a properly grounded assessment and then start to fully classify *Doctor Who* fans' consumer tribes, but no matter how fans are characterized, we have argued that psychographic and behavioural segmentation could yet prove to be very useful.

Table 16.1 *A Theoretical Typology of* Doctor Who *Fans*

The Positive Completist	The Optimistic Enthusiast	The Nostalgia Buff
• Enjoys all the series equally, without criticism • Buys all the merchandise • Embraces the series' values in their entirety • Is a 'public' fan – family, friends and colleagues are aware, attends conventions and events	• Enjoys the series and always looks forward to the next thing, which will be even better • Doesn't buy all merchandise but hopes to be able to buy more in the future • Embraces the series' values and hopes these will affect society at large • Has been to some fan events and hopes to attend more in the future	• Enjoys the original series, possibly the very early stories in particular • Makes few purchases of modern merchandise but treasures older products related to the original series • Embraces the values of the original series but may be less comfortable with (or unaware of) those of the new series • May not mix with other fans much, but is delighted when friends remember old episodes or when articles/images from the show turn up on social media

The Armchair Critic	The Pessimist	The Newcomer
• Enjoys some of the series but has some criticisms • Makes selective purchases • Embraces some of the series' values but has some criticisms • Mixes mostly in fan circles, mostly on social media, family, friends and colleagues are unaware, doesn't attend events	• Used to enjoy the series but no longer does as much • Has merchandise from earlier eras of the series but has stopped buying • Doesn't always like the writing and believes the show's long-established values have become too diluted with some of the modern changes • Remains a 'closet' fan, family may be aware but friends and colleagues at work may not know, does not attend fan events any more	• Has recently discovered the series and is keen to find out more, delighted to find there is an extensive back catalogue • Has not purchased any merchandise yet, but may do in the future • Is delighted to find that the show reflects some or all of their own values • Hasn't decided yet if they want to identify as a fan, family friends and colleagues are unaware, may be unaware of fan events

Notes

1. See Matt Hills, *Fan Cultures* (London: Routledge, 2002); Mel Stanfill, *Exploiting Fandom* (Iowa City: University of Iowa Press, 2019).
2. Robert Kozinets, 'Utopian Enterprise: Articulating the Meanings of Star Trek's Culture of Consumption', *Journal of Consumer Research* 28, no. 1 (2001): 68.
3. Steven M. Kates, 'Researching Brands Ethnographically: An Interpretive Community Approach', in *Handbook of Qualitative Research Methods in Marketing*, ed. Russell W. Belk (Cheltenham: Edward Elgar, 2006), 94–105.

4   On 'brand fans', see Henrik Linden and Sara Linden, *Fans and Fan Cultures* (London: Palgrave, 2017); on 'brandom', see Matthew Guschwan, 'Fandom, Brandom and the Limits of Participatory Culture', *Journal of Consumer Culture* 12, no. 1 (2012): 19–40.
5   Robert Kozinets, 'Fan Creep: Why Brands Suddenly Need "Fans"', in *Wired TV*, ed. Denise Mann (New Brunswick: Rutgers University Press, 2014), 162.
6   David Jobber and Fiona Ellis-Chadwick, *Principles and Practice of Marketing*, 8th edition (Maidenhead: McGraw Hill, 2016).
7   Sarah Kate Merry, 'When the Script Hits the Fan: Why Archers Fans Stop Listening (and Why They Can't Completely Keep Away)', in *Fandom Culture and The Archers*, ed. Cara Courage and Nicola Headlam (Bingley: Emerald, 2022), 43.
8   Isabelle Szmigin and Maria Piacentini, *Consumer Behaviour* (Oxford: Oxford University Press, 2015).
9   This tapestry of different fan interpretations and how fans get along despite their fannish differences are both discussed as a matter of 'convivial evaluation', in Paul Booth and Craig Owen Jones, *Watching Doctor Who: Fan Reception and Evaluation* (New York: Bloomsbury, 2020), 25.
10 Kozinets, 'Utopian Enterprise'.
11 Booth and Jones, *Watching Doctor Who*, 22–6.
12 Merry, 'When the Script Hits the Fan', 43.
13 Bernard Cova, Robert Kozinets and Avi Shankar, *Consumer Tribes* (Oxford: Routledge, 2007).
14 Strategic Business Insights, 'The VALS™ Survey' (2013): http://www.strategicbusinessinsights.com/vals/ustypes.shtml#types (accessed 28 April 2022).

Chapter 17

The controversy of the Thirteenth Doctor announcement and *Doctor Who* fandom on Tumblr by Alice de Freitas Gomes and Polyana Inácio Rezende Silva

Original to this volume

This chapter brings together the preoccupations of its two predecessors in a novel way, combining a vital sense of fandom's multiplicity with an analysis of Tumblr fandoms' responses to Whittaker's casting. Alice de Freitas Gomes and Polyana Inácio Rezende Silva analyse how, although Tumblr responses to this new Doctor were predominantly positive, there was still a wide variety of concerns raised by the 'controversy', including that yet another white actor had been cast.

Expectations surrounding casting choices are a well-known phenomenon among *Doctor Who* fans. From time to time, a new Doctor is introduced – fans create emotional bonds and follow their adventures. Then comes the news that the lead actor's departure has been confirmed. In the midst of feelings caused by this imminent change, speculation begins: who will be chosen to continue the Doctor's adventures?

On 16 July 2017, after the men's final of the Wimbledon Championships, the BBC released a video announcing actress Jodie Whittaker as the Thirteenth Doctor. This was a remarkable event for the *Doctor Who* universe: Jodie was the first woman chosen to play a character that had, for decades, been portrayed only by men. The revelation of Whittaker's casting reverberated widely within the series' fan community and rapidly divided opinions. These events motivated the original undergraduate thesis whose methodological choices and results are presented here (and for more related analysis, see the Neta Yodovich extract earlier in this section).[1] We acknowledge that *Doctor Who* is not isolated from its sociocultural context, especially considering the mobilizations, texts and conversations produced by fans. Therefore, we have sought to further unveil the tensions between *Doctor Who* and its fan community following the announcement of Jodie Whittaker as the Thirteenth Doctor.

Notes on fandom's complexities

The media depiction of fan communities has long been addressed by scholars. From the first wave of fan studies in the 1980s and 1990s, such as Henry Jenkins' prominent book, *Textual Poachers*, through to more recent writings, we find accounts of negative depictions of fans in media.[2] Two examples are the skit from *Saturday Night Live* 'Get a Life' (1986) and the web series *Con Man* (2015), which portray fan communities as groups of misfits, unbalanced and socially unfit people who live in a fantasy world.

Such depictions perpetuate the fallacy that all fans are alike and participate in homogeneous communities (see also the arguments, and the proposed fan typology, of the previous chapter). As Rhiannon Bury posits, there is a continuum of different levels of fan participation ranging from less participatory and visible practices, like searching online for information about a series, to producing fan art and fan fiction.[3] In this sense, fans don't always associate in communities. Yet even amongst those who seek connection with others with shared interests, there is no homogeneity. According to Booth and Kelly, the identity of each fan influences their participation within that community, and this accounts for great complexity in fan interactions.[4]

In *Doctor Who's* case, such complexity is also highlighted by when and where fans are located in time and space. There are older fans and younger fans; fans of the classic series and the modern series; fans from the UK and many other parts of the world. Such categories can overlap with one another, and we must also acknowledge the relevance of each fan's personal experiences. These experiences influence the connections that fans establish with media products and communities, as participation in fandom is centred around the emotional attachment to the media product, and what moves this emotional core can be very particular to each person.[5] In summary, heterogeneous identities, levels of participation and interactions are all important elements to consider when studying fan communities.

Another misconception that must be challenged is that of fans as mere escapists, immersed in the fantasy worlds of media products. Recent studies of fan activism, such as the writings of Amaral, Souza and Monteiro, Brough and Shresthova, and Jenkins et al. show that fan communities are both significantly affected by their historical context and heavily involved in social issues.[6] The points raised by these studies are very important to our research and resonate with the results of our analysis of *Doctor Who* fandom on Tumblr. Investigating *Doctor Who* fan discussions in the context of Jodie Whittaker's casting highlights the heterogeneity of fans on Tumblr and their interests in issues of social relevance such as racism, sexism and media representation. However, nuances and differences within the *Who* fandom Tumblr community also posed a challenge to our research. More than just conceiving of procedures for data collection and processing, we needed a reflexive methodology that could account for the fandom complexities that we were encountering.

Methodology

We collected data from posts published on Tumblr – this was chosen as our research locus due to the relevance of the platform to dynamics of fan communities online.[7] According to Louisa Ellen Stein, 'In the last decade, Tumblr has emerged as a dominant growth space for fan activity and authorship'.[8] Stein points out how different aspects of Tumblr, from the possibility of image sharing to the illegibility of the platform to outsiders, promote the gathering of fan communities.

We used the Tumblr Tool, developed by the Digital Methods Initiative.[9] This has a script for data extraction which allows the retrieval of posts published on the platform through a tag and a time interval. The period set for data harvesting was between 9 July 2017 and 23 July 2017, which comprised the week before and the week after the casting announcement. The tag 'Jodie Whittaker' was chosen after a few tests revealed a significant increase in posts tagged with the actress's name after the announcement. Data harvesting was then performed on 11 January 2018, retrieving information from 3488 posts. This volume of data had to be refined to constitute our empirical corpus; we selected a sample of 866 posts, all published on the casting announcement date itself, 16 July 2017, for analysis.

An exploratory evaluation of this corpus revealed a level of complexity that had not been anticipated, with multiple perspectives and themes evident in fan discussions around the announcement of the new Doctor. In light of these initial findings, we selected the method of 'cartography of controversy' to continue our analysis.[10] Cartography of controversy is useful for the visualization and investigation of online conflicts. It is a set of techniques that originated in Actor-Network Theory but do not necessarily involve in-depth incursion into this theoretical framework.[11] According to Tommaso Venturini, a controversy is a situation of shared uncertainty in which the actors (public and individuals) involved disagree about something: 'The notion of disagreement is to be taken in the widest sense: controversies begin when actors discover that they cannot ignore each other, and [...] end when actors manage to work out a solid compromise to live together. Anything between these two extremes can be called a controversy.'[12]

According to this definition, Whittaker's casting announcement generated a controversy within Tumblr fandom. When the BBC released the video sharing the news, thousands of fans on Tumblr began to express conflicting opinions. Given this scenario, how best could we explore the conflict and its consequences? Venturini's answer is to '[j]ust observe and describe the controversies'.[13] It is important to note, however, that any such description cannot be purely observational and must also involve interpretation in order to allow the mapping of data. In any case, we sought to follow the general guidelines established by Venturini: '[do] not restrain your observation to any single theory or methodology [...] observe from as many viewpoints as possible [...] listen to actors' voices more than to your own presumptions'.[14] Essentially, we tried to let our objects of study speak, acting on what we heard.

We observed and analysed each post separately, seeking to identify elements in the opinions of users regarding the casting (identifying criteria 'in favour', 'against' and 'neutral') along with different topics which were mentioned in assertions and comments on the news. To avoid imposing preconceived notions on our results, we paid close attention to this process of mapping. Then we produced a visual representation of the controversy, displaying the different opinions and points raised by fans on Tumblr.

Results

Of the 866 analysed posts, only 9 displayed negative opinions about the casting of Whittaker. And even among these, the reason for posters' disagreement was not always the gender of the new Doctor. This discrepancy between the number of negative and positive posts may relate to *Doctor Who* being, as was pointed out by one of the users, 'ahead of the curve' in matters of representation. The series has inclusively represented diverse groups before, through characters like Captain Jack Harkness (John Barrowman), an openly pansexual figure introduced in 2005, and Bill Potts (Pearl Mackie), Jenny Flint (Catrin Stewart) and Madame Vastra (Neve McIntosh), all of whom are non-straight female characters. As Jenkins points out, fans choose their media products because 'they seem to hold special potential as vehicles for expressing the fans' pre-existing social commitments and cultural interests'.[15] Therefore, it is possible that some *Doctor Who* fans have a specific stance in relation to 'social justice' issues, including the media representation of women. The choice of research locus may also have influenced these results, since Tumblr has been considered to favour the expression of non-normative identities.[16]

Starting this research, we assumed that we would encounter two basic stances: individuals in favour of or against the casting choice – viewpoints engaged, basically, with the gender of the new Doctor. In fact, in the early stages of research, expressions such as 'the casting of Jodie Whittaker' and 'the Doctor's gender change' were used as synonyms. However, our assumption was very much a misconception, as is shown by Figure 17.1, a diagram constructed from the 866 analysed posts (based on Gomes[17]). The central part of the image shows some of the main topics evoked in the discussions regarding Whittaker's casting. Around those are paraphrases synthesizing related points made by users.

The image shows that many issues expanding beyond the gender of the Thirteenth Doctor were raised during these Tumblr discussions. Among the topics identified in the sample are:

1. The fact that the new Doctor is a woman.
2. Media representation.
3. Relationships in the series.
4. The impacts of the announcement on audience ratings.
5. Former showrunner Steven Moffat.
6. Sexism.
7. The *Broadchurch* series.

This all highlights a crucial aspect of controversies: they are resistant to reduction. As Venturini posits, '[t]he difficulty of controversy is not that actors disagree on answers, but that they cannot even agree on questions'.[18]

Another element highlighting the complexity of this controversy is the fact that these themes were brought up in arguments on different sides of the dispute. Note the excerpts below, taken from posts by three different blogs in the analysed sample:

We also cannot overlook what an important moment this is for all the women and young girls who watch and adore *Doctor Who*. Young girls will finally get to see themselves as the hero of the story, an all too rare moment when most movies and TV shows – especially in science fiction – star men. Even young boys will benefit from being able to look up to a woman as their role model.

I very easily came up with this opinion, as someone who's grown up without many male role models that I could relate to, bar the Doctor, and as someone with an abundance of female role models in film, tv and books. […] I'm simply stating my opinion (which my whole family agrees with, as I've stated before) that the Doctor should not be a woman, full stop.

For fucks sake, a white woman. When will PoC get proper representation on *Doctor Who*? Fucking Chibnall and the BBC.

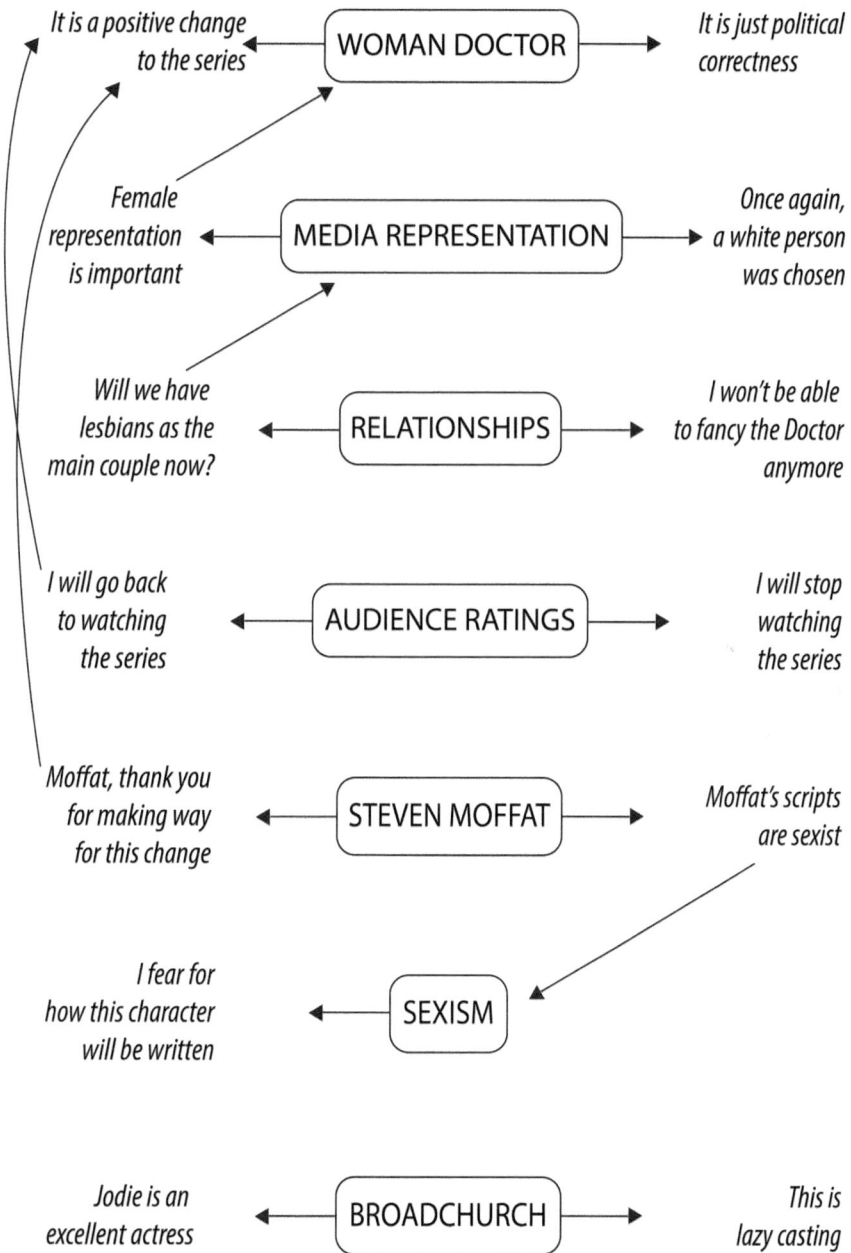

Figure 17.1 A diagram of the different topics and arguments brought up by users in the controversy surrounding the casting of Jodie Whittaker as the Thirteenth Doctor on Tumblr. Made by the authors, based on Gomes.

All the posts above deal with media representation, but from three different perspectives. The first user shows satisfaction with the new Doctor and expresses that female lead roles are still rare in TV and film. The second, who identifies herself throughout her text as a woman, says the complete opposite – that she always grew up with an abundance of female role models in the media and that the Doctor was actually her only male role model. The third user, despite also expressing dissatisfaction with the casting choice using a line of reasoning related to media representation, does so for a completely different reason again: Jodie Whittaker is the first woman to play the Doctor, but her casting means yet another white person has been chosen for the role.

Another example of how varied themes are addressed in the controversy, as well as being used in different ways by fans, are mentions of *Broadchurch*. Observe the excerpts below, taken from posts by two other blogs:

> I like Jodie Whittaker from what I've seen of her in *Broadchurch* and *Attack The Block* (w/ prince John Boyega which is +++1) so this seems like an excellent, charming pick! This is really convincing me to watch Who again. I'm more than willing to jump back in, but only as long as she's out of Moffat's grubby hands!

> […] I love Jodie Whittaker. she was brilliant in *Broadchurch* and I love her in the promo already. it's exciting. not so fun fact: Chibnall casting Whittaker is lazy af casting:)))

Broadchurch was a television crime drama series created by Chris Chibnall and starring several *Doctor Who* actors, including Jodie Whittaker in the role of Beth Latimer (the mother of the boy whose death is investigated in Series One). While some used this previous work to justify their satisfaction with the choice of Jodie, others pointed out that this casting was safe and 'lazy', considering that Whittaker and Chibnall, appointed at the time as *Doctor Who*'s showrunner, had just collaborated on *Broadchurch*.

Examples of this plurality of themes and viewpoints were abundant in the Tumblr posts. Some users mentioned how the show's ratings would plummet, saying they would stop watching *Doctor Who*. Others happily announced that they now had a reason to watch the series again. These conflicts and contradictions expose the individuality of fans and challenge any simplistic view that fandom is a homogeneous or even cohesive community. Indeed, *Doctor Who* fans may share their love for the series, but they do so by bringing unique perspectives from their individual experiences to the table. As Booth and Kelly point out, there is always a mixture of self-identity and shared interest at work in fandom.[19] The community is comprised of very different people, and it is difficult to capture its collective identity in any fixed or well-defined sense. As we found, there are constant flows, tensions and negotiations that blur how *Doctor Who* Tumblr fandom can be analytically represented.

Conclusion

The announcement of the casting of Jodie Whittaker as the Thirteenth Doctor provoked diverse reactions within *Doctor Who* fandom. The initial expectation of this research was that the discussions would be limited to the fact that a woman had been chosen to play a character previously played by men. This expectation did not materialize. Instead, multiple topics such as media representations of people of colour, previous work by the actress, sexist scripts and the possibility of lesbian relationships in the series, among others, were raised by users during their discussions. In addition to this, highly divergent opinions on the same subjects were found in our sample, as shown in Figure 17.1. Such complexity is an intrinsic feature of fan communities.

Fandoms build from emotional elements that lead to modes of identity and levels of participation around media products. The communicational flows of these dynamic, heterogeneous collectives mobilize interactions that are, in turn, complicated by the diegetic and extra-diegetic narratives of the series. Beyond the fictional reality of *Doctor Who*, these narratives reverberate with social issues, something which arguably and seemingly plays out in a specific way on Tumblr. For this reason, any critical tendency to homogenize fan behaviour is hopelessly reductive. Attempts at standardization severely underrate the organic interactions, identity processes and social media contexts of those involved. The results of this research therefore show that the heterogeneity and complexity of fandom must be taken into account in studies of these communities. Different levels of participation, when associated with the expression of identity, reveal unforeseen elements in fans' interactions: diverse knowledge practices meant that our assumptions about what and how fans would be debating in response to Jodie's casting had to be reflexively recognized and amended. As a result, we hope to have contributed to scholarly discussions with a theoretical-methodological approach that will itself be improved and amended once more in future works.

Notes

1. Alice de Freitas Gomes, *'Nobody Wants a Tardis Full of Bras': A Controvérsia da Escolha da 13ª Doutora e o Fandom de Doctor Who No Tumblr*, Bachelor's thesis, Federal University of Minas Gerais, 2018. Whittaker's casting and tenure as the Doctor have also been subsequently discussed in Brigid Cherry, Matt Hills and Andrew O'Day, eds., *Doctor Who – New Dawn* (Manchester: Manchester University Press, 2021).
2. Henry Jenkins, *Textual Poachers: Television Fans & Participatory Culture* (New York: Routledge, 1992); Casey McCormick, 'Active Fandom: Labor and Love in The Whedonverse', in *A Companion to Media Fandom and Fan Studies*, ed. Paul Booth (Hoboken: Wiley, 2018).
3. Rhiannon Bury, '"We're Not There": Fans, Fan Studies, and the Participatory Continuum', in *The Routledge Companion to Media Fandom*, ed. Melissa A. Click and Suzanne Scott (Abingdon: Routledge, 2018), 123–31.
4. Paul Booth and Peter Kelly, 'The Changing Faces of Doctor Who Fandom: New Fans, New Technologies, Old Practices?' *Participations: Journal of Audience and Reception Studies* 10, no. 1 (2013): 56–72.
5. McCormick, 'Active Fandom'.
6. Adriana Amaral, Rosana Vieira Souza and Camila Monteiro, 'De Westeros No #vemprarua à Shippagem do Beijo Gay na TV Brasileira'. Ativismo de Fãs: Conceitos, Resistências e Práticas na Cultura Digital, *Galáxia* no. 29 (June 2015): https://revistas.pucsp.br/index.php/galaxia/article/view/20250/16750 (accessed 27 April 2022), 141–54; Melissa M. Brough and Sangita Shresthova, 'Fandom Meets Activism: Rethinking Civic and Political Participation', *Transformative Works and Cultures* 10 (2012); Henry Jenkins, Sangita Shresthova, Liana Gamber-Thompson, Neta Kligler-Vilenchik and Arely Zimmerman, *By Any Media Necessary: The New Youth Activism* (New York: New York University Press, 2016); Jenkins, *Textual Poachers*.
7. See, Megan DeSouza, 'A Case of the Red Pants Mondays' (2013): https://digitalcommons.uri.edu/tmd_major_papers/3/; Melanie Kohnen, 'Tumblr Pedagogies', in *A Companion to Media Fandom and Fan Studies*, ed. Paul Booth (Hoboken: Wiley, 2018), 351–67; Louisa Stein, 'Tumblr Fan Aesthetics', in *The Routledge Companion to Media Fandom*, ed. Melissa A. Click and Suzanne Scott (Abingdon: Routledge, 2018), 86–97.
8. Stein, 'Tumblr Fan Aesthetics', 86.
9. https://labs.polsys.net/tools/tumblr/ (accessed 27 April 2022).

10. See, Tommaso Venturini, 'Diving in Magma: How to Explore Controversies with Actor-Network Theory', *Public Understanding of Science* 19, no. 3 (2010): 258–73; Tommaso Venturini, 'Building on Faults: How to Represent Controversies with Digital Methods', *Public Understanding of Science* 21, no. 7 (2012): 796–812.
11. Venturini, 'Diving in Magma'.
12. Ibid., 261.
13. Ibid., 259.
14. Ibid., 260.
15. Jenkins, *Textual Poachers,* 34.
16. See Christopher M. Cox, 'Ms. Marvel, Tumblr, and the Industrial Logics of Identity in Digital Spaces', *Transformative Works and Cultures* 27 (2018), and discussions about fandom and activism's 'silosociality' on Tumblr in Katrin Tiidenberg, Natalie Ann Hendry and Crystal Abidin, *Tumblr* (Cambridge: Polity, 2021). In terms of highlighting how our results may well have been Tumblr-specific, it is also worth comparing our findings with those that have analysed YouTube threads responding to Whittaker's casting announcement – see Sophie Eeken and Joke Hermes, '*Doctor Who,* Ma'am: YouTube Reactions to the 2017 Reveal of the New Doctor', *Television & New Media* 22, no. 5 (2021): 447–64.
17. Gomes, *'Nobody Wants'*.
18. Venturini, 'Diving in Magma', 262.
19. Booth and Kelly, "The Changing Face of Doctor Who Fandom."

Chapter 18
Marginally Fannish: Fan podcasts as alternative sites of intersectional education by Parinita Shetty

Original to this volume

A new piece that analyses the under-researched area of Doctor Who *podcasting, this chapter from Parinita Shetty analyses* Marginally Fannish*, the podcast she set up as part of her PhD. Shetty makes the case for fan podcasting as a kind of public pedagogy, where audiences can be empathetically educated about, and by, the 'restorying' of canon through fans' intersectional experiences and counternarratives.*

Popular media representations are important because they shape ideas about different cultures.[1] This plays a powerful role in influencing how people – from dominant and marginalized groups – think about themselves and others. Media can reify existing ideologies, but people can also challenge them.

The feminist theory of intersectionality investigates how multiple and complex social privileges and inequalities interact with each other.[2] The internet has played a significant role in popularizing this concept in non-academic spaces.[3] Understanding intersectional perspectives involves a process of collaboration and literacy. People can use online debates about popular culture to raise awareness about various intersectional issues. There is no monolithic experience of engaging with cultural texts, especially ones which are shared globally across different contexts.[4] Growing access to digital tools and platforms allows fans to create podcasts which cater to their own priorities, with the shared language of popular media providing opportunities to explore the intersections and interpretations of diverse identities. When groups of fans from different backgrounds discuss how their cultures are represented or erased in their favourite media, they create knowledge about intersectional experiences that can challenge mainstream representations.

Booth has proposed that fandom acts as an important space for learning.[5] In fan podcasts, collective and critical analysis emerges through a combination of fans' emotional investment in their favourite worlds as well as in their own identities. Many fan conversations use fictional characters, themes and events as a cultural shorthand to share experiences about real-world identities. Connecting fictional worlds and real-life structures helps fans consider the limitations and possibilities of both.

Creating and reading different kinds of media enables fans to develop multiple literacies outside formal academic institutions. Hills suggests that being a scholar and a fan can involve looking at theories with fresh eyes and questioning established cultural norms promoted by mainstream media.[6] At the same time, podcasting about popular fictions offers a way to make ideas more approachable to a broad range of people.[7] And it has been argued that podcasting, as a 'distinct medium', can particularly facilitate intimacy and empathy with its listeners, making it especially useful as a pedagogic tool.[8]

For my PhD project, I created a fan/research podcast called *Marginally Fannish* (*MF*) where fans used mainstream science fiction and fantasy media to co-create an alternative site of education. My co-participants and I came from a wide range of world views and backgrounds – both marginalized and privileged in different contexts. We also referred to existing fan podcasts as sources of public intersectional scholarship. This chapter features some of these co-participants and podcast episodes to examine how fans from different race, national, age and ability backgrounds navigate patterns of erasure and dominance in *Doctor Who* to develop understandings of racism, imperialism, ageism and ableism both within the show and in the real world.

Co-creating intersectional knowledge in fan podcasts

Fans' 'collective intelligence' has the potential to lead to increased insight over individual interpretations.[9] People's different personal, social, cultural, political and historical backgrounds influence the ways in which they interpret texts, so by featuring people from differently marginalized and privileged backgrounds, fan podcasts provide access to multiple fan viewpoints and offer a way to learn about diverse experiences.[10]

Many fans can balance their love of their favourite media with critiques about elements that have disappointed them.[11] Fans' emotional investment aids this critical analysis and allows them to demand better from their favourite fictional worlds and characters.[12] Analysing favourite media through the lens of their own identities allows fans to highlight different cultural perspectives. The diversity of fans of popular media like *Doctor Who* means that people can encounter ideas which they may not otherwise have considered.

The same fictional character or narrative can hold different meanings for different audiences depending on whether they're cultural insiders or outsiders. For example, Aparna and Sanjana, my fellow Indian co-participants, and I had vastly different experiences watching two *Doctor Who* episodes based on real-world histories – 'Rosa', which featured the Black US civil rights activist Rosa Parks, and 'Demons of the Punjab', which featured the Partition of India.

The three of us loved 'Rosa' when we first watched it. Since we hadn't been taught about American anti-racist activism in our schools in India, we appreciated being able to learn about a cultural history we weren't familiar with. However, the Black and Chinese-American co-hosts of US-produced fan podcast *Woke Doctor Who* had a different reaction. They discussed why they disliked the simplified depiction of Black American activist history, specifically Rosa Parks' minimized role in it. They criticized the fact that other Black women activists were largely missing in the episode, which they felt erased Black people's agency and centred white people instead. While they acknowledged that a Black writer, Malorie Blackman, had co-written the episode, they argued that her British identity led her to miss the nuances of American race-related activism.¹³ Armed with these critical perspectives, Aparna, Sanjana and I were able to come to a more contextualized, complicated understanding of both the *Doctor Who* episode and the American civil rights movement.

Fan spaces abound with examples of self-directed and interest-based education. Fans research a wide range of sources – both fictional and real-world – in order to fill gaps in their knowledge. The *Doctor Who* episode 'Demons of the Punjab' was set during the Partition of India – a violent period of history that the three of us had grown up learning about. However, the three co-hosts of *Verity!* were unfamiliar with this historical event. They therefore used the show as an opportunity to educate themselves by looking for different South Asian responses to the *Doctor Who* episode as well as historical resources about the Partition. They then used their own podcast to share the knowledge they had learned about real-world histories of British imperialism, lamenting the absence of these narratives in British classrooms.¹⁴ Such conversations within fandom can help reorient people's imaginations about real-world histories.

Having said that, while both the *Woke Doctor Who* co-hosts as well as the British, Canadian and Australian co-hosts of *Verity!* loved the 'Demons of the Punjab' episode, Aparna, Sanjana and I found it underwhelming. Sanjana highlighted the differences in our reaction to this episode and to 'Rosa' as she proposed her own theory which explained the discrepancy in different fans' responses to both episodes:

One of the things that was very evident to me is whose story is being told? Because when we watched the *Doctor Who* 'Rosa' episode for our podcast episode on race, we loved the episode [...] And when we heard the *Woke Doctor Who* episode where they spoke about the episode and all the problems with the episode, we were like, 'What?! Yeah! You're absolutely right'. With comparison to how they loved 'Demons of [the] Punjab' and we didn't quite love it [...] We did have problems with it. And I think that's basically how the way history is consumed becomes very limited and subjective to how it's being told and to the people whose story it is – who were directly affected by it.

(Sanjana, *MF* Episode 13)

While accessing *Woke Doctor Who's* response had provided the three of us with more nuanced insights about an unfamiliar culture, Sanjana pushed back against what she felt was a simplistic depiction of a traumatic part of Indian/Pakistani history. In both cases, *Doctor Who*, a British show, portrayed histories of the United States and India for a British (and global) audience. As people who had grown up with these histories and contexts as a part of their education and cultural imagination, different US/Indian fans inevitably had a more complicated perspective on the representation of their cultures. Importantly, fan podcasts offer a space to share these perspectives with a wider audience. Placing beloved media and fans' identities in conversation with each other can also draw attention to wider patterns of misrepresentation and erasure. Before our episode exploring the representations of older women in SFF media, my new co-host Deb and I listened to 'The Women Who Waited' episode of *Woke Doctor Who*. In it, the podcast's hosts analysed how, in a media and sociocultural landscape which seems to value youth, older men have more agency, status and power than older women.¹⁵

As a middle-aged *Doctor Who* fan, Deb was invested in examining how the intersections of age and gender were portrayed in the show. She focused on the examples of two female companions in *Doctor Who* – Sarah Jane Smith (Elisabeth Sladen) and Amy Pond (Karen Gillan) – who appeared as both young and older versions of themselves in the programme. Sarah Jane first appeared in the initial run of *Doctor Who*, and then returned as an older woman for an episode in the post-2005 reimagining. Amy aged up thirty-six years in an episode where she was trapped in an alternate timeline. Deb pointed out how, in both cases, their ageing was associated with bitterness, jealousy and anger. She made a connection between these emotions and how older women are perceived in general by both media and society:

> When you think about the standard maiden, mother, crone triad that you see in literature for women, the crone stage, that section is where we tend to put particularly older female characters [...] When we see women who are over fifty, we tend to see them as either angry and bitter or daffy and crazy [...] Or we don't see them at all. They just disappear entirely.
>
> (Deb, *MF* Episode 14)

Deb drew on her identities as a middle-aged female fan whose experiences were rarely at the forefront of science fiction and fantasy media. As she noted, while there have been strides made in terms of racial and gender diversity, the older woman wasn't an identity which had received the same treatment. She proposed that the absence of older writers, especially older female writers, meant that certain lives and stories were privileged at the expense of others, even when it came to *Doctor Who*. Deb signalled that having a more diverse group of media creators could do a better job of representing the diversity of the world on-screen. That way, progress wouldn't just mean progress for one group but instead would signify progress for more, or even all.

Robert, another *Doctor Who* fan, used the framework of the show's characters and storylines to describe his own experiences with disability and ableism. Initially, he was extremely excited about the introduction of Ryan Sinclair (Tosin Cole) as a companion. Ryan shared Robert's dyspraxia – a representation of his disability which Robert hadn't encountered before. In response, he wrote an essay after the first episode with Ryan aired in which he highlighted the powerful impact such fictional representations in popular TV shows can have.[16]

However, in our *MF* podcast episode, Robert spoke about how he had grown increasingly uncomfortable and upset that the show constantly privileged Graham's (Bradley Walsh) perspective – that is, Ryan's non-disabled step-grandfather – over Ryan's own needs. To Robert, this felt eerily similar to his own childhood struggles with his family where his parents' needs were prioritized over his own:

> Ryan is worried because he's caused an alien invasion. And then Graham is like, 'Oh you're going to blame the dyspraxia on that as well?' And I guess the implication there obviously is all the time that these things are going wrong for Ryan, then he's saying it's by dyspraxia, but it's not actually. If he'd had strength of will or tried hard enough, he would have been able to overcome these things that are, in fact, not possible to overcome because they are a disability.
>
> (Robert, *MF* Episode 10)

Robert drew on his own experiences to outline the problems with the way a disabled character was treated in *Doctor Who*. In the process, he drew attention to the frustrations of navigating a world which wasn't designed to accommodate his disabilities. He used the fiction to discuss real-world contexts where dyspraxia and autism were sometimes described via the perspectives of families/caregivers rather than disabled people themselves:

> I guess that the reason that autistic people are uncomfortable about things being centered on family members is because once our own voices become marginalized and once our own humanity begins to be diminished, it does leave us open to narratives that are abusive.
>
> (Robert, *MF* Episode 10)

Fan-created media offered Robert a chance to reclaim the narrative that the show and the character of Ryan told about his disability. Our podcast episode also offered neurotypical and able-bodied people valuable insights into the experiences of a disabled person.

Fan suggestions of podcasting themes based on their own identities can help others encounter perspectives they may not have analysed before. Focusing on *Doctor Who* with another co-participant who had different concerns – sexuality or religion, for example – would have resulted in different insights. Consequently, fan podcasts signpost a dynamic curriculum-in-process.

Restorying imaginations with fan counternarratives

Intersectionality is concerned not just with oppression but also with the complex ways in which marginalized people express their agency within oppressive social structures.[17] Fans find creative ways to reimagine existing narratives by inserting their own priorities into their favourite media.[18] The imaginative spaces of fan podcasts allow people to question what they have been told about the world and propose alternatives to dominant cultural narratives.[19]

Consequently, fans can transform canon in multiple creative ways by inserting their identities into narratives which didn't otherwise explicitly represent them. Stornaiuolo and Thomas have termed this fannish practice 'restorying', that is, fan responses which highlight marginalized perspectives via mainstream media and culture.[20] They argue that restorying not only challenges inequalities of representation but also offers a way of promoting empathy, respect and understanding for diverse lived experiences. Such counternarratives resist oppressive dominant cultural ideologies and seek to replace them with versions that represent diverse identities more complexly.

The internet offers these counternarratives a more widespread audience, which in turn can encourage others to imagine alternatives. Fan podcasts hence influence both those who participate in such interactions and those who encounter them as audiences.[21] Such public discussions allow listeners to access new information which can expand or change their understanding about fictional characters as well as real-world identities.

To give an example of this process, while discussing the 'Demons of the Punjab' episode, Sanjana shared some of the stories she had grown up with, stories about her grandparents and great-grandparents who had migrated from now-Pakistan to India. She used the opportunity provided by the episode's theme to recount a family story that added a South Asian response to the cultural discourse around *Doctor Who* (*MF* Episode 13). Western media fandoms tend to focus on Western political and cultural contexts; however, fans from other parts of the world can use these fictional frameworks to insert alternative narratives which draw attention to histories and cultures otherwise not given much space. In turn, fans from other cultures can better understand diverse real-world events and histories which they may not have commonly encountered. Making connections between different kinds of experiences adds to fandom's collective pool of knowledge.

Fan counternarratives also draw attention to examples which disrupt mainstream representations. While Deb complained about how older women were treated in *Doctor Who*, she also pointed to the example of River Song (Alex Kingston) who subverted the roles middle-aged female characters were generally relegated to. Deb described how the character challenged ideas of what older women are expected to do both in media and society:

> We often think of [...] women who are middle-aged and older [...] they're not sexual beings [...] River [is] the sexiest character in *Doctor Who* by a landslide. She kisses as a weapon [...] She has multiple husbands and wives [...]. She can rock a sequin gown like nobody's business. [...] She is clearly a woman who is very confident and comfortable in her body. And relishes in it in many different ways including sexuality. And [...] that's not something that we typically associate with female characters in general but particularly middle-age and older female characters.
>
> (Deb, *MF* Episode 14)

By highlighting how River subverted expectations, Deb also outlined what these stereotypical notions were. She then used the example of River to discuss the shortcomings of these tropes by appreciating representations which disrupted mainstream ideas of what an older woman was supposed to do and look like.

Different fan analyses will foreground themes most relevant to people's own priorities. Robert inserted himself into his favourite fictional world in part to take control of the narrative about his identity. He rejected unsatisfactory canonical representation of his disability and instead relied on his own imagination to recognize himself in the show. He strongly identified with Matt Smith's Doctor, who he interpreted as having dyspraxia:

> A lot of what he does in terms of falling over and causing messes and thinking he's being cool and impressive but [...] actually causing a disaster, is quite resonant to people who have dyspraxia. So we've definitely done a bit of reading that in things ourselves, in the dyspraxia *Doctor Who* community [...]. I used to like imagining how his Doctor and Ryan might work together. I think Ryan would have a bit more fun and maybe [Smith's] Doctor [would] be a bit more responsible.
>
> (Robert. *MF* Episode 10)

Even though the Eleventh Doctor wasn't explicitly identified as having dyspraxia or autism, Robert found that he represented his own identities in nuanced ways – something he didn't find in the character of Ryan, who *was* supposed to represent him. Robert's interpretation of the Matt Smith Doctor as disabled provided an alternative to the dominant norm. Instead of accepting the representation he was offered, Robert challenged and expanded *Doctor Who*'s narrative by outlining the perspectives he actually wanted in his favourite media.

By expanding the range of lives people encounter, fan podcasts offer complex opportunities to engage with diverse identities. Unless it is explicitly mentioned, people from dominant cultures don't usually consider characters or events from a marginalized lens. Fan interpretations can help make up for gaps in knowledge and expand the possibilities of people's imaginations.

Conclusion: It's bigger on the inside

Fan podcasts use popular media like *Doctor Who* to open up alternative avenues for intersectional literacy. Fan analyses expand diverse media representations, their counternarratives acting as a public pedagogy that provides access to new intersectional considerations. Discussions about the politics of representation can shed light on real-world experiences and contexts. This critical intersectional education happens in public/fan spaces outside academia. Here, knowledge emerges collectively through people's encounters with others around shared interests. Such reflections place personal identities in conversation with cultural representations. By analysing and interpreting representation in their favourite media, fan podcasts can empathetically expand understandings of diverse identities.

Fan podcast conversations restory canon in ways which speak to diverse interests and priorities. Fandom's collective intelligence helps people consider, question and expand preconceived notions about identities both in fictional and real worlds. As fans examine media through the lenses of different identities, they are able to share and learn different ways of seeing and being in the world, inviting a broader view of intersectionality with room for different identities and beliefs to co-exist.

Fan interpretations and conversations are constantly in flux and can respond to an array of social, cultural and political contexts across space and time.[22] This kind of collective, public education is important because once people begin to view media and real-world structures through a critical, intersectional gaze, it's difficult to put this awareness away. Many people's imaginations are no doubt formatively shaped by mainstream media and society – encountering new ideas via the discussions on fan podcasts can reshape the architectures of these imaginations.

Notes

1. Sara N. Gatson and Robin A. Reid, 'Race and Ethnicity in Fandom', *Transformative Works and Cultures* 8 (2012); Robin Wright and Gary Wright, '*Doctor Who* Fandom, Critical Engagement, and Transmedia Storytelling: The Public Pedagogy of the Doctor', in *Popular Culture as Pedagogy*, ed. Kaela Jubas, Nancy Taber and Tony Brown (Rotterdam: Sense Publishers, 2015), 11–30.

2. Sumi Cho, Kimberlé Crenshaw and Leslie McCall, 'Toward a Field of Intersectionality Studies: Theory, Applications, and Praxis', *Signs* 38, no. 4 (2013): 785–810; Kathy Davis, 'Intersectionality as Buzzword: A Sociology of Science Perspective on What Makes a Feminist Theory Successful', *Feminist Theory* 9, no. 1 (2008): 67–85; Mary Romero, *Introducing Intersectionality* (Cambridge: Polity Press, 2018).

3. Ange-Marie Hancock, *Intersectionality: An Intellectual History* (Oxford: Oxford University Press, 2016); Akane Kanai, 'Between the Perfect and the Problematic: Everyday Femininities, Popular Feminism, and the Negotiation of Intersectionality', *Cultural Studies* 34, no. 1 (2019): 25–48.

4. Glenn Savage, 'Chasing the Phantoms of Public Pedagogy: Political, Popular, and Concrete Publics', in *Problematizing Public Pedagogy*, ed. Jake Burdick, Jennifer A. Sandlin and Michael P. O'Malley (New York: Routledge, 2013), 103–14.

5. Paul Booth, 'Fandom: The Classroom of the Future', *Transformative Works and Cultures* 19 (2015).

6. Matt Hills, 'Foreword: "What If" – Reimagining Fandom', in *Understanding Fandom: An Introduction to the Study of Media Fan Culture*, ed. Mark Duffett (New York: Bloomsbury, 2013), vi–xii.

7. Jessie Blount and Lark Malakai Grey, 'Witch Please Meets the Gayly Prophet: An Interview with Hannah McGregor', *The Gayly Prophet* (2019). [Podcast]: https://hashtagruthless.com/listen/witchpleasemeetsthegaylyprophet (accessed 1 May 2022); Hannah McGregor, *Is Podcasting Pedagogy?: Rethinking the Teaching/Scholarship Divide* (Illinois State University, 4 March 2021). [Webinar]: https://news.illinoisstate.edu/2021/01/podcasting-toward-social-change-series/.

8. Richard Berry, '"Just Because You Play a Guitar and Are from Nashville Doesn't Mean You Are a Country Singer": The Emergence of Medium Identities in Podcasting', *Podcasting: New Aural Cultures and Digital Media*, ed. Dario Llinares, Neil Fox and Richard Berry (London: Palgrave, 2018), 24; Martin Spinelli and Lance Dann, *Podcasting: The Audio Media Revolution* (London: Bloomsbury Academic, 2019), 70.

9   Henry Jenkins, *Convergence Culture: Where Old and New Media Collide* (New York: NYU Press, 2006); Hannah McGregor, 'Yer a Reader, Harry: HP Reread Podcasts as Digital Reading Communities', *Participations Journal of Audience & Reception Studies* 16, no. 1 (2019): 366–89.

10   Sarah Bonsor Kurki, 'Investigating Adolescent Critical Literacy Engagement', *Language and Literacy* 17, no. 3 (2015): 13–33; Cait Coker, 'The Angry! Textual! Poacher! Is Angry! Fan Works as Political Statements', in *Fan Culture: Theory/Practice*, ed. Katherine Larsen and Lynn Zubernis (Newcastle upon Tyne: Cambridge Scholars Publishing, 2012), 81–96; Jen Scott Curwood, '"The Hunger Games": Literature, Literacy, and Online Affinity Spaces', *Language Arts* 90, no. 6 (2013): 417–27.

11   David Scott Diffrient, 'The Gift of Gilmore Girls' Gab: Fan Podcasts and the Task of "Talking Back" to TV', in *Screwball Television: Critical Perspectives on Gilmore Girls*, ed. David Scott Diffrient and David Lavery (Syracuse: Syracuse University Press, 2010), 79–107.

12   Sophie Hansal and Marianne Gunderson, 'Toward a Fannish Methodology: Affect as an Asset', *Transformative Works and Cultures* 33 (2020).

13   Eugenia and Toya, 'Sweep Your Own Yard', *Woke Doctor Who* (2018). [Podcast]: http://wokedoctorwho.com/index.php/2018/11/20/ep-018-sweep-your-own-yard/ (accessed 1 May 2022).

14   Deb Stanish, Erika Ensign, Katrina Griffiths, LM Myles, Lynne M. Thomas and Tansy Raynor Roberts, 'Angels and Demons of the Punjab', *Verity!* (2018) [Podcast]: https://veritypodcast.wordpress.com/2018/11/15/ep-181-angels-and-demons-of-the-punjab/ (accessed 1 May 2022).

15   Eugenia and Toya, 'The Women Who Waited', *Woke Doctor Who* (2019). [Podcast]. Available from: http://wokedoctorwho.com/index.php/2019/03/05/ep-22-the-women-who-waited/ (accessed 1 May 2022).

16   Robert Shepherd, '*People Don't Know About the Reality of Dyspraxia. That's Why We Need Fictions Like Doctor Who's Ryan Sinclair*', 2018: https://medium.com/@vegetablelove/people-dont-know-about-the-reality-of-dyspraxia-91409a8876da (accessed 1 May 2022).

17   Minoo Alinia, 'On Black Feminist Thought: Thinking Oppression and Resistance Through Intersectional Paradigm', *Ethnic and Racial Studies* 38, no. 13 (2015): 2334–40.

18   Sara Florini, 'Enclaving and Cultural Resonance in Black *Game of Thrones* Fandom', *Transformative Works and Cultures* 29 (2019).

19   Walidah Imarisha, *Dreaming New Futures: Sci-Fi and Social Change* (2018): https://www.youtube.com/watch?v=KZlmyUKiJ4I (accessed 1 May 2022).

20   Amy Stornaiuolo and Ebony Elizabeth Thomas, 'Restorying as Political Action: Authoring Resistance through Youth Media Arts', *Learning, Media and Technology* 43, no. 4 (2018): 345–58.

21   Rhiannon Bury, '"We're Not There": Fans, Fan Studies, and the Participatory Continuum', in *The Routledge Companion to Media Fandom*, ed. Melissa Click and Suzanne Scott (New York: Routledge, 2017), 123–31; McGregor, 'Yer a Reader, Harry'.

22   Stornaiuolo and Thomas, 'Restorying as Political Action'.

Marginally Fannish episodes cited:

MF Episode 10. 'Reclaiming Stories: Representations of Dyspraxia and Autism in Doctor Who/Fandom'. [Podcast]: https://marginallyfannish.org/2020/06/09/episode-10/. (accessed 1 May 2022).

MF Episode 13. 'You Want to See Yourself in That Story: The Impact of Religion and Regional Origin'. [Podcast]: https://marginallyfannish.org/2020/08/08/episode-13/. (accessed 1 May 2022).

MF Episode 14. 'We Don't Know What to Do with Them: Representations of Older Women in Media'. [Podcast]: https://marginallyfannish.org/2020/08/25/episode-14/. (accessed 1 May 2022).

Chapter 19

Casual fans and non-fans in *Flux*: The reception of 'Once, Upon Time' and *Doctor Who*'s return to serialization by Dominique Gagnon

Original to this volume

Addressing another under-explored topic, the final new chapter in this section – contributed by Dominique Gagnon – turns to 'casual' audiences for Doctor Who: Flux. *Based on a sample of contemporaneous Twitter responses to 'Once, Upon Time', Gagnon argues that, contra fan anxieties about the 'Not-We' audience, non-fan viewers were not necessarily alienated by* Flux*'s serialization, assuming that its serial narrative would later provide answers to their questions.*

The 13th series of *Doctor Who*, also known as *Doctor Who: Flux*, transported audiences on a journey across time and space where the Thirteenth Doctor (Jodie Whittaker) faced enemies old and new. In her quest to fight an unknown force called the Flux, the Time Lord was forced to face the mystery of her own past to ensure the future of the universe.

Flux was the product of a trying time for media productions all over the world, with the original plan for series 13 having to be adapted to satisfy the many safety requirements in place following the advent of the Covid-19 pandemic.[1] The most obvious change in this regard was the drop from a ten- to a six-episode series, essentially cutting short Whittaker's last full series as the Doctor. For the first time in 'New *Who*' history, audiences were presented with a fully serialized arc rather than the show's usual episodic, monster-of-the-week format. Such serials occurred in the show's original run (1963–89), but for many younger fans who had joined the Whovian ranks from 2005 onwards, *Flux* was a first in terms of serialized *Who*. Marketed as an 'epic six-part adventure',[2] *Flux* aimed to capture viewers' attention regardless of their level of fannish investment in the show. The intended focus of this analysis is to consider how this move to serialization was received by two groups scarcely studied in the show's current audience studies literature: casual fans, who do not necessarily associate with other members of a fandom and whose appreciation of a fannish object is lower in intensity,[3] and non-fans, or the 'comfortable majority', as Jonathan Gray has termed them, experiencing a production from its periphery.[4]

Doctor Who's casual and non-fans through the years

Casual and non-fans' reception of programs like *Doctor Who* matters greatly to its fans.[5] John Tulloch's interpretation of Whovians as a 'powerless elite', for example, positions them between the industry and general audiences made up of casual and non-fans (and look back at the opening extract in this section for Tulloch's influential analysis of this).[6] On the one hand, the powerless elite's expertise, as highly involved fans of the series, comes with an in-depth knowledge of the franchise that can be used to challenge the showrunner and other producers. On the other hand, fans' powerlessness stems from the fact that they are 'only a speck in [an] ocean' made up of far more casual viewers and non-fans who, in turn, due to their sheer numbers hold more power over the production team.[7] What Tulloch means, here, is that general audiences' attention and appreciation for a series like *Doctor Who*, given the force of their numbers, are crucial to guaranteeing its survival. This is a fact that fans are aware of. As such, casual and non-fans are understood as outsiders to the cultural worlds of 'elite' Whovians, yet the latter will openly worry about the 'Not-We'[8] and their opinions on the current incarnation of *Who*.

Flux's 'Tuning out point': Fear over casuals' confusion

Tulloch[9] and Brigid Cherry's[10] work on Whovians' perception of casual and non-fans' reception of the show might have been limited to the classic series and the relatively early years of the 2005 revival respectively, but a look at Twitter during the broadcast of *Doctor Who: Flux* shows that perspectives have not really changed that much since then. In the present case, fans' worries became blatantly obvious on social media during the broadcast of the third 'Chapter' of the serial 'Once, Upon Time' on 14 November 2021. This episode showed the Doctor trying to save Yaz (Mandip Gill), Dan (John Bishop) and Vinder (Jacob Anderson) from a time disruption by hiding them in their own timelines. We also meet a character named Bel (Thaddea Graham) as she tries to find her way back to her lover, who we later find out is none other than Vinder himself.

'Once, Upon Time' is narratively complex because it not only travels between these multiple timelines but also sees our main quartet appear as different characters within them, visually glitching between their actual selves and who they have become in the past. The plot was described as dizzying and confusing by some[11] and thus became an apparent cause for worry amongst Whovians online. One Twitter user even considered the episode to be a possible 'tuning out point' for casual and non-fans because, though 'Once, Upon Time' was *Flux*'s halfway point, its maze-like narrativity was perceived as being overly complicated for non-Whovian audiences. It is also the first episode of the serial that attempts to link events of the previous series to the current one, while also introducing all the characters who will prove essential to events unfolding in the serial's final three episodes.

Fans' concerned reactions to the third Chapter of *Flux* inspired me to focus my analysis on this specifically, as opposed to considering series 13 as a whole. Much like Cherry, who selected episodes 'on the basis of their predicted responses',[12] I am interested in whether 'Once, Upon Time' generated reactions among casual and non-fan audiences that mirrored fan anxieties: was this an example of overly 'complex TV'[13] that would act as a bridge too far for less committed viewers?

Method

For this study of casual viewers' reactions to *Doctor Who: Flux*, I focused my attention on the content published on the social media platform Twitter. The platform's use of hashtags to form *praeter hoc* communities, which are communities surrounding a hashtag created in anticipation of an event or, in this case, the broadcast of a programme,[14] made it easier for me to gather tweets that were published at or around the time of initial broadcast. Using the advanced search function on Twitter, which shows the most recent tweets first, I collected a total of 72 tweets[*] published in the English language on 14th November, the day the episode was broadcast on BBC One and made available on iPlayer. Though this number may seem low considering the typically high number of online posts, comments following the broadcast of a popular programme like *Doctor Who*, my aim here is not to generalize casual and non-fans' reactions. Instead, I want to explore how the move to serialization and the apparent complexity of the plot was reflected in some of these reactions. The tweets studied had to include the hashtag *#DoctorWhoFlux* and be published by a casual or non-fan.

Since I could not interview casual and non-fans to confirm their relationship to *Doctor Who*, I had to deductively infer that they were indeed in one of these two categories. To do so, I established selection criteria based on my own experiences of '*Doctor Who* Twitter'. Selected tweets had to be posted by people who did not claim to be fans of the programme in their biography, who had no reference to the show on their 'layout' (either their profile or cover photo) and appeared not to tweet regularly about the show. The latter criterion was harder to gauge, as casual fans tend to retweet content from the official *Doctor Who* Twitter account, @bbcdoctorwho. If the Twitter user had recently discussed the show in original tweets or in replies to other users, I discarded their tweets from the corpus. For the task at hand, these criteria meant I was collecting tweets from people who could be defined as casual fans or non-fans: they appeared to be solitary in their consumption of the show and did not show any clear sense of belonging to the fandom on their Twitter accounts.

'Once, Upon Time': Waiting for the 'Pay off Later'

If Whovians feared that 'Once, Upon Time' would be the tuning out point of series 13 for 'Not-We' audiences, casual and non-fans themselves may have not seen the situation in quite this way. Some tweets were obviously clear in expressing enjoyment or dislike of the instalment. Some praised the episode as well as the series, with users claiming *Flux* was epic and that the show was at its best. These compliments sometimes came at the expense of showrunner Chris Chibnall, with comments

---

[*] I collected the first sixty-five tweets published by casual and non-fans as well as occasional self-replies (also known as 'threads'), for a total of seventy-two tweets.

praising his talent in long-form storytelling while also taking a shot at his work on the previous two series: 'Story, suspense, twists, teases and development. Where the hell has this writing been?! Much much better and for the first time genuinely care about this Doctor #DoctorWhoFlux'. Others, on the other hand, disapproved of the 'disconnected plot' and felt sorry for Whittaker, who, according to them, had suffered 'some very silly plotlines' during her tenure. Not all reactions included discussion (or criticism) of Chibnall's previous work on the show. However, such comparisons with previous series show that *Flux*'s format did not alarm these audiences, but instead actually heightened *Doctor Who*'s perceived quality in their eyes in some cases.

Though a number of casual and non-fans' reactions were unequivocal, ambivalence was prevalent within the tweets that I classified as relevant and thus analysed. More often than not, these audience members' confusion about the plot of 'Once, Upon Time' was central to their arguments, and tainted their comments in unique ways. A few users, for example, mentioned that they enjoyed the episode regardless of how complex the plot was: 'I have pretty much no idea what that was about, what happened or why. But I really enjoyed it #DoctorWhoFlux.' For such viewers, the unravelling threads of the plot were not much of an issue because the episode itself remained engaging. In these cases, users never mentioned how the serialized format impacted on their enjoyment of the series, nor even specified *what* it was they enjoyed about the episode. They appeared to simply be open to what the show could offer them, regardless of the detailed workings of the story's many plot points.

Other viewers criticizing the confusing plot approached the episode with an open disdain for its disjointed nature and its 'too many incoherent threads'. Yet they still acknowledged, through their disappointment in 'Once, Upon Time', that *Flux* had got off to a great start, or that they liked 'the much harsher edge to 13's character' in this third instalment. There appeared to be an overall enjoyment of *Flux* in its more abstracted or branded sense, that is, viewed purely as a new series of *Doctor Who* regardless of its actual content. However, its novel format and the structure of its storytelling did come as a challenge to some viewers. For these Twitter users, *Flux*'s complexity was certainly perceived as a flaw and as something that needed to be dealt with by the end of the series, reflecting fans' worries about the dangers of serialization and narrative complexity.

Though some casual and non-fans were adamant that the programme had 'to undo all the threads and knots for the series to work', most in my Twitter sample presumed that the pay-off for *Flux*'s serialized arc would come at the end of the series, and were perfectly ready to wait it out. For example, one of the users said: '#DoctorWhoFlux is going well so far even if this episode was meh[,] I still think this season can pick itself up and I hope it does but so far I'm enjoying this season especially the Weaping [sic] Angels! Bring on episode 4.' Less committed audiences therefore seemed to believe that the narrative complexity of *Flux* was only temporary or, in some cases, hoped this would be the case: 'A difficult #DoctorWhoFlux to judge on its own terms. Either a lot of this is going to pay off later, if so, great. Or it's not, in which case, what's the point?'. Such expectations are logical enough; after all, a serial like *Flux* should see its main plot threads resolved by the time its ending is reached. This strongly suggested that, at least in my data set, 'Once, Upon Time' did not seem likely to be a tuning out point for casual fan and non-fan audiences. Even if the serialized format was novel for many 'New *Who*' audiences, it is hardly outlandish in the current televisual landscape, especially after the success of UK shows such as *Broadchurch*, *Vigil* or *Line of Duty* and the more general rise of long-form quality TV. The current run of episodes might have been different in terms of themes and atmosphere compared to series 11 and 12, but general audiences appeared to be well accustomed to serialization in a way that fans of the show seemed not to consider when they verbalized their worries.

Flux: A 'Jigsaw Puzzle' to piece together?

Flux's serialized format may not have been out of the ordinary for casual fans and non-fans, but perhaps Chapter 3's maze-like plot was. Because of this, some felt that the abundance of information and the complicated, multi-stranded plotlines were difficult to make sense of, with one user going so far as to remind their followers that '[y]ou can't have a series where every episode is an exhausting mess of plot'. Another user compared the series to a 'jigsaw puzzle', with this metaphor once again counterbalancing criticism of *Flux* and its narrative structure. Audiences were being given pieces of information week after week and, in time, they would be able to put together the bigger picture that was presented. It is possible that, by being more casual viewers of the show, some audience members did not possess detailed knowledge about how a *Doctor Who* story would more usually have been constructed, making it easier for them to remain open to what was coming next, and to stay along for the (narrative) ride.

Serialization, with a synchronized audience following its twists and turns, also enabled all fans – whether committed or casuals – to engage in 'predictive theories',[15] seemingly countering arguments that fan theories would be the preserve of a highly dedicated 'forensic fandom'.[16] As Cory Barker has argued in *Social TV*, audience 'behaviors once considered abnormal ... [e.g.] deep speculating on plotlines ... have been normalized over the last twenty years' or so.[17] If non-fans and fans were temporarily united by *Flux*'s serialized form, it did, however, remain the case that 'explanatory theories' of a different kind were explored by the fandom.[18] Here, longer-term narrative gaps in the show were exploited and explored; 'Once, Upon Time' was interpreted not just as a jigsaw puzzle but also as a puzzle-box TV narrative, with fans speculating that the pregnant Bel would turn out to be the Doctor's mother. But even these fan theories did not remain the sole preserve of a dedicated fandom – for instance, *Hello! Magazine*'s online coverage, certainly not known for being a subcultural fannish space, reported a week after the broadcast of 'Once, Upon Time' that 'fans think they have worked out [a] major plot twist',[19] summarizing a range of fan tweets on the subject of who Bel and Vinder may turn out to be.

Conclusion

Doctor Who: Flux's creation in unprecedented times motivated a change from episodic storytelling to a directly serialized format. After its third Chapter, 'Once, Upon Time', fans became increasingly worried about less dedicated audiences' reception of the serial. Was it all too complex for people who lacked a deeper knowledge of the show?

Without follow-up interviews, establishing whether the reactions that I have studied here were truly those of casual or non-fans was impossible to determine. The selection criteria I put in place when forming my corpus were an attempt to counter this difficulty by setting up deductive criteria through which I could at least reasonably infer casual fan or non-fan status.

And with that proviso in mind, I have analytically identified and examined casual fans' and non-fans' reactions to the third episode of *Flux* on Twitter. Although I also cannot generalize from my seventy-two tweets, it is evident that these inferred casual and non-fans were in fact not massively discouraged by *Doctor Who*'s return to serialization. Reactions were often ambivalent, with people finding good and bad things to say both about the episode and series 13 more generally. Perhaps what these results show, however tentatively, is that fans' worries were most likely an underestimation of other audiences' ability to stick around when strongly serialized plotting deviated from the show's habitual format. Rather than reading *Flux* entirely differently, both contemporaneous casual and dedicated audiences predicted and theorized series 13's future twists, reveals and resolutions. Casual fans' and non-fans' receptions of *Doctor Who* should not and cannot be read off from fan concerns about these audiences' readings, requiring (as presented) their own empirical analysis.

Notes

1. Rob Leane, '*Doctor Who* Producer Hints at Follow-up to Timeless Child Reveal in Series 13', *Radio Times* (23 October 2021): https://www.radiotimes.com/tv/sci-fi/doctor-who-series-13-timeless-child-newsupdate (accessed 9 September 2022).
2. BBC Media Centre, 'Doctor Who: Flux's Cast and Creators Tease Series 13', (24 October 2021): https://www.bbc.co.uk/mediacentre/mediapacks/doctor-who-flux (accessed 9 September 2022).
3. Vivi Theodoropoulou, '"Just to Pique Them": Taking Sides, Social Identity, and Sport Audiences', in *The Routledge Companion to Media Fandom* (New York: Routledge 2018), 221–29.
4. Jonathan Gray, 'New Audiences, New Textualities: Anti-Fans and Non-Fans', *International Journal of Cultural Studies* 6, no. 1 (2003): 74.
5. As seen in John Tulloch, '"We're Only a Speck in the Ocean": The Fans as Powerless Elite', in *Science Fiction Audiences: Watching Doctor Who and Star Trek*, ed. John Tulloch and Henry Jenkins (New York: Routledge, 1995), 144–74; Brigid Cherry, 'Squee, Retcon, Fanwank and the Not-We: Computer-Mediated Discourse and the Online Audience for NuWho', in *Ruminations, Peregrinations and Regenerations: A Critical Approach to Doctor Who*, ed. Chris Hansen (Newcastle upon Tyne: Cambridge Scholars, 2010), 209–32.
6. Tulloch, '"We're Only a Speck in the Ocean"'.
7. Ibid., 149.
8. Cherry, 'Squee, Retcon, Fanwank and the Not-We'.
9. Tulloch, '"We're Only a Speck in the Ocean"'.
10. Cherry, 'Squee, Retcon, Fanwank and the Not-We'.
11. Patrick Mulkern, '*Doctor Who* – Once, Upon Time Review: A Feverish Kaleidoscope Reveals a Few Delicious Gems', *Radio Times* (14 November 2021): https://www.radiotimes.com/tv/sci-fi/doctor-who-once-upon-time-review/ (accessed 9 September 2022).
12. Cherry, 'Squee, Retcon, Fanwank and the Not-We', 212.
13. In *Complex TV* (New York: New York University Press, 2015), Jason Mittell argues that what he terms 'forensic fandom' acts to 'dig deeper … beneath the surface' of narrative complexity (288). The fact that this has become such an accepted mode of fan engagement perhaps helps to explain why fans were concerned that more casual audiences and non-fans would, by contrast, not be interested in drilling into *Flux*'s narrative gaps, strands and mysteries in this way.
14. Axel Bruns and Jean Burgess, 'The Use of Twitter Hashtags in the Formation of Ad Hoc Publics', in *Proceedings of the 6th European Consortium for Political Research (ECPR) General Conference*, ed. Axel Bruns and P. De Wilde (UK: The European Consortium for Political Research (ECPR), 2011), 1–9.
15. José Manuel De Amo and Anastasio Garcia-Roca, 'Mechanisms for Interpretative Cooperation: Fan Theories in Virtual Communities', *Frontiers in Psychology* 12 (2021): 4.
16. Mittell, *Complex TV*, 288.
17. Cory Barker, *Social TV: Multi-Screen Content and Ephemeral Culture* (Jackson: University Press of Mississippi, 2022), 17.
18. Amo and Garcia-Roca, 'Mechanisms for Interpretative Cooperation', 4.
19. Emmy Griffiths, '*Doctor Who:* Fans Think They Have Worked out Major Plot Twist', *Hello Magazine* (22 November 2021): https://www.hellomagazine.com/film/20211122126786/doctor-who-major-plot-twist-vinder-bel/ (accessed 9 January 2022).

SECTION THREE

Doctor Who Fandom in the 21st Century

Joy Piedmont

When *Doctor Who* returned to television in 2005 it attracted an entirely new generation of fans, which isn't surprising given the 16 years that had passed since the end of the classic series. However, the fans who came of age with modern *Doctor Who* aren't only distinguishable by their age; they are unique in that their fandom grew with the rise of social media networks, and their online interactions – creating, critiquing, debating, squeeing, remixing – influenced and shaped modern fandom.

This generation of fans is diverse in practically every demographic category, and subsequently, they've given voice to a way of viewing the show that incorporates politics and identity. Feminism, queer theory and race are just a few lenses that modern viewers use to engage with the show. Likewise, fans from geographic regions usually ignored by mainstream Western markets have formed their own ways of interacting with and interpreting the show. Critical fandom is the default for this generation – accepting the show at face value is not enough for fans who crave deep thinking about *Doctor Who* in social networks.

Despite their elevation in the past decade and a half, the voices of fans who come from marginalized social groups still have to fight to be heard and validated. In-person conventions and online spaces can still be unfriendly to people who wish to examine what the show is saying about identity and politics, and how it's doing so. Inclusion in a collection of essays like this lifts up those voices and viewpoints, and will hopefully encourage future fans to continue to engage in critical fandom.

Chapter 20
Tumblr fandom is an unknowable anti-monolith cryptid by Lena Barkin

Original to this volume

Social networking sites each have unique cultures and norms. Lena Barkin takes a close look at Tumblr to explore how its niche customs interact with Doctor Who *fandom and how they inform each other.*

The *Doctor Who* universe and fandom can sometimes seem, once you dive deep enough into it, like a cosmic eldritch monster. The breadth of material available under the *Doctor Who* umbrella – including television, film, audio dramas, comics, novels and spinoffs – lends itself to strange, dark corners and infinitesimally small detours. This is also a quality that makes it an ideal fan property to map the effects and nuances of different subcommunities. The writers and artists and fans and academics just keep creating and creating and creating, adding to a behemoth that cannot be held in the mind all at once. Although around for a considerably shorter time, the massive size and influence of the social media platform Tumblr can appear a similarly impenetrable mess. The social intricacies of the website, combined with its power to broadcast to many alike minds at once, create an instantly recognizable mode of engagement while juggling multiple communities and aesthetics. The similarities between the two make them ideal for academic exploration. Using two case studies of viral Tumblr memes, I intend to illustrate how *Doctor Who* Tumblr fandom functions as both an active and evolving in-group as well as a much wider mass pop culture touchstone.

While much important scholarship has already been written about the role of fandom as part of the essential fabric of the Tumblr community, there is little about how the competing dynamics of Tumblr play out within a single fan community. A Tumblr user may only interact with one aspect of the show, such as the audio spinoff 'Faction Paradox', without ever having seen an episode of the parent series – yet their participation within the Faction Paradox community can establish norms and interpretations across the wider fandom. Classic *Doctor Who* fandom, the section of fans who focus on the show during its first run between 1963 and 1989, enjoys a limited but healthy community, as artists, writers, commenters and theorists rotate in and out of the interest and find a backlog of older posts.

Doctor Who fans on Tumblr have a unique experience that combines niche knowledge, widespread recognition and infinite iterations. Tumblr acts as a web where *Doctor Who* subcultures can observe and interact with each other, 'continually informed and reinforced' by each other, much like the wider structure of Tumblr.[1] Within smaller subsections of fandom, new interpretations and considerations of the show and its characters can be explored and solidified, creating a tight-knit community that feels inclusive and personal. *Doctor Who* posts can also take off across the site, appealing to Tumblr users through various layers and site markers that broadens the reach of the show far beyond what might be assumed.

An introduction to social media chaos: Tumblr

Many find Tumblr difficult to navigate.[2] That is because Tumblr is a cesspool of inside jokes, obscure facts, media commentary and aesthetically pleasing photography. It's important to understand this at the very beginning: tumblr dot com is a disaster area.

Instead of having all information and discussions accessible in one central place, like web forums or other popular blogs, Tumblr functions instead as an ever-shifting series of posts and pictures with changing strands of commentary. The structure of the site ensures 'potentially countless threads of constantly transforming, multimodal, multiauthored texts'.[3] The end result is a 'digital public scrapbook that users collectively create and curate'.[4] A user's Dash, or homepage, gets constantly updated with a stream of text, audio and visual. Each user who reblogs the original post creates their own thread, meaning that a single post can go in five different directions parallel to each other.

By design, the site is incapable of any sort of monolith of opinion or thought, instead branching off into corners and small groups that nevertheless feel tied to the wider imagined community through affect and style. As the editors of *a tumblr book* write in their intro, the 'experience of Tumblr is the experience of multiplicity'.[5] The site emphasizes culture jamming, the incredibly niche juxtaposed with the widely broad and popular, the aesthetic photo followed by a treatise on compulsory heterosexuality followed by a 2 a.m. shower thought that entirely upends the English language. Tumblr not only lives but *thrives* in multiplicities, each post like an alternate stream of the same initial conversation. Each additional comment slightly changes the post itself. There is no unifying experience of the site. Each user's interaction can be said to be unique to Tumblr yet creates a commonly held notion of the Tumblr experience.

Community on Tumblr can therefore be incredibly small and niche, as circles of mutuals trade posts and jokes back and forth, or unfathomably large, as a single post with broad appeal gets hundreds and thousands of comments from across the spectrum of users (Figure 20.1).

'Adric Becomes Hella Dope: Swagric'

One of the trademark experiences on Tumblr is watching popular memes reiterate across multiple fandoms. On April Fool's Day 2013, at the peak of online *Supernatural* fandom, a single image of actor Misha Collins flooded Tumblr like a tidal wave. Hundreds of fans had switched their icons to the same photo, popular posts were re-edited to include his face, and some users reported that their 'entire tumblr dash' was 'full of posts from "Misha"'.[6] Just the image of his face became a reactive source of humour. The 'Mishapocalypse' dominated posts and chatter on the site for days, equally from those who were celebratory and derogatory. The atemporal nature of Tumblr meant that detritus and straggler posts lingered around for months.

internationalspacehobo:

> *afixwithsontarans*:
>
>> unspeakable things happened in the fandom today
>
> Everyone take a moment to appreciate that New Whovians probably think of the classic who fandom like a bunch of serious old people
>
> but actually most of us have long since transcendet any notion of sanity

Figure 20.1 Accessed from smooth-mccrimmonal, reblogged from untimelylord.

Six months later, on 30 September, a much less organized but equally spirited copycat meme rippled through the *Doctor Who* fandom. The 'Adricpocalypse' drew from the 'Mishapocalypse' in the fandom's obsession with a singular character and played on the specificities of that character's position within the show and fandom, making the joke even more insular and abstract. Adric (Matthew Waterhouse), the 1980s' companion of both the Fourth (Tom Baker) and Fifth Doctor (Peter Davison), was written as a young mathematical genius. Perhaps as a reaction to seeing an emotionally turbulent, stubborn, socially awkward nerd reflected to them on screen, many fans never really took to the character. Complaints about the character being irritating and whiny often dominated conversation, when fans bothered to mention him at all. Adric, in fact, was one of the only major companions to be killed on-screen. At the end of the serial *Earthshock*, the spaceship he was stranded on crashed into Earth during the prehistoric era, killing the dinosaurs. This is all important information to know, because posts made during the Adricpocalypse ranged from light puns on his name (Adric/Radric) to 'The Adric tag has never been more alive'/'Unlike Adric'.

Sometimes other posts made weeks before by non-Whovians would get coincidentally roped into the game, such as a post including a photo from 'All My Friends Are Dead'. While not intentionally a *Doctor Who* reference, knowing the circumstances of Adric's death, and the cartoon of a sad dinosaur on the cover, meant that it would get wide circulation within the *Who* Tumblr community. In this way, 'secular' posts can take on an extra meaning to fans and become popular within fannish circles unintentionally.

Simultaneously, fandom-specific posts help generate new meanings within the fandom itself. The fandom becomes more tightly bonded as the same post might appear on your dash four or five times with slightly different commentary or insight. The proliferation of photos and texts about Adric, commonly construed as widely despised by fandom, worked to raise his social capital from whiny brat to meme hero. As humor on Tumblr often veers toward the 'dark, weird, blithe, and inappropriate', the morbid tenor of many jokes counterintuitively convey affection and even reverence for the character.[7] The memes around the gut-punch of his unfortunate and untimely demise were actually benefits to the Tumblr crowd. In creating the Adricpocalypse, the character's annoyingness became his greatest strength, and it worked as a way for the community to claim him as one of its own. His image as an outsider and the dejected loser of *Doctor Who* fandom makes him an easy character for a Tumblr user to identify with, as a social platform that positions itself as a haven for the queer, disabled, disenfranchised and abnormal (Figure 20.2).

Adric both theoretically and practically joined the ranks of other beloved Tumblr *Doctor Who* memes, recognized within fan circles for their 'cursed' energy and obscurity to non-fans. By forcing constant reiteration and reinterpretation, the Adricpocalypse ascribed new positive meanings and associations with the character. Adric was no longer simply a companion of *Doctor Who* but a symbol of the Classic *Who* fandom within the wider *Who* community. As Tumblr is less about direct interaction, and more about 'signaling shared affinities to other users', the circular broadcasting and rebroadcasting of Adric as a symbol of fandom joy and source of creativity both rehabilitated the character and made him a focal point for fandom.[8]

The cursed 1980s robot that wouldn't die: Kamelion

As much as ultra-specific memes are able to knit threads of fandom closer together, it's equally possible for a meme to go far beyond its originally intended audience.[9] A post made for aesthetic reasons could be co-opted by a popular fandom and reach new heights, or travel through multiple fandom groups as each takes their turn at interpreting it. Fandom posts are also able to achieve greater appeal through tapping into wider Tumblr trends and aesthetics.

For this case study, I'm able to use a personal example. In 2013, I spent my free time wisely by screencapping episodes of *Doctor Who* and applying quotes from the TV show *Futurama*. There was

unexpectedkeys:

An Unearthly Adric with a side of Planet of the "Asian Child" and The Colin Invasion of the 70's: a visual guide to what happened amongst Tumblr's Classic Whovians yesterday.
(Yes, that is Creeper Eight advising Adric on how to become a weird meme while Adric looks slightly uncomfortable with this whole situation.)

Figure 20.2 Accessed from smooth-mccrimmonal, reblogged from reiqenarataka.

usually some narrative or character reason to tie the scene together – one saw the Seventh Doctor (Sylvester McCoy), known for his malapropisms, quoting galactic space idiot Zapp Brannigan making a mess of a metaphor. While the blog was moderately successful with other Classic *Who* blogs, one post, in particular, exploded in popularity about a year after it was posted and never stopped. The post features the Fifth Doctor and his robot companion Kamelion. Kamelion is quoting *Futurama*'s Bender,

Figure 20.3 Accessed from doctorwhorama.

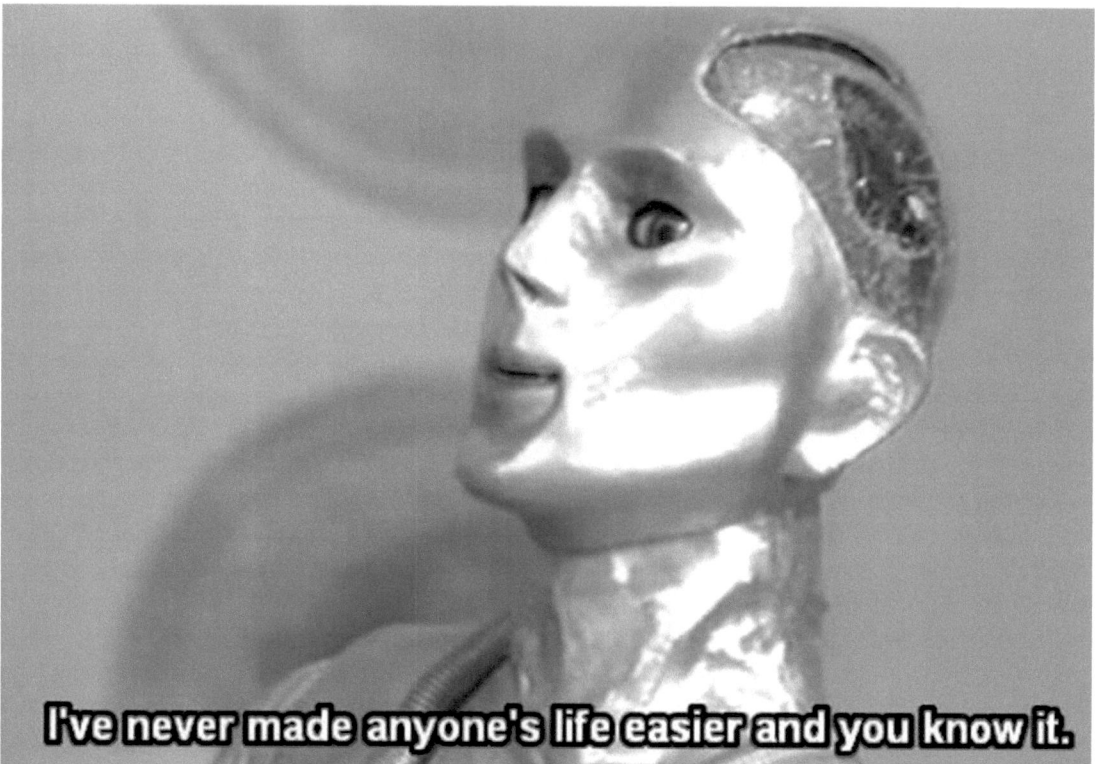

 arabellesicardi

im the robot

 titleknown

Again, this is *even funnier* if you know what a fucking *production nightmare,* with *a possible curse* attached to it no less, this robot prop was for the Doctor Who crew…

 bogleech

I want to know about the cursed robot

Figure 20.4 Accessed from doctorwhorama.

challenging Fry's (/the Doctor's) assumption that robots are supposed to be useful and belligerently claiming that he's 'never made anyone's life easier'. As of writing it has 359K notes, gaining a few each day (Figures 20.3 and 20.4).

The 'success' of the post can be attributed to multiple factors. One, the dialogue itself is humorous, even if you don't know it's stolen from *Futurama* and combined with *Doctor Who*. The belligerence of a non-human being in a 1980s vaporwave style ties into many of Tumblr's affinity for absurd, contrarian characters and post-modern comedy.[10] Even without the context of fandom or the shows it derived from, the post feels exclusively Tumblr for the effect it has on its readers. Potentially, this is why it was reblogged by a popular aesthetic Tumblr blogger and regularly gained 20k overnight.

On top of this, those in the know got added social cachet of identifying *Doctor Who* as its source. When *Star Trek* actor and internet geek king Wil Wheaton also reblogged the post, the content returned to the wider circles of Tumblr nerds and aficionados who were aware of classic *Who*, if not devoted fans. The post gained another dimension when a fan added an extensive explanation on the mysterious origins of Kamelion, how complicated the robot had been to work with and the mysterious number of production deaths connected to it, known as the 'Kamelion Curse'. While the historical details have been accurately refuted, the good story added an edge of deep lore and horror of cursed objects, two more staples of Tumblr culture, while also deepening the original message – a knowing joke that had been intentionally built into the post.

The post was flexible enough for users to appreciate it on multiple levels, as visually in line with Tumblr aesthetics, humour and the love of storytelling, as a fan of *Doctor Who* or *Futurama* who appreciated the interplay between the shows, or as a Classic *Who* fan who could dig into the deeper history hinted at by the joke. By moving back and forth between these different levels or modes of Tumblr, the post enjoyed success over and over, as different threads of conversation highlighted or played with different aspects of the original post. The most prevalent version of the post includes a detailed account of the 'haunting' as well as personal effect ('im the robot') and canonizing the '*Doctor Who*'-ishness of lore.

In many ways, the lore of Kamelion becomes less tied to *Doctor Who* and more to the lore of Tumblr itself, representative of the stories, aesthetics and humour that predominate on the site. While the origins of the post are deeply tied to the show, and couldn't have been produced by anyone other than a fan – something that Tumblr users are keenly aware of and savvy to – the ultimate effect is one where Kamelion alone is not a viral post but one piece of the viral fabric of Tumblr.

The range of aesthetics and styles that can be ascribed to a single Tumblr post highlights the flexibility and dynamics at play within the larger community. Media texts and their associated characters, jokes and fandom affectations have the opportunity to reach audiences far outside their predictable channels. Through the Kamelion post's popularity, *Doctor Who* broadly, and the Fifth Doctor era specifically, became more recognized and understood.

Conclusion

Not every Tumblr post fits neatly into the two models of viral post or secluded in-joke. But the two case studies do provide examples for how Tumblr is both a close, small community of *Doctor Who* devotees and a large ever-expanding pool of general *Doctor Who* know-how. The flexibility and breadth of Tumblr ensures that multiple truths can exist at once: the site can work to knit together small groups of people in shared interest and passions, and it can also broadcast a single thing to vast amounts of people.

Fandom experiences on Tumblr are by nature anti-monolithic – there is no one dominant way to engage with or represent fandom. Instead, many things together – art, memes, fiction, meta, historical facts – make up a steady stream of content from all kinds of tributaries. Tumblr memes, in their inscrutability and absurdity, often work both ways to reinforce smaller communities and create larger site-wide shared aesthetics and humour. The memes proliferate and permutate seemingly instantaneously, like Tribbles, always in conversation and contextualizing each other in a never-ending torrent of photos, jokes and commentary. While *Doctor Who* and Tumblr, like many ancient all-seeing all-knowing gods, should be approached carefully and respectfully, the opportunities for productive community are vast and varied.

Notes

1. Allison McCracken, Alexander Cho, Louisa Stein and Indira Neill Hoch, 'You Must Be New Here: An Introduction', in *a tumblr book*, ed. Allison McCracken, Alexander Cho, Louisa Stein and Indira Neill Hoch (Ann Arbor, MI: University of Michigan Press, 2020), 1–19.
2. Taking off the works of others, I have opted to refer to the site with a capitalized T while referring to individual user blogs as tumblrs.
3. McCracken, Cho, Stein and Hoch, 'You Must Be New Here: An Introduction'.
4. Ibid.
5. Ibid.
6. 'Mishapocalypse', in *Fanlore*: https://fanlore.org/wiki/Mishapocalypse (accessed 15 January 2020).
7. The-Cimmerrians, 'Divine Fools and Ridiculous Mystics: Tumblr Humor as an Act of Defiance', in *a tumblr book*, ed. Allison McCracken, Alexander Cho, Louisa Stein and Indira Neill Hoch (Ann Arbor, MI: University of Michigan Press, 2020), 75–80.
8. Nicholas Proferes and Katherine E. Morrissey, 'Lost in the "Dash": How Tumblr Fosters Virtuous Cycles of Content and Community', in *a tumblr book*, ed Allison McCracken, Alexander Cho, Louisa Stein and Indira Neill Hoch (Ann Arbor, MI: University of Michigan Press, 2020), 23–36.
9. The reblog function in Tumblr makes it so that on your own dash you often see posts that have travelled from the farthest reaches of the website (roughly estimated by the number of 'notes' – likes or reblogs – a post has received).
10. For a more thorough description of the style of Tumblr comedy, The-Cimmerians essay (cited above) in *a tumblr book* is a good place to start. She describes the humour of the site as 'vast and multifaceted, encompassing satire, sarcasm, meta, self-referential analysis, meme development, parody, dadaesque juxtaposition of the sacred and the profane, obscure knowledge deployment, puns, minimalism, and a thousand other forms as diverse as the posts themselves' (79). Defying any singular description, one knows Tumblr comedy when they see it, and it's hard to explain to others.

Chapter 21
The police box

From 'Doctor Who's TARDIS Has a Different Meaning for Black Fans' by Constance Gibbs[*]

First published 2018

> *Merchandise featuring the Doctor's TARDIS is ubiquitous among* Doctor Who *fans; but how can we reconcile that symbol with the violent history of policing in Black communities? Constance Gibbs explores the history of the 'police box', policing, and proposes a new way for the show to utilize the TARDIS.*

As a *Doctor Who* fan, I buy Whovian-themed merch to rep my nerd set in the streets and convention floors. One of my favourite purchases is a TARDIS bomber jacket, emblazoned with the words 'police box' on the back. With a few *Doctor Who* patches ironed on – a touch of circular Gallifreyan over the elbow completes the look – the jacket lets me wear my fandom in the most stylish way possible.

As a Black *Doctor Who* fan, my love for this jacket is something of a conundrum. I didn't realize it until my brother saw me wearing it and said with alarm, '*POLICE*?' He isn't a nerd, and hadn't even heard of *Doctor Who* when I tried to explain. All he saw was 'police box' in big white letters.

Police officers aren't a source of comfort, safety and respect in the Black community, and many others. The word 'police' instils fear. The word 'police' conjures memories of men in uniform murdering Black people for doing as little as selling loose cigarettes – or holding a wallet, violating traffic laws, jaywalking, take your pick. When a Black person sees another Black person wearing a jacket with the noun of an agitator proudly written on the back, it sends them into shock.

Doctor Who's relationship with its Black companions and characters further complicates the situation. If I could've told my brother that the show was super-inclusive and that Black characters were a central part of the series and its history, it might have been an easier sell. He might have actually heard of it before.

---

[*]Originally published on Polygon, 2018.

But the British series dates back to a time when Black actors were still anomalies on TV. In 1963, the year *Doctor Who* began and the height of the American civil rights movement, Cicely Tyson had only just become the first Black actress to star as a regular supporting character on a TV show. To *Doctor Who*'s detriment with regard to Black nerds looking for representation, Nichelle Nichols began starring as Lieutenant Nyota Uhura on *Star Trek* in 1966. British television wouldn't see its first all-Black cast until *The Fosters* in 1976.

Doctor Who didn't get its first recurring Black character until the 2005 reboot. Mickey Smith (Noel Clarke), the bumbling boyfriend of lead character Rose Tyler, was dismissed and insulted for much of his run on the show. Even after his character developed into a badass with a big gun, he was put on a bus with the rest of the Tenth Doctor's squad when actor David Tennant left the show.

Martha Jones (Freema Agyeman), the Tenth Doctor's next leading lady, lived in white companion Rose's shadow for an entire season. Her unrequited crush on the Doctor was only ever outlined in comparison to the epic, tragic love story between Rose and the Doctor. Martha's extreme competence left her sacrificing herself, saving the world and proving herself over and over again with little acknowledgement from the Doctor. Later, she was pair the spares'd with Mickey when Tennant's run came to an end. (We won't talk about how *convenient* it was for the show to marry off the two Black companions, who only maybe had one interaction prior to that point. I waffle between 'whatever, they have just enough in common for it to work' and being annoyed about it.)

Series 8's Danny Pink (Samuel Anderson) was fine (and *foinnne*) until he met the Twelfth Doctor (Peter Capaldi). Danny, boyfriend to Twelve's companion Clara, seemed to be meant as a contrast to Mickey. He was more competent and initially less irritating, but not at all interested in space travel, saving the planet or his girlfriend travelling with the Doctor.

Bill Potts (Pearl Mackie) had her stylish fashion sense, her open queerness, her amazing curiosity and her perfectly moisturized afro going for her. Yet her exit left a sour taste in my mouth. It's not enough that she was killed and turned into a Cyberman (like Danny two seasons before her) and then saved, only to run off with a supernaturally enhanced girl she'd met just once (like Clara one season before her). Worse still, she was shot in the chest by an alien with blue skin. Earlier in the season, she'd been accused of being racist against a blue-skinned alien. All this in the heat of a 'Blue Lives Matter' counter moment.

Like the United States, the UK has issues with police violence and brutality, which have been more exposed than ever in the age of smartphones and streaming video. But as my fellow Black *Doctor Who* podcast hosts witnessed firsthand in late 2016, Black Lives Matter protests are just as common there as here. Soon after, there were protests for Edson Da Costa, 25, who died in police custody in June 2017, and Sarah Reed, 32, who was found dead in her cell at London's Holloway Prison while awaiting trial. The examples don't stop there. The police violence against Black people in the UK is not as frequent or as visible as in America, but it is still an issue. If the Doctor existed in our world, could he or she land the TARDIS at the site of that protest to help or offer advice? Or would the appearance of the 'police'-branded spaceship be met with the same fear and suspicion as when real police arrive?

The police box TARDIS is a symbol I took for granted as a Whovian, a symbol I've been convinced to love by (mostly) great writing, lovable characters (even when they're *not* written well) and time travel hijinks. When my brother revealed that it could mean something else to non-fans, *even for a second*, it nearly broke my heart.

By the 1960s, there were about 685 police boxes still operating in the UK. When *Doctor Who* premiered in 1963, the TARDIS chose that form to fit with the time period. Later, the show's lore explained that the TARDIS can blend in with its surroundings because of its 'chameleon circuit', which allows it to transform into anything that would be inconspicuous in the setting to which the Doctor is traveling. But our Doctor's TARDIS has a broken chameleon circuit, forcing it to stay as the iconic blue box (though with a perception filter keeping, say, people in ancient times from finding a twentieth-century police box out of the ordinary). At one point in the series, the Doctor tried to fix the feature, to no avail. He later claimed that he likes it the way it is.

And so the police box has become a staple of *Doctor Who*. The Doctor changes. The companions cycle out. The enemies evolve and morph. The logo is updated. The theme tune gets reorchestrated. But throughout *Doctor Who*'s history, the TARDIS has been a constant. It exists in all of time and space simultaneously. It's such a staple of the show that it's the BBC, not the Metropolitan Police, that owns the image of the blue police box.

Despite it being a shapeshifting, sentient spaceship-slash-time-machine, decades of *Doctor Who* scripts have insisted that the TARDIS is always going to be a wooden blue police box that is bigger on the inside.

So instead of changing the symbol, why not grapple with it on the show itself?

Doctor Who has rarely dealt with race. The Tenth Doctor dismissed Martha's concerns about her Blackness in Shakespearean London. As Twelve, he punched a racist Victorian person. But now that the Doctor is a woman – who will likely deal with sexism she's never experienced in her previous male incarnations – there's an open door to talk about race, too. The TARDIS has landed at many different historical and cultural tipping points: the eruption of Vesuvius, various points during the Second World War, the women's suffrage movement and dozens of futuristic revolutions. I'd ask why the Doctor can't land during the 1963 Bristol Bus Boycotts or the American civil rights movement happening across the pond, but it goes back to the original point: The TARDIS wouldn't look like safety to those Black people.

This season, Tosin Cole stars as the fifth Black cast member and third Black full-time companion on *Doctor Who*. To any other character fleeing from an alien, running into a box that says 'police' might look like safety. But what if Cole's character saw the words 'police box' and hesitated to enter? Trapped between an attacking alien and presumably white law enforcement, many Black people would probably say 'screw it' and choose the alien.

I want *Doctor Who* to deal with the TARDIS' cultural meaning because, as a devout fan, I love the TARDIS and don't want it to change. The image of the Doctor's police box makes me happy (which explains how I wound up with the aforementioned jacket featuring it, as well as a blanket, a poster of van Gogh's exploding TARDIS, a light-up desk trinket, a pin, a cookie jar and a laptop decal). If I were the type to get tattoos, I'd probably get one of a TARDIS flying through the vortex. I am attached to the image.

But I also have to grapple with the TARDIS' extra meaning now. I toss my jacket on in my inner-city neighbourhood, and I wonder if someone on the elevator in my building is going to ask if I'm making a political statement in favour of police – like my brother did that day. I think of the *Doctor Who* fans who hate that the Doctor is a woman and tell me I'm 'overthinking it' because it's just a show about time travel. They don't need politics and 'PC culture' in their science fiction!

Being a Black *Doctor Who* fan is constantly wondering if it's just you seeing something as racist and dismissive or if you're thinking about it too much. It is also knowing that if the Doctor *were* to show up on your doorstep, there aren't many places in the past where you'd be welcome, but many places in the present you'd love to escape from.

Doctor Who fandom, especially for a Black viewer, is about looking to the future. Its producers are making strides in the gender problem the show has had since its inception with the introduction of the first female Doctor. They have also brought on two companions of colour, a first in itself – including the first ever South Asian actress to be a lead on the show. There will be a Black director, a Black composer, a South Asian writer and a Black woman writer on staff this year. These choices give me a lot of hope for the show, and I hope the new showrunner and direction of the series give weight to all these identities. If they can, maybe I can wear my TARDIS jacket proudly in the streets without fear.

Chapter 22

Space isn't always for everyone: How unconscious racial bias in *Doctor Who* scripts affects fan perception of companions of colour by Amanda-Rae Prescott

Original to this volume

Everyone has internal biases that influence our opinion and emotional response to media. In her essay, Amanda-Rae Prescott's close reading of the BIPOC companions in modern Doctor Who *demonstrates the effects of internalized racism and proposes solutions for the future of the show.*

Mickey Smith's (Noel Clarke) introduction in 'Rose' charted a new era in the on-screen representation of *Doctor Who*. Actors of colour for the first time were now being cast as allies and even companions of the Doctor. Despite the years, and differences in writing staff, behind each character of colour, they are still the target of racist sentiment in some sections of fandom. Why do some believe Ryan (Tosin Cole) has 'no personality'? Why do some believe Martha (Freema Agyeman) was an inferior replacement for Rose (Billie Piper)? Why are Yaz (Mandip Gill) and Bill (Pearl Mackie) often depicted only as queer women and not as queer women of colour? This chapter will examine the plot trajectories of the main companions of colour in order to highlight where white screenwriters inserted unconscious or overt racial bias along with fandom reactions from social media which highlight the result of those writing choices.

Mickey Smith was first introduced as Rose's boyfriend in 'Rose', Russell T Davies' pilot for New *Who*. At the end of the episode, the Ninth Doctor (Christopher Eccleston) refused to invite Mickey into the TARDIS because Mickey was naturally suspicious of Nine's motives and alien status. Nine calls Mickey 'the idiot' in 'Boom Town' after accidentally crashing into a woman, which solidified the negative fan perception of Mickey. Not only is this insult ableist but it's also racist when you consider the history of Black men being deemed of inferior intelligence to whites as a justification for slavery and racial discrimination. There is also the stereotyping trend of viewing Black teens and young adults as more 'mature' for their relative age compared to white teens and young adults.[1] While series 1 overall allowed Rose to make mistakes or show youthful attitudes, these same tendencies displayed by Mickey were portrayed in scripts as negatives. While Mickey was not the main companion at this point in the story, this is an early example of the kind of writing that can influence white fans' unconscious bias.

Martha Jones became the first Black companion in series 3, which began airing in March 2007. Martha's debut was ground-breaking for *Doctor Who*, as this was the first time Black Whovians could see their racial identity represented in the series. Many sci-fi fans of colour started watching the series just because Martha was introduced. While the show was promoting Martha as a positive addition to the canon, many white fans believed Martha was an 'inferior' replacement to Rose. One fan reflecting on the fifteenth anniversary of Martha's debut said her introduction was 'The moment the *Doctor Who* fandom became racist. And still to this day, is'.[2]

Racism is baked into the writing of Martha's decision to leave the TARDIS, even though it was presented as stress from saving the world. During 'The End of the World' and 'The Last of the Time Lords', the Master (John Simm) kidnapped and enslaved her family, as part of his path to world domination. In the process, the Master wiped Japan out of existence and only Martha lived to tell the tale. This action is framed as generally evil rather than a specific racial genocide. Slavery being a central plot point is important because it cannot be separated from the context of the British Empire's role in expanding chattel slavery during the seventeenth and eighteenth centuries before British involvement in the international slave trade was banned in 1807.[3] Martha's experience of extreme racial trauma has to have been part of her decision to stop travelling in the TARDIS.

Stitch, a long-time African-American fan of Martha, wrote in reflecting upon their time reading racist comments in fandom: 'Martha Jones saved the world (in a major way) and she still wasn't good enough for the Doctor or the fandom.'[4] Martha's critics still leave disparaging comments such as calling her a 'nothing character'[5] as replies to announcements for new comics or Big Finish releases.

Bill Potts was introduced as *Doctor Who*'s second Black companion and first Black queer companion in the series ten premiere 'The Pilot' in April 2017. Unlike Martha, Bill had to share screen time with Nardole (Matt Lucas). Fandom's reaction to Bill was more positive compared to Martha's debut. There are a few possible reasons for this. First, *Doctor Who* had gained millions of viewers internationally in the decade since Martha's debut. Second, antiracist efforts in *Doctor Who* fandom led by fans of colour over the years led to increased awareness of racist attitudes in fandom. During Bill's era racism was manifested through white fans' ignoring Bill's identity as a Black woman while fully perceiving her as a lesbian. Many fans of colour were horrified to watch Bill get shot and turned into a Cyberman in 'World Enough and Time'/'The Doctor Falls'. Some white fans did not understand that while this episode had good moments for other characters, the scenario would remind Black Whovians in particular of news footage from police brutality cases. While *Doctor Who* has had many characters killed in the past, these scenes are even more traumatizing for fans of colour who watch as an escape from the stress caused by racism.

Chris Chibnall took over as showrunner from Steven Moffat and expanded the diversity of the TARDIS. He introduced Jodie Whittaker as the Thirteenth Doctor as well as two new companions of colour. Ryan Sinclair was the first Black male companion and Yasmin 'Yaz' Khan was the first South Asian companion. Rounding out Thirteen's companion 'fam' was Graham O'Brien (Bradley Walsh). Graham, an older white man, was Ryan's grandfather by marriage. Graham's inclusion inevitably reduced screen time for the companions of colour.

A small but very vocal section of fandom to this day refuses to acknowledge Chibnall's era of *Doctor Who* because it is 'too woke' because of Ryan and Yaz's presence (and likely Thirteen as well).[6] 'Woke' as a phrase comes from the term 'stay woke', which was initially coined by African-American racial justice activists to mean staying vigilant to institutional racism. However, 'woke' is now regularly used as an insult to mean something is too liberal, antiracist or pro LGBTQ.[7]

Fandom's opinion on Ryan varied throughout the course of series 11 and 12. Early on, many claimed Ryan had no personality even though both Ryan and Graham grieving over Graces' death was a major subplot in series 11. Ryan critics to this day believe he was 'the worst' companion.[8] Granted, any *Doctor Who* season with more than one companion means that character development may not be evenly distributed. However, despite Ryan's contributions to the team – Ryan figured out in 'Arachnids in the UK' that the spiders didn't like the beat vibrations from the Stormzy song he played – selective memory plays a key role in how racist fans perceive plotlines.

Opinions on Yaz changed over time in fandom primarily because later episodes in series 11 and 12 hinted towards Yaz having feelings for Thirteen and vice versa. (Fans gave their relationship the nickname 'Thasmin', a portmanteau of their names.) Initially, people believed Yaz was not fully fleshed out during series 11 but complaints about her character shifted towards blaming writers for lack of development or screen time. Some Yaz critics still insist she has 'the same personality as a board of card board'[9] despite Chibnall expanding her backstory and the Thasmin plotline. The 2022 specials 'Eve of the Daleks' and 'Legend of the Sea Devils' specials solidified Yaz's status in fandom as a queer companion.

The series 13 'Flux' storyline once again reduced screen time for Yaz. Dan (John Bishop) is a middle-aged white man from Manchester who has his house disappear into time. While white fans praised Dan for representing working-class Brits, Whovians of Colour speculated that Chibnall caved to pressure from misogynist fans who didn't want Thirteen and Yaz to travel in the TARDIS by themselves.

The BBC announced in May 2022 that Ncuti Gatwa, a Black and Scottish actor, was taking over the TARDIS after Jodie Whitaker's departure. The announcement instantly led to racist backlash[10] as critics of Chibnall's diversity efforts expected Russell T Davies to roll back these efforts. One UK rightwing commentator said Gatwa's casting was the result of 'tokenistic diversity first policies'.[11]

Conclusion

Although *Doctor Who* is transmitted to a global audience, white screenwriters often write characters of colour from a white and culturally British point of view. This phenomenon is called the white gaze or white default.[12] Unconscious racial bias is commonly defined as the negative stereotypes and attitudes that people have internalized about people from a different race or ethnicity than them.[13] These phenomena influence racist attitudes in *Doctor Who* scripts which then impact fan perception of companions of colour.

Institutional racism in the UK also plays a role in the decisions white creatives make on *Doctor Who*. UK screenwriters of colour in the UK make up a very tiny fraction of the entire industry and at the BBC specifically. Data collected by the UK industry group the Creative Industry Network show that British people of colour were represented on screen 20.9 per cent of the time, while British people of colour represented 12 per cent of behind-the-scenes or off-screen talent.[14] A survey of British actors of colour conducted in 2021 revealed that 79 per cent of the actors of colour polled feel that they are offered stereotypes of their race or ethnic group.[15] The UK has no equivalent to US and international networks explicitly devoted to audiences of colour such as Black Entertainment Television and Telemundo and studios run by people of colour such as Shondaland and Tyler Perry. This is important to note not only for American Whovians of Colour but also for international Whovians of Colour living in countries where their ethnicity is the majority of the population. There are several UK efforts designed to help creatives of colour break into the television and film industry, but these initiatives are frequently targeted towards entry-level positions and/or technical behind-the-scenes jobs.

Many of the plots that have resulted in criticism from fans of colour are the result of the *Doctor Who* production largely failing to hire screenwriters of colour. It was not until series 11 that screenwriters of colour, Malorie Blackman and Vinay Patel, were hired. This is important to highlight because often racism in scripts can go unrecognized by white production staff. In some cases, *Doctor Who* scripts end up perpetuating racist stereotypes when an actor of colour is cast, because the role was written with a colourblind lens.[16] In addition, *Doctor Who* is not known to use sensitivity readers or historical consultants of colour in their screenwriting process to avoid stereotyping and insensitivity.

What can white fans do to change their way of thinking about the companions of colour? First of all, reading more blog posts, social media comments, podcasts and other fandom content by Whovians of Colour will help you understand how non-white viewers interpret storylines. This is especially important when it comes to constructive critiques of racism or unconscious bias in storytelling. Second, fans should interrogate whether their reactions to plotlines are due to double standards as a result of unconscious bias. Deciding that they would have the same reaction to a plotline or a conversation if it was a white companion isn't enough. White viewers must interrogate their internalized racism.

Russell T Davies' return to being *Doctor Who* showrunner is being hailed in some quarters as a reversal of Chibnall's era. Whovians of Colour are hoping that Davies has had time to reflect on their critiques of Martha's season and to cast more companions of colour along with the first Doctor of Colour to pilot the TARDIS.

Notes

1. Stacey Patton, 'In America, Black Children Don't Get to Be Children', *The Washington Post* (WP Company, 26 November 2014): https://www.washingtonpost.com/opinions/in-america-black-children-dont-get-to-be-children/2014/11/26/a9e24756-74ee-11e4-a755-e32227229e7b_story.html (accessed 9 Aug 2022).
2. Two T's biggest fan (@mehehhhmeh), 'The moment the Doctor Who fandom became racist. And still to this day, is'. Twitter, 30 March 2022: (3:16 p.m.), https://twitter.com/mehehhhmeh/status/1509550186892300301?s=21&t=ZvRgQWSNj50HPEAN1oTZaA (accessed 9 August 2022).
3. David Olusuga, *Black and British* (London: Macmillan, 2016), 202.
4. Stitch's Media Mix (blog), 'Flashback Friday: My Martha Jones (Fandom) Problem', 15 May 2020: https://stitchmediamix.com/2020/05/15/flashback-friday-martha-jones/ (accessed 9 August 2022).
5. MorganAndAVacuumCleaner (@morganandahalf) 'Idk, Martha Jones was such a nothing character for me. Rose was ok and Donna was amazing, RTD's track record with companions is still more positive then negative thanks to all the side characters', Twitter, 16 December 2021: (8:44 p.m), https://twitter.com/morganandahalf/status/1471582000339423240?s=21&t=7uu68vG7g07mJ1gDQAPmWg, (accessed 9 August 2022).
6. Cadfael. (@laudatedominum5), 'They Need Their Quota of Black People in Every Series, Movie or Commercials or They Cry "Racist". Dr Who Is Infected by the Woke Agenda'. Twitter, 9 February 2022, https://twitter.com/laudatedominum5/status/1491427656490831879?s=21&t=Xl02ZtNHLUDo7c3sEpeRXA, (accessed 9 August 2022).
7. Steve Rose, 'How the Word "Woke" Was Weaponised by the Right', *The Guardian* (Guardian News and Media, 21 January 2020): https://www.theguardian.com/society/shortcuts/2020/jan/21/how-the-word-woke-was-weaponised-by-the-right (accessed 9 August 2022).

8   Mark M (@tedvonpenguin), 'Rose and Smith era Clara were worse. Than Martha. Not than Ryan. Nothing is worse than Ryan'. Twitter, 2 February 2020: (11:22 a.m.) web.archive.org/web/20220430212055/https://twitter.com/tedvonpenguin/status/1509853705092448259?s=21&t=ZvRgQWSNj50HPEAN1oTZaA, (accessed 9 August 2022).

9   One-nerd (@one1nerd), 'This era makes me absolutely depressed, And when chinball Stan's are confronted with this they can barely explain and just say 'you don't get it' I had a conversation where I asked for them to explain yazs personality, they just said 'well if you didn't get it in series 11. Then your mind won't be changed, Completely side stepping the conversation cause they don't want to face the fact that Yaz has the same personality as a board of card board, and that her and Ryan could be interchanged and no one would notice', Twitter, 28 April 2022: (9:47 a.m.), https://twitter.com/one1nerd/status/1519614389871165440?s=21&t=ZvRgQWSNj50HPEAN1oTZaA, (accessed 9 August 2022).

10 Gregory Upton (@GregoryUpton6) 'Can't wait for Tom cruise to be cast as Martin Luther King and Jim Carey as Barack Obama. What about we cast a black woman to play Anne Boleyn. Oh wait how did that turn out, good luck with the lousy viewing figures, got to be favourite to finally get the show cancelled'. Twitter, 19 May 2022: (12:23 p.m.), https://twitter.com/gregoryupton6/status/1527263731859996672?s=21&t=h03dVXpBp0PpBRMoxe6_jw (accessed 9 August 2022).

11 Darren Grimes (@darrengrimes_) 'Even if new Doctor Who has been offered the role because he's the best person (I happen to think he was fantastic in Sex Education), sad reality is that years of tokenistic diversity-first policies have convinced a nation that "best person for the job" is no longer BBC policy.' Twitter, 8 May 2022: (3:29 p.m.) https://twitter.com/darrengrimes_/status/1523324309275504640, (accessed 9 August 2022).

12 American Masters, 'Toni Morrison on Writing Without the "White Gaze"', PBS, (1 June 2020), video, 2:29: https://www.pbs.org/wnet/americanmasters/toni-morrison-on-writing-without-the-white-gaze/14874/ (accessed 9 August 2022).

13 Lincoln Quillian, 'Does Unconscious Racism Exist?' *Social Psychology Quarterly* 71, no. 1 (2008): 6–11: http://www.jstor.org/stable/20141814.

14 Creative Diversity Network, The Fifth Cut: Diamond at 5. London, UK, 2022.

15 Dr Jami Rogers, *Race Between the Lines: Actors' Experience of Race and Racism in Britain's Audition and Casting Process and on Set* (Birmingham City, UK: Sir Lenny Henry Centre for Media Diversity, 2021).

16 Nicole Hill, '*Doctor Who* and the Complications of Color-Blind Casting', Den of Geek (Den of Geek US, 17 January 2020).

Chapter 23
'Martha Jones is a lesbian': Queer (re)interpretations of companions in *Doctor Who* by Océane I. Nyela and Anna Young

Original to this volume

Queer fans often have to engage with transformative fan works to see certain character relationships have romantic fulfilment. Nyela and Young describe a unique kind of queer shipping they have noticed in Doctor Who *fandom.*

Defining retroactive queering

Retroactive queering is defined as a practice through which queer fans of television shows reinterpret plots and character development through a queer lens. This reinterpretation, in turn, gives these texts and characters a new 'queer' life. While they can be affirming for queer fan communities, these creative practices allow showrunners, broadcasters and distributors to rely on audiences for queer interpretations and media production rather than investing in and developing queer characters themselves. As such, this chapter details how fans' queering of texts has evolved as some writers and producers are enticed by more demanding audiences[1] to add more explicitly queer characters and storylines to their television shows. Despite these realities, we posit that retroactive queering is a radical creative practice that allows queer viewers to assert and enact their subjectivities. We offer this chapter as a call for a greater focus on WLW in studies of *Doctor Who* fandom, as well as fan studies in general.

Queer characters on *Doctor Who* are not new. From Captain Jack Harkness (John Barrowman) to Bill Potts (Pearl Mackie), and most recently Yasmin Khan (Mandip Gill), the Doctor has had plenty of queer companions, despite its origins as a show aimed at children, shying away from outwardly discussing queerness.[2] Therefore, one might question the relevance of writing about rhetorical fan practices aimed at reimagining existing *Doctor Who* characters through a queer lens. Is there really a need for a theory of retroactive queering if many of the characters on *Doctor Who* themselves are queer? While it might seem like *Doctor Who* is an explicitly queer show, exploring how retroactive queering is mobilized by fans of the show can complicate how we understand the *Doctor Who* fandom as well as the show itself. Indeed, *Doctor Who* is one of the programmes which is often referenced under the umbrella term 'SuperWhoLock'. SuperWhoLock (also spelled superwholock) is a fan-created crossover involving *Sherlock*, another globally successful BBC show along with the CW's *Supernatural*, two shows which were embroiled in controversies surrounding queerbaiting and general contempt by the showrunners for their queer audiences.[3] *Doctor Who*, unlike these two other shows, has more readily embraced its queer audience by showcasing queer relationships and queer characters on the show. While this iteration of the show manned by Chris Chibnall has been dismissed as too 'woke' or 'politically correct' by some fans, this era of the show has been positively received.[4] Most recently, Yasmin 'Yaz' Khan, the Thirteenth Doctor's (Jodie Whittaker) companion, admitted to Dan (John Bishop), another companion of the Doctor, that she is in love with the Doctor. Yaz's admission to Dan and the audience that she harbours these romantic feelings for the Doctor was also significant for parts of the show's fanbase, since the Thirteenth Doctor, the first female incarnation, is portrayed by Jodie Whittaker.[5] Both Whittaker and Gill have seemed to embrace the enthusiasm for this potential relationship between Yaz and the Doctor. Therefore, this chapter not only defines retroactive queering but shows how the practice, which allows fans to expand on and transform the content of shows, can happen even when these shows feature existing and established queer characters.

As a theoretical framework, retroactive queering is concerned with how the interpretations that might emerge when a media text is released into the world can often move beyond the expectations and intentions of the creators of a given media text. In other words, once a media text is released, its creator is no longer in control of how it will be perceived and embraced by its audience. Framing enjoyment and playfulness as driving forces of queer creative practices that reinterpret straight texts is necessary if we want to move beyond the positivistic connotations that underline most academic approaches to how queer audiences engage with media texts that are not explicitly queer. Developing new ways to study and theorize how marginalized audiences engage with mainstream media texts creates ways to think about queer visuality beyond pathologizing queer audiences. Therefore, a theory of retroactive queering is needed since most of the writing on how queer audiences engage with heteronormative media does not adequately engage with the

> agency of the reading practices of media fans – not only in being able to identify (and define what constitutes) actual subtext, but also in being able to enjoy the process, to engage in play with the mainstream text, and not be harmed by it.[6]

As a rhetorical and creative fan practice, retroactive queering allows audiences to reinterpret existing texts and characters through creative fan practices such as vidding, fanfiction writing and discussions of a character's personality and character arc. Perhaps one of the most popular pairings resulting from this process is MARTHADONNA, a romantic pairing featuring two of the Tenth Doctor's (David Tennant) companions Martha Jones (Freema Agyeman) and Donna Noble (Catherine Tate). While Martha and Donna's relationships with the Doctor were drastically different, they both were both considered close friends of the *Doctor Who* was still grieving the loss of Rose Tyler (Billie Piper) – a loss which precluded him from forming a romantic attachment with Martha or Donna. While the portrayal and treatment of Martha,

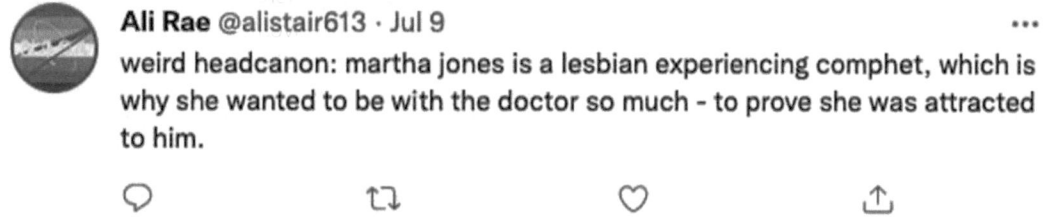

Figure 23.1 Screen capture of a tweet by Ali Rae (@alistair613) discussing the idea that Martha Jones' infatuation with the Doctor is the result of compulsory heterosexuality.

the Doctor's first Black companion, has recently been critiqued for its instances of racial insensitivity and covert racism (see previous chapter),[7] attempts have been made at romantically pairing Martha Jones and Donna Noble. In fact, queer fans have sometimes reinterpreted Martha's perceived infatuation with the Doctor because of compulsory heterosexuality (Figure 23.1).

Other fans have also noted that the Doctor's lack of attraction to Donna Noble might also be the result of fatphobia on the show's part, portraying her character as someone not even the pansexual Captain Jack Harkness, who seemingly never turns down anyone, could possibly be attracted to.[8] Nevertheless, some fans have used fanfiction and vidding to create retroactively queer portrayals of a romantic relationship between Martha and Donna.

#MARTHADONNA: A case study of retroactive queering in the *Doctor Who* fandom

The earliest Twitter mentions of #MARTHADONNA confirm that it is indeed a recent phenomenon. According to the discussions which we observed on '*Doctor Who* Twitter' fans who engaged in the retroactive queering of these two characters often did so in part because viewers were often reminded of the inherently romantic incompatibility of either Martha or Donna with the Doctor. On the one hand, Martha is incompatible with the Doctor because he could not see her or her infatuation because of his lingering feelings for Rose Tyler and, on the other, Donna Noble because early she expressed her lack of romantic or physical attraction to the Doctor. For fans of MARTHADONNA the impossibility of a romantic relationship between the Doctor and these companions allows them to reimagine them through a queer lens. For example, a fancam by Twitter user @lesbiantardis, captioned: 'MARTHADONNA: Don't pretend that you don't want me' (Figure 23.2); crops and edits scenes together where the Doctor is either supposed to be on screen or his voice is heard off screen.

As fans of the romantic pairing engage with media texts which reinterpret these characters through a retroactive queer lens, they are aware that Martha Jones and Donna Noble have both been characterized as straight and have never been engaged in a romantic relationship. It is, in part, that combination of these edited clips, the caption and the song choice creates the possibility for the romantic pairing to exist. Because queer audiences already engage in this kind of close reading when engaging with media texts where the characters are assumed to be heterosexual, things such as glances and longing looks

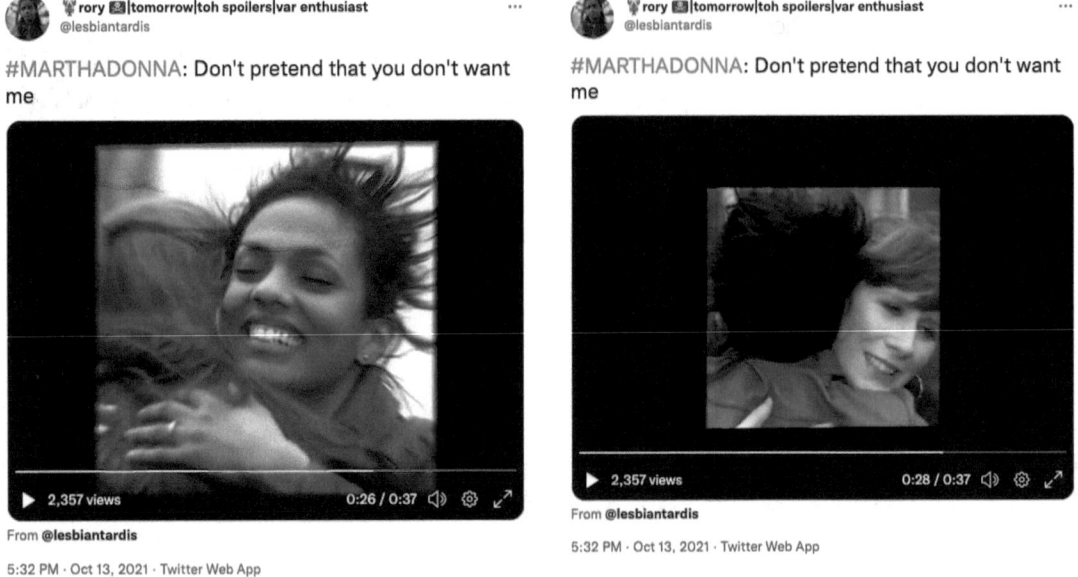

Figure 23.2 Screen captures of a MARTHADONNA fan edit by Rory (@lesbiantardis).

are already codified as signifying queer potential.[9] As such, this instance of retroactive queering works because the codes become the focus of these videos. This kind of close reading is only possible because of the ability to review, pause and rewind segments of a media text. This manner of watching involves both the fan's own perspective and the 'deep textual reading and broad understanding of the nuances of a canon are only possible when the texts themselves are available for study'.[10] Engaging in retroactive queering does not necessitate imagining a queer alternative for an existing media text. Rather, the queer subtext that was already present in each media text is brought to the fore through the close reading of the text and the ability to edit and splice scenes together. Accordingly, 'the textual boundary has already been breached',[11] and by sharing these fancams, the potential queerness of a character is made explicit.

Playfulness, power and retroactive queering

This section will discuss the implications of retroactive queering within the *Doctor Who* fandom: how these readings embody a thriving tradition within queer fan communities. Retroactive queering is an agentic fan practice, an example of Jenkins' 'textual poaching' by which 'fans raid mass culture, claiming its materials for their own use, reworking them as the basis for their cultural creations and social interactions'.[12] Moreover, the fact that the process of queering is *retroactive* means that fans do not have to be satisfied with the explicitly queer representations shown in canon (such as Yaz and Bill): they continue to assert their own prerogative to make and remake the text according to their own desires. Both Jenkins and Brennan highlight the disruptive, anti-hegemonic potentiality of queer fandom pairings like MARTHADONNA.

In this chapter's discussion of retroactive queerness, we have purposefully chosen to draw exclusively on WLW ('women-loving-women') relationships and characterizations. Despite the overwhelming presence of women and femmes in online fandom communities, including *Doctor Who*, the literature around fan queering practices focuses heavily on MLM ('men-loving-men') representations. Some reasons for this include the fact that societal perceptions of male friendships versus sexual/romantic relationships draw a sharper line than those between women, as well as the dominance of MLM content in slash fiction.[13]

Jenkins notes that heterosexual female K/S (erotic pairings of *Star Trek*'s Kirk and Spock) slash writing 'represents a reaction against the construction of male sexuality on television and in pornography [...] a refusal of fixed-object choices in favour of a fluidity of erotic identification' – a means for women to imagine a sexual encounter without the power dynamic inherent in heterosexual pairings.[14] Brennan's contemporary observation highlights the *fun* of fan queering practices: fans are not only 'able to identify (and define what constitutes) *actual* subtext, but also [are] able to enjoy the process, to engage in play with the mainstream text'.[15] We argue that when positioning retroactive queering within *Doctor Who* (such as MARTHADONNA) alongside the canon WLW queer representations on the show, it is this twin dynamic of playfulness and power that emerges as the draw for fans to engage in the practice.

Retroactive queering can be seen as a playful engagement with the text of *Doctor Who* due to the fact that there is no 'actual' possibility of the pairings becoming realized. Martha and Donna are retired companions, and are unlikely to return full-time to the show – even less so for a romantic relationship to be written for them. Their dynamic is not a result of 'queerbaiting' – described by Brennan as 'a tactic by which media producers suggest homoerotic subtext between characters [...] that is never intended to be actualized on screen'[16] – as they rarely shared a scene together, nor were either suggested to be anything other than heterosexual in the text. In fact, MARTHADONNA could be seen as an almost absurd stretching of the source material in order to imagine a queer potentiality. The fact that queer fans have nevertheless managed to find queerness here shows the playfulness inherent in retroactive queering.

Rather than see MARTHADONNA as absurd, we position it as an example of the way in which queer fans exert their agency over mainstream televisual texts. Agreeing with Brennan in his assessment that the concept of queerbaiting can rob fans of power, such as in questions like 'when will the writers *give us* a lesbian character?', we view retroactive queering as a way to retake this power. Instead of either asking for greater representation or else being satisfied with the queer representations actualized on *Doctor Who*, MARTHADONNA demonstrates the fact that fans will always centre their own creativity, desires and imaginings when engaging with texts in this manner.

Conclusion

This chapter has explored examples of our term 'retroactive queering' as it has been put into practice in *Doctor Who*. Despite the fact that the programme has depicted WLW relationships explicitly, especially in recent years, fans continue to look for and create sexual/romantic dynamics between women. We have also discussed some of the implications of these practices of retroactive queering, in relation to the work of Jenkins and Brennan, viewing them as a means of fans to engage playfully with a show that they love, as well as to assert their right to interpretation and creativity. Retroactive queering in *Doctor Who* shows that the 'work' of queer representation in television is never over: it is an ongoing, ambivalent, sometimes contradictory and fundamentally optimistic process.

Notes

The Day of the Doctor was simulcast in over ninety countries when it aired in 2013. The reach of Doctor Who as a brand is obviously wide, and social media has made it easier to connect fans from all over the globe, but it would be myopic to assume that fan communities in every country are exactly the same. In Chapters 24, 25 and 26, authors from Poland, Brazil and China demonstrate that being a Doctor Who fan in those countries requires a special kind of committed passion.

1. Amanda Cataldo, 'From "Stranger Things" to "Sherlock": 10 TV Shows That Queerbaited Their Fans' *Collider* (13 July 2022): https://collider.com/tv-shows-that-queerbaited-their-fans/ (accessed 9 August 2022); Stephanie Soteriou, '"Stranger Things" Has Sparked a Conversation about "Queerbaiting" After Noah Schnapp Confirmed That Will Is Gay', *BuzzFeed* News (18 July 2022): https://www.buzzfeednews.com/article/stephaniesoteriou/stranger-things-noah-schnapp-will-gay-queer-baiting (accessed 9 August 2022); Jennifer Still, 'Killing Eve Fans Hated the Finale – But They're Taking the Final Word for Themselves' *Vanity Fair* (13 April 2022): https://www.vanityfair.com/hollywood/2022/04/killing-eve-finale-backlash (accessed 9 August 2022).
2. 'Queer Representation in *Doctor Who*', *TARDIS Data Core: The Doctor Who Wiki* (16 April 2022): https://tardis.fandom.com/wiki/Queer_representation_in_Doctor_Who (accessed 9 August 2022).
3. Michael McDermott, 'The (Broken) Promise of Queerbaiting: Happiness and Futurity in Politics of Queer Representation', *International Journal of Cultural Studies* 24, no. 5 (2020): http://journals.sagepub.com/doi/full/10.1177/1367877920984170.
4. Jordan Robledo, '*Doctor Who* Confirms Long Awaited Queer Romance in Latest Episode', *Gay Times* (4 January 2022): https://www.gaytimes.co.uk/television/doctor-who-confirms-long-awaited-queer-romance-in-latest-episode/ (accessed 9 August 2022).
5. David Craig, '*Doctor Who*'s "Thasmin" Romance Wasn't Originally Planned, Says Producer', *Radio Times* (20 February 2022): https://www.radiotimes.com/tv/sci-fi/doctor-who-thasmin-romance-unplanned-newsupdate/ (accessed 9 August 2022).
6. Joseph Brennan, 'Queerbaiting: The "Playful" Possibilities of Homoeroticism', *International Journal of Cultural Studies* 21, no. 2 (2018): 189–206.
7. Amit Gupta, '*Doctor Who* and Race: Reflections on the Change of Britain's Status in the International System', *Round Table (London)* 102, no. 1 (2013): 41–50; Saljooq M. Asif and Cindy Saenz, 'Colonialist Pasts and Afrosurrealist Futures: Decolonizing Race and Doctorhood in Doctor Who', *Journal of Medical Humanities* 40, no. 3 (2019): 315–28.
8. thisisthinprivilege, '*Doctor Who* Fatphobia', Tumblr, *This Is Thin Privilege* (blog): https://thisisthinprivilege.tumblr.com/post/76428557045/doctor-who-fatphobia (accessed 18 April 2022).
9. Camille Bacon-Smith, *Enterprising Women: Television Fandom and the Creation of Popular Myth* (Philadelphia, PA: University of Pennsylvania Press, 1992); Joseph Brennan, '"If Duchamp's Toilet Can Be a Masterpiece…": Slash Manips as Fannish Readymades', *The Journal of Fandom Studies* 4, no. 1 (2016): 3–21.
10. Bacon-Smith, *Enterprising Women*, 131.
11. Tisha Turk, 'Metalepsis in Fan Vids and Fan Fiction', in *Metalepsis in Fan Vids and Fan Fiction* (Berlin: De Gruyter, 2011), 92.
12. Henry Jenkins, *Textual Poachers: Television Fans and Participatory Culture* (New York, NY: Routledge, 1992), 18.
13. Ibid., 186.
14. Ibid., 189.
15. Brennan, 'Queerbaiting', 194–5.
16. Ibid., 189.

Chapter 24
Fandom DIY: *Doctor Who* fans in Poland by Magdalena Stonawska

Original to this volume

Geography and demographics play a large role in how Polish fandom connects as a community. Magdalena Stonawska surveys and analyses the current landscape and notes what makes Polish fandom unique.

Two students finding a Dalek toy with a British flag pattern in an off-price retailer store and passing it from one Whovian to another for years.[1] A handyman using diagrams found on the internet and his own engineering skills to construct a fully operational Dalek with motor and operator seat. A young married couple organizing photo sessions at conventions in their exact TARDIS replica, initially a photo booth constructed for their wedding.[2] Scarves knitted by grandmas, handmade fezzes, hand-sewn Adiposes, outfits and cosplays, hand-painted T-shirts and bags; fan translations, subtitles, reviews, essays, fanfiction, fanart, fanvids, academic papers and events. In Polish *Doctor Who* fandom, creativity is essential. Seldom will anyone mention such things as merchandise collections, books, DVDs, comic books or signed photos; if someone like this shows up, they seem to come from another planet.

It's not easy to be a Whovian in Poland

In 2015, having been a Whovian for several years, inspired by Henry Jenkins' and John Tulloch's *Science Fiction Audiences*, I carried out ethnographic research on the fandom.[3] I was lucky – it was the show's peak of popularity. I found almost a thousand respondents. Seven years later, in 2022, reaching people with a follow-up was much harder to achieve.

Doctor Who is broadcast in Poland rarely and irregularly. The new series would appear on several TV channels; series 5–10 are currently airing repeatedly on BBC First.[4] Other series are not to be found in the scheduling. There are not any other means to watch *Doctor Who*. It is not offered by any streaming service (although it was on Netflix in 2016–18) and only series 1 and *a part* of series 6 were released on

DVD. The only way to watch the Christopher Eccleston and David Tennant eras is to order DVDs from abroad (without Polish subtitles) or obtain the episodes illegally. In a world of streaming services, people would rather just watch something else.

Other elements of Whoniverse are also hard to come by. There is no means to access Classic *Who* (apart from ordering DVDs from the UK). Some remember films with Peter Cushing aired on TV in 1979, Paul McGann in 1999 and several episodes of Fourth Doctor (Tom Baker) in 2002–3. There was also a quite surprising incident of three *Doctor Who* novels being published in the 1990s in a truly terrible translation. Interestingly, *The Sarah Jane Adventures* were once broadcast on a popular children's channel and many young viewers were surprised to discover that there is more to see.

No one in Polish *Doctor Who* fandom grew up with the classic series. Most fans started with 'Rose'; their Doctor is a young action hero. This can be the reason why the show's popularity started to decline with Peter Capaldi's series. There is also no culture of showing *Doctor Who* to the kids – the youngest fans are usually late teens (not counting children of faithful fans, always the best cosplayers). Demographically a typical Polish Whovian is probably a woman in her late twenties who discovered the show through friends, got intrigued by fans on the internet, came across a random episode on TV or watched an episode while getting acquainted with someone's filmography. She knows New *Who* but watching Classic *Who*, reading comics, listening to Big Finish – it probably does not interest her that much. People passionate about the Expanded Universe form almost another, separate fandom. Maybe the transmedial universe does not speak to people not accustomed to seeking more stories in different media (see Evans' chapter in the next section) – or maybe the cause is the language or financial barrier.

What is there to do?

Once a person somehow manages to watch the episodes and becomes a fan, they want to extend the experience and this is not easy. Ordering DVDs, a piece of merchandise or clothing from abroad is expensive. One of fans' favourite sports is hunting for random gadgets and T-shirts in vintage and charity shops; my collection of Dalek toys comes entirely from my mother's arrangements with sellers in such stores in a small town in Subcarpathian Province. Moreover, cosplayers declare it is sometimes easier and more fun to hunt for pieces for their costumes in charity shops or to make it themselves. It is quite easy to buy a T-shirt with a print, but a Polish fan will rather look for it in Polish online shops than order licensed merchandise from abroad.

As Tisha Turk wrote, only some fans are creators.[5] There are more fan consumers and more than one way to be a fan. Some want to get involved more, whereas some do not; if someone considers themselves a fan, they are one. Among fan activities, writing – fanfiction, fan journalism, translating – and making art stand out. Most fans enjoy other people's creations and share them on social media. There is space to become famous thanks to one's creativity.

Personally, I find creating and managing online communities also an essential fan activity. It is community that people seek: a place to talk, share experiences and joy, meet other people. Fans declared in the survey that it is easier to get in touch with people in fandom:

> Fandom gives the key topic, the reason to gather, and then … it's just fun. Outgoing, enthusiastic people and an unusually pleasant world. Things that are important here are … different. It's not about breaking away from our reality, but at least for a moment to do something *really* engaging.

Minorities and dreamers

Seventy-five per cent of my respondents were women, about 10 per cent nonbinary people and 25 per cent identified as LGBTQ+. It suggests that the *Doctor Who* fandom is considered a friendly group. Some places openly declare themselves as feminist and LGBTQ+ friendly; others usually have a code of conduct protecting against discrimination. *Doctor Who*, preaching equality and respect for every being, attracts people from various minority groups:

> There is a kind of science fiction that is inclusive, open, I think *Doctor Who* is a very good example of that. It promotes deliberately notions that attracts people who would not feel comfortable in that other SF fandoms.

One level of fan activity, according to Henry Jenkins, is *an alternative social community*.[6] Fandom, with its peculiar norms and rules, is appealing for marginalized people. One of my respondents stated that the *Doctor Who* fandom is a place 'for those discriminated against and dreamers'. The world view promoted by the show is personally important for some fans and affects them in a good way:

> One day I looked at the Doctor delighted by some monster and I thought: this is such a good attitude towards life – not to grumble but to be delighted with everything. It changed my life. I've always been an optimist but the Doctor made me realize I lacked enthusiasm.

For some, it is just freedom to be themselves:

> Fandom gives me joy of community and sharing. No one will tell me I'm too old for something or that it is just a TV show.

For all that, fandoms are also prone to conflict. Quarrels usually break out over personal matters and non-fandom issues, such as political polarization about LGBTQ+ rights or racism. Arguments over the show itself are much calmer.

Language – A wall and a ladder

My respondents generally enjoy British popular culture and 60 per cent of them have high language proficiency. Still, one of the major fan activities is translating news, interviews and subtitles. The official translations of episodes aired on TV are always analysed and criticized. They are also an enormous source of memes since the series' technobabble and neologisms pose quite a challenge for translators. How to translate *timey-wimey* or what grammatical gender is TARDIS? These are popular topics, especially since *timey-wimey* got an official translation evoking probably unplanned (NSFW) associations.
Cultural content is another thing:

> Some meanings and cultural allusions elude the Polish fans, especially the younger ones – simply because they belong to a different culture. Our mentality and humour are different, we pay attention to different things.[7]

The feeling of distance and alienation leads to a funny trend of *polonizing* the Whoniverse, for example by wondering what moments of Polish history the Doctor should visit.

> I like to think how would *Doctor Who* look like if made in Poland. How would the TARDIS look like? (My favourite theory is that it would look like a *kiosk*). Trying to find alternatives for British actors in Polish film is also a lot of fun (my great achievement is coming up with Roman Wilhelmi as the Doctor – just look at him!). Who has *it* in them?

There are also fanfiction and parodies placing elements of the show in a Polish context.

> One day we came up with a very affectionate parody of *Doctor Who*. In *Ksiądz Kto* (*Priest Who*) the protagonist is a Catholic priest wearing a red tourban and heavy boots. We aimed to reference some naïve and coarse Polish TV series and just life in Poland. After many years it is still quite popular on Tumblr …

Polish culture impacts everything fans do and create – their discussions and the way they talk about the show. It binds the group together. Some interviewees described Polish fandom as a part of the global community, but it does not seem quite true; Polish fans add a lot to the base of their interest and do not reach to the English-speaking areas very often. Only one in a dozen declares to have regular interactions with fans from other countries.

Whovians offline (rarely)

During the peak of *Doctor Who* popularity, Whovians, wearing fezzes and bowties, stood out from the crowd at SF&F conventions. The growing popularity of the show encouraged them to run their own event.

Two editions of Whomanikon took place in Kraków in 2016 and 2017, and 500 attendees took part in talks (on such topics as transhumanism in *Doctor Who*, Time Lords' neurobiology or history of art in the show), contests and debates. BBC did not contribute in any way, and there were also no guests connected to the show. Whovians also organized parts of other events, such as Serialis in 2016 and Warsaw Comic Con in 2017, promoting the community and the show.

However, one event was different: SerialCon, a part of OFF Camera Festival of Independent Cinema in Kraków, hosted guests from the *Doctor Who* production team twice: Toby Whithouse and James Moran in 2017 and Sarah Dollard in 2018. Their panels were met with moderate attendance – it could have been that they were not promoted enough or maybe meeting the screenwriters during a stiff film festival was too far from what the fans are used to – a direct contact and casual atmosphere of fan-made convention.

Whovians online (usually)

Doctor Who fandom is mostly an online community, with partial identities connected to virtual spaces – groups, websites, chats. Probably the first online community had formed on drwho.pl forum in 2008 or

2009 (now inactive). Then Facebook took over and debates moved there. In 2012–15 such groups as Doktor Who Polska, Obywatele Gallifrey, *Doctor Who* Polska, Whosome and several smaller communities were founded, as well as a few blogs and websites, most notably Gallifrey.pl (2014) and then Whosome.pl (2020) by the same editorial board. Every time a new website or group comes out, its creators are accused of breaking up the community.

Disappointments

In recent years, Whovians' enthusiasm has noticeably declined. My respondents state clearly their disappointment in the quality of Chris Chibnall era. Many fans went into a sleep mode but are looking forward to the future. It is also clear that streaming services changed profoundly the way we consume television. It is very difficult nowadays to catch the viewers' attention for long enough for them to form communities.

Limited access to the show and poor official distribution can sometimes motivate to create but it is also a source of frustration and discouragement. Polish fans of *Doctor Who* feel disregarded, treated like second-class viewers, separated from their favourite franchise by a thick wall.

What is there to gain?

Both the show and its fandom have educational value. Fans share their knowledge and experience. They learn English to gain a better understanding of the show itself and references it contains. Some of my respondents were grateful to the fandom for its friendly audience, the opportunity to overcome shyness, learn to speak publicly (that's me!) or organize events and cooperate in a group. And, of course, for friendships they have developed over the time:

> I have a group of friends … We've met in the Travelling Dalek group. My friend … well, she wasn't my friend yet … found a Dalek in a shop and thought it would be cool for it to pass from one person to another. We had a meeting in Warsaw, then we went to the cinema, met again and again. Now we stick together.

Polish *Doctor Who* fandom is an example of how crucial it is to consider cultural determinants while analysing social phenomena – including fan communities. History, language, wealth, media policy – everything influences the shape of the group that formed rather in spite of the conditions than thanks to them. There are some things to compensate for, but it is just a part of it – being close to the show is not necessary to form a strong, colourful, creative and surprising community.

Notes

1. Travelling Dalek: https://www.facebook.com/TravellingDalek.
2. TARDIS Replica: https://www.facebook.com/TARDISReplica.

3   Magdalena Stonawska, *Fandom większy w środku? Charakterystyka polskiego fandomu serialu Doctor Who w oparciu o badania etnograficzne* [Fandom Bigger on the Inside? Ethnographic Research on Polish *Doctor Who* Fandom] Jagiellonian University, 2015: https://bit.ly/fandomDW.

4   It is offered by private TV providers; 118th place in terms of viewership. *TVP1 i TVN liderami w 2020 roku. Rekordowe wyniki TVN24, TVP Info i Polsat News (top 171 stacji)*, Wirtualne Media, (1 April 2021): https://www.wirtualnemedia.pl/artykul/ogladalnosc-telewizji-2020-tvp1-tvn-ranking-170-stacji-rekord-tvn24-tvp-info-i-polsat-news (accessed 9 August 2022).

5   Tisha Turk, 'Fan Work: Labor, Worth, and Participation in Fandom's Gift Economy', *Transformative Works and Cultures* 15 (2014): http://journal.transformativeworks.org/index.php/twc/article/view/518/428.

6   Henry Jenkins, *Textual Poachers: Television Fans and Participatory Culture* (New York, NY: Routledge, 1992), 286.

7   All quotes come from interviews conducted with Polish Whovians in 2015.

Chapter 25

'The Day of The Doctor' and *'Flux'* in Latin America: The relationship between BBC's strategies and Brazilian Whovians by Eloy Vieira and Lilian França

Original to this volume

Engagement with official events and promotions from BBC Worldwide will be part of any fan's experience of the show if they live outside the UK. In this chapter, Vieira and França wonder what happens to the local fandom when the quality of the official brand promotion waxes and wanes in a specific country.

Introduction

The relation between fans and producers is being intensified due to our media scenario. In November 2013, when *Doctor Who* celebrated its fiftieth anniversary, fandoms all over the world got involved in a global mobilization watch of 'The Day of The Doctor'. It was aired simultaneously on TV and in movie theatres engaging fans all over the world. In Brazil, the two most important *Doctor Who* fandoms participated intensively, ensuring an outstanding role in the media production process.

Despite all of BBC's effort to engage Latin American fans, we were able to observe in the following years that something had changed as stated by some Brazilian Whovians.

See also Eloy Vieira and Lilian França, 'How Brazilian Whovians Influenced BBC's Strategies through Twitter: Fifty Years of *"Doctor Who"* and Fan Engagement', *Transformative Works and Culture* 26 (2018): https://journal.transformativeworks.org/index.php/twc/article/view/1288.

Brazilian Whovians during the fiftieth anniversary

According to the BBC, 'The Day of the Doctor' was broadcast in ninety-four countries simultaneously gathering, at least, 10 million Whovians together to watch: a Guinness World Record as 'the world's largest ever simulcast of a TV drama'.[1]

BBC first announced an exhibition in Brazil – a country of 200 million habitants – in three main cities. What they did not expect – because they probably did not know about the fandom size – was that tickets would sell out so quickly.

Another thing that the BBC and Cinemark did not expect was that Whovians all over Brazil, led by the founders of 'Doctor Who Brasil' and 'Universo Who', demanded rooms in every region, and they were contacted by BBC producers and encouraged to engage on Twitter hashtags #DoctorWhonaCMK and #SaveTheDay (Figure 25.1).

According to Thaís Auxílio, co-founder of 'Doctor Who Brasil', the division of BBC Worldwide for Latin America contacted them:

> In our case (Brazil), the division that rules here is BBC Worldwide (Miami-USA). They first contacted us in 2013, and we've been partners ever since. They want to understand the fans (…) what events are interesting to participate in. Our work is just about publicity (…) and there was never any money involved either. The only situation close to it was at the 2014th CCXP when they provided us 30 tickets to give away and organize a flash mob in front of Tardis. But that was our initiative.
>
> (AUXÍLIO, 2016)[2]

Right after that, Auxílio also revealed, through the fandom website, that the campaigns in Argentina and Mexico were coordinated by them and the BBC Worldwide.

> Together with the BBC, we organized a campaign with Argentina and Mexico. We created the hashtags #DoctorWho50noCinemark and #WhoviansUnidos to get them into Trending Topics. The BBC showed our engagement, and then Cinemark finally launched a campaign on Twitter.
>
> (DOCTOR WHO BRASIL, 2013, online)[3]

BBC Worldwide also reached out to Augusto Carvalho, founder of 'Universo Who':

> I got a call from Miami. Since then, the site was called to the BBC Showcase (…) and participated to bring 'The Day of the Doctor' to Brazilian cinemas. We became in fact responsible for BBC Latin America's social media in Brazil.
>
> (CARVALHO, 2016)[4]

As shown, the mobilization was not isolated and, at some point, was part of BBC strategy to pressure Cinemark:

> In the specific case of the 50-year anniversary, they called us to engage in a great mobilization on Twitter. When it reached Trending Topics, Cinemark got in touch and 33 theaters screened the special.
>
> (AUXÍLIO, 2016)[5]

After that move, Brazilian Whovians believed that BBC was about to get closer to the fandoms overseas, but what they saw after Peter Capaldi's era was exactly the opposite.

Doctor Who Brasil @doctorwhobrasil · 4 de nov de 2013
NERDS DE TODO O BRASIL!!! Ajudem o especial de Doctor Who a ser exibido em mais salas de cinema! #DoctorWhonaCMK
↩ ⇄ 42 ★ 2 ⋯

Doctor Who Brasil @doctorwhobrasil · 4 de nov de 2013
.@tvcultura Ajude os whovians a subirem a hashtag #DoctorWhonaCMK !! Contamos com o apoio de vocês! <3 <3
↩ ⇄ 11 ★ 2 ⋯   Ver conversa

Doctor Who Brasil @doctorwhobrasil · 4 de nov de 2013
Doctor Who tem 50 anos de história e faz parte da cultura britânica, e sua série favorita, faz o que mesmo? #DoctorWhonaCMK
↩ ⇄ 33 ★ 10 ⋯

Doctor Who Brasil @doctorwhobrasil · 4 de nov de 2013
Bieber trata mal as fãs, tirem ele dos Trending Topics, coloquem #DoctorWhonaCMK !!
↩ ⇄ 19 ★ 1 ⋯

👤 Comic Con Experience e 13 outros seguem

Doctor Who Brasil @doctorwhobrasil · 4 de nov de 2013
O especial An Adventure in Space and Time do @Markgatiss vai ao ar em 21 de novembro! #DoctorWhonaCMK #fikdik #vouchorar #veritylambetdeusa
↩ ⇄ 12 ★ 2 ⋯

Doctor Who Brasil @doctorwhobrasil · 4 de nov de 2013
Não esqueçam de usar a hashtag #DoctorWhonaCMK! Queremos salas EM TODO O BRASIL!
↩ ⇄ 15 ★ 3 ⋯

Doctor Who Brasil @doctorwhobrasil · 4 de nov de 2013
One Direction no Trending Topics NÃÃÃÃÃO! Queremos outra parte da cultura britânica nos TTs!!!! #DoctorWhonaCMK
↩ ⇄ 12 ★ 3 ⋯

Doctor Who Brasil @doctorwhobrasil · 4 de nov de 2013
Vamos tirar o Luan Santana dos Trending Topics! #DoctorWhonaCMK
↩ ⇄ 9 ★ 3 ⋯

Doctor Who Brasil @doctorwhobrasil · 4 de nov de 2013
VAMOS SUBIR ESSA HASHTAG PROS TRENDING TOPICS DE NOVO COM SALAS EM TODO O BRASIL!!!!!! #DoctorWhonaCMK
↩ ⇄ 24 ★ 2 ⋯

Figure 25.1 Screenshot of tweets from account @DoctorWhoBrasil, indicating presence in Trending Topics list.
Source: VIEIRA & FRANÇA (2018).

Brazilian Whovians: What changed with *'Flux'* strategy

Brazilian Whovians[6] generated over 16,000 posts about *Doctor Who* between November and December 2021. Most of them on Twitter (93 per cent) and dedicated to celebrating the fifty-eighth anniversary. Additionally, some conversation was speculation about the next season and the debut of Jodie Whittaker as the Doctor, the syndication announced by Globoplay and a few complaints about BBC's neglect to Brazilian audiences (Figures 25.2, 25.3 and 25.4).

Among these complaints, Rafaela Akerman, known as @akerwho and an active Whovian community member at 'Puxadinho da Tardis'[7] and FluxSubs,[8] posted on her personal profile on Twitter on 1 November a brief thread (Figure 16.5).

In the thread, Akerman highlights the neglect of the BBC towards 'the rest of world' once the company seems to prioritize the UK audience:

> The lack of communication has been the mark of BBC in the last few years. If I'm not mistaken, there used to be a profile for the BBC in Latin America. Nowadays we basically beg for any piece of information. I can cite countless examples such as (…) the mobilization with #CadeDoctorWho on Twitter that intended to demand Globoplay an official answer, but we literally only found out that the first 11 seasons would be out of streaming because a fan saw the notice on the platform (…). It's very frustrating (…) our relation did not used to be like that.
>
> (AKERMAN, 2021)[10]

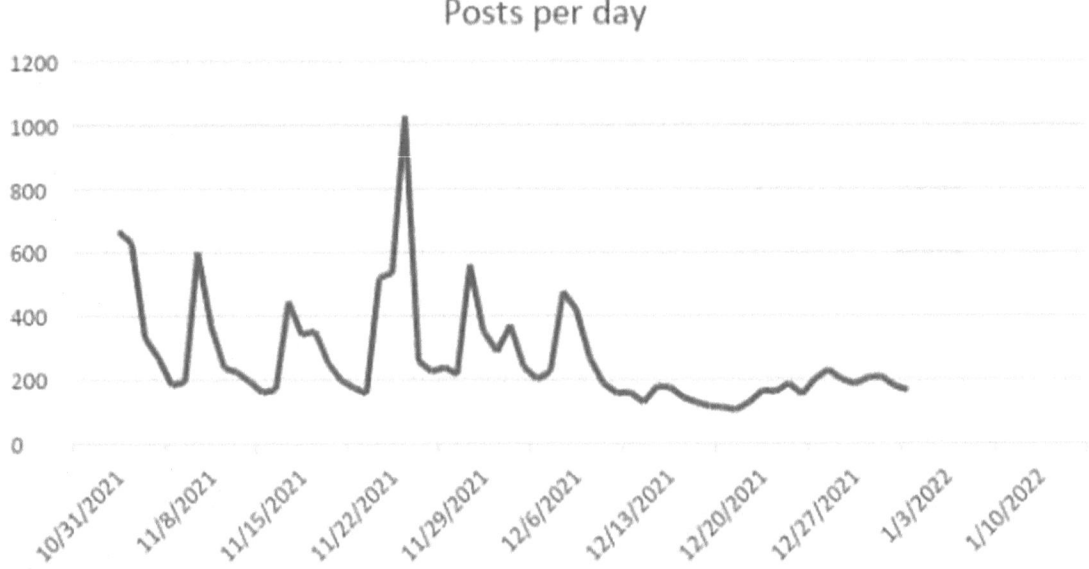

Figure 25.2 Screenshots of main results to the Boolean research combination on Stilingue: *'Doctor Who'* OR 'the flux' OR 'jodie whittaker' OR #doctorwhobr OR #doctorwho OR #DoctorWhoDay. Date: nov/dez/2021. Source: Stilingue (edited).

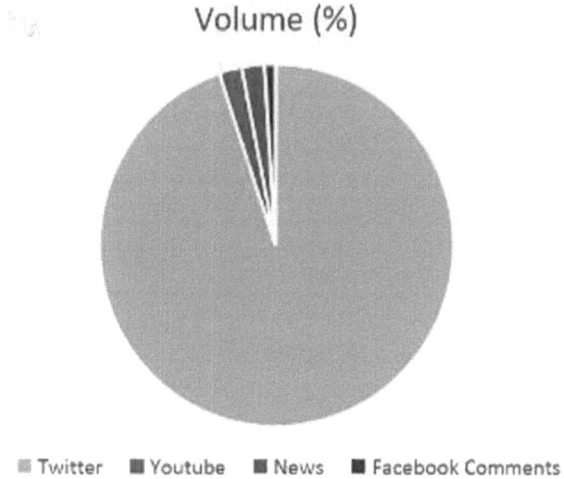

Figure 25.3 Screenshots of main results to the Boolean research combination on Stilingue: '*Doctor Who*' OR 'the flux' OR 'jodie whittaker' OR #doctorwhobr OR #doctorwho OR #DoctorWhoDay. Date: nov/dez/2021.
Source: Stilingue (edited).

Figure 25.4 Screenshots of main results to the Boolean research combination on Stilingue: '*Doctor Who*' OR 'the flux' OR 'jodie whittaker' OR #doctorwhobr OR #doctorwho OR #DoctorWhoDay. Date: nov/dez/2021.
Source: Stilingue (edited).

Figure 25.5 Akerman tweets.
Source: Twitter[9]

In a new interview with '*Doctor Who* Brasil' founders, Auxílio and Pavão (2022) echoed most of Akerman complaints. According to them, between the fiftieth anniversary and the end of Capaldi's era, the BBC Studios had a very clear PR strategy with fandoms, news portals and blogs, directly or through their press office.

> After Capaldi's era, the BBC's interest in Latin American countries decreased until it became non-existent. (...) It seems that the series has decided to focus its efforts only on UK. And this is from before the pandemic, so we can't even say that the two moments are even related.
> (AUXÍLIO & PAVÃO, 2022)[11]

Besides that, they also gave a detailed explanation about the situation in Brazil, especially regarding to syndication.

> From the 11th season, the series faced a series of criticisms. (...) the uncertainty generated by the different syndicated channels in a very short period: Crackle, Looke and then Globoplay, which never got enough attention, leaving fans unanswered in terms of airing dates, for example. (...) we tried to contact either directly with the BBC or with Globoplay, and there was never any response. It's like we don't exist as a market.
> (AUXÍLIO & PAVÃO, 2022)[12]

Finally, they also shared their expectations to the next anniversaries:

> With the 60th anniversary of the series, fans expect (...) the return of the BBC's attention. There are rumors that Davies could put *Doctor Who* in the same terms of the Marvel's (...) the series will begin production outside the BBC, with Bad Wolf Studios. These changes may or may not offer hope for Brazilian fans, but we must wait and see.
> (AUXÍLIO & PAVÃO, 2022)[13]

What becomes very clear with both interviews is, on the one hand, the consequences of the change of BBC's strategy towards Latin America, and, on the other hand, the resentment among Whovians, especially the Brazilians that used to have a close relation through the press office.

Conclusion

Although we are not able to answer why the BBC decided to withdraw from Latin America and other markets overseas, the interviews with the Brazilian Whovian community point to a few possibilities. The first one relates directly to the editorial changes, suggesting that Capaldi's era could mark the beginning of strategic changes, but it seemed more like a first step, but with a following withdrawal during Whittaker's era, known as 'Flux'.

This observation, that Whittaker could become an important asset to BBC since she was the first woman in the main role, also raises a question about why the company did not use this as a strategy to promote the series overseas. Another point would be about UK political context, with Brexit, the 'closure' and the isolation might be one of the cultural consequences that could be affecting BBC's international strategies.

Nevertheless, disregarding those subjective hypotheses, the neglect of producers is sowing resentment among international fandom communities that could reflect in the next international audience ratings, a subject that other researchers can follow up.

Notes

1. BBC, 'Millions Tune in for *Doctor Who* 50th Anniversary Show' (2013): https://www.bbc.com/news/entertainment-arts-25076912 (accessed 9 August 2022).
2. The original version of this interview was made and published in Portuguese as part of the master thesis: VIEIRA, 2015.
3. *DOCTOR WHO* BRASIL. #DoctorWhonaCMK: o dia em que fomos parar nos Trending Topics! (2013): http://doctorwhobrasil.com.br/2013/11/doctorwhonacmk-o-dia-em-que-fomos-parar-nos-trending-topics (accessed 9 August 2022).
4. The original version of this interview was made and published in Portuguese as part of the master thesis: VIEIRA, 2015.
5. Ibid.
6. According to Stilingue, 'Brazilian Social Listening Research Platform'. Available at: https://warroom.stilingue.com.br/central.
7. Available at: https://puxadinhodatardis.com/.
8. Available at: https://twitter.com/fluxsubs.
9. Available at: https://twitter.com/akerwho/status/1455297811717791750.
10. Private interview.
11. Ibid.
12. Ibid.
13. Ibid.

Chapter 26

Translating *Doctor Who* into Chinese: Fansubbing and *Doctor Who* fandom in China by Ting Guo

Original to this volume

Translation as fan work may be an unfamiliar concept to any Doctor Who *fan whose native language is English. Ting Guo demonstrates in this chapter that for those who need translated subtitles to enjoy the show, this is vital, creative work that creates subcommunities within Chinese fandom.*

If the success of *Doctor Who* has been a recurring topic among Anglophone Whovian scholars,[1] the issue often debated among Chinese Whovians is why the show is not '火' (*huo*, hot or popular) in China.[2] While whether a show is 'hot' or 'popular' is a subjective perception, depending on whom you ask, it is probably not incorrect to say that *Doctor Who* is less known to the general Chinese public than other British TV programmes such as *Sherlock* or *Downton Abbey*. On Douban.com (a Chinese interest-based social media platform with mixed functions of Reddit and IMDB), *Doctor Who* (2005 series) has only received 23,361 reviews by April 2022, while *Sherlock* has received 441,025 and *Downton Abbey* 177,087. Despite its relatively smaller number of 'followers' in mainland China, the show does have a hard-core audience, who have played a significant role in translating and disseminating *Doctor Who* in Chinese.

This, of course, does not mean that the show has not been officially distributed in China.[3] In fact, from 2006, Season 1 to 3 of the re-booted *Doctor Who* (translated as 异世奇人, literally meaning *a legendary person in a strange world*) was broadcast to Chinese audiences in Guangdong province through Asian Television Limited World Channel,[4] constituting some Chinese Whovians' initial encounter with the Doctor.[5] In the following decade, more seasons of the new *Doctor Who* (神秘博士, *the mysterious doctor*) was broadcast by China Central TV channels and some local TV channels in Shanghai in either subtitled or dubbed version at various occasions.[6] Apart from broadcast TV, some Chinese online streaming platforms such as Youku.com, Le.com, BesTV and bilibili.com, with permissions from BBC Worldwide, also provided time-limited access to the new *Doctor Who*. However, like many Western media texts, the informal dissemination of *Doctor Who* in China (e.g. through pirate DVDs, unauthorized online streaming sites or fan communities) is much wider compared to the official channels because of various limits and censorship by the Chinese authorities[7] and potentially more influential because of its intersection with Chinese fans' practices, especially their translation of relevant media texts. These fans' enthusiasm in translating *Doctor Who* is related to, and part of, the surging fansubbing culture and online translation communities in China since 2001.

Benefiting from technologies such as Web 2.0 and peer-to-peer file sharing, fansubbing has been one of the major channels for Chinese audience to access foreign media contents (at least before 2009 when the Chinese government began to tighten up its control of cyberspace), constituting one of the most widespread fan activities in China.[8] Subtitling is not only a form for Chinese fans to engage with their favourite texts but also a way to connect with others with similar interest and initiate cultural and social changes.[9] Several Chinese subtitling groups have translated *Doctor Who*, including some major Anglophone-focused subtitling groups such as ZiMuZu (人人影视), FRTVS or 1000FR (聲灵风软字幕组), BTM (波特猴字幕组) and sci-fi fansubbing groups such as Flyine subtitling group (幻翔字幕组) and SS Chaoneng xiaofengdui (超能小分队). To date, these subtitling groups together produced the Chinese translations of almost all new *Doctor Who* shows (seasons 1–13), *Doctor Who* films (e.g. *The Television Movie* (1996)), the three official spin-off series (*The Sarah Jane Adventures*, *Class* and *Torchwood*) and various special episodes (e.g. the fiftieth anniversary 'The Day of the Doctor'). There are also individual Whovians and Whovian groups such as the Fansub Group of *Doctor Who* Chinese Community (DW华社字幕组), Classic Who, Schrodinggoose (薛记烧鹅铺) and iCelery Legion (iCelery军团) dedicated to the translation of the less translated texts, including the Classic *Doctor Who* series, mini-episodes (e.g. Tardisode by iCelery), parodies (the Hillywood show's *Doctor Who* parody by 图安一记), audio plays (the Big Finish series by Fansub Group of DW Chinese Community) and fan-made media contents (e.g. 'Devious (*Doctor Who*)' and 'The Timeless Doctor' by iCelery). Their translations fill the gap left by the official limited distribution of *Doctor Who* in China, greatly enriching Chinese fans' experience of the show as well as their knowledge of international *Doctor Who* fandom.

Ostensibly, these fan-produced translations might seem to be repetitive and dispersed, because there are multiple versions of fan translation for one episode apart from the official translation[10] and these translations are scattered online in various social media platforms (e.g. Zhihu.com and bilibili.com) and individual blogs. The situation is, however, more complicated. The existence of multiple versions of translation is not simply the result of competition between fans and the industry, or within different fan groups but an indication of the pleasure for fans in translating and sharing their favourite media texts as well as fans' intolerance for poor quality translations of the show, including those generated by machine translation. Also, translation can be an important means for some Whovians to exercise their fan identity and connect with their communities. For example, a well-known feature of Flyine's translation of *Doctor Who* is its translator's notes. Appearing at the top of the screen, these notes explain references to previous seasons or concepts/terms unfamiliar to general Chinese audiences. This kind of headnotes is not an uncommon practice in fansubbing circles.[11] What is special is that these notes are created by Flyine's 'consultant', a specific role assigned to those with extensive knowledge of the show, who oversees the production of the translation and intervenes in when appropriate.[12] The setting of this role demonstrates the efforts of the fan translators made to facilitate and enhance viewers' experience of the show on the one hand; on the other hand, it also mirrors these fans' recognition of specific knowledge associated with the show and creates opportunities for them to exercise their fan identity.

The fact that these fan translations are scattered in cyberspace is a direct consequence of the short life of Chinese subtitling groups in general (from a few months to a few years), usually because of the shortage of volunteer translators and/or constant pressure from Chinese authorities. However, the closure or inactivity of a Whovian subtitling group does not necessarily mean discontinuation of their translation activities. Because of their demonstrated knowledge of the show, core members of an inactive Whovian subtitling group are very likely to be recruited by another subtitling group or even found their own group. For example, the recently re-organized Flyine has taken members from other subtitling groups such as Classic Who, while the latter also had members recruited from the already inactive S&K subtitling group.[13] This kind of self-regeneration within these Whovian fansubbing groups enables the continuation and sharing of fans' knowledge of the show; at the same time, it also helps sustain fans' experience and interest in engaging with their favourite media texts and fan communities.

The instability of fansubbing groups has also stimulated some fans to collect, categorize and archive the existing fan translations of *Doctor Who*. These digital archives, usually accompanied by commentaries by the fan founders, are freely accessible to the public across a range of online spaces from individual blogs/posts (e.g. Morrisa Tohsaka's posts at Zhihu.com[14]) to streaming sites (e.g. bilibili.com, Zhihu.com.cn) and sites founded by individual Whovians (e.g. doctorwho.doctor/). While providing opportunities for others to access and enjoy the texts related to the show, this kind of 'affective archiving'[15] established and maintained by fans constitutes an expression of fans' active and intentional recognition and preservation of the history of Chinese Whovians' love for the show as well as their desire to enrich and expand current *Doctor Who* fanbase by inviting new comers to participate in ongoing translation projects. These archives make the Chinese *Doctor Who* fandom more visible online and attract attention from the media industry, which in turn began to engage and integrate these Whovians in its marketing strategies, including through translation.

A good example is the *Doctor Who* project launched by Eight Light Minutes Culture (hereafter ELMC), a Chengdu (Sichuan)-based Chinese company focusing on sci-fi-related cultural and media products.[16] From the very beginning, ELMC's target users have included Chinese Whovians. Not only are many of its own staff Whovians themselves, ELMC has also tried to recruit Who fan as its translators and invite them as guest speakers in various marketing events. This model might not exactly fit with the situation of 'fan go pro' in UK creative industry,[17] but the niche-marketing of ELMC does provide opportunities for Chinese fans to reach out to the general public and participate in official media production. This movement of fans into the industry might not change the existing 'unsatisfying' reception of the show in China but opens up new opportunities for Chinese Whovians to participate in transnational *Doctor Who* fandom and interact with the Chinese media industry.

Acknowledgements

This chapter and the research behind it would not have been possible without the support of many Chinese Whovians. The author would like to particularly thank 串串, 晏晏, 假装在伦敦, 神户小尊, 瓦片, 允悲 and Nina for their comments and/or reading of an earlier version of the chapter.

Notes

1. See Kieran Tranter, 'In and Out of Time: Memory and Chronology', in *Doctor Who in Time and Space: Essays on Themes, Characters, History and Fandom (1963–2012)*, ed. Gillian Leitch (Jefferson, NC: MacFarland, 2013), 82–96; John Tulloch and Manuel Alvarado, *Doctor Who: The Unfolding Text* (New York: Macmillan, 1983).

2. See the post '神秘博士为什么在中国不火', (Why Is *Doctor Who* Not Popular in China) *Zhihu.com*, last modified 9 December 2019: https://www.zhihu.com/question/66942220.

3. The classic *Doctor Who* series have been shown in local TV channels in Hong Kong and Taiwan, since the 1960s. See 'HongKong', *Broadwcast.org*, last modified 13 March 2022: https://broadwcast.org/index.php/Hong_Kong and 'Taiwan', *Broadwcast.org*, last modified 29 September 2021: https://broadwcast.org/index.php/Taiwan. However, due to the limitation of space, this chapter's discussion only limits to the context of mainland China.

4. A Hong Kong-based TV channel but with permission to broadcast to audience in Guangdong province since 2002.

5. See the post by a Zhihua user, who commented that he/she became a Whovian because of the show broadcast by ATV, *Zhihu.com*, accessed 8 April 2022: https://www.zhihu.com/question/31816147/answer/82511280.

6. Shanghai International Channel showed the first episode of Season 5 of the rebooted *Doctor Who* in the 14th Shanghai International Film Festival in 2011. In 2013, China Central TV broadcast the new *Doctor Who* series (Season 5–6, plus a Christmas Special episode) in its Zhengda Drama Channel (正大剧场) and Fengyun Drama Channel (风云剧场). In 2015 and 2019, Season 8 of the new *Doctor Who* were shown during the 22nd and 25th Shanghai TV Festival by Shanghai Art and Humanities Channel and International Channel. These are just some examples, and it is not this chapter's intention to provide an exhaustive list of the official distribution of the show in mainland China.

7. Apart from the restrictions on the total number of imported foreign TV and films in China, there are also various regulations on the exhibition of foreign media contents in mainstream media. For example, since 2012, foreign films and TV are not allowed to be broadcasted between 7.00 and 10.00 pm in Chinese TV channels and the broadcasting time of foreign media can't exceed 25 per cent of the total time allocated for TV and films in any TV stations. See '广电总局:境外影视剧不得在黄金时段播出' (National Radio and Television Administration: Foreign media contents should not be shown during the peak hours), *Chinanews.com.cn*, accessed 7 April 2022: https://www.chinanews.com.cn/yl/2012/02-13/3665334.shtml.

8. Tianxiang He, 'Fansubs and Market Access of Foreign Audiovisual Products in China: The Copyright Predicament and the Use of No Action Policy', *Oregon Review of International Law* 16 (2014): 310.

9. See Dingkun Wang and Xiaochun Zhang, 'Fansubbing in China: Technology Facilitated Activism in Translation', *Target. International Journal for Translation Studies* 29, no. 2 (2017): 301–18. Ting Guo and Jonathan Evans, 'Translational and Transnational Queer Fandom in China: The Fansubbing of Carol', *Feminist Media Studies* 20, no. 4 (2020): 515–29.

10. For example, there are at least three versions of translation for all seasons (1–11) of the rebooted *Doctor Who* programme, respectively produced by ZiMuZu, FRTVS/1000FR and Flyine.

11. See Luis Pérez-González, *Audiovisual Translation: Theories, Methods and Issues* (London & New York: Routledge, 2014), 80.

12. '重启人生—时间旅行者的多重人生' (Regeneration: The Time Traveller's Multiple Lives), 八光分文化 (Eight Light Minutes Culture), 25 September 2019, accessed 8 April 2022: https://mp.weixin.qq.com/s/J0XF8c9HwcFuOUdkcLSwZA.

13. 串串, Wechat message to author, 18 April 2022.

14 Morrisa Tohsaka, '快看.神秘老博士又摔倒了' (Look, the Old *Doctor Who* Fell Down Again), *Zhihu.com*, accessed 27 March 2022: https://zhuanlan.zhihu.com/p/31004102.

15 Sarah Baker, 'Identifying Do-It-Yourself Places of Popular Music Preservation', in *Preserving Popular Music Heritage: Do-It-Yourself, Do-It-Together*, ed. Sarah Baker (New York: Routledge, 2015), 59.

16 In collaboration with New Star Press, ELMC has published twenty-four books on the Doctor in Chinese translation by March 2022, including twenty-one official *Doctor Who* novels (e.g. *Only Human, Touched by an Angel* and *Beautiful Chaos),* collections and derivatives such as and *Doctor Who: The Story of Martha* (2008), *Doctor Who: Who-Ology, Regenerated Edition: The Official Miscellany* (2013) and *Doctor Who: The Legends of River Song* (2016). This does not mean that there haven't been any published Chinese translations of *Doctor Who* novels. For example, Shanghai Translation Publishing House published the two *Doctor Who* novels, *Shada* and *City of Death* in Chinese translation, respectively in 2014 and 2017.

17 As described by Matt Hills, *Triumph of a Time Lord: Regenerating in the Twenty-First Century*, ed. Matt Hills (London: I.B. Tauris, 2010), 56.

Chapter 27

The girl who ~~waited~~ survived: Fan rewritings of Amy Pond by Bethan Jones

Original to this volume

Most fans of Doctor Who *will have a strongly negative reaction to at least one storyline or character choice in the show's long history. Bethan Jones analyses the different paths fans can take to engage with problematic or upsetting storylines via fanfiction.*

Introduction

The depiction of female characters under Steven Moffat's tenure as *Doctor Who* showrunner has long been a bone of contention among fans and critics. Jane Clare Jones writes that his 'tendency to write women plucked straight from a box marked "tired old tropes" has seriously affected the show's dramatic power', while Foz Meadows argues that Moffat has a habit of depowering his female characters to make his male protagonists look stronger.[1] Conversely, Michael Hogan considered Amy (Karen Gillan) 'far superior to Catherine Tate and Freema Agyeman, equally as excellent as Billie Piper', and Patrick Mulkern states that Moffat 'seems compelled to bamboozle us with enigmatic women', Amy among them.[2] This polarization of opinion, however, seemed to come to a head with the sixth season episode 'The Girl Who Waited'. IGN's Matt Risley praised writer Tom McRae for giving a 'simple yet refreshingly new examination of Amy Pond', yet Lindsay Miller argues that 'the writers cannot seem to come up with anything for [Amy] to do that doesn't involve being a sexual or romantic object, a damsel in distress'.[3]

Along with these episode reviews, however, fans also took more active steps to address their problems with Amy. In this chapter I examine fanfiction based on 'The Girl Who Waited', undertaking a textual analysis of stories posted to FanFiction.net and An Archive of Our Own (also known as AO3). While there were many works which examined the Eleventh Doctor (Matt Smith) or Rory's (Arthur Darvill) responses to the events of the episode, I focused exclusively on fics told from Amy's point of view. In total, I analysed eight stories, ranging in length from drabbles of around 100 words to multi-chapter fics of over 10,000 words. I will suggest that, rather than fanfiction writers 'poaching' from the text,[4] they actively seek out the weaknesses of the episode in order to address them. Adapting Stuart Hall's 1980 encoding/decoding model I argue that fanfiction writers *recode* Amy through writing fanfiction that addresses the perceived slights against her character, and depict her as a strong intelligent woman, worthy of being saved by the Doctor (or, better yet, saving herself).[5]

Filling in the blanks with character growth

'The Girl Who Waited' is the tenth episode of season six, in which Amy, Rory and the Doctor travel to the planet Apalapucia. They find the planet under quarantine due to the Chen7 plague, which kills two-hearted beings within twenty-four hours. Amy gets separated from the Doctor and Rory and ends up in an accelerated time stream, from which she needs to be rescued. When the Doctor and Rory eventually latch on to Amy's time stream and attempt to save her they realize they're in the wrong time frame. Amy is thirty-six years older than when they left her and refuses to trust the Doctor. Initially Old!Amy, as fans have termed her, refuses to help the Doctor and Rory rescue her younger self: she knows if she does, she will cease to exist. She later changes her mind, on the condition that the Doctor takes her as well, but on reaching the TARDIS the Doctor slams the door and Old!Amy is left to die.

Many fan reactions drew attention to what we don't see in the episode: namely the thirty-six years Amy spends on Apalapucia developing her fighting skills and surviving. A post on the Tumblr blog feministwhoniverse epitomizes fans' frustrations that the character development afforded Amy through the course of the episode was removed by the ending:

> In fact, the only time we get to see any substantial character growth, in The Girl Who Waited, it is snatched from her and she reverts back to the Amy we see at the beginning of the episode.[6]

Several of the fics I analysed dealt with this aspect of the episode, drawing on canon to fill in the blanks of Amy's life on Apalapucia. In Ace of Emeralds' 'One more minute and he doesn't love you' Old!Amy and Rory discuss why Old!Amy won't help her younger self. Old!Amy has come to the realization that she can't keep expecting the world to wait for her:

> Amy looked at Rory and said, 'I don't want it because being here alone all this time has made me understand a lot of things, Rory. It made me see that I'm not a little girl anymore and that I can't keep running and expecting that the world will just stop and wait until I'm finished. Sometimes things happen to trip you up and the world won't stop. I wrote on that door that I'm waiting. I'm not waiting anymore, I'm just surviving. I'm trying to keep up with the world so I don't get left behind again'.[7]

A clear distinction is made between the Amy who was – young, feisty, sexy but also reactive and reliant on the Doctor – and the Amy who is – older, wiser, stronger and capable of surviving on her own. Of particular interest, relevant not only to this episode but Amy's entire character arc throughout the series, is her decision to stop waiting. Given Amy's position as the girl who waited, a repeating theme within the text, this functions as a comment on the passive nature of the character. Now, however, rather than waiting, reacting, Amy is active, making decisions that fundamentally change her nature.

This emphasis on survival is made clear in two other fics which focus on Amy's Apalapucia years. The first of these is 'Rule Number 1' by EachPeachPearPlum, a series of snippets detailing Amy's life waiting for the Doctor. The seventeenth extract, approximately two thirds of the way into the fic, demonstrates that Amy has learnt a great deal during her time on the planet. She builds herself armour from whatever she can find, including a helmet, 'modelled on some she found with the weapons, mostly Roman, some Greek, a very few Medieval ones' evidencing her ability to actively protect herself. She is capable of using her own ingenuity to fashion armour even while traces of the old Amy – dressing up in Kate Middleton's wedding dress – are apparent. Though this snippet comes at a point in the fic where she still believes the Doctor will come for her, the final lines suggest a change in her attitude towards the Doctor:

> She was stronger. She was armed and well-armoured. She was more than capable of defending herself.
> *Good*, the voice said. *You need to be.*
> She didn't argue back.

Amy has to defend herself because no one else will.[8]

Henry Jenkins notes that recontextualization is one of the approaches employed by fan writers, placing this in the context of interpretation, appropriation and reconstruction.[9] The function of these 'filling in the blanks' stories is to add meaning to the text and encourage other readers to revisit certain characters and plots in order to understand them differently. The fics I have discussed so far follow this pattern. They engage closely with details of the original episode, the authors repeating words and phrases used in the episode, and conform to rules of chronology. Yet I would suggest that these missing scene stories cannot be categorized as textual poaching in the way that Jenkins argues as they are not necessarily operating from a position of resistance. The fics dealing with Amy's time in Two Streams fit almost seamlessly with what we see in canon: Amy survives, Amy learns to fight, and Amy begins to hate the Doctor. But by the stories' conclusions nothing has really changed.

Recoding resistance at the end

This is different in the second sets of fic I want to examine. In these, the way the story ends is fundamentally different. In the episode, when the Doctor suggests that they rescue Old!Amy from her past, rewriting her out of existence, she says no. The Doctor and Rory, however, both insist that Amy's isolation is 'wrong'. Despite Rory's apparent discomfort at the Doctor's actions towards the end of the episode, there is no choice between which woman is worth saving: no matter how much Old!Amy wants to survive, young!Amy must be rescued. Old!Amy's survival appeared to be an important aspect of fic writers' reimaginings of 'The Girl Who Waited', and the ways in which she survived were many and varied. In CJ Burns' 'Paradox Schmaradox', for example, Amy is visited by the Doctor as she lies dying. He tells her that no one should die alone, but Amy has already programmed the Rory Bot to inject her with an antidote to the Handbots' medication. The Doctor decides to take Amy with him in the TARDIS, ignoring the paradox that was such a feature of the original episode.[10] 'Paradox Schmaradox' is perhaps the most straightforward alternative ending of the fics I have examined, but it still functions to demonstrate the possibilities fans find in rewriting their objects of fandom. A more substantial rewriting, however, comes in 'The Way We Live Now' by zlot, in which Old!Amy is the one to survive.[11]

As with the other fics discussed, this mirrors some aspects of the episode, but the premise and the way in which the fic plays out are markedly different. Rory makes the decision to save Old!Amy and leave the TARDIS, thus his relationship with Old!Amy becomes the focus. Old!Amy has to rely on Rory in ways that young!Amy didn't – calculating a tip, making small talk, going to the bank. The parameters of her relationship with Rory have thus shifted and she remains more reliant on herself than we saw at any other point during the series. Of particular note is the way in which she disappears every few months. Parallels can be drawn with young!Amy through various points of the series of course, running away on the night before her wedding, for example, but Old!Amy in this fic appears much more aware of her and Rory's relationship:

> There was a time she would have worried about him. She doesn't now. He might even go back for one last fling in the TARDIS. And she's very aware how long that last fling could last. A billion places to go, and the Doctor's terribly lonely. Amy gets that now, at least.

Rory's desire to save Old!Amy also plays a part in the next fic, though the ending is different to both 'The Way We Live Now' and 'The Girl Who Waited'. In 'The Doctor: out of time' by Heliopause Old!Amy tells Rory not to let her into the TARDIS, as in the episode, but asks him to let her take a final look at him and young!Amy. Rory relents and opens the door to the TARDIS, allowing Old!Amy to burst in and attack the Doctor. The hatred Old!Amy feels is palpable; she almost growls at him 'And you ... and *you*, Doctor ... I have had thirty-six years to learn how to hate the man who is *so sorry*'. Old!Amy then ejects the Doctor, Rory and young!Amy from the TARDIS and appropriates it for her own ends. It is clear from the fic that she feels no pity for any of the characters who left her in the situation.[12]

Unlike the episode, in which her love for Rory results in her sacrifice, the Old!Amy of this fic is resolutely looking after herself. This is perhaps the most clear example of a 'recoding', that is a decoding of the original text which is encoded into a new format by fans. In this case, fans decoded the episode and found it lacking, creating fanfiction which addresses those issues and changes the meaning of the episode. The author's notes, provided at the end of the fic, make this clear:

> I have only just seen the episode entitled 'The Girl Who Waited', and ... you can tell what I thought of it. And okay, there's another possible ending, fitting all the rules, saving all of them, but I am so fed up with S. Moffat's recurrent sexism that I am getting rid of his self-insert here and now. Out of time, Doctor!

Jenkins has argued fan responses to texts do not simply involve fascination or adoration, but also encompass frustration and antagonism, and the combination of these responses motivates fan engagement with the media. As we can see in these examples, however, much of the frustration with the episode comes from sources *beyond* the text – in this case Steven Moffat. Fans see a pattern in the way women are depicted in media created by Moffat and argue that this is encoded into the text of *Doctor Who*. Writing stories in which Old!Amy kills the Doctor and leaves Rory and young!Amy on Apalapucia thus recodes the character into a woman who no longer waits but proactively designs the future she wants.

Conclusion

In this chapter I've looked at two kinds of fanfiction – those which fill in the blanks and those which recode meaning into the story. I suggest that neither of these is textual poaching in the way that Jenkins theorises it: the fans rewriting Amy Pond in the first set of stories are doing so within the confines of the episode. Although the character experiences growth within the fics, this is mirrored in the changes we see in the episode itself. In this sense, poaching is a passive action: it is a reaction to a text, a retrospective attempt to change. Recoding, however, is active: it is fans seeking out issues within and beyond the text and deliberately reworking them to create an alternative story. It is Old!Amy learning to fight, hacking the interface, killing the Doctor and making her own meaning from her experiences.

Notes

1. Jane Clare Jones, 'Is Sherlock Sexist? Steven Moffat's Wanton Women', *The Guardian* (3 January 2012): https://www.theguardian.com/commentisfree/2012/jan/03/sherlock-sexist-steven-moffat (accessed 9 August 2022); Foz Meadows, 'Imaginary Interview with Imaginary Steven Moffat', *Shattersnipe: Malcontent & Rainbows* (8 January 2012): https://fozmeadows.wordpress.com/2012/01/08/imaginary-interview-with-imaginary-steven-moffat/ (accessed 9 August 2022).

2. Michael Hogan, '*Doctor Who* Its Sad To See Amy Pond Leave', *The Telegraph* (16 December 2011): https://www.telegraph.co.uk/culture/tvandradio/doctor-who/8960682/Doctor-Who-Its-sad-to-see-Amy-Pond-leave.htm (accessed 9 August 2022); Patrick Mulkern, '*Doctor Who*: The Bells of Saint John ★★★★', *Radio Times* (21 October 2013): https://www.radiotimes.com/tv/sci-fi/doctor-who-guide/the-bells-of-saint-john/ (accessed 9 August 2022).

3. Matt Risley, '*Doctor Who*: "The Girl Who Waited" Review', *IGN* (11 September 2011): https://www.ign.com/articles/2011/09/11/doctor-who-the-girl-who-waited-review (accessed 9 August 2022); Lindsay Miller, 'The Girl Who Waited: Why I Hate Amy Pond', *Tiger Beatdown* (4 August 2011): http://tigerbeatdown.com/2011/08/04/the-girl-who-waited-why-i-hate-amy-pond/ (accessed 9 August 2022).

4. Henry Jenkins, *Textual Poachers* (New York, NY: Routledge, 1992).

5. Stuart Hall, 'Encoding/Decoding', in *Culture, Media and Language*, ed. Stuart Hall, Dorothy Hobson, Andrew Lowe, and Paul Willis (London: Hutchinson, 1980), 128–38.

6. Feministwhoniverse, 'Steven Moffat is a Douchebag – The Masterlist', *Tumblr* (21 June 2013): http://feministwhoniverse.tumblr.com/post/25598314408/steven-moffat-is-a-douchebag-the-masterlist (accessed 9 August 2022).

7. Ace of Emeralds, 'Another Minute and He Doesn't Love You', *Fanfiction.net* (11 September 2011): http://www.fanfiction.net/s/7372257/1/Another-minute-and-he-doesnt-love-you (accessed 9 August 2022).

8. EachPeachPearPlum, 'Rule Number 1', *Fanfiction.net*. (13 September 2011): http://www.fanfiction.net/s/7379717/1/Rule-Number-1 (accessed 9 August 2022).

9. Jenkins, *Textual Poachers,* 162.

10. CJ Burns, 'Paradox Schmaradox', *Fanfiction.net* (23 October 2011): https://www.fanfiction.net/s/7487391/1/Paradox-Schmaradox (accessed 9 August 2022).

11. zlot, 'The Way We Live Now', *Archive of Our Own* (17 September 2011): http://archiveofourown.org/works/254416 (accessed 9 August 2022).

12. Heliopause, 'The Doctor: Out of Time', *Archive of Our Own* (25 May 2013): http://archiveofourown.org/works/816310 (accessed 9 August 2022).

Chapter 28

Forks in the fandom road: Divergent views on the social politics of *Doctor Who* by Talia Franks

Original to this volume

Doctor Who returned to television in 2005, one year after the invention of Facebook, and Twitter launches one year later, in 2006. These public online spaces have made it easier for marginalized voices to be heard, and as the show has evolved to be more inclusive of BIPOC and queer identities, fans who see themselves represented through these changes are empowered to take up more space and speak louder about Doctor Who viewed through a socio-political lens. Talia Franks examines how this change has impacted the way fans interact, both online and in real spaces, and where we go from here.

Sixty years and counting, *Doctor Who* is a show that embodies change, adaptability and regeneration. Whether on screen or behind the scenes, there has always been a constant ebb and flow in the way that the show presents itself and the kinds of stories it tells. Fan reactions to these changes have been, and continue to be, wide, varied and constant – a testament to how the fanbase's culture has changed and grown in step with the show it revolves around. The advent of the internet created one of the largest and most notable shifts in the ways people interact with the show and each other.

For this chapter, I reached out to over a dozen fans from multiple countries who are varied in age, racial and ethnic background, ability, gender identity and sexual orientation. I also reached out to people who have been fans of *Doctor Who* for varying lengths of time. My small sample size cannot hope to encompass the entirety of fandom, but I hope that in lifting the voices of other fans in this chapter alongside my own, I can provide a fuller picture of the ways that fandom has become increasingly diverse and intersectional in the nearly sixty years it has been running, and the effects of that diversification.[1]

Representation matters

Doctor Who has always been political; however, since its revival in 2005 the show has made an effort towards more progressive politics by including more main cast and characters of colour, queer characters and disabled characters. Martha Jones (Freema Agyeman), introduced in series three, was the first full-time Black companion in the TARDIS. Bill Potts (Pearl Mackie), in series 10, was the first queer person of colour. When Chris Chibnall began as showrunner in series 11, Jodie Whittaker debuted as the first woman Doctor, Yaz (Mandip Gill) became the first South Asian and Muslim companion (she has subsequently been confirmed as a queer character as well) and Ryan (Tosin Cole) was the first Black man to be a main cast companion and the first companion with a named disability. The 2020 reveal of Jo Martin's character as the first Black woman Doctor was another large milestone for *Doctor Who*.

All these characters and the identities they represent have been incredibly meaningful and important to fans. Shortly after 'Legend of the Sea Devils' aired – the episode where a textual romantic relationship between the Thirteenth Doctor and her companion Yaz was confirmed – one Twitter user wrote:

> literally sobbing at the fact that not only did mandip portray such a important character on screen for all of us who relate but also she showed me as a queer muslim woman that it's okay to be yourself and love who you want to love. I will forever be thankful.[2]
> that while parts of my culture are still totally against the idea of wlw [women loving women] relationships there is not enough representation on screen for people like me. this era has given me so much hope and validation. Yasmin Khan will always be an icon [pleading emoji]'.[3]

The Chibnall-era decision to include characters with visibly marginalized identities has not been without its foibles; however, the benefits that come from this inclusive approach far outweigh its sometimes-messy execution. One of these benefits is how discussions of power, or lack thereof, come up naturally, both in the show itself and in fan spaces. As Skye Jones of *The Queer Archive* podcast puts it:

> The visibility of these topics has provided more opportunities for marginalized fans to be represented and feel connected to the show.
> It makes a difference when disability is seen in the main cast and talked about positively on screen. It makes a difference when the Doctor, not only claims they do not subscribe to the gender binary, but actually emboies [sic] genderqueer joy. When the queer relationship is canon. When stories about immigrants explicitly critique Western Imperialism. When these stories are created by writers, directors and actors with those lived experiences. When our narratives are named – not just limited to metaphor. This has allowed me to take up more space in the *Doctor Who* fandom.[4]

Taking up space is not something traditionally afforded to people who are on the margins of our society. The increased diversity in the show, and the validation it provides to queer fans and fans of colour, has opened the door for a more inclusive dialogue about the show and allows marginalized fans the opportunity to use their voices to become a part of the narrative about and around the show.

Fan spaces, on- and offline

Many people became fans of *Doctor Who* in 2005, when the show was revived, with others joining and leaving the fandom in the seventeen years since then. There are fans who might be quietly appreciative of the show, but not active in the fandom because they have nowhere to express themselves. As Nicole Hill, the founder of Black TARDIS, put it:

> When I became a fan of *Doctor Who*, there weren't spaces where I felt I could express or discuss my specific experience with the show and with the characters. I created a space first and foremost for myself and my friends, to address our own need and desire for a community of fans who could understand our perspectives.[5]

There can be a huge disconnect when people try to talk about the same show from vastly different experiences. The need for a space of one's own to have conversations is incredibly important for many fans. Fan spaces are changing both in person and online. According to writer Riley J. Silverman:

> speaking as a visibly trans queer person, it's been really lovely to see how much more queer the crowds at *Doctor Who* events have become. There's still a long way to go towards making everyone comfortable and safe but it's still nice to see the direction it's been moving. The more negative side is that as the show has been pushing into a more and more progressive era, the voices of people in opposition to change have gotten more vocal and hostile. So there's a greater need now to ensure that fandom spaces are explicitly welcoming and friendly to marginalized people.[6]

Online fan spaces can vary greatly depending on whether someone is interacting with the show on public platforms such as Twitter alone, as opposed to in a private Discord server. There is also a large difference in how people interact online and in person at conventions for example. As one fan, Rebecca Farren, put it:

> I love going to in-person conventions, as there is a warmth and a joy that we all share in coming together and celebrating our show. I frequently call conventions my 'happy place'. However, I tend to enjoy the general vibe and the excitement of engaging with cast and crew at in-person conventions, rather than making new friends or having in-depth discussion about *Doctor Who*. Online spaces such as the Quiz of Rassilon and the Black [Nerds] Create community have allowed me to make friends and connect with other fans on a much more interpersonal level. Online, I can discuss ideas, have fun, and create community, without needing to spend a whole weekend's worth of energy, or without being forced to navigate inaccessible/partially accessible transport, hotel, or convention spaces.[7]

The accessibility of online fan spaces is particularly key, as Rebecca notes, and is something that has provided the ability for more people in more places to connect. The advent of Covid-19 in particular opened many doors in that regard. While communities such as Black Nerds Create are almost entirely online to begin with, the Quiz of Rassilon was run as an in-person pub quiz starting in 2010 and transitioned to an online event during lockdown.

The 'threat' of diversity and 'wokeness'

Regarding casting, *Doctor Who* in the Chibnall era has been referred to as 'PC Gone Wrong' and 'liberal BS' and accused of 'checking PC boxes'.[8] Certain watchers of the show feel threatened by having women and people of colour as primary forces in telling the story, with the prevalence of the #NotMyDoctor #PCGoneMad and #SaveDoctorWho hashtags in social media.

When Jodie Whittaker was cast as the Thirteenth Doctor, there were voices who insisted that the Doctor could only be a man, and that 'wokeness' was ruining *Doctor Who*; however, Whittaker's Doctor has been the exact same character we have always known them to be. As journalist and author Laurie Penny put it on Twitter:

> Jodie Whittaker has done a bang-up job of embodying the character, and the writers have given her material that rings true- and for some fans, I think, that's the problem. The traits that make The Doctor admirable and adorable as a man make her 'annoying' as a woman. #DoctorWho[9]

Despite a remarkable lack of change in how the character interacts and engages with the world and wider universe, many people's dislike of the Thirteenth Doctor is based almost entirely in her gender presentation, and how they view it as fundamentally different from the male incarnations of the Doctor.

When asked about his opinion of how fan communities have changed in the past few years, actor, writer and producer Dominic G. Martin responded:

> *Doctor Who* fandom has massively changed from when I started being a fan. [...] Over the last 10 or so years especially however, it has felt like it has gotten generally more toxic in places. **Not everywhere, but especially with the 13th Doctor**, the controversies surrounding her very quickly become highly volatile, toxic and can lead to people getting quite hurt for no good reason. Right now I think DW fandom is at a very dangerous place, and the next era will determine whether it topples over entirely or not.[10]

(emphasis added)

Fan response to the Thirteenth Doctor and her episodes has been particularly harsh, with users commenting on the BBC America *Doctor Who* Instagram account post of the Centenary special trailer: 'Jodie Whittaker is a great actress, but the writers have really taken her character and the show as a whole, completely downhill.'[11] 'Goodbye nobody miss you … You desteoy[sic] the doctors[sic] mythology … ' and 'Doctor Woke' under the same Instagram post of the Centenary trailer.[12]

While there are also fans with positive messages, the vitriol piled onto the Thirteenth Doctor's era is notable because so much of it is criticizing the show for 'wokeness' – that is to say for daring to have characters of colour. Even criticism of the writing can be seen in a different light when one considers that Chibnall hired the first people of colour to be writers on the show, as well as more women writers generally.

In the wake of the confirmation of 'Thasmin' in 'Legend of the Sea Devils', there were people who actively suppressed and/or ignored the ship by posting pictures of past heterosexual pairings in the show such as the Tenth Doctor (David Tennant) and Rose (Billie Piper) or the Twelfth Doctor (Peter Capaldi) and Missy (Michelle Gomez), after the episode aired. While undoubtedly there are many people who do not ship Thasmin to the same degree, or at all, compared to 'Thassies', the posting and promotion of alternative pairings in the wake of Thasmin shippers having their moment left a sour note. They erased not only a queer relationship but also the presence of a queer woman of colour specifically.

Conclusion

Doctor Who fandom is varied and complex. Given its rich history of almost six decades and the way that its fans span the entire planet, I could not hope to gather all of the ways it has impacted people's lives and relationships with one another. The show is meant to encompass the universe and has infinite potential, so why should it be focused around representing only certain kinds of people? The show has made increasing efforts towards diversity and inclusion and making fans feel seen, but so much work is yet to be done.

The return of Russell T Davies as showrunner and his casting of Ncuti Gatwa as the first Black main cast Doctor is an important step. Gatwa's casting along with the casting of Yasmin Finney, a young Black trans actress, are indicative that Davies is continuing to diversify the show. Many fans responded positively to these cast announcements, with others acting incredibly critical of the casting decisions. Some white fans claimed Gatwa didn't have 'enough experience' despite the fact that at the time of casting he is older than Matt Smith was at the beginning of his run and is an award-winning stage, film and television actor.

As people continue to decry the directions the show has been taken in, the need for inclusive narrative is more important than ever. It will be important for Davies to follow through with these castings to not only account for who is on screen physically but also how their stories are told in order to accurately represent fans. Davies and the BBC will also need to provide support for their actors and push back against anti-diversity narratives. Marketing for the series needs to account for and be more inclusive of fans who support diversity and the fandom beyond the UK.

As fans continue to gather both on- and offline, it's important for us to remember what brings us together – the evolving and shifting story, where there is something for everyone to love and which we love in our own ways.

Notes

1. List of those interviewed whose words influenced this work: Beth Axford, Deborah Stanish, Dominic G. Martin, Erika Ensign, Ioan, Kayti Burt, Michael, Nicole Hill, Rebecca Farren, Remi, Riley J. Silverman, Skye Seitz and Tansy Roberts.
2. sonia (@awhoviantimtrv), 'literally sobbing at the fact that not only did mandip portray such a important character on screen for all of us who relate but also she showed me as a queer', Twitter, (22 April 2022), 4:50 p.m.: https://web.archive.org/web/20220429200421/https://twitter.com/awhoviantimetrv/status/1517606796634038273 (accessed 9 August 2022).
3. sonia (@awhoviantimtrv), 'that while parts of my culture are still totally against the idea of wlw relationships there is not enough representation on screen for people like me', Twitter, (22 April 2022), 4:54 p.m.: http://web.archive.org/web/20220422205507/https://twitter.com/awhoviantimetrv/status/1517607860590596101 (accessed 9 August 2022).

4   Skye Jones, document shared with author via email, 14 April 2022.
5   Nicole Hill, email message to author, 9 April 2022.
6   Riley J. Silverman, email message to author, 4 April 2022.
7   Rebecca Farren, document shared in email message to author, 12 April 2022.
8   Jack Pusey, 'Woke-N Record *Doctor Who* Viewers Rage at "Unbearable Political Correctness" as Another Female Doctor Revealed', *The Sun*, (27 January 2020): https://web.archive.org/web/20220429202518/https://www.thesun.ie/tvandshowbiz/television/5032530/doctor-who-viewers-rage-at-unbearable-political-correctness-as-another-female-doctor-revealed/ (accessed 9 August 2022).
9   Laurie Penny (@PennyRed), 'Jodie Whittaker has done a bang-up job of embodying the character, and the writers have given her material that rings true- and for some fans, I think, that's', Twitter, (18 April 2022), 7:07 a.m.: http://web.archive.org/web/20220429201418/https://twitter.com/PennyRed/status/1516010513951600644 (accessed 9 August 2022).
10 Dominic G. Martin, email message to author, 7 April 2022.
11 Verified *Doctor Who* on BBC America Account (@doctorwho_bbca), '"This is the day you die … " [fire emoji] The Thirteenth Doctor faces the forces that mass against her in her final adventure', Autumn 2022. #DoctorWho Instagram, (17 April 2022): https://www.instagram.com/p/Ccdr69GsJ86/ (accessed 9 August 2022).
12 Ibid.

Chapter 29
Postcolonial *Doctor Who*

From 'Through Coloured Eyes: An Alternative Viewing of Postcolonial Transition' by Vanessa de Kauwe[*]

First published 2013

> Vanessa de Kauwe's essay, excerpted here, offers two ways of analysing The Ark. *In doing so, she demonstrates that those with a personal history of postcolonial experience can't help but read the show through that lens, and seeks to merge this with a more critically focused reading.*

Cultural contamination

There are still more complex representations of postcolonial transition which an experiential viewing can uncover. Most generally, the Monoids, having overcome their oppression by the Guardians, do *not* return to their original way of life. Rather, they demonstrate elements of the transitional experience that I call cultural contamination – a notion I have developed through a lifelong observation of my own family and friends. I propose cultural contamination as a phenomenon that occurs after severe, systematic and prolonged oppression by another culture. It is the phenomenon by which the freedom, progress and power that the oppressor is seen to enjoy become conflated with the culture of the oppressor. I can still hear my parents and grandparents declaring that they went to 'the best schools' because said schools were run by 'Europeans' who would not teach the native subjects. The fact that only British language, history and culture were taught was enough for this to be declared 'the best' education. Conversely, as Fanon demonstrates, the degradation, sociopolitical impotence and suppression that the subjugated experience are so intense that they become psychologically (even pathologically) linked with their own culture and physical traits.[1]

I suggest that this double conflation of colonialism with superiority, and the colonized with inferiority, triggers a form of performative cultural contamination such that the colonized, in seeking the freedoms and

---

[*]Originally published in *Doctor Who and Race*, ed. Lindy Orthia (Bristol, UK: Intellect, 2013), 141–57.

benefits that their oppressors possess, seek to emulate the latter's culture and way of life. Thus cultural contamination can be defined as both a psychological and enacted phenomenon. At a psychological level, the culture of the colonizer is mixed with ideals of freedom, greatness, strength and desirability, while the colonized have a view of their own culture which is contaminated with Fanonian ideas of inferiority. Hence at a practical level, even after the colonized have gained political independence, the enactment of their lives is contaminated with elements of their former oppressor's culture and ideals. In *The Ark*, my notion of cultural contamination is inadvertently represented in the way the Monoids go to great lengths to mimic Guardian traits.

Postcolonial theorist Homi Bhabha points out that this 'mimicry' is typical of those attempting to transition from colonial or similar oppression.[2] In the case of *The Ark* this is most vividly seen in the devices of the statue and the voice box. Most noticeably to the Doctor and his companions, the Monoids continue building the Guardians' statue. However, they cap it with their own one-eyed head. If we are to take this as symbolism for Bhabha's mimicry, then we may interpret it as suggesting that the Monoids have taken on, as their own, various aspects of the work, culture and even future projects and expectations of their former oppressors, while now heading these things themselves – they, the Monoids, are now at the head of Guardian cultural indicators. More potent is the symbolism of the voice box. Even in a state of liberation, the Monoids do not revert to their own voice, or even use their commonly understood sign language. Rather, they develop a voice box so their thoughts can be understood in the voice and language of their oppressors – English. Here we have an implicit indication that human English is still the language of power, and the voice of the oppressor is still the voice of authority.

At this point, Bhabha may disagree with me. Rather than seeing mimicry as purely a self-deprecating acknowledgement of the superiority of the oppressor, Bhabha declares that 'mimicry is both resemblance and menace'.[3] For, as Bhabha has been summarized by Nayar, through mimicry the native shows the white man that the former can match the latter in every way.[4] Thus for Bhabha, mimicry can be useful in undermining notions of colonial superiority.[5] While this experience of mimicry as an equalizer may resonate with some postcolonial survivors, there are logical implications that should be mentioned. Again it is Nayar who summarizes the alleged equalizing qualities of Bhabha's mimicry:

> He is a mimic who can now respond in English and argue rationally (rather than sentimentally, which would be a stereotypical 'native' or Oriental form of argumentation) because of Western education [...] He appeals to the English in the language of logic, reason, administrative convenience and expediency.[6]

Note the implicit suggestions in this argument. The native shows he is equal to the colonizer by mimicking all the positive attributes of the colonizer. The implication is that the native is naturally unable to 'argue rationally', nor can he demonstrate 'logic, reason, administrative convenience and expediency', without the influence of white colonization. This is clearly an implicit affirmation of the superiority of the colonizer, which is highly problematic, and is yet another reason why the colonized may experience Fanonian inferiority.

Perhaps this too, is the reality of the postcolonial transitional experience: that the colonized only feel equal to the colonizer when they can successfully mimic the latter. Perhaps it is more subtle than that. Perhaps even postcolonial individuals who realize their self-worth feel they can only *prove* their equality to the colonizing race through thorough and accurate mimicry. This seems to be Fanon's diagnosis, for he declares, 'Black men want to prove to white men, *at all costs*, the richness of their thought, the equal value of their intellect'.[7] And it seems that part of the cost of this mimicry is that the subjugated begin to treat each other in the same way as their oppressors.[8] To take a final example from *The Ark*, the Monoids not only attempt to enslave and dominate each other as the Guardians did to their entire race but they even continue to deny each other names, referring to each other by numbers.

From the various examples given above, it is possible to view the representations of the Monoids in *The Ark* as analogous of the non-fictional postcolonial transitional experience. Yet this experiential viewing alone, like the purely critical viewing before it, remains incomplete. What seems missing is a complex viewing which reveals the relation between the colonial injustices highlighted by the critical viewing and the transitional experiences illustrated by the experiential viewing.

The complex viewing

A complex viewing acknowledges the realities of both the critical and experiential viewing, and seeks to establish the relation between the two.

For example, a complex viewing notes the disarray the Monoids find themselves in, through the experiential viewing; but it is able to causally link this phenomenon to the Guardians' colonial-like regime, as revealed by the critical viewing. Thus a complex viewing allows us to realize that racial oppression is never simply a matter of political or military control, as it appears to be in *The Ark*. Rather, as Fanon points out, it is heavily based on economic oppression, educational manipulation and segregation, and a self-serving bureaucratic system.[9] In this manner, a complex viewing traces the tragedies and instabilities of postcolonial transition back to their colonial causes. Thus colonialism is forced to bear the responsibility (and even blame) for the consequences of its injustices.

Similarly, a complex viewing sees the violence and in-fighting of transitional races, as represented in the Monoids, not as a condemnation of the race in question. Rather, a complex viewing recognizes that such violence is the consequence of the situation the race finds itself in.[10] I have already discussed Fanon's argument that the whole system of colonial oppression is based on the threat of imperial violence, and how decolonization leaves the native with little means other than violence with which to run the transitioning nation. But at this point Fanon can add more. Here Fanon claims that, at a racial level, the subjugated fight because oppression has turned their entire existence into a fight for survival: a fight against poverty, starvation, disease and hopelessness.[11] At a personal level, he famously declared that 'violence is a cleansing force' – a psychologically necessary reclaiming of life and vigour after one has been completely downtrodden.[12] While both Fanon and I regret such transition violence, we both acknowledge its reality. And recognizing the reality of transitional violence facilitates a complex viewing of representations of transitional peoples. With regard to *The Ark*, the violence of the Monoids can be recognized as the practical and psychological consequence of their oppression, rather than a slur against their inherent nature.

The complex viewing and mimicry

A further use of the complex viewing is that it facilitates a closer scrutiny of Bhabha's theory of mimicry. Bhabha proposes that mimicry renders colonial discourses ambiguous; for rather than bringing pure oppression, colonialism also bears benefits that the native would otherwise lack.[13] I have already discussed the derogatory implications that may be drawn from such a theory of ambiguity. Moreover, claiming that colonial discourses are ambiguous hinders us from making value judgements regarding colonial policies, attitudes and actions. Consequently, colonialism is protected from much of the responsibility and blame that may be attached to it. However, a complex viewing reveals a reality that is closer to Fanon's argument. That is, elements that appear to be deficiencies in the colonized are actually the consequences of colonial discourses and regimes. Fanon goes so far as to indicate that the seemingly superior wealth, progress and civilization of colonizing empires were built from the ravaged resources and enslaved labour that were taken from the lands they colonized.[14] Thus a complex viewing reveals that the struggles and apparent failings of oppressed peoples are not due to an inherent flaw in the people themselves, but are a consequence of colonialism and its discourses. Likewise, mimicry too can be causally traced to colonial discourses, rather than an alleged lacking in the oppressed. I will illustrate this point with a further example from *Doctor Who*.

Since I have focused on *The Ark*, which occurs near the beginning of the original series, I will attempt a broader view by taking an example from very late in the original series: *Ghost Light* (1989). In this serial we meet the long oppressed and enslaved character called Control. Upon gaining release from her downtrodden state, Control yearns after only two things: her 'freeness' and to be 'ladylike'. Why only these two things? Because these are the two things her oppression denied her. She was not free to achieve self-actualization, and she was certainly not permitted to attain to what she believed was the highest standard of existence: British gentry. Here we have a form of mimicry that is based on cultural contamination. For in the character of Control, freedom has become equated with the culture and social status of the British ruling class. This illustrates a postcolonial phenomenon which is commonly termed 'more British than the British'. It is the phenomenon by which the subjugated seek to emulate and even exceed the linguistic, cultural and often religious traits of the oppressors.[15]

Why is this so important to postcolonial transition? Because, as Fanon has already suggested, the language and culture of the native then become conflated with inferiority. The subjugated suspect that to stand on equal ground with their former masters, they must become masters of the oppressor's culture. But as Fanon points out, in emulating the white man, the coloured lose elements of their own cultural identity.[16] This can be seen in the example of my parents and grandparents who glorified all things British. But I also recognize it in myself: my passing suspicions that Sri Lankan ways are outdated ways, and even the fact that my accent changes when I'm not in coloured company. I was gratified to learn that my friends from other Asian and some African countries have the same experience. The result? In artificially whitening ourselves we grow increasingly forgetful of our natural heritage.

So while the postcolonial situation may be complex, it is not, as Bhabha suggests, ambiguous. That is, it is not ambiguous to the extent that we can't make value judgements regarding colonial discourses and their consequences.

Finally, I suggest that a complex viewing allows us to strip Bhabha's mimicry to a more basic level. This allows us to see that mimicry is often employed by the colonized as a necessity for survival. While Control engages in mimicry to satisfy her personal aspirations, in other circumstances colonized people have no choice but to engage in mimicry because of the way colonialism has restructured their world. To illustrate, we need only look at the 1975 serial *The Ark in Space*.

In *The Ark in Space* the humans again take the role of the colonizers. In a backstory that is quickly glossed over and therefore easily overlooked, the human race have attempted to colonize several planets and in doing so have almost wiped out the race known as Wirrn. The remaining handful of Wirrn have since journeyed towards the Earth in hope of a means to survive, possibly via the same route that the humans used to decimate the Wirrn home planets.

Yet this is not the focus of *The Ark in Space*. Rather, the storyline shows how one of the Wirrn takes over the body of the human captain Noah, but retains Noah's human voice and language in an attempt to communicate with human authorities and the Doctor. Here again we have an implicit recognition of the authority and power of the colonizer's voice and language. However, in this example of vocal mimicry, the reasoning of the Wirrn seems purely practical. It may be interpreted as indicating that any chance of survival in the colonizers' realm requires adapting oneself to their language, customs and ultimately their political control. This is surely the experience of all postcolonial peoples whose diasporic journey brings them to their colonizers' homeland. The colonizer's influence and culture continues to dominate, even after decolonization.

At a superficial level, the monstrous representation of the Wirrn leads the audience to react towards them as a powerful, foreign threat capable of wiping out human civilization. But a closer look at their backstory lets us realize that they are the dispossessed – those who are nearly annihilated by an invading human force.

A complex viewing suggests that while the Monoids take the form of the slave, the Wirrn offer an image of the refugee or migrant. In her contribution to the recent volume *Doctor Who and Philosophy*, Deborah Pless complains that Britain is 'practically bursting at the seams' with migrants from the colonies.[17] But by Pless's own logic, Britain would not be 'bursting at the seams' if it had not attempted to swallow the resources of over half the globe; just as Noah (the captain of the space station that the Wirrn take residence upon) would not be bursting with Wirrn tissue if the humans hadn't invaded the latter's planet.

It must be acknowledged that, in actuality, many postcolonial migrants are able to maintain elements of their language and cultures. Yet a tension always remains. There is always the juggle of freely expressing their heritage and integrating successfully into the new lifestyle they find themselves in. The transition is never smooth. Rather, the reality of postcolonial transition seems filled with trauma, uncertainty and, as Orthia suggests, abscesses and chasms.

Notes

1 This has been described by Nayar as 'Fanon's major contribution' to understanding the postcolonial experience. Pramod K. Nayar, *Postcolonialism: A Guide for the Perplexed* (London: Continuum, 2010), 9. The details of Fanon's thesis develop throughout his works, particularly in chapters 5, 6 and 7 of *Black Skin, White Masks*.

2 Homi K. Bhabha, 'Of Mimicry and Man: The Ambivalence of Colonial Discourse', in *The Location of Culture* (London: Routledge, 1994), 85–92.

3 Bhabha, 'Of Mimicry and Man', 86.

4 Nayar, *Postcolonialism*, 27–8.

5 Bhabha, 'Of Mimicry and Man', 87–8.

6 Nayar, *Postcolonialism*, 28.

7 Frantz Fanon, *Black Skin, White Masks*, trans. Charles Lam Markmann (New York: Grove Press, 1967 [1952]), 12, emphasis added.

8 Fanon, *Black Skin, White Masks*, 228.

9 Frantz Fanon, *Wretched of the Earth*, trans. Constance Farrington (Harmondsworth: Penguin Books, 1967 [1963]), 77, 81–2 and 134.

10 Fanon, *Wretched of the Earth*, 28.

11 Fanon, *Black Skin, White Masks*, 224.

12 Fanon, *Wretched of the Earth*, 74.

13 Bhabha, 'Of Mimicry and Man'. See also Homi K. Bhabha, 'Signs Taken for Wonders: Questions of Ambivalence and Authority under a Tree outside Delhi, May 1817', in *The Location of Culture* (New York: Routledge, 1994), 145–75.

14 Fanon, *Wretched of the Earth*, 41.

15 It is the phenomenon Fanon describes when he says 'The Black man wants to be white'. Fanon, *Black Skin, White Masks*, 11. The details of the argument follow throughout that book.

16 Fanon, *Black Skin, White Masks*, 11.

17 Deborah Pless, 'The Decline and Fall of the British Empire, Sponsored by TARDIS', in *Doctor Who and Philosophy: Bigger on the Inside*, ed. Courtland Lewis and Paula Smithka (Chicago: Open Court, 2010), 353.

SECTION FOUR

Doctor Who's creative intersections

Tansy Rayner Roberts

Because of its longevity, *Doctor Who* presents a fascinating case study for the intersections and crossovers that can exist between 'fan' and 'professional'. Writers, actors and other contributors to the show's official content are often grilled on their fannish history – did they love the show as kids? Did they write letters to the editor about Daleks, or complain about their favourite show on live TV?

There's a discomfort to those crossovers sometimes, when pros intrude on fannish spaces and vice versa. Are you allowed back to the Fitzroy Tavern once you're a writer on the show, or worse … a showrunner? Do you still count as a fan yourself when you're making the show?

Then there's the other side of it – creative professionals who don't work on *Doctor Who* (yet), but whose fandom of the show has informed and shaped their own professional trajectory. From *Inspector Spacetime* to *Outlander*, this nearly-60-year-old show has left fingerprints across popular media and beyond.

Doctor Who is a cultural product synonymous with creators who have one foot in fandom, and one in the professional world. Has this made the mythology of the show stronger, or has it fractured the growing, changing fandom? Are some fannish professionals, or professional fans, given different status to others?

Who is allowed to critique the show, and who is not?

The reprints in this chapter explore the fine line between creator and fan. Eddie Robson discusses one of the first showrunners of *Doctor Who* who was also a fan – Douglas Adams. Nolan Feeney explores the fanzine roots of *Doctor Who* in honour of its fiftieth anniversary in 2013. Following those chapters, we reprint two works of *Doctor Who criticism* from none other than future Doctor Peter Capaldi (writing into the *Radio Times*) and future showrunner Steven Moffat. Finally, Mary Robinette Kowal explains how she weaves the Doctor into her original fiction.

The original chapters in this section explore this tension as well. If fandom poaches and consumes the media it loves, then what happens when it gets poached in return? Ian Potter looks at the history of writing and publishing about *Doctor Who* from the 1960s onward, and the influence of these texts on the show over the decades. Following this, Archivist Lynne M Thomas shows how being a *Doctor Who* fan can often change lives in unexpected ways. She looks back on how her fandom not only shaped her family and social life, but also led her to a new professional path as an award-winning editor and publisher. Julia Henken has some theories about how the different fannish philosophies of the three twenty-first-century *Doctor Who* showrunners influence their respective eras of the show. The section continues with Paul Driscoll's discussion of how the fandom itself has been written into New Who by its fanboy showrunners. Driscoll examines how fandom responds when they see themselves reflected, positively and negatively, in their favourite show. And Leslie McMurtry concludes the section by discussing the fanzine Renaissance of the 2000s as a reflection of 21st century *Doctor Who* fandom.

Chapter 30
Fans for hire

From 'Douglas Adams: The First Professional *Doctor Who* Fan' by Eddie Robson*

First published 2017

It's rare these days to find scriptwriters on Doctor Who *that didn't grow up loving the show as a kid. In the 1970s, they were a little harder to find ... until young Douglas Adams caught the attention of the BBC.*

For a long time Douglas Adams was the most famous writer ever to have written for *Doctor Who*, and it's possible he still is. (More recently, you could make a strong case for Neil Gaiman or Richard Curtis.) The fact that Adams went on to be a very famous writer makes his work on the programme inherently interesting, in the way that a home recording of The Beatles noodling on their guitars in 1959 is interesting simply because it's by The Beatles. But even if Adams' career had foundered and he became one of those writers only *Doctor Who* fans have heard of, he would still be a hugely important writer in *Doctor Who*'s history.

In 1977, Adams sent the pilot script for his radio comedy *The Hitchhiker's Guide to the Galaxy* to the new *Doctor Who* script editor, Anthony Read. Adams had been recommended to Read as a writer to watch by Read's predecessor, Robert Holmes, who had generally struggled to find writers who could deliver a good *Doctor Who* script. Meanwhile *his* predecessor, Terrance Dicks, had put together a reliable stable of writers over his first three years which he then kept using for the next three. The upshot of all this was that only two new writers had joined *Doctor Who* in the past seven seasons, and both of them were in their thirties. Nobody writing for the show was young enough to have grown up with it.

Adams was twenty-five when he was commissioned to write his first *Doctor Who* serial, *The Pirate Planet* – nearly a decade younger than any other *Doctor Who* writer at that time. In 1963, he'd been eleven and *Doctor Who* was a big formative influence on him – he later said it was the only TV programme he refused to miss, religiously heading to the TV lounge at Brentwood boarding school every Saturday.

---

*Originally published in *Hero Collector*, January 2017.

The extent to which the William Hartnell episodes imprinted on Adams can be seen in his 1982 novel *Life, The Universe and Everything*: the scene where Arthur and Ford arrive at Lord's cricket ground on a sofa, which is narrated from the perspective of the commentary team, reads like direct homage to a scene in the 1966 episode 'Volcano', part of *The Daleks' Master Plan*.

Douglas Adams was the first *Doctor Who* writer to be a fan of the show. This was a significant moment. *Doctor Who* had subverted itself before, but Adams came to it from a comedy background, having written and performed in revues at Cambridge and forged a mostly unsuccessful writing partnership with Graham Chapman before finally getting the commission for *Hitchhiker's*. And he had long since absorbed *Doctor Who*'s conventions – his first response to it as a schoolboy had been to make a spoof version on cassette tape called *Doctor Which?* which he presented as part of the entertainment at a school Christmas party in 1964. Subverting *Doctor Who* was second nature to him.

The Pirate Planet gives us an over-the-top *Doctor Who* villain to distract us from the real villain, and a corridor the Doctor doesn't need to run down, because it has its own propulsion system. *City of Death* runs parallel plots through different time zones by presenting a villain who's been split between several of them (until this there had been remarkably few stories where the plot actually hinged on time travel) and, by pairing Romana with Duggan, gives us a glimpse of *Doctor Who* with a female Doctor and a dim male assistant. In the unfinished and never-broadcast *Shada*, a Cambridge professor turns out to be a Time Lord whose rooms are his TARDIS. Adams constantly took what the audience knew about *Doctor Who* and twisted it in new ways.

This isn't to say Adams was a perfect fit for *Doctor Who*. He struggled to work within its limitations. His original scripts for *The Pirate Planet* were wildly overambitious (he was working on this and the first series of *Hitchhiker's* simultaneously, and later reflected that 'I did notice one odd thing: I was writing episodes of *Hitchhiker* which all seemed to happen in corridors, and writing episodes of *Doctor Who* which called for huge, enormous, impossibly elaborate sets. I thought, "I've got this the wrong way round"'). He was appointed script editor for the following season, but he was never the most structured writer and fixing other people's scripts was not his strong suit. Instead, he tended to put more jokes in.

Whilst Adams was working on *Doctor Who*, he wrote and published the first *Hitchhiker's* novel, which was an immediate success. As he became financially secure, his output became more leisurely, which means his *Doctor Who* scripts are part of a fairly small body of work. And you can follow a line from those through everything he did afterwards – the notes in the back of James Goss' novelization of *The Pirate Planet* reveal how the key *Hitchhiker's* idea of Earth being commissioned by mice evolved from his ideas for the resolution of the Key to Time storyline.

In fact, all Adams' major works feel like *Doctor Who* stories to some extent, and some of them literally were. *Life, The Universe and Everything* was based on a *Doctor Who* storyline rejected for being too expensive and/or silly. *Dirk Gently's Holistic Detective Agency* reused ideas from both *Shada* and *City of Death*, whilst Dirk himself is heavily reminiscent of Tom Baker's Doctor. *Doctor Who* feels deeply embedded into how Adams conceived and told stories: many young fans have written the wish-fulfilment story where the Doctor lands the TARDIS in their street and takes them off for a trip around the universe. What is *The Hitchhiker's Guide to the Galaxy* if not that, but transposed onto an adult man, with Ford Prefect in place of the Doctor? (Adams acknowledged Ford was 'a reaction against *Doctor Who*', a space traveller who will always avoid the opportunity to be heroic in favour of going to a party instead.)

Over the past decade and a bit, *Doctor Who* has been run by a fan, who then handed over to another fan, who is about to hand over to another fan. Most of the writers they've brought in also grew up with *Doctor Who*. In that sense, Douglas Adams was the prototype modern *Doctor Who* writer. It's a shame he didn't live to see it.

Chapter 31
The Doctor effect

From 'How Fanzines Helped Put *Doctor Who* Fans in Charge of *Doctor Who*' by Nolan Feeney[*]

First Published 2013

Have you ever loved something so much you wrote about it, photocopied it (or mimeographed it!) and distributed it to your fellow fans? The rising wave of printed Doctor Who *fanzines in the 1980s built a pool of writing talent that would ultimately shape and influence the show.*

When the BBC announced Scottish actor Peter Capaldi would play the Twelfth Doctor in its beloved sci-fi series *Doctor Who*, superfans quickly dug up a crucial fact about the actor: He's a superfan, too. Capaldi, who takes over Doctor duties from Matt Smith in a Christmas Day special, has an enthusiasm for the show that dates back to the 1970s, when he authored stories for *Doctor Who* fanzines – small-circulation publications made and distributed by fans. See, for example, this 1976 article[1] about the show's title sequences.

'Watching the abstracted light forms & patterns which appear in the opening sequence of *Dr. Who* has become a familiar ritual for all of us', eighteen-year-old Capaldi wrote. 'The wonder of the opening is that it manages to capture in only a very few moments of screen time the atmosphere of *Dr. Who*.'

Capaldi isn't the only amateur *Who* geek to go professional. Because of the programme's unusual history – it ran from 1963 to 1989 and then returned in 2005 – many of its original fans are now its writers and producers. Showrunner Steven Moffat told *The Guardian* this year that he was 'the original angry *Doctor Who* fan',[2] and his earliest internet postings about possible story ideas are still online[3] today (and those ideas occasionally find their way into the show). Writers like Paul Cornell and Matt Jones graduated from zines to official *Doctor Who* novelizations and, eventually, episodes of the reboot itself.

'When the new show comes out, there's almost this feeling of, "We've contributed to the success of this"', says Paul Booth, an assistant professor of new media and technology at DePaul University and

---

[*]Originally published in *The Atlantic*, December 2013, https://www.theatlantic.com/entertainment/archive/2013/12/how-fanzines-helped-put-em-doctor-who-em-fans-in-charge-of-em-doctor-who-em/282631/.

the editor of *Fan Phenomena: Doctor Who*. 'There's a co-production feeling to it that, without the fans, it wouldn't have come back.'

As the longest-running science fiction series ever, whose generation-spanning viewer base has often been named one of the most intense[4] and devoted fandoms[5] ever, *Who* offers an case study in the way that modern fandom has evolved. The fanzines where Capaldi and others got their start may have seen their numbers decline over the years, but their DNA is all over the modern fandom in a way that distinguishes it from other sci-fi fanzine communities like that of *Star Trek*. *Doctor Who* fanzines not only helped keep the fandom alive during its hiatus, they've been a long-standing venue for fans to debate and police the limits of the *Doctor Who* universe – and these debates have had a direct and noticeable influence on the show itself.

The golden age of *Doctor Who* fanzines, when the number of zines peaked in the hundreds and their most famous writers were most active, lasted from the mid-1980s and into the 1990s. The explosion was enabled in part by new technology: In addition to the advent of desktop publishing that made producing quality zines at home easier, the rise of VCRs and commercial video releases by the BBC allowed fans to rewatch and catch-up on episodes, facilitating detailed, in-depth discussions about the show, according to Matt Hills, a professor of film and TV studies at the University of Aberystwyth.

Those discussions were also enlivened, paradoxically, by the show's struggle to survive. While *Doctor Who*'s ratings were underwhelming in the years leading up to the show's 1989 cancellation, the fanzine community's interest intensified and its publications flourished, which Hills says isn't unusual for a fandom that feels its favourite show or its fan identity is threatened. Once the BBC closed the book on *Doctor Who*, it also prompted more fans to take up fan fiction and articles that playfully tackled the 'what-ifs' they might have refrained from if the show had continued.

These publications didn't just thrive then; they also played a major role in getting the show back on the air. During the hiatus, some of the most prolific and well-known zine writers were hired to pen novelizations of the show, which pushed *Doctor Who* into new territory. 'The stories were longer, they were more adult, they were expansive, and, certainly, right after the series ended, they fleshed out the mythology of the Doctor and the Time Lords very much', Booth says.

Screenwriter and television producer Russell T. Davies, who lobbied for and later led the 2005 reboot, authored some of these novelizations and paid close attention to the writing coming out of this period. 'He was aware that *Doctor Who* was capable of handling more complex themes, capable of handling more than just adventure tales', Booth says. 'The novels absolutely showed that *Doctor Who* was robust enough to handle the type of material needed to make it appeal to adult audiences.' Paul Cornell, for example, adapted his 1995 novel *Human Nature* into two episodes in 2007 that were named by *The Daily Telegraph*,[6] *Doctor Who Magazine*[7] and *IGN*[8] as some of the best *Who* episodes ever for the way they humanized the Doctor, then played by David Tennant.

In some ways, the zines' success may have also led to a loss in relevance. Leslie McMurtry, the editor of *The Terrible Zodin* zine who's studied the *Doctor Who* fandom, says the prestige of writing for fan publications declined in the 1990s as opportunities to take part in official channels opened up. In the 1970s and 1980s, official *Doctor Who* publications operated without much fan involvement, but in the 1990s, *Doctor Who Magazine* became more inclusive, and the novelization publishers' had open-call submissions, causing a shift in attitudes towards fanzines.

'If you had an opinion and wrote well, you aspired to write for the best zines, and once the gates were open to be in an official publication, then the cream of the crop could have money and recognition',

McMurtry says. '[While] they got absorbed into the official machinery, the second-tier writers filled in the fanzines, and maybe that's why it was perceived as less prestigious than before.'

Unsurprisingly, the internet is also to blame for the drop in the number of fanzines. The end of the *Doctor Who* zines' golden age coincides with the rise of some of its early Internet communities, where many of the conversations among fans migrated.

'There's often a temptation to see contemporary digital fandom as something radically new, but there are a lot of strong continuities between what fans did then and what they do now', Hills says. Fans won't find animated gifs in the Xeroxed pages of zines as they would on Tumblr today, but the same kinds of content – fan art, illustrations, fan fiction, reviews and essays, all in varying proportions depending on the publication – have appeared in both print and online spaces.

Who scholars say the main difference between the fanzine community and the online fandom – and there is some overlap between the two – is simply a matter of speed. A zine writer would submit a piece, wait for it to be published and wait even longer for rebuttals – conversations would take place over months, and rarely across international borders. Today, fans can bang out reviews immediately after episodes air, or flip out in real time over casting news about the new Doctor. They even can report and respond to breaking news about the show's production, though there were a few *Who* zines that operated in a more journalistic role and actively sought scoops.

Disdain for that immediacy – and a new generation of *Who* fans brought in by the reboot – has led to a small zine renaissance with titles like *Fish Fingers and Custard*, started by Daniel Gee in 2010 and available in both print and PDF editions (the latter of which gets more than 3,000 downloads per issue). 'You get people posting opinions *during* the episode sometimes, passing judgments on writers, producers and actors before they get a chance to digest it and listen to other opinions', writes Gee. 'The main thing that I like about fanzines is that each piece has (generally) been thought-out, researched, and is intriguing to read.'

Because of the show's intergenerational fan base and the openness of the internet – it rarely takes more than a username to hang with other superfans and see their work – the online *Doctor Who* fandom is somewhat decentralized, gathering around particular interests the way zines had their own preferences. Gallifrey Base, for example, is one of the largest *Doctor Who* fan forums online, but it's focused more on the classic series, and it's not a main hub for fanfiction. 'People become linked to certain venues they see as their home', Hills says. 'Some [spaces] might be more welcoming to younger fans or female fans, while some might be dominated by older generations or masculine fandoms.'

That's important, because the *Doctor Who* fandom hasn't always been, and sometimes still isn't, friendly to female fans. By McMurtry's estimates, male fans outnumbered female fans around three to one during the classic series' run, and as fan Karen Dunn wrote in McMurtry's zine *The Terrible Zodin*, 'There was nothing more likely to bring the Juke Box at the Fitzroy Tavern [a longtime gathering place for *Who* fans] scraping to a halt than a woman in a Tom Baker T-shirt strolling in'. The perception was that female fans didn't care about the show's writing or its science-fiction elements as much as they cared about the attractiveness of the Doctor or potential romantic relationships – a perception that still lingers in some circles.[9] Some zines provided a gender-blind space to participate in the fandom without having to confront these attitudes, while other zines provided a welcome outlet for women who *were* interested in writing, say, romantic fan fiction.

The series reboot has attracted considerable more female fans, possibly because the show, compared to the classic series, has taken on a higher emotional intelligence that McMurtry suggests attracts more women. But during the classic *Who* era, it was actually both male and female writers on both sides of the Atlantic who were paying close attention to the emotional subtext of the show in zines like *Frontier Worlds* (edited by Peter Anghelides, who went on to write *Doctor Who* novelizations), *Queen Bat* and *Jelly Baby Chronicles*.

'Perhaps the fanzines were anticipating the way the show has gone', McMurtry says.

Or perhaps the show was just paying attention to conversations happening in its fanzines – it wouldn't be the first time. Debates about the *Doctor Who* universe that unfolded in zines in the 1970s and 1980s are not only still relevant, they've often influenced or been incorporated into the show itself.

The Doctor's sidekicks – the companions – have long been a part of the series as mostly platonic pals, but two Doctors in particular inspired a number of conversations in fanzines about whether that could or should ever change: the Fourth Doctor (Tom Baker), who had a number of female companions, and the Fifth Doctor (Peter Davison), who was one of the younger and better-looking Doctors. Jackie Marshall, an editor of *Queen Bat*, wrote in an issue of *Stock Footage* that the Doctor wasn't 'above' attraction to his companions, and that the relationship between the Fifth Doctor and companion Tegan in particular went 'beyond mere friendship'. Writing for *Paisley Pattern*, David J. Darlington argued that while the Fifth Doctor had a particularly close bond with another companion, Peri, they certainly weren't in love.

'A lot of the fan debates that were going about whether the Doctor should have relationships with his companions, about the history of the Time Lords, the history of the Doctor and his enemies, you can see those debates emerging today', Booth says. 'In the 80s you have people talking about "The Doctor should never have a relationship!" or "It's very obvious they have a relationship!" Today, when we see the Doctor kissing his companion, that's almost the product of the fandom from the early days. The fans today are taking that into account'.

In the run-up to Peter Capaldi's casting announcement, many *Who* fans wondered whether it would be good for the show to break out of its usual white, male Doctor[10] and increase diversity – some have accused Moffat and the show of being inherently sexist in their treatment of female characters. (As a member of the Time Lords race, The Doctor, when mortally injured, can take on a new physical form and personality.) Those conversations aren't new. Articles about whether the Doctor could ever be Black or female, and what that would mean for the show, can be found in zines like *Aggedor 5*, which in 1984 ran two articles about the topic: 'The Doctor: Should She Be Black?' by Simon Lydiard and 'Woman Is the N*****r of the World' by Pam Baddeley.

The Twelfth Doctor turned out to be another white guy, but there are other fan debates that Moffat has taken into account, as seen in the fiftieth anniversary special, 'The Day of the Doctor', which featured just a handful of Doctors. 'Steven Moffat's decision to pare down the number of Doctors and really focus on the story is telling', Hills says. 'I would suggest that's because he's been so aware of fan criticism of multiple Doctor stories in his role in the show.'

The current production of *Doctor Who* is a particularly self-referential show, filled with often-subtle nods and winks to previous incarnations of the series. There's an economic motivation behind their inclusion – they can encourage older fans to tune in while spurring younger fans to play catch-up by buying *Doctor Who* DVDs and books – but it's also sentimental, too. *Doctor Who* has plenty in common with major media brands, but Hills calls it a 'fan brand' because the responsibility of maintaining the fictional universe's consistency and coherence falls to them, even the ones running the series in an official capacity. Fans don't always agree about what *Doctor Who* should be, and in fact, that's part of what makes them special – 'You know you're at a *Doctor Who* convention when you can't agree on what you like about *Doctor Who*', Booth says – but determining the boundaries of its universe and debating what's official *Doctor Who* canon are activities that fans have the most stake in, and they're activities that often played out in the pages of fanzines before they did on the internet.

'Fans do the same type of things they used to do offline, and they do it for the same reasons – to meet people, form communities, be creative, and show their appreciation for something they love', Booth says. 'It's a show and a fandom that thrives on growth and expansion, and fans want to share that with people.'

Growth, expansion, transformation – the theme of evolution naturally comes up a lot when talking about *Doctor Who* and its regenerating hero. And as Capaldi ushers in the next evolution of one of television's most beloved characters, it's hard to imagine what the show would look like if zines didn't give him and others the space to do those very things.

Notes

1. Peter Capaldi, '*Dr Who* Titles', *Radio Times* 1976.
2. 'Steven Moffat, '"I Was the Original Angry *Doctor Who* Fan"', interview in *The Guardian* (November 2013): https://www.theguardian.com/tv-and-radio/2013/nov/18/steven-moffat-doctor-who-interview.
3. Digital Spy, Forum Discussion about Steven Moffat's rec.arts.drwho Comment on 'The Doctor's Name' (6 May 2011): https://forums.digitalspy.com/discussion/1486706/steven-moffat-posting-spoilers-16-years-ago.
4. Aja Romano, '*Doctor Who* vs One Direction: Who Owns Fandom's Biggest Day?', *Daily Dot* (10 October 2013): https://www.dailydot.com/parsec/fandom/doctor-who-one-direction-november-23/.
5. 'The 25 Most Devoted Fan Bases Ever', *Vulture* (25 October 2012): https://www.vulture.com/2012/10/25-most-devoted-fans.html#photo=17x00016.
6. '*Doctor Who*: The 57 Best Stories & Episodes Ranked', *The Telegraph* (1 January 2021).
7. '*Doctor Who* Fans Name Best Episode Ever', *The Register* (17 September 2009): https://www.telegraph.co.uk/tv/0/doctor-best-stories-episodes-ranked/.
8. 'Top 10 Tennant *Doctor Who* Stories', *IGN* (10 May 2012): https://www.ign.com/articles/2010/01/05/top-10-tennant-doctor-who-stories?page=3.
9. 'Peter Capaldi Getting Backlash from Fangirls for Being Too Old and Ugly', *Game FAQS* (n.d.): https://gamefaqs.gamespot.com/boards/296-doctor-who/66904260.
10. Ted B. Kissel, 'The Depressing, Disappointing Maleness of *Doctor Who*'s New Time Lord', *The Atlantic* (6 August 2013): https://www.theatlantic.com/entertainment/archive/2013/08/the-depressing-disappointing-maleness-of-i-doctor-who-i-s-new-time-lord/278380/.

Chapter 32
Fannish origin stories

From 'Dalek-Builders' by Peter Capaldi*

First Published 1973

In 1978, future Doctor Who *lead actor Peter Capaldi was writing letters about* Doctor Who *to publications like the* Radio Times *... and in the 1990s, future* Doctor Who *showrunner Steven Moffat shared a fannish 'silly idea' to fellow fans on rec.arts.drwho.*

May I congratulate you on your excellent *Dr Who Special*. The articles, photos and especially the Terry Nation Dalek story with the twist in the tail were excellent.

The Dalek construction plans will have no doubt inspired many a school to build their own Daleks. Who knows, the country could be invaded by an army of school Daleks! Ah, but we'd be safe, as we'd have Dr Who to protect us!

Your Special has certainly made the year for *Dr Who* fans. A rather sad year due to the untimely death of the Master, alias Roger Delgado. But I hope that in fifteen years' time, in 1988, you will publish another Special to celebrate twenty-five years of wandering in time with the Doctor.

Peter Capaldi
(aged 15)
Glasgow

From rec.arts.drwho Post by Steven Moffat†

First published 1995

Steven Moffat (10004 ... @CompuServe.COM) wrote:

---

*Originally published in the *Radio Times*, 1973.
†Originally published on rec.arts.drwho, 1995.

: Here's a particularly stupid theory. If we take 'The Doctor' to
: be the Doctor's name – even if it is in the form of a title no
: doubt meaning something deep and Gallifreyan – perhaps our
: earthly use of the word 'doctor' meaning healer or wise man is
: direct result of the Doctor's multiple interventions in our
: history as a healer and wise man. In other words, we got it from
: him. This is a very silly idea and I'm consequently rather proud
: of it.

Dalek-builders

May I congratulate you on your excellent *Dr Who Special*. The articles, photos, and especially the Terry Nation Dalek story with the twist in the tail, were excellent.

The Dalek construction plans will have no doubt inspired many a school to build their own Daleks. Who knows, the country could be invaded by an army of school Daleks! Ah, but we'd be safe, as we'd have Dr Who to protect us!

Your Special has certainly made the year for *Dr Who* fans. A rather sad year due to the untimely death of the Master, alias Roger Delgado. But I hope that in 15 years' time, in 1988, you will publish another Special to celebrate 25 years of wandering in time with the Doctor.

Peter Capaldi (aged 15)

Glasgow

Dalek-builders at Highbury Grove School

Figure 32.1 Reprint of letter from Peter Capaldi, *Radio Times*.

Chapter 33
Poachers turned cartographers
by Ian Potter

Original to this volume

If fandom poaches and consumes the media it loves, then what happens when it gets poached in return? Ian Potter looks at the history of writing and publishing about Doctor Who *from the 1960s onwards, and the influence of these texts on the show over the decades.*

> *They want to portray fans as mad consumers, people who accept everything the television gives us, without question. That's them, I'm afraid. Fandom is the culture that takes what television gives us, laughs at it, pulls it apart, makes its own art with it, and eats it.*
>
> – Paul Cornell.[1]

In his book *Textual Poachers*,[2] academic (or aca/fan as he describes himself[3]) Henry Jenkins writes extensively on fan cultures, predominantly science fiction and fantasy media fandoms, and their engagement with the shows they follow. It's a work that seeks to redress assumptions about the nature of media consumption, shedding light on the level and depth of fan creativity and analysis within fandoms and challenging prevailing notions of TV audiences as essentially passive receivers of entertainment. Jenkins' metaphor of fans as poachers allows him to explore how they take properties that they have no legal rights to and use them as they see fit. Although Jenkins touches on *Doctor Who*, his primary study is of fans of US media and it's striking that he sees the borderline between fan and professional as clearly delineated, something that it's harder to say about *Doctor Who*, which often seems to invite its fans into the creative process.

It shouldn't be remarkable that a long-running TV series, specifically designed to appeal to children while retaining adult viewers, should go on to attract contributors who had first enjoyed it as children. Nor does it seem unreasonable that a number of viewers who later found their way into the TV industry would have grown up as active and analytical fans of the medium. What is of note is just how many fans-turned-creators *Doctor Who* has. *Doctor Who* contributors to have begun as fans of the series include writers Andrew Smith, Marc Platt, Mark Gatiss, Robert Shearman, Paul Cornell, Gareth Roberts, Matt Jones and Neil Cross, script editors Douglas Adams,[4] Gary Russell and Simon Winstone, FX designers Mike

Tucker and Susan Moore and Stephen Mansfield, composer Mark Ayres, monster voice actor Nicholas Briggs, producer Phil Collinson, lead writers and showrunners Russell T Davies, Steven Moffat and Chris Chibnall and two of the programme's lead actors, David Tennant and Peter Capaldi.

There are essentially two waves of activity here – fans of *Doctor Who* in the 1960s and 1970s coming to work on the programme in the 1970s and 1980s (Adams, Smith, Platt, Ayres, Tucker, Moore and Mansfield), and the generation of fandom that contributed to the series revival in the 2000s.[5] So, why are fan creators so prominent in *Doctor Who*?

One key factor is how open to interaction with its core fandom *Doctor Who* became in the 1980s, while also becoming more invested in its own history than ever before. The production team discovered how much this loyal audience enjoyed references to the programme's history and engaged prominent fan Ian Levine as an unofficial continuity advisor (a phrase echoing the Doctor's role as UNIT's unpaid scientific advisor in the 1970s). This was a period in which archive repeats began to be screened on BBC 2 (in part as a strategy to reassure viewers that there was such a thing as *Doctor Who* without the departing long-term Doctor, Tom Baker). *Doctor Who Magazine*,[6] which had launched in 1979 as a mainstream children's comic, now developed into a title aimed at an older fan audience, regularly running substantial features and interviews exploring *Doctor Who*'s past. The magazine's writers were themselves largely from fandom: the BBC authorized tip of an iceberg of fan analysis, discussion and creativity in a booming fanzine scene. Large conventions were held in the United States where actors' anecdotes and after dinner turns found huge, appreciative audiences. Old costume elements, flashback montages and references to previous stories appeared on screen to reward the core fandom. Dialogue that originated as lines from fan interviews or convention stories found their way into the programme as knowing winks to a subset of the fan audience. The line 'reverse the polarity of the neutron flow' became an oft-repeated phrase, in deference to its position in fan folklore.[7] Similarly, Nicholas Courtney's politic reply as to which Doctor he preferred, having performed with them all, became on screen dialogue for his character the Brigadier.[8] After surpassing twenty years on air, there was a definite sense that *Doctor Who* had become consciously self-celebrating and a heritage brand. The programme's makers actively sought to reward fan following, arguably to the detriment of engaging with wider audiences, and during this period in which fans felt listened to, they became vocal both in praise and criticism. Fans were socializing with programme makers, some were now working on the programme and other fans knew it. A sense of entitlement developed. I would argue it was in this period that *Doctor Who* fans first began to move beyond being 'poachers' in Jenkins' terms. They'd been invited onto the BBC's property and *Doctor Who* was now being made for them.

Another shift from consumer to creator occurs in the period between *Doctor Who*'s cancellation as an ongoing TV series in 1989 and its revival in 2005. Deprived of an ongoing TV series, *Doctor Who* became a niche product composed of ancillary merchandise entirely aimed at its fandom. The idea of 'ownership' of the brand, and even the concept of the TV show being *Doctor Who*'s primary text, began to break down.

Back in the 1960s, *Doctor Who* had spin-offs in other media within a year of its first broadcast, notably the first TV novelization, *Doctor Who in an Exciting Adventure with the Daleks* (1964), and TV Comic's *Doctor Who* comic strip, launched in November 1964, both translations into new media that established variants on the continuity of the TV series (see Section III in this volume). A feature film, *Doctor Who and the Daleks*, a Daleks strip in the comic *TV Century 21* and two further novels followed in 1965. These again deviated significantly from the TV version of *Doctor Who*[9] (see Chapter 5).

In an age before home video recorders and when domestic TV repeats were vanishingly rare in the UK, these film and print versions of *Doctor Who* were to become some of its most accessible texts and this undoubtedly coloured fan response to the series as a whole. The book and film versions of *Doctor Who* could be reread or rewatched with relative ease, granting them a presence and permanence not gifted to the more ephemeral medium of TV.

One example of how the ancillary material affected fandom and ultimately the TV show can be found in the way that both the novel and film adaptations of the first Dalek serial (by *Doctor Who*'s original story editor David Whitaker) posit a romantic connection between the Doctor's companions, Ian and Barbara, a relationship which TV's Ian, the actor William Russell, denied was originally intended.[10] Barbara and Ian 'shipping' has been embraced by fandom ever since. The notion of a Barbara/Ian romance was expanded upon in later BBC licensed *Doctor Who* novels,[11] and was ultimately acknowledged with a reference to them as a married couple in an episode of the *The Sarah Jane Adventures*.[12]

To further understand how novels came to shape modern *Doctor Who*, and became an avenue for fans to become *Doctor Who* creators, we need to take a brief look at the history of *Doctor Who* publishing. In 1972 Pan Books' children's imprint Piccolo published a paperback entitled *The Making of Doctor Who* by regular *Doctor Who* writers Malcolm Hulke and Terrance Dicks (see Chapter 3 in this volume). Two small aspects of established *Doctor Who* lore appear for the first time in this book – the first name of the regular character Brigadier Alastair Lethbridge Stewart, which was not spoken on screen until 1974, and an alien mathematical formula said to be the Doctor's real name.[13] This book was at the forefront of a wave of fresh interest in *Doctor Who* and awareness of its history as the programme approached its tenth anniversary. In 1973, Universal-Tandem republished the 1960s *Doctor Who* novelizations under its imprint Target, commissioning more when they proved to be popular. This successful range, spearheaded by Hulke and Dicks, eventually extended to over 150 titles in just under twentyyears, producing a parallel book series of *Doctor Who* that was accessible for repeat consumption. The books, covering almost all of the broadcast stories, were almost exclusively written by the show's TV authors (predominantly Dicks), and often reshaped elements of the TV stories, both by accident and design.[14] In addition, Target produced a handful of other *Doctor Who* related factual titles including 1981's *The Doctor Who Programme Guide*.

When the Target book series came to an end in 1991, having exhausted the available TV titles, Virgin Publishing successfully pursued a license to produce new *Doctor Who* fiction. The ensuing range of novels, the New Adventures (later expanded to include the Missing Adventures), aimed at the programme's older core fandom, was marketed as the official continuation of *Doctor Who*, following on directly from the end of its final season. It was instilled with an additional aura of legitimacy through the use of established writers for the novelization range – TV writers Terrance Dicks, Ben Aaronovitch, Marc Platt and the programme's final script editor Andrew Cartmel. The rest of the authors were to come from fandom: operating an open submissions policy, Virgin attracted work from many prominent writers from *Doctor Who* fanzines.

An attempt was made to create a coherent future history (based on one originally published in Target's *The Doctor Who Programme Guide*) in a move designed to encourage readers see the range as a single entity rather than one from which titles might be picked and chosen. There was collaboration and cross promotion with *Doctor Who Magazine*, the other main surviving *Who* platform. Notably, the magazine began to feature the new Virgin book companion Bernice Summerfield in its comic strip and the Virgin books in return introduced the magazine's cult anti-hero Abslom Daak to its series. Increasingly, the book series began to construct its own fictional universe, combining that of the TV series with elements taken from the Target range, the various comics and fan theories.[15]

It was here in the Virgin books that Paul Cornell, Mark Gatiss, Gareth Roberts, Matt Jones and Russell T Davies came to write their first licensed *Doctor Who* fiction.

In 1996, the BBC took *Doctor Who* fiction back in house under the BBC Books imprint, anticipating increased sales following the US *Doctor Who TV Movie*. An attempt was made to divorce the new book series from its Virgin predecessors and create a more inclusive and less 'fannish' range, but a new wider audience for *Doctor Who* books failed to emerge. With the new books drawing on much the same talent pool, and with a fannish predilection towards linked narratives and playing with existing texts, the separation quickly broke down. Soon, the BBC books borrowed *Doctor Who* lore from various sources as enthusiastically as the Virgin books had, even publishing an unabashed sequel to a book from the Virgin series in 1999.[16]

When *Doctor Who* returned to TV in 2005 with writers who had both written and read the novel series of the 1990s,[17] this approach continued. Not only did the new series adapt previously published stories from other media (e.g. 'What I Did on My Christmas Holidays by Sally Sparrow'/'Blink' by Steven Moffat, *Jubilee*/'Dalek' by Robert Shearman, *Spare Parts* by Marc Platt, Gareth Roberts' 'A Groatsworth of Wit' and 'The Lodger' comic strips and most notably Paul Cornell's Virgin novel *Human Nature*), it was peppered with references to the expanded *Doctor Who* universe.

In the first modern season alone *Doctor Who* (2005) drew design cues from the Dalek redesigns and TARDIS interior of the 1960s films, glancingly referred to Venom Grubs (named in the 1965 novelization *Doctor Who and The Zarbi*), featured Kronkburgers, a fast-food snack from *Doctor Who Magazine*'s opening comic strip in 1979, quoted the Doctor's legendary title The Oncoming Storm devised by Paul Cornell in the Virgin novel *Timewyrm: Revelation* (1991) and even had the Doctor paraphrasing Abslom Daak dialogue as he cursed 'every stinking Dalek in the galaxy'. The series' explanation of the mysterious 'Time Lord gift' of tongues that means everyone in the cosmos seems to speak English came from the fan interpretations in *Doctor Who Magazine* and the novel series. Even the revived series' great innovation – the Time War – may have been inspired by a speculative attempt to make sense of conflicting Dalek histories in the playful 1995 reference work, *Doctor Who – The Discontinuity Guide* by Virgin novelists Paul Cornell, Keith Topping and Martin Day or by Alan Moore's *4-D War* comic strip for *Doctor Who Magazine*. *Doctor Who* has subsequently gone on to embrace the idea originating in the first Target novelization that Time Lord names are secret and of mystical significance to them,[18] use the Dalek measurement unit 'Rels',[19] display Abslom Daak's image on screen,[20] mention companion characters only featured in *Doctor Who* audio dramas on screen[21] and repeatedly reference Terrance Dicks' phrase 'neither cowardly nor cruel' from Target's revised *Making of Doctor Who*, making it the Doctor's personal credo.[22] Most recently, *Doctor Who* has introduced the idea of Doctors before those we saw on screen, previously touched on in the Virgin novels and discussed in *The Discontinuity Guide*.

Strikingly, there is no policed continuity (or canon) in *Doctor Who*, perhaps a convenient result of the series having been written by many hands and set in a universe in which the past and future can and do change regularly. A glee in referencing elements from across all incarnations of the series is as strong in recent *Doctor Who* as the desire to include TV continuity references was in the mid-1980s.

This embracing of multiple texts and medias is not common in television or film production, and one suspects a fear of litigation prohibits it in many circumstances.[23] One only has to look at the decanonization of *Star Wars* spin-off fiction when the film series was revived in 2004. A cohesive and collaborative Expanded Universe fannishly developed by multiple creators over nearly thirty years was abandoned and rebranded. The shift was a logical reframing as the property's owners sought to direct *Star Wars* away from being beholden to a smaller but deeply engaged audience and back towards mass appeal, and to free its writers from the potential limitations of a Byzantine continuity most new viewers would not know.

With *Doctor Who*, it's the fan creators who now decide what counts, and they don't count anything out. They have made a sequel to the twentieth-century experience of *Doctor Who* not the TV show. This may not perhaps seem a big deal to those outside fandom, yet here we are devoting considerable time to it in an academic work and this leads me to my final observation. *Doctor Who* fandom hasn't just taken over the programme. It has also significantly colonized media studies. A good number of prominent figures active in the study of British TV openly admit to being or having been fans of *Doctor Who* and I suspect many of this book's contributors are *Doctor Who* fan-aca/fans like Jenkins and me.

There are many reasons *Doctor Who* is worthy of study. It's a piece of what we might class as 'ordinary' television – a show not conceived of as high art or afforded large budgets for most of its history. As a series that routinely deals with the fantastic, it's also a TV show that repeatedly pushes visual effects to the medium's limits of what can be achieved within its budget and time constraints. The 1963–89 run clearly displays the techniques, styles, limitations and strengths of BBC TV production over a 26-year period and international sales have resulted in the series having an excellent survival rate in the archives and its devoted fandom has made its complete release on home media commercially viable. On top of all that, the series has been written about and discussed in ever-increasing depth since the mid-1970s in a series of books, fan publications, magazines and documentaries. The programme's files at the BBC's Written Archive at Caversham have been scoured for publication like no other, and hundreds of key figures involved in the programme have given innumerable interviews to fans. *Doctor Who* forms an excellent primer for anyone wanting to develop an understanding how television was made in the late twentieth century and at the beginning of the twenty-first. It is a show that attracts those with an interest in how TV is and was made, exactly as it has attracted those who seek to make television.

However, the weight of *Doctor Who*, and the way it is sometimes used as a yardstick to help us make sense of other TV, may have subtly reshaped the world of writing on British television. Until the 1990s, there were few satisfying and reader-friendly general works on UK TV. Academic works at that time tended to focus on audiences or draw on heavily on literary theory or film studies in a way that often seemed unapproachable, but within the fanzines of the 1980s and 1990s, an increasing level of scrutiny of TV beyond *Doctor Who* had begun to develop. A wave of publications emerged spearheaded by *Time Screen* that took TV seriously but approached it in a way that was more accessible to non-academics. It was from this fanzine culture that *The Guinness Book of Classic British TV* emerged in 1993, the first book, in my view, to help shape a new canon of popular and significant UK TV. This approachable guide to the territory, particularly in its revised second edition in 1996, has been built on by others since, though it's arguable many of the notable directors, writers, cast members and others mentioned within are largely considered so thanks to their connections to *Doctor Who*, subtly shifting the programme to the centre of UK TV. The book was, of course, written by *Doctor Who* fans, critics and creators, Cornell, Topping and Day.

We have redrawn the map to claim the land as our own.

Notes

1. Paul Cornell, *Licence Denied: Rumblings from the Doctor Who Underground* (London: Virgin Books, 1997).
2. Henry Jenkins, *Textual Poachers: Television Fans and Participatory Culture* (New York: Routledge, 1992).
3. A composite of both academic and fan. http://henryjenkins.org/aboutmehtml.
4. Douglas Adams' 1960s fandom is attested to in several places including MJ Simpson's biography *Hitchhiker*.
5. Ayres and Tucker bridge the gap. Tucker was a BBC special effects assistant in the 1980s who by the time of the series revival in 2005 headed the miniature effects company The Model Unit. Ayres, an enthusiast for the music produced by the BBC Radiophonic Workshop since childhood, worked as a freelance composer for the series in the late 1980s. By 2005 he was the Workshop's archivist and had become a specialist in sound restoration. He produced a stereo remaster of the original Delia Derbyshire arrangement of *Doctor Who*'s title theme for the 2005 revival that went unbroadcast but formed the basis of Murray Gold's version as well as sourcing archive Radiophonic effects for the series.
6. Initially as *Doctor Who Weekly*, then *Doctor Who Monthly* and a variety of different title permutations.
7. The line occurs once in 1972's *The Sea Devils*. It appears in three 1980s stories – *Castrovalva*, *Mawdryn Undead* and *The Five Doctors*.
8. 'Wonderful chap. All of them' and 'Splendid fellows. All of you' in *The Five Doctors*.
9. 'Nothing at the End of the Lane', Issue 3 (2012): http://www.endofthelane.co.uk/Issue3PDF.html.
10. Russell expressed this in the interview that accompanies his 2004 reading of *Doctor Who in an Exciting Adventure with the Daleks* for BBC Audiobooks. He reiterated this in conversation with me at the recording of the Big Finish audio story *Doctor Who – The Revenants* on 19 November 2011, though he has subsequently come around the idea of the relationship through performing further scripts that feature it.
11. Primarily in the tie-in fiction by authors Keith Topping and David McIntee, though references to Johnny Chess, a pop star son of Ian and Barbara first developed in fanfiction by Keith Topping, occur as early as 1991 in the work of Paul Cornell. See also the Tara Samms short story 'Distance' (2003) and Simon Guerrier's *The Time Travellers* (2005).
12. *The Sarah Jane Adventures* – 'Death of the Doctor part 2', CBBC, 26th October 2010. Russell T. Davies' script refers to '… this couple in Cambridge, both professors, Ian and Barbara Chesterton'.
13. This curious mixture of Greek letters and mathematical notation appears on TV as ancient Gallifreyan writing on a piece of set dressing in *The Five Doctors* (1983).
14. Dicks routinely tidied up plot holes, character motivations and intentions he felt were unclear in his novelizations, and expanded on elements he felt were lacking. Other authors reworked the original TV scripts to better fit their original intentions or in service of what they now considered better ideas. Occasionally writers adapting another's scripts radically reshaped the materials.
15. Most prominently in Steve Lyons' novels featuring the Land of Fiction, and Jim Mortimore's *Blood Heat*, which followed details established in a Target novelization rather than its TV version.
16. *Millennium Shock* by Justin Richards.
17. The complete collection of Virgin *Doctor Who* novels in Russell T. Davies' office was regularly seen in press photos.
18. *The Auton Invasion* (1973).
19. Rels originate in the 1964 spin-off *The Dalek Book* before appearing in the second *Doctor Who* feature film *Daleks: Invasion Earth 2150*.
20. 'Time Heist', 2015.
21. 'Night of the Doctor', 2013.

22 This passage, a particular favourite of writer Paul Cornell, had also appeared in the New Adventures. Steven Moffat previously used it in 'The Curse of Fatal Death' (1999), a *Doctor Who* spoof for the charity Comic Relief. Reference to it became a recurring theme in Steven Moffat's writing for Peter Capaldi's Doctor.

23 Even *Star Trek*, which has regularly toyed with alternative realities and rewritten continuity over its history, has a demarcated canon. Only the live action film and TV series versions of *Star Trek* were 'official' for some time, not the books, comics or the animated series featuring original cast and writers. This latter series was essentially 'not true' *Star Trek*, except one bit about Spock's childhood that everyone seemed to like.

Chapter 34
Within any fan's dream

In 1995, Kate Orman was one of many Doctor Who fans who had made the leap to professional author, thanks to the open reading policy of the Virgin New Adventures books ... and in 2012, Elizabeth Sandifer looked back on the 1990s, that odd decade where Doctor Who fans and pros overlapped online, in print and at the Fitzroy Tavern.

From David J Richardson interviews Kate Orman

First published 1995*

We last talked to Kate Orman back in *Sonic Screwdriver* #80 – since then, *The Left-Handed Hummingbird* has come out; she's taken over running the *Doctor Who* Fan Club of Australia, and written her second *New Adventure*, *Set Piece*. So we thought it was time we caught up with her again ...

The obvious place to start was with *The Left-Handed Hummingbird*, or *Hummer* as it has come to be known (as we all know, the only reason Kate gave it such a long title was to ensure it used two lines on the 'Also Available' page in the *New Adventures*!). I asked her what the response to *Hummer* had been – this interviewer certainly enjoyed it! 'Feedback comes in all sorts of ways – as I've said before, the best thing about writing for a fan audience is that you can be sure they'll tell you what they think! I've had reams of e-mail, several letters passed on by Virgin or sent to the DWFCA address, and of course zine reviews and articles. I was knocked out by the very positive response to the book. In fact, it was far better than a first-time author deserves! Now I'll have to wait and see whether *Set Piece* does as well. It's a very different book, and was much tougher to write'.

The popular success of *Hummer* (it gained a rapid re-print) obviously helped with getting her second *New Adventure*, *Set Piece*, accepted. How much easier, I asked? 'Once *Hummer* was published, I didn't need to keep sending in sample chapters with every proposal – Rebecca knows I can write. I wasn't exactly asked to submit a second novel, but it was made very clear that they'd be happy to see more from me. So it was up to me what I did next. I think some of the authors, including myself, are very keen in continuing to write for the series – and those are the names you keep seeing. (Alas, Paul Cornell has decided that *Human Nature* will be his last.)

---

*Originally published in *Sonic Screwdriver* 88, January 1995.

'I've been learning a lot by re-writing the latest submission, *Storm and Stress*, over and over – I'm terrible at plotting, and Rebecca doesn't let me get away with weak storylines.

'I gather there was a huge rush of fan submissions when the series was first announced, and that the rush has slowed down – probably because everyone in fandom has gotten at least one rejection slip by now! Writing an NA is within any fan's reach if they've got talent, whereas writing scripts for the TV series was a distant dream ...'

So the next question was: how did *Set Piece* come about? 'While *Hummer* was something I'd had in mind for a long time – some Australian fans may remember the original short story in Jason Towers' *Pirate Planet* [Ed: Yes, it's in the only issue I don't have!] – *Set Piece* was entirely new, except for the first two chapters.

'Those first chapters are something I've been trying to get onto paper since I was ten (I can remember hammering out the introduction to a novel on a golf ball typewriter). I kept tacking them onto various different submissions – they're more or less self-contained. You'll see what I'm talking about when you read the book, but they're obviously drawn from some deep subconscious terror of mine. If *The Most Toys* or *Frame of Mind* or *The Prisoner* give you the creeps, you're on the same wavelength as I am.

'The rest of the book began at a meeting of *New Adventures* authors waaaay back in September 1993. We were asked to think of ways in which Ace could depart the series, without violating the continuity of the *Fenric* novelisation. I came up with a way of doing it, and that formed the core of the story. That night I also said to Rebecca, "You must have had so many submissions set in Ancient Egypt!" and she said, "No, we haven't had any at all!".

'It's a shame John Peel already did Mesopotamia – I was fascinated by it as a child. Oh well, I have to get out of the habit of visiting ancient civilisations anyway ... *Storm and Stress* is set in Sydney in the year 2000.'

I'd heard that *Set Piece* had been much harder to write than *Hummer*, largely because Kate had tried to get *everything* into it, and ended up with little left for anything new. Kate elaborated. '*Set Piece* was the hardest thing to write I've ever done. It just seemed to take forever. There were several reasons. One was that I didn't do my homework before starting – unlike *Hummer*, I hadn't worked the plot out rigorously before starting.

'Another reason was Ben Aaronovitch's very helpful suggestions (I brilliantly forgot to thank him in the book). I rang him up all a-tremble, only to discover I'd gotten him out of the shower! When I rang back, he told me all sorts of amazing things about the back story for the Doctor which was being developed during the Cartmel era (lots of it is in *Time's Crucible* and *Transit*.) It was fascinating – I still have all the notes – but it necessitated a major re-plot of the last third of the novel! I think that threw me – I was confused for the rest of the book ...'

Getting a *New Adventure* must throw an awful lot of attention on to you. Kate has done book signings as any other writer might at bookstores in Sydney, and when people know you've got a book in the works, you'd expect extra comment from those around her. I asked Kate how this had affected her. 'I had far less input from my writer's circle while writing *Set Piece* – our meetings have become very irregular indeed. Nonetheless, they (and several others) battled through a complete reading of the novel one weekend, which allowed me to ferret out all sorts of mistakes. Nathan Bottomley, who now edits the reviews section of *Data Extract*, was invaluable in providing French translations.

'I don't think writing an *NA* makes you particularly famous ... people do get a bit jealous if their *NA* is rejected and yours isn't [Ed: Hopefully not the people you live with – ex-*Burnt Toast* creator David Carroll, to those not in the know], especially if they didn't think yours was very good! I've met a lot of people I wouldn't have if I hadn't written the book, which has been fabulous'.

Kate's first *NA* really stood out because of the research that had obviously been done on the historical backgrounds. Now, we see that *Set Piece* is to have a distinctly Egyptian flavour. Should we therefore conclude something about the author? 'Too much – I'm a research junkie! I'm still working at Macquarie University Library, which has a very strong Egyptology Department – I was just buried in information, as I was with *Hummer*. France was much harder – for some reason it's easier to find out the everyday details of life three thousand years ago than two hundred years ago. (Here's a game for *Star Trek* fans. See if you can spot the French references to *Family* and *Time's Arrow* which I managed to totally misspell.)'

As for *Set Piece* (out next month), Kate tells us Ace dies and gets married – in that order!

I moved on to ask Kate about the other *New Adventures*, and her opinions on them: has Benny tired on her at all, like Ace and the Doctor have in some circles? 'Not at all – I think there's so much that can be done with the character. If I had to choose the "perfect" companion, it'd be her'. Her fave recent *New* and *Missing Adventures*? 'Oh gosh, I'm so bad at remembering which book comes where ... *Strange England* and the terrifying *Falls the Shadow*, definitely. *Goth Opera* turned me back into a Davison fan. I can't wait for *Warlock*!'

To finish, I asked her how things had been going at *Data Extract*. 'I'll answer that when I crawl out from under this pile of letters! Producing *DE* is *tons* of work, and I'm lucky that there's such a large group of people participating. I keep the subscriptions database up to date, write the news, do the layout and fret.

'Our project for this year is to increase the membership – now we've got the hang of actually producing and mailing the issues, which is the bulk of the work. We've had lots and lots of feedback, especially on the re-subscription forms, which is tremendously helpful – it's good to be able to gauge whether what you're doing is working, what people do and don't like, and so on. There'll be more of that in the survey, too, which will be in the next issue'.

And before we go, her favourite colour? 'Red'.

From 'Pop Between Realities, Home in Time for Tea 41 (rec.arts.drwho)' by Elizabeth Sandifer[†]

First published 2012

The major thing to realize about the Virgin era is that the fan/production distinction was almost completely erased. One of the most notable things about Virgin was that they had a completely open submissions policy. They'd read a proposal from anyone, you didn't need a literary agent to pitch to them, and if they

---

[†]From 'Pop Between Realities, Home in Time for Tea 41 (rec.arts.drwho)', https://www.eruditorumpress.com/blog/pop-between-realities-home-in-time-for-tea-41-rec-arts-drwho (26 September 2012).

liked it they bought it. This isn't quite unheard of, but it's very unusual. And what it meant was that a large number of writers came to write for Virgin coming through fandom. As I'm pretty sure I mentioned in passing, *Timewyrm: Revelation* was originally a piece of fanzine-published fanfic. Multiple writers – Daniel Blythe, Steve Lyons, Justin Richards and Lance Parkin at the very least – have their fanzine writing mentioned, whether implicitly or explicitly, on the back-cover author blurbs of their first books.

This is, of course, the only way it was going to work. The Virgin line was financially successful primarily because of existing *Doctor Who* fans. The novels weren't bringing in substantial numbers of new fans. That's not to say that there weren't anecdotal-level exceptions here and there, but for the most part during the so-called wilderness years the only path into the books was from the existing fan base. And when your only meaningful audience is existing fans that's also your only probable pool to draw writers from.

And in the Virgin era this was a particularly weird mix. Because Virgin, as an editorial presence, was quite permissive about what could go on in the books, but relatively down on reusing old concepts. (They did more in the Missing Adventures, but in the New Adventures there were actually very few 'sequel' stories, *Blood Heat* being quite an exception.) This meant that the authors it attracted and groomed came out of *Doctor Who* fandom, but were the sorts of writers who were comfortable doing original science fiction instead of *Doctor Who* continuity porn. Many were writers who would happily move on to other things eventually. This was in and of itself a different environment, and explains why the new series has drawn writers from the Virgin pool at all.

But this is what characterized *Doctor Who* fandom in the early 1990s. There wasn't a firm line between fans and professionals. People jumped from one category to another, sometimes based on social connections, but equally often based on raw talent. And big names who did *Doctor Who* professionally mingled with the hoi polloi, both on rec.arts.drwho and in social gatherings like the Fitzroy Tavern. Plenty of fans were also making strides in real television production as well, and so you occasionally get someone like Steven Moffat, who did a short story for Virgin, was a real name in television, and also was a regular at the Fitzroy Tavern and has some rec.arts.drwho posts – indeed, people found and dusted off one of his posts after 'A Good Man Goes to War' aired and it turned out he'd recycled an idea he'd dashed off in 1995.

This meant that *Doctor Who* fandom in the early 1990s wasn't like other fandoms. We've stressed several times in the programme's history that it's not, in normal circumstances, a cult television show as we understand that term. And nothing exemplifies that quite like 1990s *Doctor Who* fandom. It's instructive to dig up Paul Cornell's *License Denied* and read through the stuff there and how at times aggressively mocking it is. That's par for the course. Bitchy humour was a part of 1990s fandom. So was openly disliking large swaths of the show. Yes, some of this was just a defence mechanism against the show's cancellation, and it often went a bit too far in trashing things. But another part of it was just that *Doctor Who* fans weren't the worshipful cult television fans that other franchises had. (If nothing else, the infamous Moffat interview that gets casually cited as evidence of Moffat's views on *Doctor Who* needs to be taken in light of the nature of 1990s fandom and a few drinks.)[1]

Much of this came from the peculiarities of the early 1990s, with a side of the peculiarities of the UK and the fact that it's just not that big an island and that the Fitzroy Tavern can be close enough to drop by at least occasionally for a relatively large amount of the population in a way that no place in America ever could be for Star Trek fans. The United States' sense of fandom was always more based on conventions, which existed in the UK, but didn't have the same status. And when Usenet and rec.arts.drwho made it possible to have a community that connected Australians, Americans, Brits and other English-speaking fans in a fast-moving, always-on discussion the norms of odd British fandom survived the transition. That could only have happened in the early 1990s, when the internet was large enough to connect, say, Kate Orman to Jon Blum (to pick a particularly significant example) but still small enough to allow the social norms of the Fitzroy Tavern to survive the transition. And so we got a fandom not quite like any other.

Note

1   https://doctorwho.org.nz/archive/tsv43/onediscussion.html.

Chapter 35
Run fast, love hard, be kind: Twenty years in *Doctor Who* fandom by Lynne M. Thomas

Original to this volume

Being a Doctor Who *fan can often change lives in unexpected ways. Archivist Lynne M. Thomas looks back on how her fandom not only shaped her family and social life but also led her to a new professional path as an award-winning editor and publisher.*

Being a *Doctor Who* fan profoundly changed the trajectory of my life. I would not be the person that I am as an adult without it, personally or professionally.

Marrying in

Unlike many American fans, I didn't watch *Doctor Who* on my local PBS station growing up. WGBH (my local Boston affiliate) ran *The Ark in Space* at least five different times from 1980 to 1983; I missed it. The first time my hazy childhood sense memory of flipping past the image of a tall man in a long scarf wandering down a starlit corridor meant anything to me was when Michael, who is now my spouse, showed me that story, and several others, lovingly acquired on VHS over the years at Suncoast Video, Borders or Best Buy. This was at the beginning of our relationship in 1999, during that intense initial period where we were figuring out how we worked as a couple.

    Michael became a *Doctor Who* fan at the age of twelve; the Doctor was a formative role model that he was far more comfortable with than the other popular heroic character options available in the 1980s and 1990s, the cultural height of toxically masculine action movies starring Stallone, Schwarzenegger and the like. Sharing these stories was his way of explaining how he viewed the world, and how he wanted to move through it.

My initial *Who* education reflected what was then mostly Received Fan Wisdom about The Best Stories, tightly curated to match up with my personal interests. We watched *Genesis of the Daleks, The Ark in Space, Earthshock, Robot, Black Orchid, The Robots of Death, Remembrance of the Daleks, Spearhead from Space, The Mind Robber, Battlefield, The Talons of Weng-Chiang* and *City of Death*. Looking at this list, I see Michael reflecting my love of historical fiction and literature, *Phantom of the Opera*, costume dramas, British mysteries and my Junior Year Abroad experience in Paris.

I connected with the companions – *especially* Ace – and the relative optimism of *Doctor Who* compared to a lot of the 'darker is better storytelling' approach of other 1990s media. The professional librarian in me can now deeply appreciate the outcomes of an excellent reference interview. Now more than twenty years into this robust romantic and creative partnership, I'd expect nothing less from Michael. When he loves, he loves *hard*, whether people or fandoms; my adult life took a turn for the better because of that love.

The Wilderness Years fandom experience

Becoming fannish about a media property in the comfort of one's own home is not the same thing as entering and participating in active fandom. I attended my first fan-run convention with a *Doctor Who* guest, United Fan Con, in 2000, awash in enthusiasm so deep that I literally spoke to everyone we met. Chided since childhood for showing excessive enthusiasm, I now entered a space full of people who welcomed my entire lack of chill. They, too, loved this series hard.

That love gets expressed in different ways: cosplay, conversations and panels, fan films and audio adventures, fanfiction, convention running, fan clubs, group viewings, crafting and more. At its heart, the fandom impulse is 'I love this *so much* that I made this thing to express my love'. We take our fannish joy, and we make it manifest by sharing it with one another.

Doctor Who conventions during the Wilderness Years had a particularly interesting dynamic because of the permeable social barrier between the fans of the property and the actors, writers and those involved in the production team. Fans become friends with those involved in the making of the show; fan productions of audio and film adventures often featured actors from the series, and numerous fans who wrote or produced fanworks or licensed tie-ins during the Wilderness Years ended up working formally for the series when it was brought back in 2005.

I fell in love with the fandom experience nearly as hard as I fell in love with Michael. Most of our dearest friends to this day are geeky, fannish or both.

Our daughter, Caitlin, was born with Aicardi Syndrome, in 2002. She is profoundly disabled, including severe epilepsy and significant cognitive and physical delays.[1] Navigating her disabilities as a family changed every single interpersonal relationship we had. There were relationships that splintered and dissolved because people didn't know how to handle this level of disability, and so they chose to avoid it. And us.

That has not been our experience in fandom.

Caitlin has literally grown up in *Doctor Who* fandom. We became regulars at the Chicago TARDIS convention, and periodic Gallifrey One attendees. We made dear friends. Year after year, we see them at these conventions, like family reunions. Our family gave up on school photos quite a while ago; the photos that track our growth and change as a family are primarily from *Doctor Who* conventions, from Peter Davison and Katy Manning each holding Caitlin as a baby to us taking family photos with Sacha Dhawan and Jo Martin in 2021.

Many of the *Who* actors have watched Caitlin grow up as they repeatedly guest at these conventions. They often make a point to spend extra time with her if they see us in the lobby or the audience between panels. Caitlin's disability is visible, which makes us easy to spot. Louise Jameson, Sophie Aldred, Nicola Bryant and Katy Manning all make beelines for Caitlin when they spot her to say hello. Mark Sheppard once spent nearly half an hour chatting with her. Caitlin firmly believes that this is just how her fandom experience works.

Chicks Dig Time Lords

My day job as a Rare Books and Special Collections librarian at Northern Illinois University, where I worked from 2004 to 2017, created an opportunity to attend literary SF/F conventions as part of my work. Among my responsibilities was a collection of science fiction and fantasy literature. I spent my time at NIU building a collection of literary archives from SF/F writers, attending conventions as an allied professional and asking writers to consider placing their literary papers with us. As a result, I spent several years being known as 'Archivist Lynne' at literary SF/F conventions (as opposed to media fandom) before I became an editor.

At Chicago TARDIS 2005, Lars Pearson, publisher of Mad Norwegian Press, along with his wife and co-writer Christa Dickson were doing a panel for *Dusted*, a book about Buffy. Michael and I were in the panel audience, and asked good-enough questions that Lars and Christa invited us to serve as associate editors on *Redeemed*, their guide to *Angel*.

After completing a book-length project in 2008–9 at my day job, this relationship led to my invitation to co-edit *Chicks Dig Time Lords: A Celebration of Doctor Who by the Women Who Love It*, with Tara O'Shea, who had initially pitched the project. This collection of essays about the experience of being a female *Doctor Who* fan documented that we had been active in fandom all along, not just joining with the New Series (which was, at the time, the popular narrative).

My two fandoms began to connect. A good strong handful of the SF/F writers I was working with in my day job also happened to be *Doctor Who* fans, and I was able to convince them to write essays for *Chicks*. Elizabeth Bear, Catherynne M. Valente, K. Tempest Bradford, Jody Lynn Nye and Mary Robinette Kowal joined the roster of essayists. I was now editing authors' work in addition to archiving it. I had become part of the story.

We didn't understand just how large the impact of the book would be. We did a panel at Chicago TARDIS in 2009 to promote the book and someone (who later became a friend) cosplayed the cover. *Chicks Dig Time Lords* officially launched with a panel including multiple contributors at the Gallifrey One convention in 2010. Tara and numerous fandom friends raised the funds for me to attend. Paul Cornell, who after publishing licensed tie-in novels had actually written for the New Series, came to the panel, to my astonishment. I had only just met him at the convention. He declared the book 'a sea change' during panel Q&A. After the panel, the contributors all passed around and signed copies like yearbooks, and there was a crush of people getting our autographs outside the panel room. We did multiple podcast interviews, including *Two-Minute Time Lord*, *Radio Free Skaro* and *Doctor Who: Podshock*, which helped us reach a much broader audience. Fans showed up for the book; many have become dear friends since. We did our best to provide a snapshot of female *Doctor Who* fandom at the time. The next few years of packed panels and signings demonstrated how many women fans felt finally seen. Although the fandom has grown and changed since, *Chicks* proved that women have been part of *Doctor Who* fandom all along. It's been taught as a primary source for university courses on fandom, and it is still in print, which is no small feat for a small press book of essays.

The following year, I was a guest at Chicago TARDIS and Gallifrey One.

I was now on the other side of the table as a professional. I *had* fans in addition to being a fan.

From fan to public professional

The next ten years are, in all honesty, a bit of a blur. All of these things happened while Michael and I were still parenting Caitlin, and I was working towards tenure at my day job.

In March 2011, *Chicks Dig Time Lords* was a finalist for a Hugo Award for Best Related Work. I had turned in the follow-up volume to *Chicks*: *Whedonistas*, co-edited with Deborah Stanish. *Chicks Dig Comics*, co-edited with Sigrid Ellis, was getting underway.

A month later, I was having dinner with Catherynne M. Valente, in my archivist role, at Harold's Chicken on the South side of Chicago. She was the editor for the dark SF/F/H magazine *Apex Magazine.* As we ate fried chicken covered in hot sauce, she mentioned that she was looking to step down so that she could focus on novel writing. She asked if, given my Hugo nomination, literature background and industry contacts, I'd be interested in interviewing with the publisher to succeed her. I eventually said yes, interviewed with publisher Jason Sizemore and got the gig.

In June, the SF Squeecast Podcast, with me, Elizabeth Bear, Paul Cornell, Catherynne Valente and Seanan McGuire, where we discussed SF/F things we enjoyed, premiered.

In August, Tara and I won the Hugo Award for *Chicks Dig Time Lords*, the first time a nonfiction book about a media property had ever done so. I spent that entire evening in shock. I was now an award-winning editor. In November, I was a literary guest at Chicago TARDIS for the first time, eleven years after attending the first one as a fan. I was asked back again for the next two years. It was disconcerting to go from getting autographs from Paul McGann to giving him the wifi password for the green room when he asked me.

My debut issue of *Apex Magazine* appeared that month. Michael was associate editor on all three of my Mad Norwegian books and unofficially helped with *Apex* as well that first year; he publicly joined the masthead as managing editor in 2012. Michael has worked on every single fandom science fictional project that I have done, although his visibility has varied greatly in his efforts to ensure that my work wasn't erased.

I wrote essays for Mad Norwegian Press, including an essay defending Season 24 of *Doctor Who* in *Chicks Unravel Time* and an essay on *Torchwood* in *Time Unincorporated 2*. In late 2012, I joined the cast of the Verity! Podcast. At the time, we were the first all-women *Doctor Who* podcast. Thankfully, that particular distinction didn't last long. (*Verity* is currently going strong in its ninth year, and I'm deeply grateful to count each of these exceptional women as dear friends.)

In August 2012, the SF Squeecast won the inaugural Hugo Award for Best Fancast. We won again in August 2013. I announced that I was stepping down as editor-in-chief of *Apex Magazine* later that year, in preparation for a major surgery that Caitlin needed in early 2014.

After Caitlin's recovery, Michael and I began planning *Uncanny Magazine* because we missed editing short fiction so much. Many of the fandom folks who had followed our family since *Chicks Dig Time Lords* showed up to support *Uncanny*'s first Kickstarter in July–August; the first issue of *Uncanny* debuted in

November. *Uncanny* is deeply influenced by *Doctor Who* in its overall aesthetic and tone, and routinely features writers who are fans of (or have written for) the series.

Michael and I renewed our wedding vows in 2015 at CONvergence. *Uncanny* went on to win five straight Hugo Awards for Best Semiprozine beginning in 2015, and in 2018 Michael and I also won in the Best Editor, Short Form category. I have now won nine Hugo Awards across four categories over a decade. As of this writing, I am second in all-time Hugo Awards won by women, behind Connie Willis (11) and tied with Ellen Datlow (10), and *Uncanny* won the 2022 Hugo Award for Best Semiprozine. Caitlin has attended most conventions with us since 2014, and has been onstage with us during one of our Hugo Award wins.

I think the best way to describe my current experience in fandom is 'situationally famous'. I have a Wikipedia page. I'm on a popular *Doctor Who* podcast. I edit a well-known online science fiction magazine. I was asked to submit a video clip for the BBC America launch of the Jodie Whittaker era and it made it on air. At fan-run science fiction conventions and *Doctor Who* conventions folks will routinely recognize me and want to chat or have me sign a book. I periodically serve as an onstage interviewer for actor appearances at *Doctor Who* conventions. We still attend bigger gate shows like C2E2 as fans. Actors doing autographs and photographs there don't have a clue who I am, so when I'm utterly tongue-tied during the thirty seconds of photoshoot with David Tennant, we all shrug and move on with our lives. The folks who *do* recognize me – or, more accurately, *us* – are mostly already dear friends or warm acquaintances.

In 2017, I accepted a position as the head of the Rare Book & Manuscript Library at the University of Illinois at Urbana-Champaign. Although I was no longer working directly with science fiction collections for my day job, the university was perfectly fine with my professional geekdom. In 2018 I was asked to be the Opening Convocation Faculty Speaker; my talk framed the college experience as regeneration. (My personal college experience was a series of rapid regenerations in the style of *The Curse of the Fatal Death*, but the point stands.)

Multiple aspects of my professional and fannish life have now come together in a way that feels as though I planned it all along. *Doctor Who* fandom and being a professional editor have helped grow my ability to think critically about storytelling, and to articulate those ideas. I submitted my first scholarly work about *Doctor Who* last year, a book chapter about Ace as an accidental anarcha-feminist. After two decades of fan and professional involvement in *Doctor Who*, I approached the topic from multiple facets, looking at discussions of Ace in academic critique, fan sites and directly interviewing Sophie Aldred (who played Ace) and Ian Briggs (who co-created Ace as a character) for their perspectives on the character.

My current contracted book project, *The Infinite Loop: Time Travel and Archives in the Popular Imagination*, co-authored with Katy Rawdon (Society of American Archivists, 2024), will explore the intersections of time travel narratives across multiple media (including *Doctor Who*, naturally) with archives and archivists, both real and imagined.

As a family, we count ourselves deeply lucky to have found a community of dear friends across fandom. Over the last two decades, when Caitlin has struggled with her health, we've had incredible support from folks across the globe. This fandom community has spent twenty years showing up for Caitlin and our family in all kinds of ways, from moral support and funding our projects to feeding us when she was hospitalized for months and nearly died in both 2019 and 2021.

Becoming a science fiction professional didn't stop me from being a fan. My fannish enthusiasm for the things I love hasn't abated; it has just grown broader, and more intense, because it is now deeply tied to all of the personal and professional relationships that have come out of it. My professional experiences have given me the opportunity – and the platforms – to show this community the same love that they have so generously given our family for twenty years.

Chicks Dig Time Lords brought us firmly into communities that, to paraphrase the Twelfth Doctor, showed us what 'run fast, love hard, be kind' looked like.

Save each other; save the universe. The Doctor would expect no less.

Note

1. Caitlin approves everything that is posted publicly or written about her. Any discussion of her life and experiences that we publicly share is one that she has consented to.

Chapter 36
Popping into fiction

From 'Where to Find the Doctor in All of My Historical Fantasy Novels' by Mary Robinette Kowal*

First published 2013

Just because you're a creative professional doesn't mean you stop being a fan! Just like Douglas Adams with The Hitchhiker's Guide to the Galaxy *series, many current SFF writers like Mary Robinette Kowal wear their love of* Doctor Who *on their sleeve – and sneak references into their books.*

I have had a long-standing love for *Doctor Who*, dating back to middle school when I was watching Tom Baker episodes. The nice thing about a time traveller is that he can turn up anywhere so ... in each of my historical fantasy novels – *Shades of Milk and Honey, Glamour in Glass,* and *Without a Summer* – I've inserted an unspoken cameo from the Doctor. My rule is that I can slide these private jokes in only if they don't interrupt the story. For instance, in *Shades of Milk and Honey*: '*It seemed forever before the surgeon arrived. When he did, Dr. Smythe strode straight into the room, without so much as taking off his greatcoat.*'

The good doctor often uses the pseudonym Dr. John Smith. In my head, this was the Third Doctor, living in the Regency for a time. I thought that Lady FitzCameron would find the name 'Smith' too common and insist on spelling it Smythe. It's sheer silliness, of course, but the Doctor has hopped universes before, so what's to say that he couldn't wind up in my version of the Regency? It's subtle and mostly in my head.

However ... when it came time to write the sequel, *Glamour in Glass*, I was a little bolder and inserted the Tenth Doctor into the novel. '*Before Jane could decide on the merits of this argument, voices and footsteps in the hall announced the arrival of the doctor, a tall, slender fellow, with a shock of dark hair. He was younger than she expected a doctor to be, but exuded such an air of confidence that Jane could*

---

*Previously published on *Tor.com*, April 2013.

not help but trust him. Settling himself on a chair at her bedside, he produced a pair of horn spectacles and slipped them over his ears.'

Yes. I am a complete geek.

In *Without a Summer*, the Second Doctor makes an appearance as 'a man in his middle years with ruffled black hair' and uses one of his other pseudonyms, Dr. McCrimmon. Now, I'm normally a stickler for attempting to use language that is period correct. When I showed this scene to my editor, she flagged a word as being an anachronism by a hundred years or so. That's because I had decided to allow the doctor to use language from the future.

That's not as much of a giveaway as this next bit: '*The doctor stood and cleared his throat. "I have some things to attend to in the back, if you will pardon me". No one paid him any mind as he slipped behind the curtain leading to the back of the shop, which appeared to be bigger on the inside than Jane would have suspected.*'

I don't expect anyone to notice these, unless I point them out. In fact, if you do, then I've done it wrong. But still … how can you not want a little bit of *Doctor Who* in your Regency fantasy? I mean, as an author I'm given license to create a universe as I see fit. It's not complete without a Time Lord.

Is there a Doctor planned for the fourth book? Yes, and Lord Byron is his companion.

Chapter 37
Sexism in fandom

From 'The Uncomfortable Truth about Fandom Sexism' by Claudia Boleyn[*]

First published 2019

> Doctor Who *fans are known for being as outspoken about what they don't like about the show as they are about what they love – and not everyone's voice, critical or otherwise, is given equal weight, or respect. Claudia Boleyn discusses the nuances of critiquing sexism, misogyny and other difficult topics in* Doctor Who *fannish spaces.*

We need to start talking about sexism in fandom.

This week, the subject has come up yet again in the *Doctor Who* fandom, with the convention Panopticon making some extremely dodgy comments in their 'mission statement', one of which references humorous upskirting (an oxymoron if I ever heard one). Understandably, they've come under fire for inappropriate remarks and for not providing an inclusive and safe environment for fans. All sorts of voices are coming forth to condemn the convention, as they should, and the show of solidarity against this conduct is indeed heartening.

What does surprise me, however, is the outpouring of supposed shock being expressed by those within fandom. The problem is this: a lot of fans, predominantly white men, perceive fandom as a space they have ownership of, which is already a place of perfect equality, which does not need to be fixed. In fact, any move to attempt to make the space more inclusive to women and minorities is often met with anger and scorn.

We all know this unfortunate group of fans exist, and most are happy to condemn them. This is, however, an easy move, and not where change takes place. In my view, it is those men of power and influence in fandom, those who claim to be progressive, to support change and growth, who are currently the biggest obstacle to reaching our fandom utopia. When the ideal is a vague image of harmony and equality, it is easy for many to agree to this aim, yet when this ideal starts to become a

---

[*]*The Digital Fix*, 2019. https://www.thedigitalfix.com/life/feature/the-uncomfortable-truth-about-fandom-sexism/.

reality, with women and minorities gaining more power in fandom, and starting to lead conversations of their own, about sexism and racism in the show and fandom, there are few of these so-called allies who don't become uncomfortable. Many, it seems, are unused to not having control in such situations, and of them not taking place on their terms. This turns valuable conversations from the growing fandom of women and minorities into what can be easily dismissed as invalid and on the fringes, instead of at the very heart of fandom.

No matter what some might pretend, the *Doctor Who* fandom is absolutely dripping in sexism. And this latest Panopticon 'scandal' is merely the latest in a continuing trend. What we cannot do is pretend it is an isolated incident.

Panopticon's 'joke' about upskirting has no place in a convention which is supposed to be a safe and inclusive place for all, and most can agree the wording was outrageous. However, as a non-white woman who's been talking about sexism both within fandom and the show for many years now, I have to admit I am exhausted by the faux outrage. Not because I am one of those *anti-political-correctness-damn-those-woke-snowflake* types but because I find it hypocritical that the very same members of fandom who are speaking out about this now it has become popular for them to do so (and because there is no risk to them or their careers by taking this view) won't accept that the very show they love has directly perpetuated these same ideas for a long time now. They also seem perfectly happy to villainize those women and minorities who have put their necks on the line to call this out, while they retain their 'progressive' reputations.

On the subject of Panopticon and fan conventions, there is also an argument to be made, which was brought up by Reality Bomb podcast co-producer Joy Piedmont, that although Panopticon is one of the more loudly obnoxious examples of casual sexism, we need to scrutinize more convention spaces, look at how they deal with harassment complaints and give that same energy to making them more inclusive. As Joy pointed out on Twitter, it is easier to condemn Panopticon's language while that's in vogue than to actually check how each convention stands in terms of their stance on protecting attendees. It is less about performative outrage, more about a consistent dedication to making fandom an equal and welcoming place.

To me it is pure hypocrisy that the people who will (rightly) condemn this heinous joke about upskirting will not stand up and accept that the show itself has formerly been littered with this exact sort of 'humour', and is worthy of the same scorn and criticism.

The truth is, there is a *Doctor Who* mini episode written by former showrunner Steven Moffat, based around the premise of a male companion looking up the female companion's skirt, subsequently messing everything up, which ends in the Doctor not telling the usually lovely Rory Williams to get a grip, but instead telling Amy to put on some trousers.

The same people that are happy to declare this fan convention despicable are those that believe the women and minorities that were vocal in their criticisms at the time were taking things 'too far', and even now dismiss their complaints. My question is this. Is it any wonder that a fan convention would make a joke about upskirting when that very same joke appears as the premise of an official episode?

Where were these voices when *Doctor Who* saw fit to include such sexist tropes and 'jokes' regularly? When a previous showrunner saw fit, in a programme aimed at children and families, to present the objectification and shaming of women, and use the Doctor himself as a mouthpiece to support the idea that women need to cover up, otherwise they're responsible for the reactions of the men around them?

We were here, and we were making noise, yet we were dismissed as radicals, and denied our status as 'real fans'. We were painted as a group of pesky, man-hating feminists, who had somehow infiltrated the fandom, a fandom we were not entitled to, and thus had to be bullied out again.

I don't need to list the many reasons in which I find the Moffat era of the show distasteful from a feminist standpoint here, as my point is not that all have to agree. Despite adoring the Russell T Davies era, I do not believe that means the era is unworthy of criticism. In fact, I also think that those who criticize the current era, provided they do not use misogyny, are entirely valid in their responses. Criticism cannot be the enemy of fandom. I often see criticism of media that I do not agree with, but that is the price we must pay in order to allow those from oppressed and minority groups to speak. A member of a minority group speaking their opinion is not 'fandom drama', nor is it necessarily 'toxic' (within reason). It is merely an opinion, and it *must* be allowed to stand.

If it is acceptable for white male fans to critique the show, as is common (I hear no end of complaints about the Sixth Doctor era), then it cannot be seen as an insult when minorities do the same. You see certain 'acceptable' complaints, which most take part in, ones which have been mutually decided upon by white male fandom, and then you see the unacceptable complaints, which, surprise surprise, are usually the ones made by minority groups about social justice issues. Many older fans relish the picking apart of classic episodes, and in many cases do so with witty aplomb, yet it is always the complaints about real world issues such as sexism, racism and homophobia which create the sudden irrational cries for an end to 'negativity'.

If the show is entering a new, forward-thinking era, in which we have a woman in the lead role and the show is making a pointed effort to represent a more broad spectrum of people, then we have to accept what comes with that. It means the voices of women and minorities in fandom being taken seriously, and not just when they say what older male members of fandom find palatable.

I hasten to add that although in my personal perspective, I take particular issue with the Moffat era, for its constant sexist tone, tropes, lad banter, objectification and what I perceive to be an era specifically aimed at boys and men, as well as his own sexist comments, all eras can and should be reassessed with our modern outlook, and stories can still be enjoyed while acknowledging that we can do better. This should not be seen, as it is by many, as some form of heresy or rebellion. In order to create an inclusive and diverse fan space, it means more than simply having us women and minorities present, it means listening to what new perspectives our identities have shaped, and what the show might mean to us. Whether we agree with them or not. The outrage at some fans describing *The Talons of Weng-Chiang* as racist in their view speaks volumes about the real intolerance within fandom spaces.

On this subject, I have an interesting personal experience to share. I am a YouTuber who first gained a following among the *Doctor Who* fandom for writing a number of critiques of Steven Moffat's sexism, and the Moffat era in general, as well as making videos on the subject, along with other videos which discussed feminist and social justice issues in popular media and beyond. I was not looking for a following, but I felt I could be silent no longer as I watched my favourite show become the home of lad banter, where the women were objectified and only defined by the Doctor, the characters were overwhelmingly white and LGBT people were simply passing jokes. (The fat gay married Anglican marines, anyone?)

Of course harassment followed, but as a woman with an opinion in a popular fandom, I quickly grew to accept it. The misogynistic harassment set a clear message: put up with things as they are, or go.

Unluckily for those charming people, they only made me more determined to speak my truth, and demonstrated to me quite how far the fandom still had to go.

When I was asked to be on the revamped *Doctor Who Magazine Time Team* feature some years later by Benjamin Cook, I was thrilled. I was excited to see a diverse lineup (although admittedly not in age), and was surprised and rather impressed that as someone so vocal about sexism within the show (my brother Dan and I have made several YouTube videos touching on these subjects and our disgust at

Moffat's repeated sexism), we had been chosen. As a teenager I had emailed *Doctor Who Magazine*, during Steven Moffat's tenure, pitching a feminist analysis feature, which I was not surprised received no response. To be scouted personally by Benjamin for the feature was a dream-come-true for my young self. The fact he delighted in our Moffat critique and enjoyed our videos on the subject made me hope that perhaps things really might be changing, and new voices might well be rising in fandom, where after so long they had been ignored.

The reaction to the new *Time Team* was exactly what I had anticipated. In a show about a time travelling alien who tries to do good and promote equality, it is baffling that there is such a huge group of fandom that so completely misses the point. People complained about how 'woke' it was, how it was simply 'diversity for show', and despite later coming to a similar conclusion myself, it was for utterly different reasons. Many are quick to forget the likes of Verity Lambert and Waris Hussein, a woman and British-Indian man, without whom the show would not exist.

My experience on the *Time Team*, although enjoyable, while it lasted, began to go sour as I found myself repeatedly given taps on the wrist for comments about the sexism in Steven Moffat's work. My continuing instance that as a woman I had a right to be vocal, and even angry about this, without being restricted by the men around me, was something that became something of a battle, and ultimately led to me being blacklisted from the team without my knowledge. Initially (after considerable radio silence), I was informed this exclusion was due to my mental health issues, something which alarmed me for entirely different reasons. Quite clearly, this was not the appropriate or adequate response to a person with mental illness, and ableism is not befitting of the magazine, nor condoned by it. When I put this to Ben, the real reason quickly came to light. It was indeed my refusal to stop talking about the sexism in previous eras of the show that was making me rather too much of a wildcard. In fact, I was even accused of 'putting people in danger' by refusing to back down on this particular issue, not to mention informed that I needed to pipe down or else the dreaded *Daily Mail* were going to target me. Here lies the problem. Instead of supporting a woman against this, it was far easier to put pressure on me to be silent.

I was informed that Steven Moffat was an important man in terms of the magazine, and that although speaking truth to power was apparently supported, it wasn't when calling out particular men. Sadly, I was unsurprised by this reaction, which included describing me as 'slagging off the production team' and 'publicly sh*tting on Steven Moffat'. Presumably the more palatable thing to do was make such criticisms in private, where nobody might hear me, and where the delusional ideal of total equality in fandom and the show could continue. Certainly I was hearing these same criticisms from certain individuals privately, and actually some I found distasteful, but there was an acceptable fandom face we clearly had to put on. Yes, we all agreed the sexism was bad, but heaven forfend we come out and say so. In fact, when I explained that I could not possibly censor myself to be more palatable, I was informed that 'representing the show with dignity, diplomacy and class shouldn't be an imposition' which rather speaks for itself.

It is important for me to note that in spite of this, it was a great privilege to be in the feature, and that the editor, Marcus Hearn, was unaware of this, and when made aware, treated me with admirable respect. I cannot say if *Doctor Who Magazine* itself is at fault here, or if the blame lies with those in charge of individual features, but what it *does* confirm is that uncomfortable bias we still have in society, a desire to protect the powerful. A fear of being dismissed for expressing discomfort. And I am not the only person to have experienced such an incident within this particular fandom.

When criticism is perceived as a personal attack, as 'classless' or lacking in 'dignity', this leaves women and minorities in a very sticky situation indeed. It is of course the white men of fandom who are allowed to determine what constitutes valid critique, and what they believe is simply taking things too far and making a scene. My opinions about said sexism were described as 'mean spirited', which of course implies that keeping quiet is what makes a minority 'nice' and valuable. We have heard these attitudes time and time again. The oppressed and marginalized must be dignified, which means don't rock the boat, and those in power can in turn reward them for this, while retaining a progressive exterior. Too many of us hear these same complaints daily, being told that it is cruel to point out what is our own dehumanization.

To this day, we, as women and minorities, have an uncertain place within fandom. It is not a space in which we are believed to belong. We are outsiders who need to toe the line and go along with established thought in order to be respected. Otherwise, we are merely troublemakers, snowflakes and figures of ridicule.

It is also notable in my personal circumstances that my brother was kept on the team in spite of his own comments about Moffat's misogyny, as we all know that when a man dares to voice such an opinion, it is far more palatable than those awful shrieking, overdramatic women. It was also interesting to see that the backlash to the team as a whole was almost exclusively aimed at the female members, with a few of us picked out for extra special scorn. Some of the women on the team found this constant level of harassment extremely difficult to handle, and it caused a great deal of stress.

I applaud Chris Chibnall and his team for pushing for better representation and diversity, and I am delighted by his choice to have a woman play the Doctor, but progress is still slow. While the show itself is leaping forward, fandom is at a standstill. The same white male figures are still in charge of attitudes and narratives, with opinions being deemed as acceptable or disgraceful based on the validation of these men.

In fact, I worry that as in society, sexism in fandom is increasing rather than dying out, perhaps as a panicked response by those who preferred a time of inequality. True 'toxic fandom' is rising, and it looks nothing like impassioned critiques. We now have the #NotMyDoctor lot, who apparently cannot accept that a time travelling alien who can completely regenerate their body might at some point not be a white man. You cannot go on YouTube to find good *Doctor Who* fan content without having some sexist video essay pop up, in which a faceless person describes how *Doctor Who* has gone to the dogs due to a 'PC agenda', and bizarrely, Jodie Whittaker herself.

My theory is that this hotbed of sexism has been allowed to grow and flourish, and has become ever more emboldened, because so many in fandom, and indeed the so-called 'progressives' have decided to stand by and say nothing when faced with the growing sexism of both show and fandom in recent times. What we see is an explosion of pure misogyny, a sneering, seething hatred of anyone who isn't a white male in fandom, and this group is unfortunately going nowhere fast.

So what can we do to change things? Sadly, it isn't something I can see happening overnight.

The first is issue is that instead of this being a rogue group of particularly misogynistic fans, their attitudes are seen within the source material itself. As I have previously touched on, when the show itself has, at times, been accused of having a 'women problem' and has been known to use sexist tropes and jokes with no real consequences, how can we possibly eliminate sexism from our fandom? It is my belief that the repeated sexist jokes and themes of the Moffat era only emboldened many disgruntled fans, who were starting to worry about the growing numbers of women and people of colour making themselves heard in fandom. Many *Doctor Who* fan forums were full of posts discussing the so-called 'gay agenda' of the RTD era (aka representing non-straight people), and relishing the fact that they, white men, were the most important type of fan again. This entitlement is a poison in any fandom.

The second issue is that many supposed progressives in the *Doctor Who* fandom are happy to talk the talk, but when it comes to actually doing something about it, we see a very different story.

Having been told while on the Time Team that I needed to choose what was important to me, being on the team or continuing to call Moffat's work sexist, and that calling out said sexism wasn't 'classy', as well as others being routinely told off for not quite toeing the line, it was startling to see some of the same figures publicly posting about their support of women in fandom. It would still seem that in 2019, the preferred feminists in fandom are those that are (a) white men, and (b) charmingly silent when it comes to those in power.

What I am saying is that diversity cannot just be for show. Fandom needs to make a choice, do we make an effort to be progressive, or are we not brave enough? That doesn't mean just seeing more brown faces and women (which I might add have been here all along) but *listening* to those people. It means accepting criticisms from those people that might seem radical to a fandom so predominantly ruled by white men. It does not mean total agreement, of course, as fandom is a space for discussion and debate, and always, respect. But it does mean that these white men need to relinquish control of our narratives and conversations. Listening is key.

The lie of criticism 'feeding toxic fandom' is as ridiculous as it is insulting. Surely the nature of said criticism must be taken into account? What we see here is a new and insidious form of silencing. What on the surface seems to be all about positivity and love is really an unspoken ultimatum to minorities that speak out. Be positive constantly, no matter the content, or be dismissed. Clever manipulation is taking place to retain the status quo. The lie that all criticism is automatically toxic, and that the sexist #NotMyDoctor brigade, and those who oppose them and other forms of sexism are equally at fault, is a dangerous precedent to set. In a situation of misogyny, there is no middle ground.

Those more extreme misogynistic voices are easy to focus on, but the point Joy Piedmont made in reference to the Panopticon convention is, I believe, relevant to the state of fandom, and social justice as a whole. As the saying goes, talk is cheap. And there are a lot of people talking who really ought to be practicing such ideals in their everyday interactions with fandom and the show.

While the validity of criticism depends on the acceptance of white male faces in fandom, there is no progression. It is not for the *Doctor Who* fandom to graciously open itself up to minorities and women; it is for those popular voices to step back instead of taking ownership, to amplify our voices, to listen, to respect and accept that we are not intruders. We may be louder now, but I promise you, we have been here all along.

Chapter 38
When fans become showrunners
by Julia Henken

Original to this volume

How have the different fannish philosophies of the three twenty-first-century Doctor Who *showrunners influenced their respective eras of the show? Julia Henken has some theories.*

Beginning with Russell T Davies' revival, *Doctor Who* (2005–) has had designated showrunners: central decision makers with distinct creative visions. Davies, Steven Moffat and Chris Chibnall have all positioned themselves not only as the artists responsible for the narrative direction during their era but as lifelong *Doctor Who* fans. Each showrunner has been influenced by the Classic series, making creative connections with the past. As members of the original fandom, they straddled the line between being a fan of *Doctor Who*'s content and creating it. These showrunners have each capitalized on their fan knowledge in different ways, and in doing so have each had a unique impact on the series' narrative direction.

Russell T Davies

When the *Doctor Who* revival was announced in 2003, Davies was fully established as a talented industry professional.[1] His work on both children and adult television series, such as *On the Waterfront* (BBC1 1988–9) and *Queer as Folk* (Channel 4, 1999–2000), made him a good choice for the family-oriented programme, which would hopefully appeal to all ages. This experience would be emphasized later with the *Doctor Who* spin-offs, *Torchwood* and *The Sarah Jane Adventures*, which were aimed exclusively at adults and children respectively and further opened up the *Doctor Who*-niverse. Davies' reputation as a talented writer even drew Christopher Eccleston to the role of the Ninth Doctor as he did not hold any particular childhood fondness for the series.[2]

While Davies preferred at times to downplay his fannish credentials and pitch the new *Doctor Who* (2005–) to a wider mainstream audience, his history as a fan was often mentioned as a form of reassurance that the beloved property was in good hands.

Suzanne Scott classifies Davies as a 'fanboy auteur'.[3] The term refers to any media professional already established in the industry that is hired to act as the creative driving force behind the property of which they are a fan. The fanboy auteur is able to use their status both as a fan and as a showrunner to assure audiences and industry professionals that an intellectual property is in qualified hands.[4] In *Doctor Who*'s case, many attribute the revival's success to the foundation laid during the Davies Era[5] – and this is also why so many are excited to see him return as showrunner in 2023.[6]

As a lifelong fan, Davies' understanding of the Classic series gets filtered through a lens of childlike wonder and nostalgia. He has acknowledged that his own emotional attachment to *Doctor Who* goes back to his childhood,[7] and how he treats the Doctor throughout the series reflects that childlike idolization. During the early years of Davies' 2005–9 revival, the Doctor is a figure to be idolized, a romantic fantasy.

Davies depicts the Doctor as a nearly godlike character, capable of overcoming any obstacle, regardless of size. Perhaps the most visible example of this is the series 3 finale, when the Doctor uses Time Lord psychic abilities to gain superpowers and defeat the Master. This solution doesn't depict the Doctor outwitting a foe with cleverness. Instead, the conflict is resolved because the Doctor can do anything and always wins. Rather than framing the Doctor as a messianic hero,[8] I believe this reflects Davies' childhood adulation – comparable to how a small child thinks their parents are infallible when they are young.

Compared to Classic *Who*, the Doctor also becomes a romantic figure in the revival. The kiss between the Ninth Doctor (Christopher Eccelston) and Rose (Billie Piper) in the series 1 finale is the culmination of a season-long flirtation and leads into more overt romance in later seasons. The Tenth Doctor (David Tennant) continues this romance with Rose in series 2, and at the end of series 4, Rose gets to spend the rest of her life with a duplicate of the Doctor Who will age and die just as a human does. Matt Hills argues that Rose is actually a stand-in for Davies, reflecting his own love for the Doctor[9] and, in this ending, his character gets her own Doctor to love.

Davies explores other aspects of his fandom in the spin-offs. *The Sarah Jane Adventures* (*SJA* 2007–11) features Classic characters Sarah Jane Smith (Elisabeth Sladen) and K9 (John Leeson), after their guest appearance in series 2. Not only do Doctors Ten and Eleven (Matt Smith) appear in *SJA* but it also includes guest appearances by Jo Grant (Katy Manning) and Brigadier Lethbridge-Stewart (Nicholas Courtney), Classic-era allies. In *Torchwood* (2006–11), which similarly opens up the *Doctor Who* narrative universe, Captain Jack Harkness, (John Barrowman) another Davies creation, leads his team as a queer man.

As the first showrunner for *Doctor Who* (2005–), Davies was responsible for reviving *Doctor Who* and steering the narrative during the first five years. What he chose to include or ignore affected the other writers. As the first showrunner, Davies opened up the series to new audiences and possible fans, but the next showrunner proved to be more exclusive and protective of the *Doctor Who* fandom.

Steven Moffat

Steven Moffat began his tenure as showrunner with the freedom to reinvent *Doctor Who*, with new actors and a new TARDIS interior. Moffat presented himself as a fanboy auteur from the outset and was vocal about his lifelong passion for *Doctor Who*. In interviews, Moffat describes the weight of responsibility, even as he presents himself as having a superior understanding of what is best for *Doctor Who*.[10] As a BBC-sanctioned fan, he was able to temporarily take ownership of the canon and increase the complexity.[11] He took seriality and canonicity to new heights by sowing seeds for complex plots across multiple episodes, where the viewer needed to keep up in order to understand what was going on. In making the series less approachable, Moffat effectively became a gatekeeper, guarding the entrance to the *Doctor Who* fandom from the general masses. Under Moffat's guidance, to understand the story a true fan needed be faithful and devoted, not a casual viewer.

River Song (Alex Kingston) is one example of Moffat's approach to *Doctor Who* as a BBC-sanctioned fan. River Song first makes her appearance in series 4 (Davies' last full season) as an important character from the Doctor's future. This begins a plot arc that leads directly into Moffat's era. While the mystery surrounding River Song is revealed in series 6, her last appearance is in the 2015 Christmas Special, which precedes Moffat's last full season, series 10.

River Song is a Moffat-creation built on narrative complexity. Each of her appearances builds on the ones before. She and the Doctor live their lives in reverse: the first time he meets her is the same day she dies. There is little to catch an unfamiliar viewer up to speed. For example, her last appearance directly references dialogue from series 4, but is meaningless without context. The episode remains entertaining, but might be confusing for a viewer who only recently began watching *Doctor Who* or watched intermittently.

River Song's last appearance demonstrates Moffat's possessiveness over his creations. He specifically includes narrative details that make it challenging to use her in future episodes. Because *Doctor Who* is about time travel, there are ways in which the Doctor can reunite with past companions, even if the companions are dead. However, all of the Moffat-era companions are diegetically isolated from time travel. This approach to the show's ongoing canon could be called an 'Original Character Do Not Steal' mentality, a phrase that was coined by members of various fandoms posting fanart online. It indicates possessiveness of a fan-made character within the scope of a non-fan-owned IP and embodies Moffat's assertion of sole control over his creations, which he solidifies by creating narrative reasons why they cannot return. Circumventing any of their deaths would result in a paradox, which could destroy the universe. For many of Moffat's characters, their future and ultimate end are already decided – even within the flexibility of time travel – and cannot be altered as a result. No other writer can use Moffat's companions outside of the narrative he wrote for them, only as a brief appearance that would not impact their timeline.

Moffat's companions are each uniquely special in some way, and many are firsts for *Doctor Who*. Amy (Karen Gillan) and Rory (Arthur Darvill) are the first married couple to travel with the Doctor (series 5 through 7); Clara (Jenna Coleman) jumped into the Doctor's personal timeline which enabled him to meet other versions of her (series 7 through 9); Bill Potts (Pearl Mackie) is the first openly gay female companion (series 10); and Nardole (Matt Lucas) is the first alien to become an official companion since the 1980s (series 10). Davies and Chibnall created companions that generally defer to the Doctor, but Moffat's companions are more willing to challenge them.

Perhaps this was Moffat's version of self-insert[12] as so many of his plot arcs revolved around the companions, his creations. The resolutions of long narrative arcs are tied directly to each of the Moffat-era companions and their histories and identities. In series 5, Amy Pond lives in a very large house with only her aunt because there is a crack in time in her wall that has been devouring pieces of her life. In closing this crack in time, the Doctor ends up trapped outside of time and memory. Because Amy's brain has been altered by growing up with a crack in time, she maintains her memories of him which enables the Doctor and the TARDIS return to existence. In series 7, Clara becomes an integral part of the Doctor's past in 'The Name of the Doctor' by stepping into his timeline and creating helpful copies of herself. She only becomes his companion because he meets these copies and thus seeks her out, but it is canonically suggested that she could have been present during the Classic era.

In the fiftieth anniversary special, Moffat further asserts his creative control over *Doctor Who*'s past, present and (at that time) future. He fills in the blanks Davies left about the Time War, providing a definitive canonical account of what happened, whereas Davies left it open to the imagination.[13] Moffat's answer includes appearances (old footage) of all previous Doctors and a cameo of the (then) recently announced Twelfth Doctor (Peter Capaldi). It retroactively erases an implied part of canon (that the Doctor had acted unconscionably during the Time War) and replaces it with a much tidier, heroic version of events – and ensures every version of the Doctor is there to witness it. This is how Moffat exerts his sanctioned control over even the Classic-era canon. A parody released as part of the fiftieth anniversary special, 'The Five(ish) Doctors', jokes that Moffat writes his scripts by playing with *Doctor Who* toys, literally controlling the Doctor's movements.

The next showrunner, Chris Chibnall, created lore that would redefine the Doctor's identity.

Chris Chibnall

When Chris Chibnall was selected as showrunner, it had almost been assumed that the next *Doctor Who* showrunner would be another fan. Being a *Doctor Who* fan and the next *Doctor Who* showrunner was no longer a novel concept. However, with his authorial powers and fan knowledge,[14] Chibnall's era has proven to be more faithful to the Classic series in multiple ways.[15]

This is evident in how he tells the Doctor's stories. Davies and Moffat both utilized overarching season-long plots. Chibnall's first season, series 11, was considerably more episodic, with the biggest connection being the same antagonist in the premier and the finale. Series 11 returned to the pseudo-hard science fiction reminiscent of Classic *Who*, but specifically left out any planets, characters or species that the Doctor had encountered on screen before. Series 12 introduced more seriality, but remained largely episodic. It also reintroduced the Master (Sacha Dhawan).

In Classic *Who*, the Master was a recurring villain characterized by their hatred for the Doctor. Under Davies, the Master and the Doctor gained a level of camaraderie as the last of their species. Under Moffat, Missy (Michelle Gomez), the female Master, flirted with the Doctor. In both eras, the Master found a level of redemption before the Doctor regenerated. Chibnall returned the relationship to a more Classic *Who* balance of hostility and civility; in between trying to harm each other, they could talk as equals. Chibnall's Master was also much more keen to inflict violence on the Doctor specifically.

Series 13 reintroduced the serial storytelling format that was the norm during Classic *Who*. Under this format, stories were told over the course of typically three to six episodes. 'Flux' is one such story. While 'Flux' could be considered an overarching plot similar to other seasons, BBC promotion took care to position it as a single story.[16] As for why 'Flux' took up an entire season, the average episode count for a modern British TV series is significantly fewer than in the Classic series and further episodes were cut due to the Covid-19 pandemic.

Another way Chibnall focuses on Classic *Who* is by addressing the lore behind the Doctor. While Davies sought to build on canon and Moffat sought to control canon, Chibnall turned his attention to the lore, changing how the viewer sees the Doctor without changing the events that have already occurred within the show. This creative decision also has some basis in the Classic era. A 2004 issue of the *Doctor Who Magazine* details a proposed story arc from the 1980s that would further distinguish the Doctor as special or unique among the Time Lords: The Cartmel Masterplan. Former script editor Andrew Cartmel wanted to establish the Doctor as being a mysterious founder of Gallifrey.[17] As a lifelong fan, Chibnall was familiar with the Cartmel era.[18] 'The Timeless Children' (2020) revisits this plotline by establishing that the Doctor herself is actually a being from a parallel universe whose DNA contains the secret to regeneration. In other words, the Doctor is responsible for creating the Time Lord race.

Chibnall's era also is also more overtly political than Davies' or Moffat's tenures.[19] Discrimination based on race, gender and age are all explored with the female Doctor and her companions:[20] a retired older white man, his grandson who is a young Black man, a young Muslim woman of Indian descent and a working-class white man. Additionally, Chibnall addresses capitalistic corruption and environmentalism. *Doctor Who* has always been political,[21] and the Classic serials often included political issues. There are Classic *Who* stories that address exploitation of workers,[22] environmentalism, racism and capitalism[23] in addition to concerns regarding globalization of the economy.[24] Chibnall draws on this tradition in his era, arguably as a result of his faithfulness to the Classic series.

Doctor Who (2005–) is unusual in that all three of its showrunners have been pre-existing fans of the show as well as industry professionals given the opportunity to work on the object of their fandom. Russell T Davies, as the first showrunner of the revival, had the difficult task of appealing to both old and new audiences. By drawing on his own fan memories, he was able to create a foundation for future showrunners. Steven Moffat admitted that working on *Doctor Who* was a dream-come-true for him,[25] but in increasing the narrative complexity, made the series less approachable for a new viewer. However, this did not stop the audience from continuing to grow. Chris Chibnall took *Doctor Who* back to its roots, reexamining what makes the Doctor so special and using science fiction as an allegory to comment on the current state of our world. All three men are considered 'fanboy auteurs' because they used their fandom to assure both the industry and their audience that the *Doctor Who* property was in capable hands. There is much more to be examined about each showrunner and his tenure, particularly as Davies is set to return in 2023. It is unclear what the future holds for *Doctor Who*, but it rests once again in the hands of a fan.

Notes

1. Associated Press, 'Cult Favorite "*Doctor Who*" Coming Back', *The Doctor Who Cuttings Archive* (27 September 2003).
2. 'Interview with Christopher Eccleston (BBC Breakfast)', *Disk 1, Special Features*, *Doctor Who Series 1 DVD Boxset* (BBCVideo, 2005).
3. Suzanne Scott, *Fake Geek Girls: Fandom, Gender, and the Convergence Culture Industry* (New York: New York University Press, 2019), 162.
4. Ibid., 161.
5. James Chapman, *Inside the TARDIS* (New York: I.B. Tauris, 2013 [2006]), 184–208.
6. Mia Johnson, 'With Russell T Davies' Return, BBC Loses Creative Control of "*Doctor Who*"', *Salon* (28 November 2021): https://www.salon.com/2021/11/28/with-russell-t-davies-return-bbc-loses-creative-control-of-doctor-who_partner/ (accessed 9 February 2022).
7. Matt Hills, *Triumph of a Timelord: Regenerating Doctor Who in the Twenty-First Century* (New York: I.B. Tauris, 2010), 65.

8   Chapman, *Inside*, 216.
9   Hills, *Triumph*, 65.
10 Andrew Harrison, 'Steven Moffat: "I Ws the Original Angry *Doctor Who* Fan', *The Guardian* (18 November 2013): https://www.theguardian.com/tv-and-radio/2013/nov/18/steven-moffat-doctor-who-interview (accessed 18 April 2021).
11 Chapman, *Inside*, 280.
12 Ibid., 273.
13 Hills, *Triumph*, 64–5.
14 Matt Greenfield, 'Interview: Chris Chibnall Talks Past, Future and the Audience', *BlogtorWho* (18 September 2018): https://www.blogtorwho.com/interview-chris-chibnall-s11/ (accessed 26 April 2021).
15 'Regenerating *Doctor Who*' Disk 1, *Doctor Who Series 11 BluRay Boxset* (BBC, 2019).
16 BBC America, 'Official New Season Trailer | *Doctor Who*: Flux Premieres October 31st | BBC America', *YouTube* (15 October 2021). Accessed 27 April 2022.
17 'Cartmel Masterplan', *TARDIS Data Core*: https://tardis.fandom.com/wiki/Cartmel_Masterplan (accessed 18 April 2021).
18 Chapman, *Inside*, 163–4.
19 Ciarán Treacy, 'The Chibnall Centrism of *Doctor Who* | Politics on TV', *HeadStuff* (8 January 2021).
20 Katharine Harris and Peter Ridley, 'I Never Did This when I Was a Man': Review of Season 11, Doctor Who, BBC 2018. *Soundings: A Journal of Politics and Culture,* no. 71 (2019): 107–15.
21 Danny Nicol, *Doctor Who*: A British Alien? (Cham: Palgrave Macmillan, 2018).
22 Ibid., 91.
23 Ibid., 212.
24 Ibid., 218.
25 Chapman, *Inside*, 273.

Chapter 39
Scripting fandom in twenty-first-century *Doctor Who* by Paul Driscoll

Original to this volume

How has fandom itself been written into New Who by its fanboy showrunners? Paul Driscoll examines how fandom responds when they see themselves reflected, positively and negatively, in their favourite show.

The three showrunners of twenty–first-century *Doctor Who* have all been fans of the series since childhood. Fans, not only according to the most inclusive definition of the word (which would aptly describe every contributor apparently obligated to reassure fans of their prior commitment to the programme)[1] but those who have travelled far along Abercrombie and Longhurst's continuum of consumer, fan, enthusiast, cultist and petty producer.[2] To the readers of *Doctor Who Magazine*, and those who frequent fan forums and social media sites, those fan credentials are indelibly enshrined in a series of often shared images. Davies' collection of *Doctor Who* memorabilia, including a life-size Dalek which would go on to appear in 'Asylum of the Daleks', a photograph of Moffat as a child reading a Target novelization and stills of Chibnall's appearance on *Open Air* (1986) as a somewhat disgruntled adolescent fan, all serve as evidence of their allegiance. They function to demystify, disempower and deconstruct the auteur, by returning them to their roots and reminding them that they are expected to reflect and represent the fanbase.[3]

All three showrunners are coded by fans as more than the romanticized auteurs of their beloved series. To be sure, their public presence and official role help to impute and preserve a cult-like status onto *Doctor Who*,[4] making them an essential part of the fan object, but nonetheless they are treated as flawed custodians, those who have crossed over from the strongly hierarchical realm of fandom. Undemocratically, they have been given licence to play with toys that belong to fandom as a whole, and so they are seen as fair game to be pilloried if their perceived agendas are at odds with any metanarrative created by a particular fan base. The showrunners stand in a liminal position between membership and non-membership, recognized as part of the fold, for example through affectionate nicknames (Rusty,

The Moff, Chibbers), yet at the same time set apart as those with the power to sell (and sell out) the series to the widest possible marketplace.⁵

When *Doctor Who* returned in 2005, the British press frequently emphasized that it was now being run by the fans, for good or ill. Russell T Davies in particular was singled out for his fanboy credentials: 'Davies is a devoted fan of *Doctor Who* […] Such is the strength of [his] feeling that, were he not involved in the new series, he too would be on the internet, trying to read the runes with all the other obsessives.'⁶ Davies may have embraced the label with enthusiasm, but he also took steps to distance himself from the 'diehards', even going as far as to adopt an othering nickname for them – 'the ming mongs': 'They're like members of the Flat Earth Society. It would be mad to take them too seriously […] The fans are hugely vocal, but there are only about 2,000 of them, maximum.'⁷ Davies may have existed in that 'parallel universe' of *Doctor Who* fandom, where the show was still at the forefront of the imagination as if it had never been cancelled, but he had to divorce himself from *Doctor Who* and see it through the albeit affectionate eyes of the more disinterested general public. For the majority, *Doctor Who* was a nostalgic artefact, one remembered fondly for being very much a product of its time. Privately and sometimes for readers of *Doctor Who Magazine*, Davies could still write his own fanfic and continue to obsess over matters of continuity,⁸ but as showrunner little of that attention to detail would be helpful. 'The fiction of the Doctor has got 40 years of back-story … Which we'll ignore. Except for the good bits.'⁹ More importantly, all three new series showrunners, instead of being obsessed by existing canon (including their contributions to it), have created their own versions of what Matt Hills calls the 'endlessly deferred narrative' (many of the series long arcs are left unresolved, such as the identity of the hybrid and the Doctor's quest to uncover her forgotten lives; numerous characters remain open to interpretation, such as Davies' Woman in White; and death itself is repeatedly held back).¹⁰ These less prescriptive and more creative moves ironically do more to preserve the cult-like status of *Doctor Who* than any narrow appeal to fandom, even when they do create shockwaves and trigger yet more division between fans. A number of pre-existing deferred narratives that fandom had long since closed with their own largely uncontested pseudo-canonical resolutions are also provocatively reopened (Is the Doctor Half-Human, How Many Times Can a Time Lord Regenerate, Is the Doctor Called *Doctor Who*). Knowledge of these once fixed elements of *Doctor Who* lore could no longer be used to distinguish the 'true fan' from the casual viewer.

The relationship of the showrunner to the fan is a complex one, made more complicated by their own fan self-identities. Echoes of their experiences of fan membership and engagement have inevitably leaked into their scripts, resulting in a dialectical spirit of provocation and reflection, antagonism and affection, and parody and celebration. The series serves to both empower its fans and put them very firmly in their place.

One aspect of fan sensibility is the desire to step inside the world of the text, a movement that can be seen in the recent trend of high art to embrace popular culture with various interactive installations, such as the Van Gogh Experience, where fans can literally step inside not only the mind of the heavily mythologized artist but also the paintings themselves.¹¹ Fans can do this through imaginative play, even in their own home, whether aided by VR and other interactive tools or by transforming an existing space into a fantasy dimension. Certain *Doctor Who* film locations have for some become places of pilgrimage, which, like the collecting of screen-used props, generates a feeling of closeness through a multi-sensual engagement with the fan object. Cosplay functions in a similar way when pre-scripted impersonation becomes playful improvisation as the fan embodies a given character.¹² But what happens when the fan is scripted by the fan auteurs into the text itself?

Both Russell T Davies and Steven Moffat have created characters who reflect certain fan sensibilities and stereotypes. Unsurprisingly, the likes of Elton Pope (Marc Warren), Malcolm Taylor (Lee Evans) and Petronella Osgood (Ingrid Oliver) have provoked the fan base into somewhat extreme reactions. These characters can be loved excessively considering their limited screen time (none of them are full time companions), perhaps even rising to cult status themselves. Conversely, they can be viewed as a personal attack, or used to cruelly denigrate other fans as if that was their intended function. Chris Chibnall has avoided the same interplay between story and fan by characterizing the Doctor as a fan of others[13] and by focusing on 'the fam' over the fan. By shifting the locus of belonging away from the spheres of religious devotion and discipleship towards those of the reconstituted nuclear family and the friendship circle, the boundaries between fan and fan object are less clearly discernible.

Davies' first *Doctor Who* story, 'Rose', is written from the perspective of Rose Tyler (Billie Piper), who lives with her mother on a London council estate. She is the prototype for Davies' new style of companion, the audience identification figure written to defy all the old stereotypes of the damsel in distress, but she also reflects his ideal *Doctor Who* fan. Her research into the Doctor leads her to Clive Finch (Mark Benton), who runs the conspiracy website 'Who is *Doctor Who*?' Clive is very much a cipher for the old guard fan, in direct contrast to Rose.[14] When she arrives, Clive's son tells him, 'it's one of your nutters', but Rose, even after becoming a fan of the Doctor, could hardly be described in such negative terms. Clive's obsession with the Doctor is, at least in theory, kept separate from the rest of his life, as symbolized spatially by his den and his family's dismissive othering of his hobby. It's a form of escape, a withdrawal from the everyday, something that he can only talk about with fellow enthusiasts. When he dies, it isn't so much the death of one type of fan that is being enacted (contra Arnold) but an attempt to put to an end the errant association between the *Doctor Who* fan and ufologists, trainspotters, conspiracy theorists and other groups labelled as 'anoraks'. Rose Tyler represents a fandom that is open to change, inclusive and not elitist, acknowledged, celebrated and integral to everyday life – a fact that her mother Jackie (Camille Coduri) and boyfriend Mickey (Noel Clarke) must learn to come to terms with. Such a fandom already existed in *Doctor Who*, despite any perception otherwise. Fandom is not portrayed here as a dysfunctional subculture and neither is the fan pathologized. Consequently, few of the 'old guard' took offense at Clive, even if Davies was making clear that his vision of *Doctor Who* would not afford them any inner circle privileges.

In 'Love and Monsters', *Doctor Who* fandom takes centre stage. The filming of the episode was double-banked with 'The Impossible Planet/The Satan Pit'. Scripted by Davies with that practical consideration in mind, the Doctor (David Tennant) and Rose would only feature in the opening and closing scenes. The adventure would instead be told from the perspective of Marc Warren's Elton Pope. The story's prehistory shows that it was not simply written as a convenient filler piece. Davies returned to a comic strip idea he had pitched to *Doctor Who Magazine* the previous year about an ordinary person whose life had been significantly affected by a number of alien invasions from past *Doctor Who* stories (including the death of a parent).[15] Far from blaming the Doctor for bringing destruction in his wake (in contrast to Clive Finch), the orphaned child would grow up idolizing the Time Lord, determined to one day meet his hero. Elton Pope is presented as a likeable figure, and together with his small band of likeminded fans, he serves as a further corrective to the negative stereotypes of fandom that Davies was so eager to counter in 'Rose'.

Although Marc Warren was once described as having 'cornered the market in sexy weirdos',[16] his character in *Doctor Who* is scripted as 'a nice, ordinary bloke … no funny voice or daft clothes. Just plain, honest, and polite'.[17] The idea that fan sensibility is a continuum, and that we can all embrace different fandoms to different extents at different stages in our lives, is an important counter to the obsessed fantasist stereotype. By making Elton 'into all sorts of things' from football to ELO, the character is normalized. During the episode commentary for the DVD release, Director Dan Zeff, Executive Producer Julie Gardner and Camille Coduri (Jackie Tyler) discuss the fact that none of the members of LINDA are social outcasts; they all have lives beyond *Doctor Who*. They come from diverse backgrounds and their fandom is expressed variously, including the academic (Skinner), the fan artist (Bliss) and the intrepid set reporter (Bridget). The overriding mood is one of joy until the black-coated Victor Kennedy (Peter Kay), clearly representing the elitist 'super fan', arrives to kill all the fun. He literally absorbs their dissenting voices, even if his inability to silence them ultimately leads to his death.

The heavily contested fan base reaction to 'Love and Monsters' re-enacts the ideological differences between Victor Kennedy and the rest of LINDA. Depending on which fan type one identifies with, the episode is a celebration or a parody of fandom. Some online respondents on fan forum Gallifrey Base felt more of an affinity to Victor than to Elton, and took offence at the episode's judgements about what makes for a good or bad fan. The following anonymized comment is representative: '*anyone who ever made a list of stories that all feature certain monsters or themes is a fat bastard, anyone who ever tried to fit everything together into a coherent timeline apparently did so out of some rigid fascist mentality and not because they were just having fun with their favourite show, and anyone who ever had a friendly chat with another fan about continuity issues was apparently wrong because they should have been singing karaoke and shagging instead.*'

The parodying of cosplayers and fans who enjoy the social and creative dimension of conventions and the like occurs within fandom as much as beyond it.[18] Although such expressions would not be out of place among the members of LINDA, the script fails to provide any ammunition for the Victor Kennedy types to laugh at their expense. This serves to double-down on the attack against a certain fan sensibility. Only one type of fan is allowed to be stereotyped. Victor Kennedy is a continuity obsessive (one deleted line from the script has him describe the Doctor as allergic to aspirin, an obscure reference to *The Mind of Evil* [1971])[19] who cannot bear any expression of emotion. This coldness reinforces the socially maladjusted stereotype of the 'anorak' fan, as well as translating onto screen the vocal aversion to Davies' alleged populist dumbing down of their show through the adoption of soap opera conventions. Initially, the LINDA members are impressed by Victor's know-how and attention to detail, amazed by the clarity of his photographs when compared to their own amateur efforts. Such admiration reflects the nascent feeling that regardless of their personality, super-fans, even as ghastly as Victor, should be treated as gifts to the community, which only adds to their sense of self-entitlement.

UNIT scientist Malcolm Taylor, created by Russell T Davies and Gareth Roberts for the 2009 Easter special 'Planet of the Dead', was expected to be a hit with the audience. Davies spoke enthusiastically about the character, suggesting Evans could star in his own spin-off series.[20] A serious flaw in this ambition is that the character was defined almost exclusively in terms of his excessive love for the Doctor. The comedian's over-the-top comic sensibilities were kept in check,[21] but his performance and role would do little to deter any mocking by the 'not-we' general audience. Once again, the fan community was split, with some interpreting Malcolm as a loving representation of fandom, and others left embarrassed by what they considered to be a geeky stereotype. Quite how such a character could work in a spin-off show without the Doctor is hard to imagine. Even within the vast array of other licenced media, Malcolm Taylor barely features,[22] and aside from being namedropped twice in 'The Day of the Doctor', where he is apparently still employed by UNIT, the TV series has completely ignored him. In fan circles, the character has similarly remained sidelined. A Facebook fan club group with only a handful of members is hardly the legacy Davies was expecting.

Rather than bring back Malcolm, Steven Moffat would effectively replace him with his own version of the scripted fan. Making her debut in the fiftieth anniversary celebratory special 'The Day of the Doctor', Ingrid Oliver's Osgood boldly affirms fandom as an intrinsic part of *Doctor Who*'s story. Although like Davies, Moffat would be highly critical of certain hypercritical and vocal elements within fandom, he was quicker to acknowledge the silent majority.[23] Davies wished he could erase the pejorative term 'mingmong', but Moffat embraced it, turning it into a positive label: '[I am] a proper list-making-borderline-autistic fan. I am head mingmong. I'm King Ming.'[24] For Moffat, a degree of enforced separation between auteur and fan is a regrettable but necessary defence against the angry mob that personalize their criticisms: 'the relationship between a fandom and a show should be permeable. They should be talking to each other. Because particularly in *Doctor Who*, where the creators [...] grew out of the fandom, the idea that the storyteller doesn't sit around the same campfire as the audience is abominable.'[25] Popular areas of debate within fandom are fully engaged with during Moffat's tenure, rather than being dismissed as dirty laundry that shouldn't be aired in public (the Davies approach). He would make them part of the 'endlessly deferred narrative', such as the name of the Doctor, the regeneration limit, hybridity and ethnicity (is the Doctor half-human?), and whether or not the Master can be redeemed. This playfulness could be regarded by his critics as goading or mocking the fans. Such activity is not beyond Moffat (he recalls how he and Davies would deliberately invent titles with rude acronyms to provoke a reaction in the *Doctor Who* forums,[26] and the framing of Clara as the star of the show in 'Death in Heaven' is clearly meant to antagonize those who feared the series was becoming 'The Clara Show'). But for the most part, Moffat is consciously writing as a fan, rather than for or against the fans.[27]

The character of Osgood is a loving representation of the fan community, a performative fan whose identity is shaped, but not defined by her love of the Doctor. However, when viewed with an a priori unconscious separation of the auteur from the fan, she becomes a more contestable figure. Some have taken offence as her appearance and poor health, pointing out that it reinforces the geeky stereotype of the fangirl as ugly, dysfunctional and inadequate. Others have heralded her as the corrective for the fanboys who present themselves as the truth-bearers, a means by which the show legitimizes cosplay, fanfic and improvisation, favouring such expressions over continuity obsessed list-makers (ignoring the fact that Moffat views himself as the latter). The intense online reactions to Osgood's death in 'Death in Heaven' highlighted the divisiveness within the fan community, with some left distraught and others gleeful. But when regarded as a character in her own right, free from authorial intention, she becomes an impersonator to impersonate, and reminds us that the Doctor is an impersonator too with a willingness to cosplay and assume the identity of others.[28]

The various efforts to bring fandom into the narrative reflect the showrunners' ambivalence towards the fan communities they belong to. The characters are unavoidably provocative and interpreted according to the viewer's sense of their own place within fandom. As transitional objects par excellence,[29] they pull the fan in two directions – into and away from the narrative world by acting as agents for both escapist fantasizing and introspective self-evaluation. They also become hooks for the conflicting moves to both other and project a fan identity onto the showrunner. Such movements also occur at a group level, as participants take up their positions in a battle not merely for the favoured interpretation and scoring of any given *Doctor Who* episode but also in the shaping and defining of their own identity as the 'fan base'. They can serve as metaphors for the inevitable death (Clive, Mr Skinner [Simon Greenall] and the other

LINDA members, see also Lorna Bucket [Christina Chong]) and the equally inevitable rebirth of the fan (Osgood). They warn us not to get too close to the fan object so that we forget who we are, while at the same time showing us exactly why we are part of the narrative.

Notes

1. Richard Curtis (writer of 'Vincent and the Doctor'), for example, despite his credentials as a screenwriter, felt it necessary to explain how he was still a fan of the show when living overseas. Newly appointed football managers make similar claims. Those who might appear to be a bad fit (whether for cultural or historical reasons) will make statements about how much they have loved the club, even as a child. Note also the tendency to praise not only the club but the fans too. Acceptance means being seen to be a fan and praising the supporters for being an intrinsic part of the club's ethos.
2. *Audiences: A Sociological Theory of Performance and Imagination* (Thousand Oaks, CA: Sage, 1988). On the usefulness and limits of Abercrombie and Longhurst's taxonomy, see Cornell Sandvoss, *Fans: The Mirror of Consumption* (Cambridge: Polity, 2005), 30ff.
3. The auteurs themselves become active in constructing their 'fan-boy' identities in order to authenticate their relationship with the audience. See Henry Jenkins, *Textual Poachers* (New York: Routledge, 2012), xvi–xvii.
4. On the relationship between the auteur and the cult, see Matt Hills, *Fan Cultures* (London: Routledge, 2002), 133ff.
5. Although the auteur's fannish credentials are important to fans, a fear of cancellation means that conversely 'In an era of seemingly blurring borders between fans and producers, intensive boundary work is carried out by fans to make sure they stay apart', Leora Hadas and Limor Shifman, 'Keeping the Elite Powerless: Fan-Producer Relations in the "Nu-Who"', *Critical Studies in Media Communications* 30, no. 4 (2013): 275–91.
6. Rachel Cooke, 'What's up Doc?' *The Observer* (6 March 2005).
7. Ibid.
8. He would at times invent theories to appease discontinuity spotters, such as using the Time War as an explanation for the Doctor being a few decades younger, *Doctor Who: The Complete History*, Vol 48 (Modena, Italy: Panini, 2016), 31.
9. Quoted in *The Complete History*, Vol 48, 31.
10. Hills, *Fan Cultures*, 134.
11. Immersion into a physical manifestation of the narrative world '[…] is a search for unmediated experience, of putting oneself, literally, in the place of the fan text and thus creating a relationship that goes beyond mere consumption and fantasy'. Sandvoss, *Fans,* 61.
12. See Hills, *Fan Cultures*, 158–71.
13. E.g. Ada Lovelace, Nikola Tesla, Byron and Shelley. A trait that the Doctor has occasionally displayed under previous showrunners (e.g. the Ninth Doctor as a fan of Dickens).
14. See Jon Arnold, *Rose, The Black Archive #1* (Edinburgh, UK: Obverse, 2016), 25.
15. *Doctor Who: The Complete History*, Vol 53 (Modena, Italy: Panini, 2017), 50.
16. *The Complete History* Vol 53, 73, quoting *Radio Times*.
17. *The Complete History* Vol 53, 54.
18. Seen for instance in the backlash by some fans against pages of the *Doctor Who Magazine* being dedicated to cosplay.
19. *The Complete History* Vol 53, 62.
20. *Doctor Who: The Complete History*, Vol 61 (Modena, Italy: Panini, 2018), 28 & 62.

21. Evans turned up on set with a set of comically oversized dentures, an idea vetoed by Davies, *The Complete History* Vol 61, 38.
22. He was selected for one of Jonathan Morris' short-lived Blogs of Doom in DWM, but the premise of the series was to consider some of the more obscure characters who had encountered the Doctor. He also features in Titan comics 'The Lost Dimension' and a DWM short-story follow-up to *Death in Heaven* – 'The Secret Diary of the Master'. Although his non-appearance to date in a Big Finish audio may be down to the actor's availability, he only once gets name-dropped even in the UNIT audios (*Ice Station Alpha*). Contrast this with the prominence given to Osgood.
23. If Davies rhetorically underestimated the number of *Doctor Who* fans during the so-called wilderness years, Moffat would overexaggerate: 'We sort of enshrine this myth that no one was a *Doctor Who* fan during those years. Loads of people were *Doctor Who* fans, almost anybody vaguely arty was a *Doctor Who* fan at some level.' 'Steven Moffat on Writing, Weeping Angels and More', *Doctor Who: The Fan Show* BBC (5 January 2018).
24. Quoted by Matt Hills, *Triumph of a Time Lord* (London: I.B. Tauris, 2010), 213.
25. 'Steven Moffat on Writing, Weeping Angels and More'.
26. Ibid.
27. Which in itself can become a reason for fans to criticize him; see Hadas and Shifman's observation that Davies isn't meant to write as a fan.
28. E.g. the Second Doctor's (Patrick Troughton) various disguises and vagabond default, the Third Doctor (Jon Pertwee) cross-dressing as a cleaner (*The Green Death*), the Fourth (Tom Baker) styled after Lautrec, the Fifth (Peter Davison) as a cricketer, the Eighth (Paul McGann) as a cross between Wild Bill Hickock and Lord Byron, the Eleventh (Matt Smith) as a geography teacher. The Doctor is also happy to mimic his past lives in fannish ways ('Time Crash'), and can even take on the physical appearance of others (the Twelfth [Peter Capaldi] as Caecilius from 'The Fires of Pompeii').
29. Winnicott's theory has been usefully applied to the fans' relationship with the object of fandom by Hills, *Fan Cultures*. The fan object itself functions as a transitional object, occupying a liminal position between the fan's self and the outside world.

Chapter 40
The legacy of the fanzine Renaissance by Leslie McMurtry

Original to this volume

What is the past, present, and future of *Doctor Who* fanzines? Leslie McMurtry, editor, examines how important fanzines have been, are, and will continue to be in *Doctor Who's* ongoing life.

In front of you, you have yet another edition of **The Terrible Zodin** *for your delectation. […] Remind yourself as you read that no one who draws or writes for* **TTZ** *gets any monetary recompense. I love my magazine, and I love that people read it and contribute to it. If all goes well our next edition is our one-year anniversary, slated for 23 November.*
– **DOCTOR WHO**'S BIRTHDAY!

Thank you to Rich for letting us interview him and use so much of his gorgeous artwork. Thanks to Steven for his willingness to write, fabricate, and coax at the drop of a hat. Thank you to Lori for letting me take a photo of her and post it on Facebook.
Let the good times roll!
– EDITOR'S NOTE TO **TERRIBLE ZODIN** #4, AUTUMN 2009

The unofficial heyday of *Doctor Who* fanzines was in the 1980s to early 1990s, both in North America and the UK.[1] Then fanzines went quiet for several decades,[2] replaced by online message boards and early social media. Then, in 2008, the improbable occurred: a *Doctor Who* fanzine Renaissance, with dozens of new titles popping onto the scene, such as *Fish Fingers and Custard, Shooty Dog Thing, Blue Box, Panic Moon, Venusian Spearmint, Rassilon's Rod,*[3] and *The Terrible Zodin,* my fanzine. Fourteen years later, however, the future of *Doctor Who* fan discussion, I feel certain, will be in podcasts and social media – not fanzines. Fanzines are ephemera in the history of fandom. Was the fanzine Renaissance actually meaningful to *Doctor Who* fans? This chapter will attempt to answer this question through autoethnography and critical analysis.

Choosing autoethnography as a method for this chapter doubtlessly highlights other methodologies in which I could have engaged. Other qualitative methods such as interviews, focus groups and questionnaires, and quantitative methods, such as analysing the number of downloads of issues of *TTZ* across time and with regard to demographics, could be extremely useful in answering the question of whether the fanzine Renaissance was actually meaningful to *Doctor Who* fans. Selecting a sample of *TTZ* readers and writers and asking for their comments on how the fanzine affected their engagement with the programme and fandom could be incredibly illustrative. Nevertheless, such methods are far beyond the scope of this chapter (which is not to say they should not be attempted in other contexts!).

Autoethnography is used here to explore how, as a reader of fanzines and as editor of *TTZ*, my feelings, attitudes and beliefs about the fanzine Renaissance and *TTZ* specifically can provide a narrative about this cultural phenomenon. Autoethnography allows for 'ground-level, intimate, and close-up perspectives on experience'.[4] In this chapter, therefore, I can aspire to an insider perspective whilst also giving a more neutral overview of the history of the engagement of *Doctor Who* fans with fanzines and how this has changed over time.

The medium is the message

Rewind to the Noughties, when the Internet was 'cemented as the hub of fandom',[5] and the medium of choice for self-expression was the blog, distinguished from other websites by its 'dynamism, reverse chronological presentation and dominant use of the first person'.[6] Why did attention turn back to the fanzine format around 2008? Fanzines as a participatory medium – something people 'do' together[7] – have appeared on topics as varied as British football (soccer), science fiction and punk music. Fanzines differ from blogs in that they are interdisciplinary. While a focus is often on writing, fanzines also require 'elementary compositional skills',[8] therefore juxtaposing graphic design, images and photographs along with the written word. In terms of genre, fanzines could also be much more wide-ranging than the average blog post or indeed what is contained in a mainstream magazine table of contents. For example, physical, cut'n'paste *Doctor Who* fanzines of the 1980s and 1990s included poetry and fan fiction, and *TTZ* has included recipes, paper dolls, spoof family trees and downloadable board games. Running parallel to the spirit of collaboration was the 'do it yourself' ethic of fanzines, reflected in the genesis of *TTZ,* as I started the fanzine in response to my frustration with my article ideas being (politely) rejected by Paul Castle, editor of fanzine *Shooty Dog Thing*. In the fanzine Renaissance, a clear dichotomy was introduced between the print copy zines and the hybrid PDF/print-at-home zines, with the latter lasting far longer than the former. Often beautifully produced and wonderfully physical objects, ranging from the tiny *Panic Moon* to full-size *Rassilon's Rod,* the print zines could be handed around at events or sent through the post. Perhaps this added complication in paying for postage and printing, in addition to a curb on length, predicated their short but exciting tenure.

The fanzine Renaissance corresponds roughly with what is known as forensic fandom, when 'strategies of complexity' began to more regularly characterize TV.[9] The level of scrutiny of granular detail engendered by forensic fandom encourages 'research collaboration, analysis, and interpretation',[10] which is something fanzines can do well. They arguably can do these things better in the digital age given the speed and ease afforded by the Internet and other digital technologies. *TTZ* arose late in David Tennant's tenure and into Matt Smith's, coinciding with the (narratively complex) era of the programme showrun by Steven Moffat, epitomized by fan- and officially created timelines attempting to reconcile River Song's and the Doctor's timelines.[11] Fanzines of this period include sometimes lengthy analyses and reflections on New Who and Classic Who. In *TTZ* this is epitomized by our policy of reviewing newly aired stories and long-running series like 'Back2theWhoture', an attempt to watch *Doctor Who* not in story release order but in chronological order (i.e. from the Big Bang to the end of the universe). These were combined with an editorial policy of 'family'-friendly fanzine writing and respectful discussion. My attitude towards editorship was to include articles with which I personally might disagree as long as they were clearly and critically written with arguments supporting opinion.

In highlighting the opportunities available to the long-form written article, I do not claim that podcasts, for example, cannot engage in detailed, meticulous and lengthy (!) analyses and fan discussions (see Shetty's chapter 18). While definitively listing podcasts is always difficult, we can be certain, at the moment of writing, that there are more than 100 podcasts about *Doctor Who*[12] from around the world, with the vast majority engaging in fan dissection – in essence, chatcasts/chumcasts.* While longer form writing makes you think critically,[13] the way in which podcasts and fanzines are consumed generally differs. While there is some evidence that podcasts require close listening and active participation[14] – another form of 'forensic fandom' – there is also evidence that many people listen to podcasts as a secondary medium, while doing something else.[15] It would be difficult to multi-task in the same way while reading a fanzine.

Sexism and social media

Nevertheless, podcasts and fanzines are reasonably similar in that they offer long-form engagement, something that researchers say appeals to younger mobile audiences.[16] Podcasts and fanzines are the antitheses to what may be seen as the frenetic pace of social media discussion on Twitter, Instagram, Snapchat, TikTok, etc. While this feverish pace has its advantages, fast-paced Twitter conversations have been known to spread like wildfire and even dupe world leaders with 'fake news'.[17] 'Toxic fandom'[18] feeds on quick reactions and the prioritization of emotional rather than intellectual responses. As argued by Donaldson with regard to *Doctor Who* fandom, 'Social media websites like Twitter feed on division, they make large amounts of money by dividing groups of people into opposing forces, entrenching them in these sorts of never-ending binary arguments'.[19] This may be a result of the so-called cultishness of fandom, which suggests that fans feel they possess 'sophistication, perseverance and cultural competence' above that of casual viewers,[20] thus they 'own' *Doctor Who* and their personal opinions are irrefutably valid.

I cannot speak for other fanzine editors, but this was not the space in which *TTZ* wished to engage with fans. Our policy was to encourage discussion, fellowship, celebration and acceptance, doing our best to refute fan hierarchies. Hadas argues that 'post-television *Doctor Who* was a quintessential cult',[21] with clear in-groups and everyone else defined as 'Johnny-come-latelies'. We attempted in *TTZ* to reject this attitude, reflected, I believe, in the makeup of our contributors, some of whom had been watching *Doctor Who* since 1963 and demographically represented the stereotypical image of pre-2005 fandom (white, male, British, middle-class), whereas others were relative newcomers, having accessed the series through the 'gateway' of New Who, many of whom were young, female and non-British.

During the fanzine Renaissance, to my knowledge, I was the only female editor of a long-running title.†
I did not know in 2008 when I started *TTZ* that I was part of an ongoing saga of female-led *Doctor Who*

---

* At their most basic, chatcasts/chumcasts can be two people talking in front of a microphone in someone's house. They are characterized by their 'chatty, familiar, personal, fluid, intimate' (M. Spinelli and L. Dann, *Podcasting: The Audio Media Revolution* (London: Bloomsbury Academic, 2019), 9) quality and account for the vast majority of available podcasts.
† Editor Lea of *Venusian Spearmint* distributed this zine at the Fitzroy Tavern between approximately 2011 and 2013.

Table 40.1 *Gender Representation in Televised* Doctor Who *Creatives Between 1963 and 2021*

	1963–2008 (45 years)	2009–2021 (12 years)
Women-directed TV stories	15	16
Women directors	8	7
Percentage of women-directed TV stories out of all TV stories	8%	17%
Women-authored or partially authored TV stories	7	10
Women scriptwriters of the TV series	6	9
Percentage of women-authored or partially authored TV stories out of all TV stories	6%	10%
Percentage of women scriptwriters TV series out of all TV story scriptwriters	5%	9%

fanzines. Female fans of *Doctor Who* have existed as long as the series has been broadcast, yet the series has a legacy of in-programme sexism that was either ignored or is maybe 'too obvious to state'.[22] Despite the perception in the 1980s and 1990s that women fans were 'an unusual phenomenon'[23] in British fandom at least, female *Who* fan identities were manifest in fanzines. Sometimes, their gender was unimportant to their self-conception as fans, seeing them adopt a homogenized 'Who-speak'[24] like Jackie Jenkins, the pseudonymous female *Who* writer commissioned by Gary Gillatt in *Doctor Who Magazine* from 1997. Sometimes, female-led fanzines manifested gender politically or in a more overtly feminized way.

I arose out of the North American *Doctor Who* experience, which differed in many salient ways from the British one, and although I was too young to be involved in the more gender-mixed fandom of the 1980s and 1990s, *TTZ* mirrored the genre-hopping freewheeling of North American female-edited titles such as *Bafflegab, Jelly Baby Chronicles, Time Log* and *Rassilon's Star*. At times, New Who could present 'a sustained critique of traditional gender dynamics and structures'[25] problematized by the post-2005 'schism' between 'anoraks' and 'rabid' female shippers.[26] I saw *TTZ* as a space to explore the continuum between these attitudes, rather than cementing their status as mutually exclusive.

The ethos of *TTZ* was a forum for all fans but particularly female ones, predicated partly on the fact that I noticed, from a very young age, that women were underrepresented in major creative roles (writers, directors) in the series.[27] In terms of gender representation,‡ we have seen a (modest) shift during the lifetime of *TTZ*. Stories directed by women have doubled.

This has culminated, of course, in the accession of Jodie Whittaker to the role of Thirteenth Doctor. Jowett pointed out in 2014 that it would be essentialist to argue that men cannot write feminist texts, though she also suggested that one reason for the dearth of women writers and directors in the new series was 'because its production is dominated by (male) fan-producers'.[28] Sadly, after all the post-2008 advances, there is still much work to do in terms of representation of women directors and writers – it is hardly impressive that only 17 per cent of the stories made between 2009 and 2021 were directed by

---

‡ Ethnic and racial representation as well as decolonization of the narrative in *Doctor Who* is an equally important subject, one which the series has been shamefully slow to address, and which *TTZ* equally has failed to address until recently.

women or that only 9 per cent of the writers on *Doctor Who* between 2009 and 2021 were women. And of course, we have yet to have a female *Doctor Who* showrunner. More worryingly, *Doctor Who* fandom's relationship to gender is *still* fraught. Matthew Jasper rather understated it by noting the 'exceptionally vitriolic outrage from a loud sect of the fandom, the motivation of which primarily seems to be rooted in their belief that a woman should never play the Doctor'.[29]

Conclusion

Did the fanzine Renaissance make a difference? It made a difference to me. The act of making my own fanzine brought me into a welcoming social scene so that I could work on something with others interested in the same thing. *TTZ* launched writing careers. I never received any financial recompense for *TTZ* (rather the opposite), which is in keeping with its status as a not-for-profit fan text. Despite this, each issue involved an incredible amount of effort from not only me but the contributors. With the speed and complexity of modern life intensifying, and faced by an increasingly monetized creative media landscape,[30] *TTZ* is itself winding down. Podcasts will, for now, inherit the long-form forensic fandom and erudite analysis that characterized the fanzine Renaissance. If there is any wider legacy, then perhaps it is this migration to podcasts where multiplicity of viewpoints and sophisticated discussion are still possible.

Notes

1. P. Cornell, *Licence Denied!: Rumblings from the Doctor Who Underground* (London: Virgin Books, 1997).
2. B.J. Robb, *Timeless Adventures: How Doctor Who Conquered TV* (Harpenden, Herts: Kamera Books, 2008).
3. L. McMurtry, 'Do It Yourself: Women, Fanzines, and Doctor Who', in *Fan Phenomena: Doctor Who*, ed. P. Booth (Bristol: Intellect, 2013), 84–95.
4. T.E. Adams, S.H. Jones and E. Ellis, *Autoethnography* (Oxford: Oxford University Press, 2015), 2.
5. R. Barnard, *Panic Moon* #1 (2010).
6. M. Tremayne, *Blogging, Citizenship, and the Future of Media* (London: Routledge, 2007), vii.
7. D. Gee, *Fish Fingers and Custard* #1 (2010), 3.
8. M.C. Kearney, *Girls Make Media* (London: Taylor & Francis, 2006), 33.
9. J. Mittell, 'Narrative Complexity in Contemporary American Television', *Velvet Light Trap* 58 (2006): 29–40.
10. J. Mittell, *Complex TV: The Poetics of Contemporary Television Storytelling* (New York: New York University Press, 2015), 277.
11. Ibid., 2015.
12. Best 90 *Doctor Who* podcasts (TV Series), *FeedSpot*, (29 January 2022): https://blog.feedspot.com/doctor_who_podcasts/
13. K. Looijesteijn, 'Replace Social Media with Blogs and RSS?' (25 August 2018): https://www.kooslooijesteijn.net/blog/replace-social-media-with-blogs-and-RSS
14. K.S. Boling and K. Hull, 'Undisclosed Information – Serial Is My Favorite Murder: Examining Motivations in the True Crime Podcast Audience', *Journal of Radio & Audio Media* 25, no. 1 (2018): 92–108, DOI: 10.1080/19376529.2017.1370714, 94
15. L.G. Perks, J.S. Turner and A.C. Tollison, 'Podcast Uses and Gratifications Scale Development', *Journal of Broadcasting & Electronic Media* 63, no. 4 (2019): 617–34, DOI: 10.1080/08838151.2019.1688817

16 J. Marino, S. Jacobson and J. R. Gutsche, 'Scrolling for Story: How Millennials Interact with Longform Journalism on Mobile Devices', Donald W. Reynolds Journalism Institute (1 August 2016): https://www.robertgutschejr.com/wp-content/uploads/2019/09/RJIWhitepaper72216.pdf

17 J.H. Lipschultz, *Social Media Communication: Concepts, Practices, Data, Law and Ethics* (New York: Routledge, 2017), 315.

18 M. Baggs, 'Toxic Fandom: Online Bullying in the Name of Your Favourite Stars', *BBC Newsbeat* (1 August 2018): https://www.bbc.co.uk/news/newsbeat-44950274

19 M. Donaldson, 'If We Fight Like Animals, We Die Like Animals: Doctor Who Fandom, Talons, the DWM Time Team and Social Media', *Doctor Who Big Blue Box Podcast* (22 August 2018): https://www.bigblueboxpodcast.co.uk/if-we-fight-like-animals-we-die-like-animals-doctor-who-fandom-talons-the-dwm-time-team-and-social-media/

20 L. Hadas, 'Resisting the Romance: "Shipping" and the Discourse of Genre Uniqueness in Doctor Who Fandom', *European Journal of Cultural Studies* 16, no. 3 (2013): 329–43, 330.

21 Hadas, 'Resisting the Romance', 333.

22 L. Jowett, 'The Girls Who Waited? Female Companions and Gender', *Doctor Who. Critical Studies in Television* 9, no. 1 (2014): 77–94, 86.

23 K. Dunn, 'When Geeks Collide!', *The Terrible Zodin* #5, (2009): 35–6.

24 B. Cherry, 'Squee, Retcon, Fanwank, and the Not-We: Computer-Mediated Discourse and the Online Audience for NuWho', in *Ruminations, Peregrinations, and Regenerations: A Critical Approach to Doctor Who*, ed. C.J. Hansen (Newcastle: Cambridge Scholars Publishing, 2010), 209–34.

25 Jowett, 'The Girls Who Waited? Female Companions and Gender', 80.

26 Hadas, 'Resisting the Romance', 335, 336.

27 Jowett, 'The Girls Who Waited? Female Companions and Gender', 87.

28 Ibid., 88.

29 M. Jasper, 'Jodie Whittaker's Doctor Who Will Be Appreciated Over Time, Says Producer', *Screen Rant* (5 February 2022): https://screenrant.com/doctor-who-jodie-whittaker-critics-chris-chibnall-praise/

30 J.L. Sullivan, 'Podcast Movement: Aspirational Labour and the Formalisation of Podcasting as a Cultural Identity', in *Podcasting: New Aural Cultures and Digital Media*, ed. D. Llinares, N. Fox and R. Berry (Hampshire: Palgrave Macmillan, 2018), 35–56, 35.

Index

Aaronovitch, Ben 43, 229, 236
Abidin, Crystal 132 n.16
Abslom Daak 229–30
Ace (fictional character) 39, 236–7, 242, 245
Adams, Douglas 77, 215, 217–18, 247
    Doctor Who and the Krikkitmen 45
    Life, The Universe and Everything 218
Adamson, Lorna 58
Affron, Charles 32
    modestly denotative 33
    Sets in Motion: Art Direction and Film Narrative 32
    taxonomic model 33
Affron, Mirella Jona, *Sets in Motion: Art Direction and Film Narrative* 32
Aggedor 5 222
Agyeman, Freema 197
Akerman, Rafaela 184
Aldred, Sophie 45, 243, 245
All Flesh is Grass 66
All My Friends Are Dead 152
Alvarado, Manuel, *Doctor Who: The Unfolding Text* 3, 26, 87
Amaral, Adriana 126
American race-related activism 135
Amy Pond (fictional character) 135, 197–200, 250, 257
Androgum variant 52 n.10
Angel 243
Anghelides, Peter, *Frontier Worlds* 222
Apalapucia (planet) 198, 200
Apex Magazine 244
archontic principle 87, 89–90, 92
Arc of Infinity 50
Ark in Space, The 212–13, 241–2
Ark, The 209–12
Armageddon Factor, The 78
Army of Ghosts 14
Asian Television Limited World Channel 191
Atkinson, Sarah 55
Attack The Block 130

audiences and fans 1, 4–5, 68, 71–3, 79, 89, 101, 141, 145, 228, 235, 243. *See also* fan(s)/fandom
Australasian *Doctor Who* Fan Club (ADWFC) 76, 235
Autoethnography 267–8
Auxílio, Thaís 182, 185
Ayres, Mark 228, 232 n.5

Baddeley, Pam 222
Baker, Colin 37
Baker, Tom 45, 78–9, 218, 221, 247
Barbara (fictional character) 9, 229, 232 n.11
Barker, Cory 145
Barkin, Lena 149
Barrowman, John 103, 105
Battlefield 39, 41, 242
Baxter, Stephen 45
BBC 5, 11, 13, 20, 39–40, 56, 61, 79, 100, 125, 143, 165, 170, 188, 220, 228, 258
    Books 40, 44, 230
    brand management 26, 51
    Editorial Policy 14
    new media division 14
    Radiophonic Workshop 232 n.5
    Studios 51, 63, 67, 185
    Visual Effects 24
    Wales 25–7
    Worldwide 181–2, 191
    Written Archive at Caversham 231
Bear, Elizabeth 243–4
Beatles, The 217
Bel (fictional character) 142, 145
Benford, Steve 64, 66
Bentham, Jeremy 76, 78
Best Stories, The 242
Beth Latimer (fictional character) 130
Bhabha, Homi, theory of mimicry 210–12
Big Finish Audios 4, 6, 9, 12–14, 37–8, 40, 44, 51, 63, 164, 176, 232 n.10, 265 n.22
Bill Potts (fictional character) 127, 160, 164, 169, 204, 257

BIPOC companions 163, 203
Black Entertainment Television 165
Black fans 159–62
Black Lives Matter 160
Blackman, Malorie 134, 166
Black Nerds Create 205
Black Orchid 242
Blue Lives Matter 160
Blum, Jon 239
Blythe, Daniel 238
Bodle, Andy 25
Boleyn, Anne 167 n.10
Boleyn, Claudia, The Uncomfortable Truth about Fandom Sexism 249–54
Booth, Paul 71, 120, 126, 130, 133, 219–20, 222–3
  Periodising Doctor Who 87–92
Booy, Miles, *Love and Monsters: The Doctor Who Experience, 1979 to the Present* 39–40, 263–4
Borad (alien creature) 47
Bottomley, Nathan 236
Bradford, K. Tempest 243
brand fans 118, 123 n.4
branding (transmedia storytelling) 67
Brazilian Whovians 181
  during fiftieth anniversary 182
  flux strategy 184–8
Brennan, Joseph 172–3
Brigadier Lethbridge-Stewart (fictional character) 256
Briggs, Ian 245
British cultural identity 103, 212
Britton, Piers 90
  Design for Doctor Who: Vision and Revision in Science Fiction Television 32–4
  TARDISBound: Navigating the Universes of Doctor Who 29–31
Broadchurch 128, 130, 144
Brough, Melissa M. 126
Bryant, Nicola 243
BTM 192
Buffini, Nuala 43
Buffy the Vampire Slayer 102
Burns, CJ, Paradox Schmaradox 199
Bury, Rhiannon 126
Butler, David 88

Candy, Arthur 45
canonicity 9, 11–12, 14, 39, 48–51, 91, 138–9, 256–7
Capaldi, Peter 2, 32, 176, 182, 185, 188, 215, 219–20, 222–3, 228, 233 n.22
  Dalek-Builders 225–6
Captain Jack Harkness (fictional character) 127, 169, 171, 256
Carey, Jim 167 n.10

Carroll, David 237
Cartmel, Andrew 26, 39, 43, 229, 259
Cartmel Masterplan, The 39, 43, 259, 260 n.17
Castle, Paul 268
casual and non-fans (*Flux*) 142, 146
  complexity 144
  fear over casuals' confusion 142–3
  jigsaw puzzle 145
  method 143
  Once, Upon Time 143–4
  on Twitter 145
casual audiences 4, 72, 141, 146 n.13
Chapman, Graham 218
Chapman, James 49
  Inside the TARDIS 6 n.2
Charles, Alec 91
Charlotte Pollard (fictional character) 37, 51
Chelonians, The 45
Cherry, Brigid 142–3
Chess, Johnny 232 n.11
Chibnall, Chris 34, 115, 130, 143–4, 164–6, 170, 179, 204, 206, 228, 253, 257–9, 261, 263
Chicks Dig Comics 244
Chicks Unravel Time 244
Chicks: Whedonistas 244
Chinese fandom 191–3
Chinese Whovians 191, 193
chronological analysis 30
City of Death, The 26–7, 78, 195 n.16, 218, 242
civil rights movement, American 135, 160–1
Clara (fictional character) 160, 257, 265
Class 44
Clive Finch (fictional character) 263
Coduri, Camille 264
Cole, Steve 43–4
Cole, Tosin 161
Collins, Misha 150
Collins, Stephen 78–9
colonialism 209, 211–12
Con Man 126
consumers, fans as 117–18, 176, 227
  describing and categorizing 118
  fan behaviour 119
  fan psychographics 119–20
  initial typology of 121
  social media and formation of consumer tribes 120–1
  theoretical typology of 117, 122
  values and lifestyles (VALS) 121
consumer tribes 117, 120–1
convivial evaluation 120, 123 n.9
Cook, Benjamin 251
Cook, John R., *Adapting Telefantasy: The Doctor Who and the Daleks Films* 35–6

Cook, Terry 59
coping strategy 81–2
Corman, Roger 32
Cornell, Paul 9, 41–3, 219, 220, 227, 230–1, 232 n.11, 233 n.22, 243–4
   Canonicity in Doctor Who 11–12
   Discontinuity Guide, The 230
   Guinness Book of Classic British TV, The 231
   Human Nature 45, 220
   License Denied 238
   Timewyrm: Revelation 42, 230, 238
Courtney, Nicholas 228
Covid-19 55–6, 141, 205, 258
Coyle, Kelly 89
Creative Industry Network 165
Creature from the Pit, The 3, 76
critical fandom 147
Cruise, Tom 167 n.10
cult audiences 83
cult text 30–1, 89
Curse of Fatal Death, The 233 n.22
Curse of Fenric, The 39, 41, 236
Curse of Peladon, The 96–7
Curtis, Richard 266 n.1
Cushing, Peter 176

Daily Mail 252
Daily Telegraph, The 220
A Dalek Awakens (TLV) 66
Dalek Book, The 232 n.19
Dalekmania 48, 52 n.3
Daleks' Master Plan, The 91, 218
Dan (fictional character) 142, 165, 170, 251
Danny Pink (fictional character) 160
dark dimension of academia 73
Darlington, David J. 222
Darvill-Evans, Peter 42
Data Extract 236–7
Datlow, Ellen 245
Davies, Russell T 4, 6, 7 n.5, 11, 14, 24–6, 33–4, 45, 71, 81–5, 90–1, 163, 165–6, 207, 220, 228, 230, 232 n.12, 232 n.17, 251, 255–65, 265 n.23
   Writer's Tale, The 3, 90–1
Davison, Peter 242
Davros (fictional character) 47, 61, 83
Day, Martin 230–1
   Discontinuity Guide, The 230
   Guinness Book of Classic British TV, The 231
Day of the Doctor, The 181–2, 222, 264–5
Deadline 38
Deadly Assassin, The 31
Death in Heaven 265, 265 n.22

De Beauvoir, Simone 114
Decalogs 44–5
decolonization 211, 213
de Kauwe, Vanessa, Through Coloured Eyes: An Alternative Viewing of Postcolonial Transition 209–13
Delgado, Roger 225
demographics (segmentation) 118, 175
Demons of the Punjab 134–5, 137
Derbyshire, Delia 232 n.5
Derecho, Abigail, archontic literature 89
Derrida, Jacques 71, 89–91
   archontic (archival textuality) 87
desirability (*Doctor Who*)
   geek chic and masculinity 101–3
   policing genre 103–6
Destiny of the Daleks 76–7
Dhawan, Sacha 242
Dickson, Christa, *Dusted* 243
Dicks, Terrance 41, 49, 217, 229–30, 232 n.14
   The Making of Doctor Who (second edition) 23–4, 229–30
digital fandom 221
Digital Methods Initiative 127
Dimensions in Time 9, 91
Dingsdale, Daniel 56–60
Dirk Gently's Holistic Detective Agency 218
discontinuity and continuity 91–2
diversification 29, 134, 137, 139, 203
Doctor Falls, The 164
Doctor: Time Lord Victorious (TLV), costs 63–4
   cognitive costs 64, 66–8
   contextual costs 64
   cost-engagement equation 67, 68
   A Dalek Awakens 66
   Dark Times, The 67
   Fractured Universe, The 67
   list of elements 65–6
   logo 67
   managing 67–8
   mapping 64, 66–7
   Release Timeline 67–8
   Story Order 67–8
   Victorious Days, The 67
Doctor Who (comic) 9, 18, 41, 228
Doctor Who (TV series) 1–2, 5, 9, 30–1, 41–2, 51, 60, 66, 76, 82, 87, 89, 131, 134–5, 138, 147, 156, 167 n.11, 170, 175, 191, 197, 203, 215–16, 223, 227, 255, 263. *See also specific Doctor Who Episodes*
   criticism 3, 215
   eras 87–8
   extravagance 78

fiftieth anniversary 181–2, 215
Forum 71
golden age of 49
legacy of 41–5
sense of canon 4, 110–11
Sixtieth Anniversary 6
structuralist-to-poststructuralist time 3–4
website 13, 64
Doctor Who and Philosophy 213
Doctor Who and the Daleks 35–6, 228
Doctor Who Annual 2020 68
Doctor Who Appreciation Society (DWAS), *The* 1–2, 77, 120–1
Doctor Who at the Proms 119
Doctor Who Brasil 182–3, 185, 189 n.3
Doctor Who Chinese Community 192
Doctor Who Escape Rooms 119
Doctor Who Experience 119
Doctor Who Figurine Collection (*DWFC*) 47–51
   Character Options 48–9
   classic history 49–50
   commerce, canonicity and transmedia historiography 48–51
   cross-media remembering 48
   cultural memory management 50–1
   immobility 48
Doctor Who: Flux 72, 141, 146 n.13, 165, 258
   casual and non-fans (*see* casual and non-fans (*Flux*))
   serialization 141, 145
Doctor Who in an Exciting Adventure with the Daleks 228, 232 n.10
Doctor Who Magazine (DWM) 3, 6, 13–14, 25, 42, 68, 220, 228–30, 251–2, 258, 261–3
   Doctor Who Monthly 4
   Time Team 251–2, 254
Doctor Who: Podshock 243
Doctor Who Reader, The 1
Doctor Who: The Complete History series 6 n.2, 266 n.8
Doctor Who: The Fan Show 265 n.23
Doctor Who: The Legends of River Song 195 n.16
Doctor Who – The Revenants 232 n.10
Doctor Who: The Story of Martha 44, 195 n.16
Doctor Who: Time Fracture (DWTF) 55, 63, 66, 119
   immersive experience design 61
   principles 59–61
   process 58–9
   sandbox phase of 57
   transmedia techniques 56–8
   UNIT Command 58
Doctor Who TV Movie 230
Doctor Who Weekly. *See Doctor Who Magazine* (DWM)

Doctor Who: Who-Ology 195 n.16
Doktor Who Polska 179
Dollard, Sarah 178
Donna Noble (fictional character) 170–1
Doomsday 14
Douban.com 191
Downton Abbey 191
Dragonfire 26, 50
Driscoll, Paul 216, 261
Dr Who Special 225
Dunn, Karen 221
Dyer, Richard 18

EachPeachPearPlum 198
Eaglemoss, Ltd. 47, 50–1. *See also Doctor Who* Figurine Collection (*DWFC*)
Earthshock 152, 242
Eccleston, Christopher 6, 91, 176, 255
Echoes of Extinction 66
Edge of Time 64
Eight Light Minutes Culture (ELMC) 193, 195 n.16
Elam, Keir 26
Ellis, John 18
Ellis, Sigrid 244
Elton Pope (fictional character) 263–4
Empty Child, The 105
endlessly deferred narrative 29–31, 262, 265
End of the World, The 164
Evans, Elizabeth 63
Dr Evelyn Smythe (fictional character) 37, 51
Eve of the Daleks 165
Expanded Universe 176

Faction Paradox 149
Falls the Shadow 237
fanbrand 27
fan(s)/fandom 1–2, 5, 14, 25, 38, 48, 72, 75, 82, 84–5, 99, 117, 125, 147, 164, 170, 204, 206–7, 215–16, 223, 231, 238, 269. *See also* Black fans; Whovians and Whovian groups
   academics and 2, 4
   blogosphere 5
   canons 49–51
   Chicks Dig Time Lords 243–4
   cohesive fictional world 27
   collaboration and prohibition 26
   as consumers (*see* consumers, fans as)
   creative fan practices 170
   criticism 33–4
   culture 25, 27, 103, 227
   fanboy auteur 256, 259, 261, 265, 266 n.3
   fan writing 1–3, 42
   gender in 270

hierarchies 269
hybridized para-academic writing 4–5
inclusion of continuity 84
intratextual analysis 88
male fans' domination 111
marrying in 241–2
new generation of 5, 110, 147, 221
and non-fans 82
poaches 215, 227
as powerless elite (*see* powerless elite (fans))
and professional 5–6, 33, 215, 227, 238
to public professional 244–6
as queer companion 165
society 75, 79
as subcultures of consumption 118
textual exegesis and 77–9
in twenty-first-century 261–5
US vs UK 270
wilderness years 242–3, 265 n.23
fanfiction 171, 178, 197, 200, 232 n.11
fangirl 85, 101–6
Fanon, Frantz 209, 211–12, 213 n.1, 214 n.15
Black Skin, White Masks 213 n.1, 214 n.15
inferiority 210, 212
Fan Phenomena: Doctor Who 220
fansubbing (China) 192–3
Fansub Group 192
Fantastic Four 111
fanwank 25, 82
re-invented 84–5
fanzines 2, 76, 219–22, 229, 231, 267–71
heyday 267
Farren, Rebecca 205
Feeney, Nolan 215
How Fanzines Helped Put Doctor Who Fans in Charge of Doctor Who 219–23
feminism 72, 109, 111, 114, 147
feminist female fans 109
backlash and 110–12
expectations of 13th Doctor 113–15
findings 110
gender and 114
traditional 114
Fenech, Pat 76
Fengyun Drama Channel 194 n.6
Finney, Yasmin 207
Fish Fingers and Custard 221
Fiske, John 2–3, 48, 98–9
'Dr Who: Ideology and the Reading of a Popular Narrative Text' 19–21
structuralist 71, 98
Five Doctors, The 40, 232 n.13
Flat Earth Society 262

Flyine subtitling group 192–3
forensic fandom 145, 146 n.13
Fosters, The 160
Foucault, Michel 87–8
4-D War 230
Frame of Mind 236
Franks, Talia 203
Frobisher the Penguin (fictional character) 40
FRTVS/1000FR 192
Futurama 152–3, 156

Gagnon, Dominique 4, 72, 141
Gallifrey (fictional planet) 31, 44, 56, 90
Gallifrey Base 221, 264
Gallifrey Chronicles, The 14, 44
Gallifrey, Obywatele 179
Gammon, Dan 60
Gardner, Julie 264
Gatiss, Mark 15 n.2, 43, 230
Gatwa, Ncuti 6, 165, 207
gay agenda 253
Gee, Daniel 221
Genesis of the Daleks 242
geography (segmentation) 118, 175
Ghost Light 39, 212
Giannachi, Gabriella 64, 66
Gibbs, Constance, Doctor Who's TARDIS Has a Different Meaning for Black Fans 159–62
Gillatt, Gary 269
Girl Who Waited, The 197–8
character growth 198–9
recoding resistance 199–200
Glamour in Glass 247
Godfrey, Pat 50
Gold, Murray 232 n.5
Gomes, Alice de Freitas 72, 125
Good Man Goes to War, A 238
Goss, James 13–14, 61 n.3, 67, 218
Goth Opera 237
Graham O'Brien (fictional character) 136, 164–5
Grant, Richard E. 91
Grimes, Darren 167 n.11
Grodin, Debra 89
Guardian, The 219
Guerrier, Simon, *The Time Travellers* 232 n.11
Guo, Ting 191

Hadas, Leora 71, 269
Keeping the Elite Powerless: Fan-Producer Relations in the "Nu Who" (and New YOU) Era 81–5, 266 n.5
Hall, Stuart 197
Han Solo (fictional character) 111

Harrigan, Pat 2
   Third Person: Authoring and Exploring Vast Narratives 30–1
Hartnell, William 218
Hearn, Marcus 252
Heartstopper (TV series) 3
Hendry, Natalie Ann 132 n.16
Henken, Julia 216, 255
Hickman, Clayton 13, 25
Hills, Matt 1, 29–30, 83–4, 87–8, 102, 134, 220–2, 256, 262, 265 n.29
   Fan Cultures 30, 265 n.29
   powerless duality 84
   Televisuality Without Television?: The Big Finish Audios and Discourses of "Tele-centric" Doctor Who 36–8
   Triumph of a Time Lord: Regenerating Doctor Who in the Twenty-First Century 24–7
Hinchcliffe, Philip 49, 76
Hitchhiker's Guide to the Galaxy, The 217–18, 247
Hobbit 32
Hogan, Michael 197
Hollows, Joanne 114
Holmes, Robert 49, 97, 217
Holmes, Tim 47
Hook, Brian 55, 60–1
Horns of Nimon, The 76
Howe, Tony 79
Hulke, Malcolm 229
   Doctor Who and the Doomsday Weapon 40
   Making of Doctor Who (first edition), *The* 23–4
Human Nature/The Family of Blood 45
Hummer 235–7
Hungry Earth/Cold Blood, The 47
Hunt, Nathan 83
Hussein, Waris 252
hyperdiegesis 29–31

Ian (fictional character) 9, 229, 232 n.11
I.B. Tauris 4
IGN 220
Impossible Planet/The Satan Pit, The 263
inclusion principle (DWTF) 50, 56, 59–61
Infinite Loop: Time Travel and Archives in the Popular Imagination, The 245
Inspector Spacetime 215
institutional racism 165
Intellectual Property (IP) 48, 56, 256
Interregnum 13, 15 n.2
intersectionality, feminist theory of 133, 139
intersections and crossovers 2, 5, 215, 245
inter-textuality 18–19

interview textual analysis 95–6
Invasion of Time 76

Jackson, Peter 32
Jameson, Louise 243
Jancovich, Mark 83
Jasper, Matthew 270
Jelly Baby Chronicles 222
Jenkins, Henry 15, 26, 50, 84, 111, 126, 127, 173, 175, 199–200, 228
   alternative social community 177
   convergence culture 12–13
   heterosexual female K/S 173
   recontextualization 199
   Science Fiction Audiences: Watching Doctor Who and Star Trek 4, 71, 75–9, 87, 175
   Textual Poachers 126, 172, 227
Jenny Flint (fictional character) 127
Jo Grant (fictional character) 256
John and Gillian (fictional characters) 9
John, Caroline 6
Johnny Storm (superhero) 111
Jones, Bethan 197
Jones, Craig Owen 120
Jones, Jane Clare 197
Jones, Matt 219, 230
Jordan, Michael B. 111
Journey's End 47
Jowett, Lorna 270

Kate Lethbridge-Stewart (fictional character) 57, 229, 256
Keidl, Phillip Dominik 50
Kelly, Peter 126, 130
Kennedy, Helen 55
Key to Time, The 78, 218
Kotturuh (ancient species) 63, 68
Kowal, Mary Robinette 215, 243
   Where to Find the Doctor in All of My Historical Fantasy Novels 247–8
Kozinets, Robert 120
Ksiądz Kto (Priest Who) 178

Lambert, Verity 24, 252
Last of the Time Lords 44, 164
Latin American fans 181
Lawson, Alison 72, 117
Lawson, David 72, 117
Leamington Spa Lifeboat Museum Website 13
Lee, Bruce 111
Lee, Jonathan Rey 48
Left-Handed Hummingbird, The 235
Legend of the Sea Devils 165, 204, 206

Letts, Barry 49
Levene, Rebecca 42
Levine, Ian 75–7, 79, 228
Liminaut (DWTF) 57, 62 n.4
Lindlof, Thomas R. 89
Line of Duty 144
line-of-succession model 30
Live Action Role Playing (LARPing) 62 n.4
LiveJournal fans 71
Lofficier, Jean-Marc, *Doctor Who Programme Guide, The* 229
Logopolis 77
Lorna Bucket (fictional character) 266
Lost Dimension, The 265 n.22
Lydiard, Simon 222
Lyons, Steve 232 n.15, 238

MacDonald, Andrea 103
Madame Vastra (fictional character) 127
Mad Norwegian Press 243–4
mainstream media 134, 170, 194 n.7
    and culture 137
    and society 139
Malcolm Taylor (fictional character) 263–5
Maltese Falcon, The 26
Manning, Katy 242–3
Marginally Fannish (*MF*), fan podcast 72, 133–4
    co-creating intersectional knowledge 134–7
    collective intelligence 134
    restorying imaginations with fan counternarratives 137–8
Marshall, Jackie 222
Marsters, James 102
MARTHADONNA process 170–2
Martha Jones (fictional character) 160, 163–4, 166, 166 n.5, 170–1, 204
Martin, Dominic G. 206
Martin, Jo 204, 242
Marvel Comics 3
Masque of Mandragora, The 32
Masque of the Red Death, The 32
McGann, Paul 37–8, 176, 244
McGuire, Seanan 244
McIntee, David 232 n.11
McKee, Alan 71
    Is Doctor Who Political? 95–100
McMurtry, Leslie 220–2
McRae, Tom 197
Meadows, Foz 197
men-loving-men (MLM) representations 173
Merry, Sarah Kate 121
Mestor (fictional character) 50–1

Michael (fan) 241–5
Mickey Smith (fictional character) 160, 163–4
Mickey's website 14
Middleton, Kate 199
Miles, Lawrence 44
Miller, Lindsay 197
Millingdale Organic Ice Cream website 13
Mind Robber, The 242
Missing Adventures (MAs) 31, 43
Mission to the Unknown 91
Mittell, Jason, *Complex TV* 143, 146 n.13
Model Unit, The 232 n.5
Moffat, Steven 23, 34, 45, 130, 164, 197, 200, 215, 219, 222, 228, 230, 233 n.22, 238, 250–9, 261, 263, 265, 265 n.23, 268
    rec.arts.drwho post 225
Monoids 50, 209–11, 213
Monteiro, Camila 126
Moorcock, Michael 45
Moore, Alan 230
Moran, James 178
Morris, Jonathan 267 n.22
Mortimore, Jim
    Blood Heat 232 n.15
    Campaign 40
Most Toys, The 236
Mulgrew, Kate 100
Mulkern, Patrick 197
multi-discursive approach 87
multi-generational audience 5
music and sound effects 24
Mutants, The 35

Name of the Doctor, The 257
Nardole (fictional character) 164, 257
Nathan-Turner, John 11, 42, 76, 79
Natural History of Fear 38
Nayar, Pramod K. 210, 213 n.1
New Adventures (NAs) 11, 13, 31, 42–5, 229, 233 n.22, 235–8
    canonicity 11–12
    ethos of 45
Newman, Kim, *Time and Relative* 40
Newman, Sydney 35–6
New Star Press 195 n.16
Nice, Liz 47
Nichols, Nichelle 160
Nightmare of Eden, The 76
Night of The Doctor, The 110
novelizations 9, 11–12, 13, 40–2, 44–5, 176, 195 n.16, 219–20, 228–30, 232 n.17
Nye, Jody Lynn 243

Nyela, Océane I. 169
Nyota Uhura (fictional character) 160

Obverse Books 4
Omega (fictional character) 31, 47
Once, Upon Time 72, 141–5
Oncoming Storm, The 230
online fandom 81, 83, 101, 173, 205, 221
On the Waterfront 255
Open Air 261
Original Character Do Not Steal 257
Orman, Kate 43, 239
    David J Richardson interviews 235–7
Orthia, Lindy 213
O'Shea, Tara, *Chicks Dig Time Lords: A Celebration of Doctor Who by the Women Who Love It* 243–4, 246
Outlander 215

Paisley Pattern 222
Pan Books 229
Pandorica Opens, The 45
Panini UK 6 n.2
Panopticon convention 249–50, 254
Parkin, Lance 26, 90, 238
Past Doctor Adventures 43–4
Patel, Vinay 166
Pearson, Lars, *Dusted* 243
Peel, John 236
peer-to-peer file sharing 192
Penny, Laurie 114, 206, 208 n.9
periodization 5, 71–2, 87–9
    archives, palimpsests and 89–92
    corpus 87–8
    as discourse 88–9
Perryman, Neil, Doctor Who and the Convergence of Media: A Case Study in "Transmedia Storytelling" 12–15
Pertwee, Jon 18
Petronella Osgood (fictional character) 263, 265, 265 n.22
Phantom of the Opera 242
Piedmont, Joy 250, 254
Pilot, The 164
Piper, Billie 197
Pirate Planet, The 217–18, 236
Pixley, Andrew 6 n.2
Planet of the Dead 264
Planet of the Spiders 78
Planet Zog 85
Platt, Marc 43, 229
Pless, Deborah 213

police box 20, 159–61
Polish fandom 175
    cultural determinants 179
    disappointments 179
    language 177–8
    minorities and dreamers 177
    Whovian 175–6, 180 n.7
    Whovians offline (rarely) 178
    Whovians online (usually) 178–9
politics of *Doctor Who* 71, 95. *See also* social politics
    Amnesty International 97
    cultural 96, 98
    extreme right 96
    identity and 5, 147
    ideology 99–100
    interpretations of the programme 97, 99
Pompadour, Madame De 13–14
popularity and ideological problem 19–21, 49, 176, 178
postcolonial transition 209
    complex viewing 211
    cultural contamination 209–11
    mimicry, complex viewing and 211–13
poststructuralist 4, 71, 87, 89, 95–6, 98–100
Potter, Ian 215, 227
powerless duality 84
powerless elite (fans) 5, 71–2, 75, 81, 142
    community's perception 81–2
    fanwank re-invented 84–5
    golden ages and unforgivable 75–6
    self-disempowered elite 82–4
    textual exegesis and 77–9
Prescott, Amanda-Rae 163
Prisoner, The 236
psychographics, fan 117, 119–20
Punchdrunk 57

Quantum Leap 103
Queen Bat 222
Queer Archive, The 204
Queer as Folk 255
queer fans 169, 171–3, 204

racism 163–5
    institutional 165
    sexism and 250
Radio Free Skaro 243
Radio Times 2, 37, 40, 225
Rassilon (fictional character) 31, 56
Rawdon, Katy 245
Real Time 51
Redeemed 243
Regenerated Edition: The Official Miscellany 195 n.16

regeneration theory 79
relativity and relativism 91
Rels (*Dalek Book*) 230, 232 n.19
Remembrance of the Daleks 39, 41, 242
Resurrection 95
retroactive queering 169–71, 173
    #MARTHADONNA case 171–2
    playfulness, power and 172–3
Richards, Justin 38, 44, 238
Richfield, Edwin 50
Rinpoche, K'anpo 78
Risley, Matt 197
River Song (fictional character) 137–8, 257, 268
River Song's Guide to the Dark Times 68
Roberts, Gareth 43, 230, 264
Robot 78, 242
Robot of Sherwood 33
Robots of Death, The 242
Robson, Eddie 215
    Douglas Adams: The First Professional Doctor Who Fan 217–18
Rory Williams (fictional character) 197–200, 250, 257
Rosa 32–3, 134–5
Rosa Parks (fictional character) 134
Rose Tyler (fictional character) 3, 31, 85, 160, 163–4, 170–1, 176, 206, 256, 263
Royal Shakespeare Company 103
RTD. *See* Davies, Russell T
Russell, Gary 77, 79
    Placebo Effect 40
Russell, William 229, 232 n.10
Ryan Sinclair (fictional character) 136–8, 163–5, 167 n.9, 204

Sam Jones (fictional character) 31
Samms, Tara, Distance 232 n.11
Sandifer, Elizabeth 87, 235, 237
    Pop Between Realities, Home in Time for Tea 41 (rec.arts.drwho) 237–9
Sandvoss, Cornel 112
Sarah Jane Adventures, The 176, 229, 232 n.12, 255–6
Sarah Jane Smith (fictional character) 79, 135, 256
Saturday Night Live 'Get a Life' 126
Saunders, David 77, 79
Schrodinggoose 192
Scott, Suzanne 256
Scream of the Shalka, The 91
Secret Diary of the Master, The 265 n.22
segmentation 117–18
    behaviour 118, 121
    demographics 118
    geographic 118
    psychographics 118, 121
    socio-economics 118
Seitz, Skye 204
semiotic thickness of text 26–7
SerialCon 178
Set Piece 235–7
Sex Education (TV series) 3
sexism (fandom) 249–54, 267–70
Shada 40, 195 n.16, 218
Shades of Milk and Honey 247
Shakedown 13
Shalka Doctor (fictional character) 91
Shanghai Art and Humanities Channel 194 n.6
Shanghai International Channel 194 n.6
Shanghai International Film Festival 194 n.6
Shearman, Rob 38
Sheppard, Mark 243
Sherlock 170, 191
Shetty, Parinita 72, 133
Shifman, Limor 71
    Keeping the Elite Powerless: Fan-Producer Relations in the "Nu Who" (and New YOU) Era 81–5, 266 n.5
showrunners, fans as 255–9, 265
    Chibnall, Chris 130, 143, 164, 204, 258–9
    Davies, Russell T 71, 90, 166, 207, 228, 255–6
    Moffat, Steven 164, 197, 215, 219, 225, 250, 256–8
Shresthova, Sangita 126
Silva, Polyana Inácio Rezende 72, 125
Silverman, Riley J. 205
similarity and difference 17–19
Sizemore, Jason 244
S&K subtitling group 193
Smith, Matt 47, 104–5, 138, 207, 219, 268
social hierarchy 89
social media 119–20, 131, 143, 147, 149, 174, 191–2, 206, 261, 269. *See also* Tumblr fandom
    chaos 150
    and consumer tribes 72, 120–1
social politics 203
    fan spaces, on- and offline 205
    representation matters 204
    threat of diversity and wokeness 206–7
Sonic Screwdriver 235
Souza, Rosana Vieira 126
Spearhead from Space 242
SS Chaoneng xiaofengdui 192
Stanish, Deborah 244
Star Trek 29, 100, 120, 156, 160, 220, 233 n.23
Star Wars 230–1

stay woke 164
Stein, Louisa Ellen 126
Stock Footage 222
Stonawska, Magdalena 175
Stones of Blood 78
Storm and Stress 236
Storm Warning 38
Stornaiuolo, Amy 137
Story of Martha, The 44
Strange England 237
structuralist 3, 21, 71, 87, 98–9. *See also* poststructuralist
structured polysemy 18
Subotsky, Milton 35–6
Summerfield, Bernice 43, 229
Sun Makers, The 96–7
Supernatural fandom 150, 170
SuperWhoLock 170
Susan (fictional character) 9
Swaffield, Luke 56, 58–9

Talons of Weng-Chiang, The 242, 251
TARDIS 20, 24, 33, 40, 42, 47, 104, 159–66, 175, 198–200, 204–5, 218, 230, 242–4, 256–7
Tate, Catherine 197
Tegan Jovanka (fictional character) 79
tele-centric 38
Telemundo 165
televisuality 37–8
Telos Publishing 44
Tennant, David 24, 67, 71–2, 84, 101, 104–6, 160, 176, 220, 228, 245, 268
    geek chic and masculinity 101–3
    irritation with female fans 104
Terrible Zodin, The 220–1, 267–71
textual conservationism 37
textual meaning 18–19
Thasmin 206–7
theoretical-methodological approach 131
Thomas, Ebony Elizabeth 137
Thomas, Lynne M 215, 241
    Chicks Dig Time Lords: A Celebration of Doctor Who by the Women Who Love It 243–4, 246
360-degree commissioning 25
Three Doctors, The 31, 47
Tiidenberg, Katrin 132 n.16
Timeless Children, The 259
Timeless Doctor, The 192
Time Lord Guide 61
Time Lords (fictional character) 23, 31, 67, 76, 178, 220, 222

Time Monster 77
Time Screen 231
Time Unincorporated 2 244
Time War 12, 230, 258, 266 n.8
Timewyrm: Genesis 13
tokenistic diversity 165, 167 n.11
Topping, Keith 230–1, 232 n.11
    Discontinuity Guide, The 230
    Guinness Book of Classic British TV, The 231
Torchwood (Cyberwoman) 14, 105–6, 244, 255–6
Towers, Jason 236
toxic fandom 253–4
transformations 30, 223
transitions, model of 64, 66–7
translations 177, 191–3, 195 n.16
transmedia 2, 4–5, 47, 55, 63
    historiography (DWFC) 48–51
    storytelling 9–10, 12–15, 15 n.4, 50, 63–4, 67–8
    techniques 56–8
    texts 9–10
Troughton, Patrick 38, 40
Tucker, Mike 227–8, 232 n.5
Tulloch, John 2–5, 26, 71–2, 81, 87, 111, 113, 142, 175
    Doctor Who: The Unfolding Text 3, 26, 87, 89
    Dr Who: Similarity and Difference 17–19
    pure science 20
    Science Fiction Audiences: Watching Doctor Who and Star Trek 4, 75–9, 87, 175
Tumblr fandom 72, 125, 198, 221
    activism's silosociality 132 n.16
    Adric 150–2
    anti-monolithic 157
    cartography of controversy 127
    complexities 126, 131
    Kamelion Curse 152–6
    methodology 126–7
    reblog function 157 n.9
    results 127–30
    social media chaos 150
    The-Cimmerians essay 157 n.10
    topics and arguments 129
Tumblr Tool 127
Turk, Tisha 176
TV Century 21 228
TV Movie 38, 43, 91
Twice Upon a Time 32
Twin Dilemma, The 50
Two Doctors, The 52 n.10
Two-Minute Time Lord 243
Tyson, Cicely 160

Uncanny Magazine 244–5
Universal-Tandem 229
Universo Who 182
Upton, Gregory 167 n.10

Valente, Catherynne M. 243–4
Van Gogh Experience 262
vast narrative 29–31, 92
Venom Grubs 230
Venturini, Tommaso 127–8
Victor Kennedy (fictional character) 264
Vigil 144
Vinder (fictional character) 145
Virgin New Adventures 13, 235
Volcano 218
Voord (alien creature) 47

Wardrip-Fruin, Noah 2
   Third Person: Authoring and Exploring Vast Narratives 30–1
Warren, Marc 263
Warsaw Comic Con 178
Waters of Mars, The 63
Way We Live Now, The 199–200
Web 2.0 192
Weeping Angels 47
Whispers of Terror 38
Whitaker, David 24
white male entitlement 111
Whithouse, Toby 178
Whittaker, Jodie 5, 72, 109, 114, 125–8, 130–1, 132 n.16, 164–5, 170, 206, 208 n.9, 245, 253, 270
Whosome.pl 179
Whovians and Whovian groups 192–3
   Black 164
   Brazilian 181–8
   Chinese 191, 193
   offline (rarely) 178
   online (usually) 178–9
   Poland 175–6
   as powerless elite 142
Whovians of Colour 165–6
William (Doctor Who) Hartnell Fan Club 2
Williams, Graham 18, 76–7
   errors in continuity 76, 79
Williams, Rebecca 71, 83–4, 85, 102
   Desiring the Doctor: Identity, Gender and Genre in Online Fandom 101–6
Willis, Connie 245
Winnicott's theory 265 n.29
Wirrn (insect race) 212–13
Without a Summer 247–8
Woke Doctor Who 134–5
women-loving-women (WLW) relationships 172–3, 204
Women Who Waited, The 135
World Enough and Time 164

Yaz/Yasmin Khan (fictional character) 142, 163–5, 167 n.9, 169–170, 204
Yodovich, Neta 72
   Finally, we get to play the Doctor: Feminist Female Fans' Reactions to the First Female Doctor Who 109–15
   Women Negotiating Feminism and Science Fiction Fandom 72
Young, Anna 169

Zapp Brannigan (TV character) 153
Zeff, Dan 264
Zerinza 76, 79
Zhengda Drama Channel 194 n.6
ZiMuZu 192
Zygon Invasion, The 32
Zygon Inversion, The 32